NECESSARY CONDITIONS OF LEARNING

"Marton has provided an outstanding exposition of his lifetime's thought. Through describing research and teaching in a variety of subjects, he exemplifies the theory of learning through discernment of variation. This stimulating and scholarly book acts both as a handbook for design of teaching and teaching materials and as a basis for understanding more about learning in educational contexts."

Anne Watson, University of Oxford, UK

Necessary Conditions of Learning presents a research approach (phenomenography) and a theory (the variation theory of learning) introduced and developed by Ference Marton and taken up by his wide and varied following around the world—together with their practical applications in educational contexts. Reflecting Marton's whole lifetime's work, the unique and significant contribution of this book is to offer an evidence-based answer to the questions, "How do we make novel meanings our own?" and "How do we learn to see things in more powerful ways?"

The presentation makes use of hundreds of empirical studies carried out in Europe and Asia that build on the theory. The line of reasoning and the way in which the examples are put together is consistent with the theory—it is both presented and applied. The main argument is that in order to learn we have to discern, and to discern the intended ideas we must be presented with carefully structured variation, against a background of invariance. We then go through processes of contrast, generalization and fusion in order to make sense. These insights form a practical framework for those who design teaching and teaching materials. *Necessary Conditions of Learning* is a major original work for which scholars of pedagogical theory have been waiting a long time.

Ference Marton is Professor of Education at the Göteborg University, Sweden, and Honorary Professor on the Faculty of Education at the University of Hong Kong. He is internationally known for introducing the distinction between deep and surface approaches to learning, for developing phenomenography as a methodology for educational research and, more recently, for developing the variation theory of learning. Both the methodology and theory were developed by Marton together with research groups in Sweden, the UK, Australia and China.

NECESSARY CONDITIONS OF LEARNING

Ference Marton

NEW YORK AND LONDON

First published 2015
by Routledge
711 Third Avenue, New York, NY 10017

and by Routledge
2 Park Square, Milton Park, Abingdon, Oxon OX14 4RN

Routledge is an imprint of the Taylor & Francis Group, an informa business

© 2015 Taylor & Francis

The right of Ference Marton to be identified as author of this work has been asserted by him in accordance with sections 77 and 78 of the Copyright, Designs and Patents Act 1988.

All rights reserved. No part of this book may be reprinted or reproduced or utilized in any form or by any electronic, mechanical, or other means, now known or hereafter invented, including photocopying and recording, or in any information storage or retrieval system, without permission in writing from the publishers.

Trademark notice: Product or corporate names may be trademarks or registered trademarks, and are used only for identification and explanation without intent to infringe.

Library of Congress Cataloging-in-Publication Data
Marton, Ference.
 Necessary conditions of learning / Ference Marton.
  pages cm
 Includes bibliographical references and index.
 1. Learning, Psychology of. 2. Phenomenological psychology. I. Title.
  LB1060.M3383 2014
  370.15'23—dc23
  2014000268

ISBN: 978-0-415-73913-9 (hbk)
ISBN: 978-0-415-73914-6 (pbk)
ISBN: 978-1-315-81687-6 (ebk)

Typeset in Bembo
by Apex CoVantage, LLC

For Birgitta

CONTENTS

Preface   xi
Acknowledgments   xv

1. What Makes Humans Human?   1
   Cultural Evolution   1
   The Species That Teaches Its Offspring   2
   The Origin of Pedagogy   3
   Learning From Others   5
   Learning as a By-Product and Learning as an Aim   9
   "De-Pedagogizing" Learning   11
   Pedagogies of Learning   13
   Teachers' Professional Knowledge   16

2. What Is to Be Learned?   20
   What Matters?   20
   Organizing Learning   21
   What Is to Be Learned?   22
   Learning as Differentiation   33
   Different Meanings of What Is to Be Learned   37

3. Sameness and Difference in Learning   39
   The Problem With Direct Reference   39
   Discerning Features That Have Been Discerned Previously   40
   Discerning Features That Have Not Been Discerned Previously   41
   We Do Have to Learn to Discern Features Whether or Not They Are Innate   43
   Learning to Discern Novel Features and Aspects   44

	Dimensions of Variation and Values	47
	Neither From the Specific to the General, Nor the Other Way Around	48
	Patterns of Variation and Invariance	48
	The Path of Learning	52
	Critical Aspects and Critical Features, Again	54
	Why Is the Experience of Difference, Against a Background of the Experience of Sameness, Necessary for Learning to Discern Novel Features and Novel Aspects?	56
	Delimitation	60
	Grouping	61
	Differences and Experienced Differences	64
	Discernment, Difference, Simultaneity	66
	Discerning and Learning to Discern	67
	Using the Known to Prepare for the Unknown	67
	The Transfer of Learning	72
4	What Does the World Look Like to Others?	82
	The Revelation of Jonas Emanuelsson	82
	What Is to Be Learned, Again: Ways of Seeing	83
	Finding Critical Aspects	85
	The Learner's Perspective and the Observer's Perspective	87
	Logic and Understanding	88
	Asking Questions	89
	Analyzing Answers	91
	The Idea of Phenomenography	106
	Qualitative Differences in Learning, Specific to Specific Objects of Learning	115
5	The Art of Learning	128
	Learners Generating Patterns of Variation and Invariance	128
	Discoveries as Discernments	154
	Innovations and the Opening Up of New Dimensions of Variation	160
	Finding Novel Meanings	161
6	Making Learning Possible	164
	Three Faces of the Object of Learning	164
	Necessary Conditions of Necessary Conditions of Learning	165
	The Origin of Differences	166
	Analyzing Lessons	175
	Comparing Teaching	180
	Relating Learning and Teaching to Each Other	190
	Bringing About Learning: Patterns of Variation and Invariance as Tools for Planning and Conducting Teaching	196

	Bringing Learning About: Implementing Patterns of Variation and Invariance	206
	Bringing About Learning: The Order of Things	213
	Hierarchical and Sequential Structure in Reading and Writing	221
	Can the "Art of Learning" Be Learned?	226
	There Are No Teaching Experiments	231
	Putting Conjectures to the Test	237
	The Chinese Connection	245
7	Learning to Help Others to Learn	255
	What Teachers Have to Be Good At	255
	What Is to Be Done	257
	Learning to Handle Pedagogical Units in More Powerful Ways	257
	Lesson Study	258
	Design Research	259
	Learning Study	260
	Examples of Learning Studies	265
	"Learning Study in a Wider Sense"	274
	Effects of Learning Studies	275
	Teachers' Research	277
	In School	280

References — *283*
Author Index — *299*
Subject Index — *303*

PREFACE

When we learn, we learn to do things, to say things and to see things. The latter is meant in the sense that when we learn, the meanings of things, words and acts come into being or change and we make new meanings our own. This is frequently assumed to happen by means of the learner encountering different instances of the same concept, different examples of the same principle. The new meaning is supposed to be that which the different things have in common. This invariant meaning, it is assumed, is seen against a background of variation in other respects. In this book, I argue that we make new meanings our own in exactly the opposite way. We cannot grasp just one meaning; it takes at least two. We can only find a new meaning through the difference between meanings. The difference between meanings thus becomes visible against a background of invariance in other respects. We cannot understand what "dry wine" is by drinking dry wine only, we cannot understand what linear equations are by seeing linear equations only and we cannot experience "flow" if it is flow that we experience all the time.

But we can learn what dry wine is through the contrast with sweet wine, and we can understand what linear equations are by comparing them with quadratic equations. And we can find out what "flow" is through experiencing how it differs from the lack of it. The secret of learning is to be found in the pattern of variation and invariance experienced by the learners.

Students are doing better in school in some countries than in others, and even in the same country, students in some schools are doing better than in others. Discussions about education are dominated by questions as to why this should be so. The answers to these questions tend to focus on the number of hours spent in school; the amount of homework given; how much fun the students have in school; how much they work in whole classes, in groups or independently; what resources are spent per student on average; how the resources are distributed; how many students there are per class and so on.

Important as these questions may be, none of them is discussed in this book. These are general questions that are supposed to apply to the learning of all of the many things that students are expected to learn. But whatever the students are trying to learn, whatever object of learning they are trying to make their own, there are specific keys that are necessary for learning just that. Once those specific keys (in this book, called "critical aspects" of the object of learning) are found and used by both the teacher and the students, the latter will be much more likely to make the object of learning their own and to handle relevant situations in the future in more powerful ways, because they will see them in more powerful ways. If the specific keys are not found, or not used, the students will in all likelihood miss the learning target. And this holds true regardless of whether the students are working in whole classes, in groups or on their own; regardless of whether their style of learning is predominantly visual or auditory; and regardless of whether or not the teacher is firm, or fair, or charismatic.

As mentioned previously, each object of learning will have its own particular critical aspects: if students do not find out about part–whole relationships between the numbers from 1 to 10, they will fail to learn arithmetic; if they do not see the difference between *s* signaling genitive and signaling plural in English, they will confuse the two when the distinction is called for; if they do not separate the perspective from what is seen, they will not be able to describe a historical event from different perspectives; if they have not distinguished weight from volume, they cannot grasp the idea of density, and without density as a conceptual tool they cannot possibly explain why some things float and others sink; if students have not learned to distinguish punctuation marks from one another, or to vary the lengths of sentences, or to make use of synonyms, or to describe the same thing in different ways, it is hardly likely that their review of a film they have seen will communicate their impression of the film in a powerful way.

There is more to learning than appropriating such specific keys, of course. But without them, students cannot make an object of learning their own. And as for general threats to a good and meaningful existence in school, such as feelings of boredom, a lack of self-confidence, an absence of joy in learning, for instance—could there be a better way of making learning more powerful, life in school more interesting and the students' self-confidence stronger than helping them to see how things make sense, how novel situations can be handled in powerful ways and how the world around them can be seen and understood better, by means of what they learn in school?

Specific objects of learning have specific keys, and, without them, the intended learning cannot take place. These keys are what this book is about.

What This Book Is About

This book is about the relationship between learning and the conditions of learning. There are some necessary, general conditions. It is very difficult to teach someone who does not want to learn. Students do not learn from the teacher if they do not pay attention to what she says. Sometimes it is impossible to find out something on your own; sometimes you have to find out something by yourself, in order to learn. It is hard to learn when it is too cold, too hot, too noisy or when you are very hungry. These are general, necessary conditions for learning, conditions that apply to all kinds of learning. This book is not about them. It is not about differences in how learning is organized. It is not about whether, or when, learning without pedagogy is better than learning with pedagogy. It is not about whether it is better to learn together with others or on your own. It is not about whether it is better to learn outdoors rather than indoors, by listening and looking or by doing.

This book is about necessary, content-related aspects of learning, aspects without which the learning aimed at just cannot happen. You cannot understand in a powerful way how the algorithm for the multiplication of three-digit numbers works if you do not understand the distributive law and if you do not understand place value in terms of basic units. You cannot understand currency exchange if you cannot see sums of money as products of numbers and currency units, nor can you exchange currency with any understanding of what you are doing. And you cannot measure anything without a unit of measurement.

Such aspects are specific to different objects of learning. They are the kind of things that have to be learned in different cases. Whether or not it is possible for the learners to discern and make such aspects their own determines whether or not learning can happen.[1] This is why I firmly believe that the kind of differences exemplified by how the multiplication of three-digit numbers might be taught, as described in Ma Liping's (1999) study are differences of unconditional importance for learning, and this is why this book is about such differences.

Note

1. The aspects mentioned in the example are not necessary conditions for learning to multiply two three-digit numbers with each other by using a pocket calculator, but they are necessary for seeing the logic of the multiplication algorithm and for being able to explain it to someone who has not yet learned to see it as such.

ACKNOWLEDGMENTS

Research is mostly a collective endeavor; for me this has always been very much the case. I have always had the good fortune to be able to work with wonderful and wonderfully brilliant people. In addition to our research group in the Department of Pedagogical, Curricular and Professional Studies at Gothenburg University, in Sweden, I have been lucky enough to have other intellectual homes as well, during different periods in different places: in the UK, in Australia, in Hong Kong. Everything in this book we have found together. Thank you, dear friends! Some of these great people have even taken the trouble to read the manuscript and comment on it. I thank them in particular: Maria Bergqvist, Shirley Booth, Christine Bruce, Yrjö Engeström, Noel Entwistle, Henrik Hansson, Mona Holmqvist Olander, Angelika Kullberg, John Mason, Tuula Maunula, Airi Rovio-Johansson, Ulla Runesson, Lennart Svensson, Anne Watson, Eva Wennås Brante. Furthermore, I had the luck of having Catherine MacHale to turn my manuscript into readable English. She has worked under the very attractive assumption that I meant something comparatively sensible, even when it did not look to be so at all. More luck: this is the third book on which I have worked with Naomi Silverman, publisher at Routledge. It has been a sheer pleasure every time. Daniel Schwartz has provided further editorial support at critical moments. Lisbeth Söderberg manifested great skill and efficiency, and willingness to help, in putting the manuscript into an acceptable form. The Swedish Research Council has financially supported the writing of the book.

This book is dedicated to Birgitta Marton, my better half and my soul mate. I love her dearly—always and in all ways.

1
WHAT MAKES HUMANS HUMAN?

Cultural Evolution

Humans are unique among species in that each generation teaches the next. And what makes humans human is what they learn. Knowledge and skills that have been passed from one generation to the next, through learning, have been humanity's most important and, to begin with, only competitive advantage for survival. The development of knowledge and skills has been driven by the development of tools (Säljö, 2000; Vygotsky, 1986). Tools can be tools in a literal sense, such as a hammer, a computer or an airplane; or tools might be tools in a metaphorical sense, such as language, concepts, theories and so on. Tools are developed by humans and the ability to use them is not a part of our genetic endowment. We have to learn how to handle them and we have to learn it from other humans.

Gould (1997) compared natural and cultural evolution (p. 219ff.). According to Darwin's theory, the former works by means of natural variation in different characteristics of a species. Members of the species who possess characteristics that are critical for survival under certain conditions have a greater probability of surviving under those conditions than do members of the same species who lack those characteristics, or who have them only to a lesser extent.

Greater likelihood of survival means greater likelihood of having offspring. Offspring of parents with those particular characteristics are more likely to have the same characteristics than offspring of parents who have them to a lesser degree. Hence, the characteristics critical for survival will in all likelihood be more frequent in the next generation. And if the same conditions prevail, these kinds of changes will also prevail from generation to generation, and the species will change in that particular respect. If the environment were to change again, making some other characteristics critical for survival, then the species would adjust to the changing environment, as more members equipped with these new critical characteristics would survive and produce similarly endowed offspring. Thus, the proportion of members of the species equipped with these characteristics will increase; in this way, the species keeps changing with changing conditions but through a very slow process, across many generations.

It would be so much more efficient, Gould says, if members of a species could figure out for themselves what characteristics are most important, develop those during their lifetime and then pass on the improvements genetically to the next generation (1997, p. 221). Actually, this is exactly how the French biologist Jean-Baptiste Lamarck thought that evolution happened. But he was mistaken. Even if a giraffe's neck gets longer by being stretched again and again, the "improvement" cannot be passed on to the offspring directly, because the genetic material is not affected by what the individual does or does not do. The same thing goes for the right arm of the blacksmith, which grows strong through his work. The effects of training cannot be transmitted biologically.[1] Cultural evolution is, in contrast, fundamentally Lamarckian, in the sense that knowledge and skills developed by one generation can be passed on directly to the next one, through learning. And as this is going on all the time, a culture can accumulate successful innovations from earlier generations and from other cultures. In this way, development towards more powerful ways of handling the world around us can take place very rapidly. The cultural evolution of humankind is much faster—and increasingly so—than its natural evolution. Pedagogy, in its widest sense, is the servant of cultural evolution.[2]

The Species That Teaches Its Offspring

Barnett (1973) argued that there is a stark difference between humans and animals as regards the way in which they help—or do not help—their offspring to learn. It is pedagogy that makes humans human. Therefore we might speak of *Homo docens*—the teaching human being.

Premack (1984) pointed out, however, that members of other species may also support younger members' learning, but without living up to his three criteria of pedagogy:

1) There is a goal for learning.
2) There is a systematic attempt (by the "teacher") to help the learner to reach that goal.
3) The systematic attempt is guided by the teacher's perception of the learner's progress (or lack of progress).

Adult chimpanzees might very well train younger members of their species. They might set a goal for the youngsters' learning (picking fruit, walking in pairs, etc.). Two criteria of pedagogy are then satisfied: a specific target is set for someone else, on the one hand, and systematic efforts are made to reach it, on the other.

But the chimpanzees fail on Premack's third criterion of pedagogy: they do not observe possible changes in the pupil's way of acting and make use of them as clues for further support in learning.

Over a period of 10 years, Tetsuro Matsuzawa and his team observed and filmed in the wild how infant chimpanzees learned to crack nuts in a group that was good at cracking nuts (Inoue-Nakumura & Matsuzawa, 1997). In this learning process, that in fact took some 10 years (from being a novice to becoming an expert nutcracker), the infant observed intently as the mother placed a nut on an anvil and cracked it by striking it with a rock; the infant tried to imitate—for a long time with no success—continued observing, tried again and so on. There was not a single instance of a mother showing any interest in an infant's attempts, nor was any initiative taken to show them how to crack nuts, in the hundreds and hundreds of hours of film that were recorded. And the 10 years that it took for the youngsters to learn to crack nuts could have been reduced by a factor of 20, according to Premack and Premack's (2003) estimate, had the mothers instructed their offspring.

There are many animals that provide opportunities for their offspring to acquire skills necessary for their survival. Cats arrange for their kittens to learn to kill mice: they bring mice to the kittens to allow them to practice, and they may even seriously injure a mouse to make it easier for the kitten to stalk in the initial training. But the behavior of cats is driven by a rather rigid biological mechanism. They do not take the kitten's progress into consideration and adjust the training accordingly (Premack and Premack, 2003, p. 70), and thus they do not live up to Premack's third criterion of pedagogy. According to that criterion, there has to be interaction between "pupil" and "teacher" in order for the former to learn from the latter, and at the same time, the teacher has to learn from the pupil in order to help the pupil to learn better.

Pedagogy is, then, unique to humans—animals do not have it. It is only for humans that learning has become "pedagogized" and that finding ways to help others to learn has become a necessary condition for the survival of the species. This is exactly what teachers are supposed to do well. There are cases, however, when teachers do not live up to the three criteria of pedagogy: they may not set goals for the students, they may not use a systematic way of trying to help the students to learn or they may not pay sufficient attention to the learners to be able to learn from them.

The Origin of Pedagogy

Pedagogy—in Premack's sense of the word—is something that humans in all likelihood have to learn. But there must be a readiness for learning it, a readiness for learning how to help others to learn, a readiness that animals appear to lack. We might then ask: How early can humans engage in the practice of pedagogy? Frankly, I know of only a few studies of this question; it seems to be something of a virgin territory. Or maybe I am just more ignorant in this respect than I should be. One relevant study is that of Eva Ekeblad, who carried out pioneering work in Sweden in the context of using computer games to develop arithmetic skills in 7-year-old children (Ekeblad, 1996). The children worked in pairs, in which one of them (the teacher) had already learned how to play a game and was supposed to instruct the other child (the pupil). The researcher was sitting next to the children during the lesson. They seemed to slip into their roles easily enough: the teacher took responsibility for helping the pupil and the latter was prepared to learn from the former.

The situation was layered in the sense that the children separated one layer (the teacher and the pupil, and their pedagogical interaction) from another layer (the two children and the researcher), ignoring the researcher sitting next to them as far as pedagogical matters were concerned, but consulting her about matters that had to do with other things—the computer, in particular. Occasionally, the teacher who did the consulting reported to the pupil what the researcher had said, in spite of the fact that both had heard it clearly. The distinction between the two layers was also a distinction between the pedagogical aspect and other aspects of the situation. Sometimes, however, in competitive games, some children failed to make the distinction between teaching to play and playing, and instead of teaching the pupil how to play a game, they opted for trying to beat her instead (Ekeblad, 1996, p. 154).[3]

Additionally, the children made even more subtle distinctions, for instance, helping someone to learn to play the game in contrast to helping someone to learn *from* playing the game. The game consisted of identifying the number of objects shown on the screen, while the sets of objects were moving in patterns on the screen in such a way as to make it difficult to count the objects (see Figure 1.1). The children gave their answers by pressing that number of keys on a specially made keyboard. In this case, the children had to learn to play the game in order to learn (to identify the "manyness" of the patterns and pressing that many keys, as fast as possible). The teacher explained to the pupil how to play the game and while demonstrating it, saying something such as, "You have to see how many there are" when the pattern appeared, waiting for the pupil's answer ("three," for instance), and then saying "OK, then you have to press three keys." The teacher thus told the pupil everything about how to play the game, but did not say what someone playing the game had to find out each time she played. Helping the pupil to learn the game was the teacher's responsibility, but learning to figure out how many things were on the screen was the responsibility of the pupil. In other cases, however, this distinction was not made and the pupil was not afforded the opportunity to discern the pattern. The teacher provided the answer. When the pattern appeared the teacher might have said, "There are three things there, you have to press three keys" (Ekeblad, 1993). This study showed two things: first, that 7-year-old children may be able to distinguish between pedagogical and non-pedagogical aspects of their interactions with their peers and, second, that they do so to varying degrees.

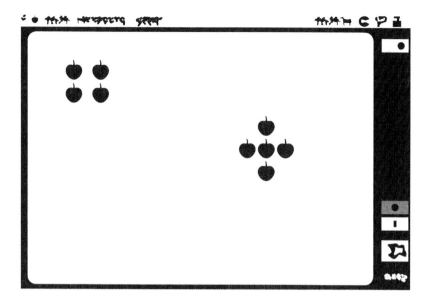

FIGURE 1.1 Screen dump from the number practice game (Lindström et al., 2011, p. 126).

But pedagogical sensitivity may actually appear much earlier in life. Reis (2011) studied how toddlers (1 to 3 years old) learn to order nested cups and the rings of a ring tower, taking these as expressions of the children's early mathematization. A little girl, of 3 years of age, who had found out how to put the rings in order on the peg, from the largest to the smallest, then helped her peers to do the same, by pointing out which rings they had put in the wrong order. But not only that: she deliberately put rings in the wrong order on the peg and handed it over to other children as a task in which they had to put the rings in the correct order. When doing this, she seemed to vary the difficulty of the tasks, by giving simpler tasks (fewer rings to change) to children whose ways of ordering the rings was "less advanced" (pp. 155–158).

It is not known how exceptional this little teacher is among her peers, but by describing Ekeblad and Reis's studies, I just want to show that what is being called pedagogy here is a species-specific adjustment that might appear very early in life.

Learning From Others

Pedagogy assumes the existence of someone who is ready to help others to learn, but also someone who is ready to learn from others. Recently, psychologists studying learning and teaching from an evolutionary point of view have demonstrated that even very young children exhibit such readiness. Gergely and Csibra (2006a), for example, presented a bold hypothesis: that the ability to teach, and the ability to learn from someone who is teaching, are primary, independent, species-specific adaptations, which, in the evolution of humans, probably precede the ability to use language.

They then asked what kind of factors might have brought about selective pressure to develop this specific ability (or rather these specific abilities). Let us consider the use of tools. The predecessors of *Homo sapiens* (the early hominids), as with some primates existing today, especially chimpanzees, were on occasion capable of using objects as tools. Such an act suggests a certain attitude towards the object, indicating that the user may be thinking: "This object could be used for a particular purpose." Testing the object in question is preceded by the desire to attain a goal, that is to say, something lying in the future. In other words, the act has a teleological structure. It appears, however, that in the case of the early hominids and today's primates, when the tool has actually been used—successfully or otherwise—the user does not bother about it any longer. In other words, the object has not been categorized as a tool of a permanent nature with stable functional properties.

We know, however, that several million years ago our predecessors had already progressed to a qualitatively different view of tools. Archaeological findings show that objects came to be regarded as tools with a consistent function. Tools were kept, stored in special places and could be made at one place to be used much later at another place. This presupposed a change of perspective from *simple teleology* (What object can I use to achieve this goal?) to *inverse teleology* (What can I use this object for?).

The next stage is *recursive teleology,* as Gergely and Csibra called it. This refers to the use of tools to produce tools. As opposed to the case of simple teleology (for example, using a stone to crack nuts) the means-end structure of recursive teleology is not visible to the learner. If, for example, one individual observes another using a tool to remove the hard rind of a fruit, it might be obvious that the tool is being used to obtain the edible parts. Let us imagine, in contrast, a child observing someone using a tool to remove parts of a piece of wood (to make a tool for cutting or boring holes, for example), resulting in a smaller piece of wood, as well as other by-products and sound effects. In this case, it is impossible for the child to know the purpose of the activity.

When the learner can see the relationship between the means and the end of an act, what can be called the means-end structure, she can learn by *emulation*. In this case the learner focuses on the relationship between the outcome of an action (for example, the removal of the hard rind of a fruit) and how this is achieved (by using a certain tool in a certain way). Based on this insight into the relationship between means and end, the learner can reach the same goal in her own way by bearing in mind and recreating what is critical in the observed action in order to achieve the goal. This implies that the same outcome (the same end) can be achieved in different ways (by different means), if what is critical is reconstructed.

When the means-end structure of the situation is not visible (as in the case of using tools to make other tools), the only way to learn the skill in question is to imitate the example. Not knowing what is critical in what she is doing, the learner cannot but repeat the imitated act as closely as possible. Emulation is a more advanced—or at least more rational—way of learning than imitation. In emulation the critical steps for achieving a certain goal are discerned, in which case the exact procedure does not need to be followed. This means that skills that are learned in this way are more flexible, generalizable and more widely applicable than those that are learned by slavishly following a certain fixed procedure through imitation. You could say that in emulation, the learner's focus is on the relation between her acts (the means) and their expected outcome (the end), while in imitation, her focus is on the acts themselves (the means). Infants of 12 months use emulation spontaneously when the means-end structure of the situation is visible and imitation only if the adult makes special efforts to make a kind of learning pact with the child by ostensive communication (establishing eye contact with the child, fixing her eyes on the object in question, saying the child's name, etc.; Gergely & Csibra, 2006b). Nevertheless, 3- to 4-year-old chimpanzees use emulation to a greater extent than human children of the same age when the means-end structure of the situation is visible (Horner & Whiten, 2005). Since emulation is a more rational and advanced form of learning than imitation, it seems paradoxical that it would be more common among young apes than among children.

The paradox is resolved in the fact that imitation in children is of a qualitatively different nature from that in animals. First, it occurs in parallel with emulation (the children can do either); second, children continue to be able to use both imitation and emulation even long after emulation has replaced imitation as the primary form of learning. What then is the function of this qualitatively different imitation?

Let us return to the example of recursive teleology, learning to use tools to make tools or, more generally, learning to handle situations when the means-end structure is not visible. As pointed out previously, imitation is the only way to learn in such cases.

In the example on which the previously mentioned studies are based, the goal could be perceived in any case, even if the means-end structure could not. Gergely and Csibra (2006b) used a modified form of Meltzoff's (1988) procedure, where the leader of the investigation sat on the floor with a 14-month-old child and a partially transparent cardboard box between them. Suddenly, the investigator bent down and knocked on the surface of the box with her head—and a lamp came on inside the box. This was done only once. When these children returned to the same situation one week later, 67% of them repeated the investigator's action. But none of the children in a control group, who had never seen anyone switch on the light in the cardboard box by knocking on it with her head, did so. This means that the children used imitation instead of emulation, since emulation would have seen them doing something more familiar, namely, pressing the top of the box with their hands (as the children in the control group did). Gergely, Bekkering and Kiraly (2002) showed that the outcome was a function of the situation not being cognitively understandable (the means-end structure was not visible). In this study, two conditions were compared—first, when the investigator had her hands engaged and second, when she had her hands free, as in Meltzoff's original study. In the first case the means-end structure is visible and the children do indeed use emulation. They use their hands to light up the box when they get a chance to do so. In the other case the means-end structure is not visible, and the result is about the same as in the original study. This occurs on condition that a learning pact is made, in accordance with what was said previously.

In the case of recursive teleology (and the example of using tools to make tools), not only the means-end structure but also the goal itself is invisible to the learner. It is in such cases that children's ability to imitate in a qualitatively different way comes into its own. They can get involved in imitating behavior without being able to see what it leads to. Animals rarely do that. We could say that humans' ability to learn things that do not appear at that moment to serve any purpose gives them a gigantic advantage over animals.

At the same time, this is what school is always criticized for, namely, teaching things whose relevance is far from being obvious to the learners. But if one cannot see the goal, let alone the means-end structure, one is, as is previously shown, restricted to using imitation, blind imitation, if one is to learn. Even if the readiness to enter into such a process is a prerequisite for the continued existence of humankind, the learning itself is not of the powerful kind; it is blind, inflexible and non-generalizable. What is missing is precisely what the learners can do on their own when the means-end structure is visible: distinguish what is critical and important from what is not. When the means-end structure is not apparent, the teacher is necessary to bring about the same function. The pupil, who cannot tell what is critical and what is not, must be helped by someone who knows how to do so. Csibra and Gergely (2006) believe that it is education that distinguishes humans from animals, and that education presumes two abilities in humans: the ability to make explicit what one knows—the ability to teach—on the one hand, and the ability to learn from someone who is teaching, on the other.

In the previous two sections of this chapter I have given examples that suggest that humans can engage in behavior that fulfills Premack's third criterion of pedagogy, and that they might do so surprisingly early in life. In this section I also wanted to point out that the readiness and ability to teach is matched by a readiness and ability to learn from teaching. It is as if the teacher said to the student: "I will teach you," and the student responded: "I will learn from you." It is as if a learning pact were sealed, the two parties taking their different, but related, responsibilities.

The message that this first part of this chapter is supposed to convey is that pedagogy is—as it was called previously—a species-specific adjustment, fundamental for our existence as human beings.

Learning as a By-Product and Learning as an Aim

Pedagogy is, however, far from a necessary condition for all learning. The young chimpanzees learn to crack nuts anyway (even if it takes an awfully long time) and—just as Premack and Barnett point out—all animals learn in their natural habitat without pedagogy. Even humans do this to a great extent. Mostly, you do not need to decide "I am going to learn this" in order to learn. Nor do you always need someone to help you to learn. Whatever you do, you learn. Learning is frequently a by-product of doing things for reasons other than learning to do them. In such cases, learning is not the result of systematic efforts to learn or to help others to learn.

This point was made clearly by the anthropologist Jean Lave, who had studied the master-apprentice form of learning among Vai tailors in Liberia (Lave, 1988). Although there was, in this situation, something that someone was supposed to learn (making clothes), and so the first criterion of pedagogy was met, there was no systematic effort to contribute to making this happen: things were arranged for *making* clothes, and not for *learning* to make clothes; the second criterion of pedagogy was thus *not* met.

In the case discussed by Lave, learning can hardly be described as an intended effect of systematic efforts to bring it about, but rather as a by-product of the apprentices' participation in the clothes-producing practice of the masters. Although the conditions were not set up for helping the apprentices to learn to make clothes, they nevertheless learned to do so, because they participated in the making of clothes. They participated in the same practice as the masters, the apprentices being "legitimate peripheral participants", while the masters were central participants. Learning can thus be seen (in this case, and in general) as a change in the pattern of participation, from someone being a peripheral participant to becoming a central participant (Lave & Wenger, 1991). Such a change amounts to the apprentice learning a great number of things: to talk like a tailor, to dress like one and, above all, to be one. And in addition, almost by accident, the apprentice learns to make clothes as well. The technical skills of a tailor are acquired as a part of the apprentice's acquisition of the identity of a tailor. Learning specific skills is just part of the transformation of the person, according to this view.

Lave's point is well taken. Much of what we learn, we learn without systematic effort on anyone's part to make it happen. A child growing up on a farm learns to milk cows by milking cows. Children learn to walk better by walking, learn to talk (mainly) by talking and learn to ride a bike by doing so. They learn by doing, by being involved. The most efficient and most successful cases of learning are of this kind. In addition to learning to sit, to walk, to run, to jump and so on, we might think of how children learn their mother tongue. Although adults usually do their utmost to help them, children mainly learn to speak as a by-product of their efforts to communicate.

In all these cases, you do not learn one thing in one place, in order to use what you have learned in other places and at other times, as is the case in school. You learn what is needed, when it is needed, and where it is needed. Learning something and making use of what you have learned are not separated. When learning is a by-product, you do not have the problem of learning for life, as in the case of learning in school, where the relevance of what you learn may not always be obvious.

On the other hand, I would argue that help in the form of systematic efforts by others is necessary for the learning of certain things. Although some children may become literate largely by themselves if they grow up in an intensely literate environment, other children need help, in the form of instruction, in order to do so. Learning to handle numbers, money, and tools in general, learning a second or third language, Newtonian mechanics, the theory of evolution, traffic signs and millions of other things; these are necessarily learned thanks to the systematic help of others.

But according to Lave and Wenger (1991), skills and knowledge are best learned (or, possibly, can only be learned) by participating in relevant practice. Skills and knowledge cannot (or, perhaps, cannot easily) be separated from the practice to which they belong.

Now if this is a fact, what can we say about schooling, the purpose of which is to prepare students to handle future novel situations in powerful ways? Lave and Wenger (1991) chose a group of high-school students studying physics as an example. What kind of practice are they participating in, what kind of community do they form? To the extent that "the practice of physics is . . . being reproduced in some form, there are vast differences between the ways high school students participate in and give meaning to their activity and the way professional physicists do" (p. 99). And the authors draw the conclusion: "In this view, problems of schooling are not, at their most fundamental level, pedagogical" (p. 100).[4] Instead, as I understand this conclusion, problems of schooling have to do with relations between different practices and between different communities. But how does this apply to the relationship between the practice of the high-school students studying physics and the practice of the physicists? In Lave and Wenger's view, it seems that the former can be improved by making it more like the latter. I would argue, however, that making the practice of learning physics more like the practice of creating physics, without addressing pedagogical issues, will not improve the learner's chances of acquiring new knowledge.

It thus seems reasonable to conclude that we can distinguish between two forms of learning: learning as a by-product of being involved in certain activities, on the one hand, and learning as an achievement brought about by systematic efforts (of the learners and/or of others), on the other hand. It also seems reasonable to conclude that certain things are learned primarily in one way, while other things are learned primarily in another way. Furthermore, the same thing might be learned in one way by some learners, and in another by others.

But even if they are clearly distinguishable, these two forms of learning are usually intertwined. When humans learn in the company of others, they almost always get some support from others, and if they learn by being taught, they frequently get involved in activities with purposes other than learning (traveling to foreign countries, reading books, watching TV for fun, etc.), which nevertheless help them to learn.

"De-Pedagogizing" Learning

These two forms of learning, however, are not usually seen as two equally legitimate options, applicable in different cases. Mostly, one of the options is seen as superior to the other, and attempts to improve learning spring from a preference for one or the other. During the last two decades or so, practice-based learning (learning by participation) has been considered by many to be a more powerful form of learning than school-based learning, and, in consequence, efforts to improve learning in schools have frequently involved trying to make school-based learning more like practice-based learning. This may be grounded in a view of learning in school, such as that of White (1989):

> We move the would-be learner out of the complex, dynamic life of everyday activities and sit him or her down in front of workbooks, drill-and-practice exercises, problem sets, reinforcement schedules, and so forth, and then try to build new skills and habits. Then carefully, we try to reinsert both the learner and learning back into the real world.
>
> (p. xiv)

Authentic and Non-Authentic Learning?

In a highly influential paper, Brown, Collins and Duguid (1989) defined learning through participation, or practice-based learning, *authentic* learning, while learning due to systematic efforts, such as learning in school, is by implication *inauthentic* learning. Obviously, what is authentic is the real thing, it is good; what is inauthentic is fake, it is bad. It may seem a bit ironic that the pedagogical acts that are seen by some as a distinguishing attribute of humans (Barnett, Premack, for instance) are seen by others (Brown et al., for instance) as "inauthentic learning."

But the world outside school is, after all, no more real than the world inside school, just as the people outside school are no more real than those inside school. As Ireson, Mortimore and Hallam (1999) point out, "for young pupils, it is *school* . . . that is the 'real world.'" The reason that learning in school is seen as unreal or unproductive is that students are expected to learn to handle situations other than the ones in which learning is taking place. This separation between the act of learning and the use of what is learned is a consequence of the institutionalization of learning in our society. If you are unhappy with the negative effects of this separation, there are basically two approaches to the problem. First, you might argue for "de-schooling society," either by doing away with schools in accordance with Illich's (1971) less than fully realistic suggestion, or by reducing the pedagogical function of the school and emphasizing its role in connecting people, in creating opportunities for children to learn about nature and society in situ. The second option is just the opposite of the first—we might try to develop the school's pedagogical function far beyond its current level. By helping the students to see the world around them in more powerful ways, we promote an understanding that the world talked about in school and the world surrounding school is the very same world.[5]

Does De-Pedagogization Affect Learning in School?

Two questions are relevant here: 1) Does the rhetorical de-pedagogization of learning correspond to a real de-pedagogization of learning in schools? and 2) If the first question can be answered in the affirmative, is it the case that such a de-pedagogization has shown adverse effects on the quality of learning in schools?

Let us look at the first question in the Swedish context. If de-pedagogization can be measured in terms of less teacher-led learning, the answer to this question is definitely yes. Also, if the diminishing importance of teaching, the planning of teaching and the following up of teaching relative to the teachers' other duties, can be seen as an indication of a de facto de-pedagogization taking place, the answer is yes, again (Skolverket, 2009, p. 211). As far as the second question is concerned, let us start by considering achievement in Swedish schools, by looking at information in the form in which it is available. Scores have gone down over the past two decades (Skolverket, 2004, 2009, pp. 15–16), whether measured by means of international comparisons or by comparing the performance on the same tests of different cohorts, at the same age but in different years. Can we then conclude that declining standards in Sweden are related mainly to the de-pedagogization of learning? We cannot say for sure, since there are a host of other things that have changed during that period. But the facts are indeed consistent with such a conjecture. In the special case of mathematics learning in (Swedish) multilingual classrooms, for instance, Hansson (2010) has identified a substantial positive influence on mathematics achievement of teachers taking responsibility for students' learning processes by organizing and offering a learning environment where the teacher actively and openly supports the students in their mathematics learning; and—as Hansson (2011) shows—by using more class time for teacher-led learning. She arrived at her conclusions by comparing different classes at the same point in time. But if we look at all Swedish classes together at different points in time, teacher-led learning has not increased but decreased during the last two decades, a period during which achievement in mathematics has gone down as well. Hence, a decrease in teacher-led learning has been (statistically) associated with lower achievement in mathematics, a fact consistent with Hansson's results.[6]

Pedagogies of Learning

As mentioned previously, learning with pedagogy is not necessarily better than learning without pedagogy, and the differences between learning with different pedagogies (i.e., between different ways of helping others to learn) are as important as the differences between learning with and without pedagogy. The pedagogization of learning might actually have serious side effects, if institutional factors (such as grades, selection of students, school rankings, etc.) dominate over the idea of learning as an empowerment of the learners.[7]

Demands on Teachers, Demands on Students

Brousseau (1997) introduced the concept of the didactic contract, referring to the teacher's expectations of the students and the students' expectations of the teacher, a kind of school-based form of the learning pact between child and adult, mentioned earlier. The teacher expects the students to learn, the students expect the teacher to help them to do so. The sign that learning has taken is that the students answer the questions and solve the problems presented by the teacher. But the teacher is facing a paradox: the more the teacher does to enable the students to answer the questions asked, to solve the problems given, the fewer opportunities may be left for the students to learn to understand that which they are expected to learn to understand. The reason is that the more clearly the teacher tells the students what is to be done, the less chance the students get to make the necessary distinctions (for instance, between what is critical and what is not). If the students were supposed to learn to discern what is to be taken into consideration, to make distinctions between what should be done and what should not be done, there might be nothing left to be learned; if the teacher has made the distinction already, the student can only repeat it. The students also face a paradox. They are expected to learn (to understand), but the more the teacher points out what they have to do or say, the less opportunity they have to learn (to understand), as they have fewer distinctions to make. On the other hand, they cannot decline to listen to the teacher either, as that would mean breaking the didactic contract (according to which they are supposed to learn from the teacher).

This double-sided paradox has to do with the distinction between two ways of learning in school. One way is to make the object of learning (that which is to be learned) your own, to discern the important aspects of the content of learning and the relations between them. The other way is to learn what to do and say in order to meet the demands imposed upon the learner by the teacher or the test. This distinction resembles other distinctions, named differently, but capturing the same—or similar—differences in learning and teaching, such as, for instance, Skemp's (1976) distinction between relational and instrumental understanding, or Marton and Säljö's (1976a, 1976b) distinction between deep and surface approaches to learning (see Chapter 5). The object of learning might be to learn to grasp how things are related to each other and to act accordingly (called "relational understanding" by Skemp) or it might be to learn to do things and to do them in a certain order, because this is what the teacher has told the students to do (this is what Skemp calls "instrumental understanding"). In the case of the former the learner is trying to learn to see (and do); in the case of the latter she is trying to learn to do. Skemp (1987) offers a simple example: learning to move from one point to another in a town where you have never been before. You can learn the route (turn to the left when you are on the street, walk straight on, turn to the right at the third street you cross, turn to the left . . . etc.). This is learning to do. You must always start from the same point, and if you make a mistake, you are lost. The alternative is to learn the geography of the relevant part of the town. You can start from any point and get wherever you want within the confines of the known part of the town. This is learning to see. In the latter case the learner's focus is on the objects involved in her acts (on what to see), while in the former, her focus is on the acts themselves (on what to do).

Another example: you have to learn how to solve quadratic equations. Again, you might learn to *do:* you learn how to insert certain numbers in certain places in the formula, but you might have problems with setting up the equation if it is not given, or the form in which the equation appears might not be recognizable to you. Or you might learn to *see:* you get familiar with the various forms in which a quadratic equation might appear, and you learn that a quadratic equation can be solved by means of quadratic completion (which generates the known formula). In this case, you can easily deal with quadratic equations of kinds you have never seen. In other cases, some students learn what to say when asked by the teacher, while others learn what they are supposed to say (express) when asked by the teacher. Not only the students but also the teachers might have a primary focus on an instrumental understanding or on relational understanding (as a requirement for students). In this way, the teacher's focus might or might not match the students' focus.

The significance of the double-sided paradox, mentioned previously, is that the more learning that happens of the second kind (learning to do), the less might happen of the first kind (learning to see). Hence, the teacher should, above all, help the students to appropriate the necessary aspects of the object of learning and the relationships between them. What would stop the teachers from doing so?

According to Brousseau (1997), there are pressures on the teacher to help the students to meet the demands of the system, and this diminishes the space for learning in the sense of developing more powerful ways of seeing the content of learning. The very same phenomenon was described by Kilborn (1979), within an entirely different framework, as "piloting" (see also Johansson, 1975; Lundgren, 1977). Here is an example of how the teacher solves a problem that the student was supposed to solve, instead of helping him to learn how to solve it. This should be obvious from the dialogue between a year-4 student, Erik, who has struggled with a multiplication problem for a quarter of an hour, and the teacher who walks up to his bench:

$$\begin{array}{r} 16 \\ \times\ 26 \\ \hline 96 \end{array}$$

Teacher: Right now. . . . That's right, yes . . . 2 × 6, what is it?
Student: 2 × 6 it is 12, right . . .
Teacher: No, where do you put the 1?
Student: There. 2 × 1 is 2, plus 1 is 3.
Teacher: Hm.

$$\begin{array}{r} 16 \\ \times\ 26 \\ \hline 96 \\ 12 \end{array}$$

As Kilborn (p. 83) points out, the teacher avoids Erik's real problem (which is 20 × 16) by asking the direct question "2 × 6, what is it?" When Erik continues by putting the 1 directly under the 9, the teacher tells him that the 1 should not be there, but without telling him why.

Piloting is thought to derive from the constraints of the frames, the factors delimiting the space of action (what can be done) in school.[8]

In Erik's case, the problem might have been that the teacher did not have the time to explain to Erik why he had to shift 12 to the left. According to Brousseau, the problem is the student's eagerness to deliver the correct answer, in combination with his seeing the teacher as the source of that answer, on the one hand, and the teachers' eagerness to help the students to deliver the correct answer, on the other hand. For Brousseau, the main problem in schooling is the risk that learning becomes instrumental in meeting the demands of the school, instead of enabling the students to handle future novel situations in powerful ways. But the reason for a teacher to act as described in the quote from Kilborn might be entirely different: the teacher might not know why 2 has to be shifted to the left, although he knows that it should be.

Teachers' Professional Knowledge

Ma Liping (1999) compared Chinese and US teachers' understanding of fundamental mathematics. She asked them four questions in individual interviews, the second of which was this:

> Some sixth-grade teachers noticed that several of their students were making the same mistake in multiplying large numbers. In trying to calculate
>
> ```
>    123
>  × 645
> ```
>
> the students seemed to be forgetting to move the numbers (i.e., the partial products) over on each line. They were doing this:
>
> ```
>    123
>  × 645
>    615
>    492
>    738
>  1,845
> ```
>
> instead of this:
>
> ```
>     123
>   × 645
>     615
>    492
>   738
>  79,335
> ```
>
> While these teachers agreed that this was a problem, they did not agree on what to do about it. What would you do if you were teaching sixth grade and you noticed that several of your students were doing this?
>
> (pp. 28–29)

Ma Liping found that 61% of the US teachers and 8% of the Chinese teachers could not explain why we have to move the numbers. Although worded in different ways, their answers boiled down to the idea that this is what you have to do, and they described the procedure of how to line up the partial products correctly. As to the question of why the students failed to follow the correct procedure, these teachers would probably say that the students were forgetful, careless, lacked concentration. They should shape up and do more exercises of the same kind.

But the rest of the teachers (American as well as Chinese) thought otherwise. They assumed that the students in the question did not understand why the numbers had to be moved. Accordingly, in their opinion, what the students needed, above all, was an explanation of the rationale underlying the procedure. So these teachers all came up with conceptual (and mathematical) explanations, although there were differences in how powerful their explanations were. Actually, there were three different kinds of explanations presented.

The first kind of explanation builds on the insight that 123 × 645 is just one of many way of representing a product of the two numbers. We might thus choose another representation that is more handy for carrying out the multiplication. Then 123 × 645 = 123 (600 + 40 + 5) and 123 (600 + 40 + 5) = 123 × 600 + 123 × 40 + 123 × 5 (according to the distributive law, as pointed out by all the Chinese teachers, who presented this explanation, but by none of the American teachers presenting the same explanation otherwise).

Now, 123 × 600 + 123 × 40 + 123 × 5 = 73,800 + 4,920 + 615 = 79,335 and if we line the partial products under each other, we obtain

$$
\begin{array}{r}
123 \\
\times\, 645 \\
\hline
615 \\
4{,}920 \\
73{,}800 \\
\hline
79{,}335
\end{array}
$$

The zeros in the second and third partial product derive from multiplication with 10 and 100 (the specific form of multiplication with 10, 100 and so forth, carried out by putting zeros after the number multiplied) and reflects the main point of this explanation: When we multiply with 5, 4 and 6, we in actual fact multiply by 5, 40 and 600. Whether or not the zeros are included or not does not make any difference to the end sum. So they can be omitted if we wish.

According to the second explanation, however, the zeros should not be there at all. The basic unit of numbers is usually one. When we consider 123, we think of 123 ones. But there are other options: we can choose other basic units, such as tens or hundreds. This means that when we multiply with 40, we can say that we multiply with four 10s, when we multiply with 600, we can say that we multiply with six 100s. Hence, when multiplying with 5 we get a product expressed in *ones* in the ones' place. When we multiply with four 10s we get a product expressed in *tens* in the tens' place. When we multiply with six 100s we get a product expressed in *hundreds* in the hundreds' place. Here the explanation of why the numbers have to be moved builds on the meaning of place values as seen in terms of basic units.

The third kind of explanation is simply a combination of the previous two, showing that there are different ways in which the question can be handled in a mathematically decent way.

It is interesting to note that the second explanation also builds on the distributive law (a [b + c] = ab + ac), but introduces an additional element: basic units. As the third explanation is a combination of the previous two explanations, it assumes both, of course. The three explanations are thus qualitatively different, and hierarchically organized (the second one includes the first one, and the third one includes both the first one and the second one). All the US teachers who presented conceptual explanations did so by using the first one of these three kinds of explanations, although without reference to the distributive law. The Chinese teachers presenting conceptual explanations did so by using the first of the explanations, but with reference to the distributive law, or by using the second or the third kind of explanation.

The conceptual explanations build on one or two powerful mathematical ideas, the idea of the distributive law and the idea of basic units. The distributive law tells us that a product can be rewritten as a sum of partial products. By doing so, the multiplication of large numbers can be handled easily. The distributive law derives from the fact that any number can be rewritten in terms of other numbers in infinitely many ways. This means that we can differentiate between a quantity and a number, the latter being just one specific representation of the former. So what 7 represents, for instance, can be represented in infinitely many ways (such as $1 + 1 + 1 + 1 + 3$; $139 - 132$; 4×1.75, etc.).

Since we can choose any representation as long as it represents the given quantity, we can choose that which is best for our specific purpose.

The second powerful idea, the idea of basic units, is similar. We are so used to seeing numbers as multiples of one that we do not even think of numbers as multiples of one, probably because our first encounter with mathematics usually starts with counting objects, one at a time. The unit "one" is given, and in consequence, not reflected upon. As mentioned earlier, any number can be rewritten as a sum of (or difference between) other numbers, representing the same quantity in infinitely many ways. In the same way, any quantity can be represented as the product of numbers in infinitely many ways, hence also as multiples of different basic units. In the previous example of multiplication of three-digit numbers, the operations are seen in the second and third kind of explanation as using three different basic units ("ones," "tens" and "hundreds").

Interestingly, the Russian educational psychologist, Davydov (1990) has taken the choice of the basic unit as the point of departure for introducing young children (6-year-olds) to the world of mathematics. His reason for doing so is the assumption that mathematics historically originates from the need for measurement. And in order to measure, you need a unit of measurement, so that every quantity can be seen as a product of a unit of measurement and a number.

Notes

1. Though I cannot guarantee that the rapid developments in epigenetic research will not overturn this fact in the future, it is unlikely to be on a scale that would make it relevant to this book.
2. The word *pedagogy* is used in two different senses in this book: first to refer to human beings' ability to help one another to learn and second to refer to a particular field of knowledge, which in many parts of the world, not least in Europe, is considered a discipline in its own right, dealing with upbringing, teaching and education in general terms (see, for example, Svensson, 2009).
3. "She" is used as the gender-indefinite pronoun throughout the book.
4. From the mid-1980s such ideas have been widely embraced by the educational research community. For instance, Lauren Resnick (1989), former president of the American Educational Research Association, declared that "we develop habits and skills of interpretation and meaning construction through a process more usefully conceived of as *socialization* than *instruction*" (italics in original, p. 39). A few pages later, the argument is repeated in a more specific context: "We may do well to conceive of mathematics education less as an *instructional* process . . . than as a *socialization* process" (italics mine; Resnick, 1989, p. 58).
5. The emphasis on learning through participation has not been the only source of de-pedagogization of learning. Constructivism, focusing on how knowledge is construed by the learner, has been interpreted as regarding the teacher's role as a passive one (see, for instance, Bergqvist, 1990). The enormous increase in the amount of information available, through the rapid development of information technology, has been seen by many as implying that students should above all develop generic abilities to pick up information (see Carlgren & Marton, 2000; Limberg, 1998).
6. This does not imply a generalization, such as "teacher-led learning is better than learning that is not teacher-led." It simply states a historical fact about Swedish schools, from ca. 1993 to 2013.
7. Some would argue that this type of impact, far from being an accidental side effect, constitutes a main function of the educational system. Disciplining, sorting, stratifying and categorizing every new generation is "the hidden curriculum" (Gustafsson, Stigebrandt & Ljungvall, 1981; Snyder, 1973), it is argued.
8. Also described as "funnelling" by Bauersfeld (1988).

2
WHAT IS TO BE LEARNED?

In Chapter 1 I elaborated briefly on the difference between "learning as a by-product" and "learning aimed at." This chapter is about the latter, as is the rest of this book.

What Matters?

People in most societies, such as Sweden in 2014, do not seem to consider "learning aimed at" an inferior kind of learning; they take schools for granted and they want the teachers who work there to help children to learn. General elections were held in Sweden on the 19th of September 2010. The liberal–conservative ruling block was challenged by the socialist–environmentalist block in opposition. According to the pre-election polls, the electorate found questions about school to be the most important ones. In the frequently televised public debates, school was discussed largely in terms of resources: how much money would be spent on schools by different governments and how that money would be distributed among schools, whether evenly or to favor lower-achieving schools. At the same time, it was more or less taken for granted in these debates that increased resources should primarily be used to reduce class size. I found this a bit perplexing. Even if you agree that schools need more resources, the ways in which those resources should be used can hardly be seen as self-evident. Although the effects of class size can be observed for younger children, especially for those with less favorable socio-economic backgrounds, such effects are in general weak (Gustafsson, 2003; Hattie, 2009; Skolverket, 2009).

The question of what factors contribute to differences in student learning is much discussed and much researched. What is it then that makes a difference? There are two main kinds of differences that co-vary with differences in student achievement in any given year of schooling. First, we have differences in what the students can do and what they know, before they begin work for that year. And second, there are differences between the classes in which the students happen to find themselves (see Hattie, 2009). The responsibility for providing the students with powerful conditions of learning rests primarily with the teachers. The next step, then, is to consider what they do towards such an end, and what they can possibly do.

Organizing Learning

The teachers must somehow organize work in the classroom in order to make learning possible. A frequent question posed in educational research is: Which is the best arrangement for learning?

This question may take several forms, such as some of those that Hattie (2009)—and many others—point to the following:

- Is learning by yourself better than learning by being taught?
- Does homework enhance learning?
- Is problem-based learning better than lectures for big classes?
- Is individualized learning preferable to group work?
- Is project work a good idea?

Questions like these deal with ways of organizing learning: possible methods, pedagogical tools and techniques. They are usually studied by comparing two or more ways of organizing learning, implemented in different classes, with the effects being measured by a test that assesses what the students have learned about the particular content dealt with during the lessons. The outcome is normally given in quantitative terms, the readers being ignorant of exactly what the students have learned.

The problem with questions of this kind is that they cannot be answered. It is not that they cannot be answered *yet,* and it is not because of a scarcity of research funds or a scarcity of good ideas. They are simply imponderable because of the degree of generality. Asking these questions is like asking whether pills are better than operations, or whether a hammer is better than a screwdriver, or whether eating is good for your health. Could it really be the case that everything is learned better when learners work by themselves than when they are taught? Regardless of what the learners do and regardless of how they are taught? Similar doubts can be raised about all the other questions on the list.

The best that can be said with regard to the optimal arrangements for learning is that they are not fixed: one arrangement might be preferable for certain aims, in certain circumstances, while another might be better for reaching other aims, in other circumstances. If we see the different ways of organizing learning as tools that are good for different purposes, then it makes sense to start with the question What is to be learned? instead of starting with the question What is to be done?

What Is to Be Learned?

The object of learning is the answer to the question What is to be learned? and it can be formulated in three different ways of increasing precision: in terms of content, in terms of educational objectives and in terms of critical aspects.

The Content

Learning is always the learning of something: there cannot be any learning without something being learned. Focusing on what is learned implies focusing on the content of learning. So perhaps the most obvious answer to the question What is to be learned? is to refer to the content of learning (What is to be learned? Multiplication of multi-digit numbers, Systems of linear equations in two unknowns, World War II, Literary genres, Long division, etc.).

In the past, syllabuses were written in such terms; occasionally, they still are. The problem is, however, that such formulations do not tell us what the students are supposed to become able to do. Will they be expected by the end of the school year, for instance, to recall Newton's laws of motion, or will they be expected to solve problems in physics that can be solved by means of Newton's laws of motion? Will they be expected to multiply multi-digit numbers by using the standard algorithm, or will they in addition be expected to be able to explain how and why the standard algorithm works in novel cases? Is it all right to use pocket calculators?

Educational Objectives

Educational objectives (instructional objectives, learning targets, learning goals, learning outcomes, etc.) relate to what the students are expected be able to do at the end of the school year, after the course or after the lesson. The most well-known attempt to develop a system of general categories is what has become known as Bloom's taxonomy (Bloom, Engelhart, Furst, Hill & Krathwohl, 1956).

Educational objectives are, as a rule, formulated on a central, national level in the school system and at the local level in higher education, according to the following formula:

> act + content = educational objective.

"Act" refers to what the learners are expected to learn to do with the content, such as, for instance:

> recall,
> interpret,
> explain,
> describe in one's own words, and so on.

(Bloom's categories mentioned above refer to the act aspect of educational objectives.)

And "content" might then be, for example:

Newton's laws of motion,
World War II,
pricing,
baroque music,
narrative, and so on.

By combining act and content, we obtain educational objectives, such as the following:

Using Newton's laws, when they apply, for solving problems,
Explaining the relationship between World War I and World War II in writing,
Distinguishing between different styles of music,
Describing the same event as a narrative and as a documentary report.

In educational objectives relating to skills, the act and content are fused:

Adding and subtracting in the number range from 1 to 20,
swimming,
riding a bike,
hitting a target, and so on.

There can even be qualifiers to characterize the way in which the students are supposed to be able to use the skill in question:

'independently,'
'in detail,'
'with the aid of,'
'in writing,' and so on.

Educational objectives are intended and assumed to inform teachers and students about what the latter are expected to become able to do. But, in reality, they do not say what the students are expected to *learn,* much less how we can help them to learn it.

Critical Aspects

The focus of the theory elaborated in this book is on learning to handle novel situations in powerful ways. A certain class of situations (instances) corresponds to a particular educational objective. Mastering an educational objective amounts to discerning and taking into consideration its necessary aspects. A necessary aspect might be (experienced) differences in the frame of reference from which situations have to be seen when trying to solve certain kinds of problems in physics; or differences in the "manyness" of objects when dealing with the very simplest problems of arithmetic; or differences in the meaning of Chinese words differing with regard to tone but being the same with regard to sound, and so forth. To the extent that the learner has not already made a specific necessary aspect her own, it is a critical aspect for her. It is one of the things that she has to learn in order to meet the learning target (the educational objective).

"Doing Sums"

We will take the example of the simplest form of "doing sums," mentioned earlier. That the expected learning outcome is to add and subtract in the number range 1 to 20 is certainly an answer to the question What are the students supposed to be able to do? But it does not address the question What do they have to learn in order to become able to add and subtract in the number range 1 to 20? nor does it address the question What do we have to do in order to help the students to learn that?

The reader might object: What on earth are you talking about? If the students are supposed to learn addition and subtraction in the number range 1 to 20, then they have to become able to add and subtract numbers up to 20. This is exactly what they have to learn.

You might believe that your answer is straightforward and self-evident, but it is in all likelihood based on an invisible assumption, invisible because it is not seen as one assumption among other possible assumptions, but as the only possible assumption. The assumption is that what it takes to learn to add and subtract in the number range 1 to 20 is to remember the answers when either two addends or one minuend and one subtrahend are given.

Now imagine the following. We ask a 6-year old-child: "How many fingers do you have on your left hand?" She says—just as almost all 6-year-olds would say: "Five." Then you ask her: "How many fingers do you have on your right hand?" And she says—as very few other 6-year-olds would: "Ten." Maybe she has misunderstood the question, or maybe her counting skills are erratic, so perhaps you suggest she should count her fingers. She does this, but comes up with the same answer again: "five" on the left hand and "ten" on the right hand. Now we need to change track and ask ourselves whether "five" and "ten" mean the same to her as they mean to us, and assume that her answers follow logically from what "five" and "ten" mean to *her*, just as our answers follow logically from what "five" and "ten" mean to *us*. In that case, we need to find out what those different meanings are and help her to be able to see the meanings that "five" and "ten" have for us. And if she does, her answers to the two questions will in all likelihood be the same as our own.

Neuman (1987) found that in three cases out of the 105 6- to 7-year-olds that she studied, the response was exactly like that of the little girl above, and she took the step of trying to envisage how the problem appeared to the child and what "five" and "ten" meant to her in that context. Numbers have three necessary aspects, without which the four rules of arithmetic do not make much sense. First, each number refers to a place in an order (the 1st, 2nd, 3rd . . . 9th thing)—its ordinal property. Second, each number refers to a certain "manyness" (one thing, two things, three things . . . nine things)—its cardinal property. And third, numbers are wholes that can be divided into parts (for example, 8 can be split into 3 and 5, and they are parts of the whole 8, and so are 6 and 2, or 1 and 7 or 4 and 4). Children frequently discern these aspects from events where quantities are handled, and having done so, they see future, similar events in terms of those aspects, in ways that are mathematically correct. But some children might discern one aspect, and others another. If they see and handle the situation in terms of one or two aspects only, instead of all three, what they do with numbers might appear not only wrong, but even bewildering.

So what would "five fingers on the left hand" and "ten fingers on the right hand" mean if we saw numbers only in terms of the first, the ordinal, aspect (as position in sequence)? It would not mean "more" (on the right hand), because now numbers do not mean "many" or "few." They are used only as a sequence of names (the one, the two, the three, etc.), much like the way that in some cultures children are named by the order of their appearance in the family (Neuman, 1987). In addition to seeing numbers as names in a sequence, children who do this frequently learn that that name of the last thing in a sequence is used as the name for the whole sequence. When adults demonstrate counting to children, they usually emphasize the last word of the sequence. "How many apples are there, Victoria? . . . OK, I'll help you. . . . One, two, three, four . . . yes, there are *four* apples" (stressing the "four").

If numbers are seen and used in this way, the name of the last finger on the left hand is "five"; hence, all the fingers on the left hand are called "five" together. If we assume that the girl counted (or just thought about) her fingers from the left to the right, both hands together, the last finger on her right hand is named "ten," hence, all the fingers on her right hand are named "ten" together. Somewhat surprisingly, perhaps, we find that the strange statement "I have five fingers on my left hand and ten on my right hand" originates from having correctly discerned one necessary aspect of numbers, but not the other two.

What would this little girl need to learn, then, in order to become able to add and subtract within the number range 1 to 20? She would need to discern two other necessary aspects of numbers, in addition to the position in a sequence: their "manyness" and their part–whole relationships. And this was exactly what Neuman (1987) helped her to do, thereby saving her from becoming a child with math difficulties.

Learning to Swim

What does it take to learn to swim? Most people would say that you have to learn the specific movements involved in swimming. However, this does not seem to be the case. The movements are just one aspect of what we might do in the water, and it actually turns out not to be the most important aspect. According to Polanyi (1958), the sudden experience of "I can swim" has more to do with breathing than with the particular movements of arms, hands and legs. The thing is that when a child, or an adult for that matter, has that sudden feeling of being able to swim, they have just learned to float, and this comes about by learning to breathe in water, which is different from breathing on land. In water, you breathe in such a way that you always retain a certain amount of air in your lungs, thereby lowering your own density and bringing it on par with that of water. And all of a sudden, you feel that you don't sink anymore and you shout out, "I can swim!" So, for the object of learning to swim, the critical aspect that distinguishes being able to from not being able to is the way of breathing or, more correctly, the bodily awareness of different ways of breathing.

These two cases are examples of critical aspects and the critical features[1] that are discovered by every successful learner, though rarely consciously. The "fiveness" and the "tenness" in the previous example are features belonging to the cardinal aspect of numbers, and a particular way of breathing is a feature of swimming, belonging to its breathing aspect.

What Critical Aspects Are

This book looks at the kind of learning that enables learners to deal with future, novel situations in powerful ways. In order for this to happen, the learner must come to be able to discern and take certain aspects of the object of learning into consideration simultaneously. Those aspects that she has to notice, but is not yet able to, are *critical* aspects for her learning.

Following this line of reasoning, the learner must learn to discern the critical aspects of the object of learning and *some* critical features simultaneously and, by doing this, enhance the likelihood of being able to discern the same or *other* critical features of novel tasks. In helping students to do this, it is, of course, a great advantage if the teacher knows what these aspects of the object of learning are. Unfortunately, however, this is far from always the case. Critical aspects (and features) can be difficult to discover. And—as mentioned previously—they can in no way be chosen, or decided upon, as educational objectives. Critical aspects and features have to be searched for and found.

All the ways of doing and seeing something have certain necessary aspects and certain necessary features that vary from situation to situation and must be discerned. This applies to dealing with the physical as well as with the symbolic. How could, for instance, Blanka Vlasic make a 208-centimeter high jump? "Through analyzing the video recordings of [her] jumps we could find that . . . Vlasic is able to jump 2,08 m because of a combination (timing and coordination) of the speed of her approach, the radius of the turn and thus the angular momentum achieved" (Pramling & Pramling Samuelsson, 2011, p. 6). Finding that speed and that radius means being able to distinguish the necessary speed and radius from other speeds and radii.

In the same way, awareness of the distributive law and of basic units are necessary aspects of understanding the multiplication of multi-digit numbers. Without them, the same meaning will not appear, regardless of whether you work on your own, in a group, outdoors or indoors, using electronic aids or not. But there are many other necessary aspects in any given situation, and, of course, it is impossible to list them all. Those mentioned previously might be necessary for the high jump, and others for the multiplication of multi-digit numbers. Other aspects again are necessary for other objects of learning. The idea is simple enough: the constituent aspects of the whole (the object of learning) are necessary for the whole to appear. And for all objects of learning, there are many necessary aspects that we never think of, for the simple reason that they have not happened to be critical in the cases that we have encountered. Or because we have never managed to find them.

But whatever is critical, it is critical to some particular learners. The features are critical in the sense that they distinguish between being able to and not being able to, between those who can and those who cannot. It is critical for beginners in swimming to learn to breathe in a particular way. If we were to compare elite swimmers with regular visitors to the pool, we would certainly find other critical features that separate experts from novices. What is critical is relative to the object of learning, and relative to the learners as well.

There are, however, some further distinctions to be made as far as the object of learning, described in terms of critical aspects, is concerned. The critical aspects that the learner must learn to discern make up the intended object of learning. The critical aspects that it is made possible to discern (in the learning situation) make up the enacted object of learning. The critical aspects that the learner has actually discerned in that situation make up the lived object of learning (i.e., the object of learning as seen by the learner).

Discerning Aspects of the World Around Us

Let us now shift from a pedagogical perspective to a developmental one in this section. If we take a close look at the growth of various capabilities in children, we can see how they gradually discern many different aspects of potential objects of learning, by themselves. Most adults are not aware of those aspects, and thus can hardly help children who fail to discern them. We will now look at some examples of children spontaneously discerning aspects of the world around them.

Learning to Speak

As early as the age of 6 to 12 months, children start to pick up (or in our words, discern) features of the language spoken by the people around them. While the babbling of infants up to 6 months old is more or less universal, after that, their babbling starts to show distinguishing features of their language. Whalen, Lewitt and Wang (1991) have found, for instance, that at the age of 6 to 12 months, French infants and American English infants show different patterns of intonation in their babbling. While the former tend to have a falling pitch contour in each utterance, the latter tend to have an equal number of rising patterns. This means that children at that age discern an aspect of speech, namely pitch, or rather variation in pitch (i.e., they distinguish between features). People generally focus on the first word uttered by a child ("Do you know that Lisa said her first word today? It was 'cat,' actually!"), but children start "to speak French" or English, or Hungarian, long before they say any words. One would think that words are the basic units of the spoken language and that letters are the basic elements of the written language, but it seems that when learning to speak or write, it is the general characteristics of the spoken or written language that are discerned first. Learning to talk is not only—perhaps not even mainly—a question of learning one word after another. Nor is learning to write only—or mainly—a question of learning one letter after another. The units by which adults characterize the system of spoken or written language may not always correspond to the units in terms of which the spoken or written language is learned. Jusczyk (1997) argues, for instance, that there are two basic skills the infant needs to develop in speech perception: first, the skill of segmenting speech signals into words, syllables and phonetic segments and, second, that of categorizing speech sounds.

Thus, the learner must become able to discern certain differences, to make certain distinctions, to tell things apart. These differences seem to be of rather general kinds, such as the difference between the black text and the white paper, the progression from the left to the right (or the other way around) or the patterns of intonation—sounds rising and falling. Distinctions can also be more specific, such as differences between letters and differences between sounds or tones. At every point in learning something, the learner has discerned certain things and has not discerned other things. The learner's mastery of the capability is partial at every point, neither right nor wrong. This applies to all kinds of learning and indeed throws new light on the body of research about conceptions, misconceptions, beliefs and children's theories, insofar as differences between them can be characterized in terms of partially identical component parts. The little girl in Neuman's (1987) study, for instance, had discerned the ordinal (sequence) aspect of numbers, but neither the cardinal ("manyness") nor the part–whole aspect. Saying that she had 10 fingers on her right hand followed logically from this. "Ways of seeing," frequently referred to as "misconceptions," originate from the fact that we discern some critical aspects but not others.

Learning to Write

Let us consider another skill that most people in the world learn, learn successfully and learn thanks to the support of others. What does it take to learn to write? Some might think that it amounts to learning to copy one letter at a time, learning to link letters to sounds and learning to put different letters (and sounds) together. But learning to write starts much earlier than that. Children learn to use pens, chalk and the like, to make marks on paper (or walls) rather than doing something else with them, like throwing the pen or sucking the chalk. Then they learn to draw things. The sun looks different from a dog, one dog looks different from three dogs, and so on. They also learn to distinguish between drawing and writing. If you ask them to draw something (and they want to please you), they do one thing, if you ask them to write something (and they agree to that) they do something different.

Luria (1929/1978) carried out an interesting study. He asked young children who had not yet learned to read and write to "write" something. It was hard to get them to agree: after all, they could not write. But at last they produced some "writing," to please the researchers. About 50 years later, Emilio Ferreiro tried to do something very similar with children in Buenos Aires who yet had not learned to read and write: she asked them to write something. Just like the Russian children 50 years earlier, the Argentinian children were reluctant to meet the researcher's request: "How on earth could we write, when we can't?" But the researchers managed to trick the children into writing, nevertheless. "We are going to tell you a story and afterwards we are going to ask you to tell us all you remember. You are welcome to write things down while I am reading the story, so it could be easier to remember." And the children indeed wrote something (Ferreiro & Teberosky, 1979). A third case of writing without being able to comes from the French anthropologist Claude Lévi-Strauss, who, in the 1950s, lived for some time with an Indian tribe on a research trip to the Amazon. The members of the tribe could neither read nor write. Nevertheless, Lévi-Strauss gave them paper and pencils—for whatever they wanted to use them for. He sat in the shade a lot, busy with writing up his observations by hand. One day, he discovered that several members of the tribe seemed to be imitating him. They were sitting, bowed above a pile of papers, busy "writing" something, just as he was (Wilcken, 2010).

Now, what did the Russian peasants, the Argentinian children and the warriors of the Amazon "write"? Well, they "wrote" the same thing (i.e., they wrote in the same way, in spite of differences in time, space and age). What they wrote is exemplified in Figure 2.1.

One might rightfully ask whether this figure depicts writing. Well, obviously not. Those who produced the marks have definitely not demonstrated that they are capable of writing. But I would like to argue that they knew more than nothing. They had, in fact, discerned some features of writing. They knew something that everyone who can write knows. First, there is a regular alternation of

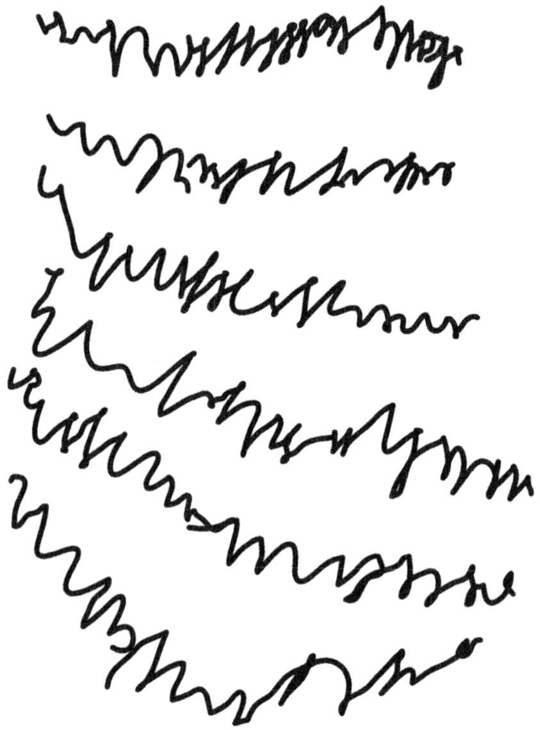

FIGURE 2.1 Illiterate "writing" (Tolchinsky, 2003, p. 57).

white (empty paper) and black (the letters). It is a necessary—but far from sufficient—component or feature of writing. Without it, there is no writing at all. Second, there is a linear growth (from the left to the right, in French, anyway) and an alternation of lines and empty spaces. This is another necessary feature of writing. Third, the movement from the left to the right is combined with short movements, alternating between up and down. This is also a necessary feature of writing (in English, Russian, French, etc.).

When it comes to young children, they clearly distinguish between drawing (produced mostly through circular movements of the hand holding the pen) and writing (produced through linear movement of the hand holding the pen). The scribble in Figure 2.1, although it certainly does not qualify as writing, shows that those who produced it have managed to capture something about writing (i.e., they have discerned some features of it).

When do children start to learn to read and write? Some children can read and write before they start school. Obviously they must have started learning earlier. But what about children who cannot read and write when they go to school? Have they not started to learn? Are they going to begin only when the teacher starts to teach them? No, I do not think so.

The picture we obtain from the observations referred to shows that children discern various necessary features of writing, one after the other, such as using pens, pencils, typewriters and computers to produce a graphic track; they make the track progress linearly, horizontally from left to right or from right to left, or vertically from top to bottom or from bottom to top, depending on the conventions of the system practiced in their surroundings; they alternate the track with white spaces. These aspects cease to be noticed as the children become literate, since all have mastered them and no differences can be observed between the children in this respect. We cannot separate aspects that are simultaneously present in each case.

Ashton-Warner (1963) described the great difficulties experienced by children who have grown up in an illiterate environment, when they start school and begin to learn to read and write. Possibly, they have not had the opportunity to grasp the idea of reading and writing and the aspects of those skills that are taken for granted by literate adults and by children growing up in a literate environment. Children can pick up such necessary and—as a rule—taken-for-granted aspects of their environment, given that those features are present in that environment. If they are not present, they cannot be picked up.

Getting Sweets

Hannula and Lehtinen (2005) set out to study young children's tendency to pay attention to quantitative aspects of the world around them. The procedure they used was as simple as it was ingenious. Thirty-nine Finnish children in the age interval 3.3 to 3.7 were asked to imitate the interviewer, who gave some sweets to a toy animal. Only small quantities of sweets were used. Twenty-four of the children gave the toy animal the right number of sweets (and brought the right number of socks to a one- or multi-legged dinosaur in another similar task) and also indicated their awareness of the number aspect of the situation by saying the number (showing it with their fingers, etc.). The difference that the researchers noticed and became interested in was to what extent the children paid attention to the number of sweets and the number of socks when trying to imitate the interviewer. All the children were followed up to 6 years of age as far as their numerical skills were concerned. The extent to which they spontaneously attended quantitative aspects of the test situation when 3.5 years old turned out to be significantly correlated with their numerical skills 2.5 years later, when the effects of non-verbal IQ, verbal comprehension and lack of enumeration and procedural skills were controlled.

This is an example of certain children discerning (noticing, attending to) a particular aspect of a situation. This aspect happens to be critical for the task to be performed (imitating the interviewer). Furthermore, the children's tendency to discern this particular aspect was found to be correlated with their numerical skills, not only at the time when the observations were made but also some years later. And, of course, how can children learn about the quantitative aspects of the world without even noticing them? On the other hand, how can they learn to notice the quantitative aspects without learning about them? Actually, Hannula and Lehtinen (2005) found that the relationship between the two was reciprocal.

What these results and this line of reasoning suggest is that noticing quantitative aspects of the world around us is a constituent part of the development of numerical skills. It is actually a critical aspect, but it is critical among children, including some who discern it and others who do not. It is not critical in groups in which all the participants are capable of discerning it. For this reason, we probably do not think of it as a part of the numerical–mathematical development, for the simple reason that it is invisible among older children. It is invisible because everybody can do it.

Discerning More Precise Meanings

In the previous examples the differences between different understandings of what it takes to read and write were described in terms of discerning—or not discerning—certain necessary aspects of reading and writing. In other cases, differences in understanding might be described in terms of discerning a certain aspect of something in a more or less precise way, which again is a function of the learner making or not making certain distinctions.

Jensen (2007) observed instances of pretending, in pre-school. In some of his observations we can see how children capture certain aspects of pretending (notably that it differs from "doing it for real") without being quite able to pretend (see p. 89). On one particular occasion, a little boy is observing someone pretending to drink. Then he picks up some thawing snow with his plastic spade and drinks a few drops. Jensen's interpretation is that the little boy has discovered one (holistic) aspect of "pretending to drink," namely, that it is drinking but drinking in a different way. He produces a different way by drinking only a very little. Later he probably discovers the more precise meaning of "pretending to drink," namely, that you do not drink at all but merely appear to be drinking. The difference between more and less precise ways of perceiving something resembles qualitative differences in understanding what you read (see, for example, Marton & Säljö, 1976a). Tolchinsky (2003) provided us with another example: at a certain stage, children realize that text is composed of different letters, and they would not accept a sequence of the same letter (e.g., AAAA) as writing. Subsequently when they have learned to write in a more conventional sense, they are aware of further restrictions on what counts as writing, above all that the letters put together are supposed to form meaningful units. Just as the meaning of "pretending" becomes more precise, the meaning of "writing" becomes more and more precise: fewer and fewer things count as writing (as the learner makes further distinctions).

But the space of what counts as "writing" may also expand, and expand without getting less precise. You might become aware that you can write in different languages, with different kinds of letters, or not using letters at all, and so on.

Aspects Critical for Making Distinctions and Aspects Critical for Generalizing

Obviously, there are aspects that must be taken into consideration by making a distinction, such as whether your body is immersed in water or not, what numbers you are trying to find the difference between, and so on. If you have not discerned these aspects, you must learn to do so in order to master certain tasks. However there are other aspects that should *not* be taken into consideration when performing a task: they are irrelevant to it. What is important here is to be able to generalize, to ignore variation in a particular aspect. In such cases, you still have to learn to discern the aspects in order to be able to disregard them. In order to recognize a triangle, you must discern its three corners, but you have to disregard its rotational orientation, its size, and so on. "This is a triangle . . . and this. . . . and this, too." Because every triangle will have a rotational orientation, you have to learn to discern (notice) this in order to be able to disregard the orientation and recognize the form as a triangle. The same goes for size, which is an inherent feature of any triangle. By discerning the size, it can be disregarded when comparing the angles of two triangles, for example.[2]

The learner thus must discern (open up) the necessary aspects of the object of learning in order to handle it in a powerful way. But she must also discern (open up) the non-necessary aspects of the object of learning in order to separate them and generalize across them. So learning, in the sense of learning to discern, may imply the narrowing or widening of the set of relevant cases (the situations that the object of learning refers to). Furthermore, aspects and features might be critical in the sense that they have to be taken into consideration or in the sense that they must not be taken into consideration (see the section "Critical Aspects and Critical Features, Again" in the next chapter).

Learning as Differentiation

Critical aspects are thus aspects of the object of learning that the learners must become able to discern in order to make the object of learning their own, as well as in order to be able to handle novel instances of the object of learning. Learning to discern critical aspects of the object of learning resembles Gibson and Gibson's (1955) view of perceptual learning. They distinguish between enrichment theories and differentiation theories. According to the former, we receive sensory information (light waves, sound waves, etc.) that has to be processed, enriched and cumulated in order to yield meaning. An internal representation or a model of "the world out there" is built up in one's mind, and it is this "inner world" that is the source of our awareness. (This is "making meaning of sense data.") According to the alternative, differentiation theories, perceptual learning entails learning to discern relevant features of the environment and thereby perceive the world in more and more differentiated ways. (This is "discerning meaning in the world.")

Enrichment or Differentiation

To put it very simply, according to enrichment theories, our perception of the world is richer than the world itself (the information we receive from the world around us has to be processed in order to become meaningful and, thus, richer), while according to differentiation theories, the world we perceive is richer than our perception of it (we pick up meaningful patterns and structures directly from the world around us, but our picture is always partial). In the first case we are cut off from the world and only its internal representation is available to us, a view called "dualism." In the second case, meaning is constituted in the relationship between humans and their world, a view called "non-dualism."

This line of argument appeared in a paper by Gibson and Gibson (1955), in which the differentiation view of perceptual learning was illustrated by a simple experiment. Eighteen scribbles were devised, varying in three dimensions 1) number of coils—3, 4 or 5, 2) horizontal compression or stretching and 3) orientation, or right–left reversal (see Figure 2.2).

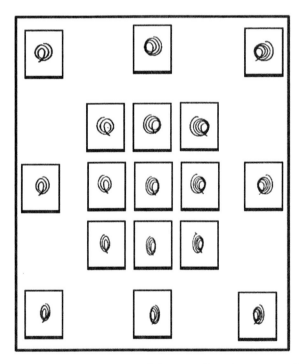

FIGURE 2.2 Nonsense items differing in three dimensions of variation (Gibson & Gibson, 1955, p. 36).

In addition, there were 12 more scribbles differing from each other and from all of the 18 scribbles in the original set in many respects, which were assumed to be sufficient for discriminating these 12 scribbles from the topical item given at the beginning. The topical item (or chosen item) was the scribble in the middle of the set in Figure 2.2. The experimenter shuffled a pack of cards with the two sets of scribbles, one scribble on each card, the topical item appearing on four of the cards. In individually administered sessions, each subject was told that she would be shown scribbles on cards, one at a time, and that every time she would have to tell if the scribble was the topical item. The subjects were also told that it would appear several times. After that they were invited to inspect the chosen scribble for 5 seconds. Then the cards were shown one at a time, and every time the subject had to tell if the scribble on the card was identical with the chosen scribble or not. Once the whole pack had been used, the experimenter showed the topical item again for 5 seconds after which the same procedure was repeated. Once the subject had identified the four occurrences of the topical item during the same trial (without mistaking any other scribble for the chosen one) the session was terminated.

Adults, children (8.5 to 11 years old) and younger children (6 to 8 years old) participated in the experiment. Eight of the 10 children in the last group failed to fulfill the given criterion during the experiment. We can see the results for all three groups in Table 2.1, in which the first line refers to the number of scribbles that the subject erroneously "recognized" (i.e., thought that she had recognized as the chosen one) during the first trial. We can conclude that all the subjects got better at distinguishing the other scribbles from the topical item, and the more a scribble differed from the topical item, the easier it was to discriminate between the two (see Table 2.1). The three dimensions in the experiment were simply critical aspects, in the sense in which the expression is used in this book, and the participants learned to discern them better and better. The experiment was set up to illustrate what learning to differentiate might be like, and this is what was shown.

TABLE 2.1 Increase in the specificity of an identifying response for three age groups (Gibson & Gibson, 1955, p. 37).

Variable	Adults (N = 12)	Older children (N = 10)	Younger children (N = 10)
Mean number of undifferentiated items on first trial	3.0	7.9	13.4
Mean number of trials required for completely specific response	3.1	4.7	6.7★
Percentage of erroneous recognitions for items differing in *one* quality	17	27	53
Percentage of erroneous recognitions for items differing in *two* qualities	2	7	35
Percentage of erroneous recognitions for items differing in *three* qualities	0.7	2	28

★ Only two of the younger children achieved a completely specific identification. The mean number of undifferentiated items on the last trial was still 3.9.

There are some interesting qualitative aspects of the experiment. The participants were encouraged to describe the scribbles, and special efforts were made to obtain and record what seven of the older children said. Their ways of describing the scribbles were of two kinds: naming responses and qualifying responses. The frequency of the latter increased during the experiment. Examples of the former are nouns like "figure 6", "curl," "spiral," "scroll." Examples of the latter are adjectival phrases like "too thin," "rounder," "reversed." These ways of referring to the scribbles do not focus on the scribble to be described, but on the relationship (read: difference) between it and the topical item. It thus seems that identifying an object amounts to identifying the difference between it and other objects—at least in the cases examined. Learning was thus described in this study as the discernment of critical aspects and critical features, and the discernment was described in terms of finding differences (i.e., as progressive differentiation).

Theories of differentiation, to which the theory presented in this book belongs, all share the view of learning described previously but may differ in other respects.

Ascending From the Abstract to the Concrete

The idea of a progressive discernment of necessary aspects of the object of learning, argued for in this book, is consistent with the second view of perceptual learning, inherent in theories of differentiation. At the same time, it is also consistent with the Hegelian idea of ascending from the abstract to the concrete. In Gibson and Gibson's (1955) experiment, mentioned in the previous section, the participants are assumed to abstract the three critical aspects (through the differences between the different instances), and the three critical features within each, bringing them together and then seeing every scribble in terms of this initial abstraction. This is in line with Ilyenkov's (2008) and Engeström's (2011) interpretation of Hegel's principle, in terms of an initial abstraction from "the sensory concrete," followed by using this initial abstraction to make sense of widely varying concrete cases, and by doing so, enriching it and developing it into a system of multiple and progressively expanding manifestations.

Theories of Differentiation and the Natural Attitude

The idea of seeing learning as "learning to see," which runs through this book, contradicts common sense. As pointed out by the phenomenologists, we mostly adopt what they refer to as the "natural attitude" (see, for instance, Spielberg, 1982). We tacitly assume that what we see is exactly what is there to be seen and that others see things in the same way we do. It is hard to realize that we have actually learned to see the world in certain ways and that others may have learned to see it differently.

According to differentiation theories, we do see the world differently, and not because the same sensory information is processed differently by the machineries of different minds, but because different persons perceive the world in different ways right from the beginning (of the perceptual act). They "pick up" or discern different features. In Markova's (1982) interpretation, the differentiation theory of perception is already inherent in Hegel's philosophy. Objects are initially not differentiated from other objects with which they have some properties in common, nor from the wholes of which they are parts. By discerning different features and by separating parts from wholes, and especially by bringing features as well as parts together, the learners arrive at a more powerful—and more concrete—understanding or perception of the object.

Heinz Werner has described the original, undivided experience of the world that a young child can be assumed to have (Werner, 1948). Let us try to imagine what such a perception of the world may be like. A human being, for example, has an infinite number of attributes. But these are not discerned by the child, as she has not yet learned to discern them. She sees an undifferentiated whole. Gradually, however, she learns to differentiate more and more aspects and features of beings and things. The aspects and features, thus discerned and differentiated, become more and more related to each other and integrated. The course of learning and development proceeds from the undivided wholes to more and more differentiated and integrated wholes, according to Werner—and the author of the present book.

Different Meanings of What Is to Be Learned

Earlier in this chapter, I mentioned three different answers to the question What is to be learned? The first answer refers to the content of learning (also called "the direct object of learning," by Marton & Booth, 1997). The second answer refers to what the learners are expected to become able to do with that content (sometimes called educational objective, learning target, intended outcome, etc., though the same concept is also referred to using a combination of the terms "direct object of learning" and "indirect object of learning," by Marton & Booth, 1997). The third answer refers to what the learners need to learn in order to achieve the goals involved in the second answer. The object of learning in this case amounts to becoming able to discern all the critical aspects and to focus on them simultaneously. There is no one-to-one correspondence between objects of learning as described on different levels. There are many different ways in which an object of learning that is characterized in terms of content can be rewritten as an educational objective or in terms of critical aspects. Nonetheless, the three ways of answering the question What is to be learned? represent three levels of increasing precision. In this book, the object of learning is described primarily in terms of critical aspects and features to be discerned.

Notes

1. As mentioned previously, the former refers to a dimension, such as numbers or colors, the latter to particular numbers, such as 1, 2, 3 . . . or to particular colors: red, blue, green . . . for example.
2. What kind of variation must be taken into consideration and what kind of variation must not be taken into consideration is relative to the authoritative definition of the object of learning; in the example of what it takes to differentiate a triangle from other geometric forms, a certain classificatory system is assumed (Anne Watson, personal communication, March 3, 2013).

3
SAMENESS AND DIFFERENCE IN LEARNING

Two of the points made in the previous chapter were as follows:

1) When trying to help someone to learn something, we should take our point of departure in what is to be learned (i.e., in the object of learning).
2) For every object of learning, and for every learner, there are critical aspects and critical features, which the learners have to become able to discern.

This chapter is about what it takes to learn to discern critical aspects and critical features.

The Problem With Direct Reference

We usually refer to aspects and features of the object of learning with words. Therefore, making the object of learning your own frequently means finding out the meaning of words.

The usual way of trying to help a child to grasp the meaning of a word is to point to what the word refers to. We say "green," point to a cucumber and hope that the child will realize that the word *green* means "green." But how can the child possibly know that the word does not mean "cucumber"? Or "vegetable"? Or "there"?

This problem was pointed out by the philosopher Quine, in his book *Word and Object* (1960). He suggests that we imagine a linguist trying to learn the language of some little-known "natives." One day he is out in the open with an informant of his, and "a rabbit scurries by, the native says 'Gavagai,' and the linguist notes down . . . 'Rabbit' . . . as a tentative translation, subject to testing in further cases" (p. 29).

Yes, of course, *gavagai* could very well mean "rabbit," but equally well "white thing," "animal," "one," "food" or even "the huckleberries are ripe" (Murphy, 2004, p. 341). Trying to communicate the meaning of a word by pointing to its referent (i.e., using direct reference) is not a powerful way of helping a fellow human being to find out what that word means. Nothing has one feature only. The question is, how the feature that a word refers to can be separated from other features and hence be made visible. You cannot draw a circle only (you draw a geometric figure, in black perhaps, in the middle of the page, or to the right or to the left; you draw a small figure or a large one, etc.). What does the word *circle,* for instance, refer to among all these features? What am I pointing to when I point to a circle?

When trying to help children to learn what a word means, an important distinction has to be made. Sometimes, the child has already discerned a particular kind of phenomena (such as circles, for instance), but she does not know what it is called. In other cases, the child has not identified the phenomenon in question: whether or not she has discerned the word, she has not discerned the phenomenon (and thus the meaning). Vygotsky's (1986) famous experiment on the learning of the meaning of words is about the first kind of situation.[1]

Discerning Features That Have Been Discerned Previously

As mentioned earlier, the meaning of a word cannot be found out by means of direct reference (pointing to something to which the word refers); it leaves too many alternative hypotheses, of which all but one have to be rejected.

There is a standard way of solving this problem, however, called "induction," that is practiced a countless number of times every day, everywhere around the globe (at home, at work, in schools, etc.). A necessary condition for learning word meanings is assumed to be the realization of what different things referred to by the same word have in common. The learner is thus invited to consider different things, having the targeted feature in common, but differing otherwise. Hypotheses can be eliminated in this way. Suppose that *gavagai* in reality means "white thing." The native would need to point to other white things, in addition to the rabbit, which are also *gavagai* (a bird, a flower, a piece of paper, etc.), all supporting the hypothesis that *gavagai* really means "white thing."

In the same way, it is not good enough to point to a cucumber saying "green" to a child who has already discerned the color green but has not yet linked the word *green* to it. What about pointing to a cucumber, on the other hand, saying "green," pointing to a green ball, saying "green," pointing to a green curtain, saying "green"? Now the learner can see that "green" does not mean "cucumber"; neither does it mean "vegetable" nor "round" nor "hanging." Perhaps, after all, it means "green." In this case, the focused feature (green), that which we want the learner to discern, is invariant (i.e., present in every instance) while other features vary (they are present in some instances, but not in others). As the right feature must be present in all instances, we can eliminate all hypotheses about features not present in all instances. This procedure can never result in absolute certainty (there are always conceivable hypotheses left that have not been ruled out). But for all practical purposes, this procedure (induction) works well enough, when direct reference does not, provided that the learner recognizes the focused feature. And if she does, it means that she has indeed discerned and seen it previously. She does not have to form a new meaning but has to select a meaning among meanings, in the new situation.

Discerning Features That Have Not Been Discerned Previously

By means of induction, you can thus select a feature with relative certainty if you have discerned that feature previously and can recognize it. The scenario suggested by Quine is an example of this: the learner (the linguist, in this case) does not have to learn a new meaning. It is assumed (by Quine and by the reader of the present text, I believe) that the linguist knows the relevant meaning (i.e., he can discern the word's referent and even knows the corresponding word in his mother tongue, English). He is trying to find out what words in the new language mean (i.e., trying to find the correspondence between words uttered and their meanings). The linking of meaning and word in the new language is mediated by the link between meaning and word in his mother tongue.

But you cannot discern a novel feature in a novel aspect for the first time, by encountering different instances having that feature in common, but differing otherwise. If you cannot discern a feature in one case, you cannot discern it in two either. Or in 22. Encountering several instances is no better than encountering one, in this respect. If the child is looking at two apples and cannot possibly discern (grasp, apprehend) their "twoness," why would she be better off when looking at two cups and two birds or looking at 100 pairs of different things at the same time? The same with discerning the color green. If you cannot discern the greenness of a watermelon, why would it help to look at a cucumber too? If you cannot see a particular feature of one thing, you cannot see the same feature of another thing, either. And then you cannot possibly see that the two things have that feature in common. Consider, for instance, a child, who does not know what democracy is and to whom a teacher describes the system for governing, in three countries that have been chosen as instances of democracy (which is supposed to be common to all of them). Will the child be able to understand what democracy is through this exercise? Well, the reader might say "No, it is not good enough to point to three instances. You have to define the concept, you have to explain what it is, in addition to giving examples." So you perhaps say something such as "democracy is a way of governing a country, people choose representatives who can decide various things on their behalf." Let us assume that this particular (Swedish) child has in fact come across general elections. Perhaps she has even heard the word *democracy,* without understanding what it refers to. And she might even have heard of choosing representatives who are members of the

Parliament and decide on the people's behalf. "This is how a country is governed," the child might have concluded. Will she now understand what it is that is called democracy? No, she will not. At least she will not understand how it differs from "governing a country." In order to separate the two, she would need to encounter at least one other way of governing a country. There is no way of discovering—or being able to explain—the meaning of *green* in an entirely green world, or the meaning of *democracy* in a world where there has never been any other way of governing a society. Induction thus presupposes that you can see a particular feature (or features)—that you can recognize it already. Induction assumes meaning; it cannot create it. So where does meaning come from to begin with?

How can we discern features that we have never discerned before? And how can we learn to discern them? The American philosopher Jerry Fodor argues that the only answer ever suggested to this question is induction, which means—as explained previously—finding out what is common to different instances having a particular feature in common but differing in other respects. As pointed out previously, however, induction works only when the feature has been discerned already, and does not work when the feature has not been discerned previously. Hence, we do not have any explanation of how people discern features initially—still less how they learn to discern them. In other words, we do not know how novel meanings are brought about (see Fodor, 1980). In other words we do not know how the most important form of learning can possibly take place.

Children do, nevertheless, learn what *two, green, large, tall* and *three* mean, and later on even what *one thousand ninety-seven* means or what *virtue* is, how we can account for the melting of ice when the temperature goes up or for the sun rising every morning, and hundreds of thousands of other things. Where do all those ideas or meanings (concepts) come from if they cannot be learned? Fodor's (1980) answer is as straightforward as it is radical: they are innate. All of them. The only learning that takes place is learning which (conceptual) capabilities to draw on in different contexts. The hypothesis of innate concepts is advanced by default: concepts cannot be learned, nevertheless we use them. Hence they must be innate.

The same basic point was actually made by Plato more than 2,000 years ago in what has become known as Meno's paradox:

> A man cannot inquire either about what he knows or about what he does not know—for he cannot inquire about what he knows, because he knows it, and in that case is in no need of inquiry; nor again can he inquire about what he does not know, since he does not know about what he is to inquire.
> (from Harman, 2011)

Learning is thus impossible. We cannot acquire new knowledge. The paradox is that we do know things nonetheless, quite a lot of things. The solution for Plato is that knowledge was already laid down in our immortal souls, when we were born (Harman, 2011; see also Day, 1994).

Fodor's thesis contradicts all theories of conceptual development, of course, such as Piaget's or Vygotsky's theories, for instance. In all those theories, a progression through different and increasingly advanced and complex levels is mapped. Usually, a certain level is considered to be more advanced than another (earlier in the succession) if the later level includes the earlier one, but not the other way around. But Fodor argued that higher—or more complex—ways of understanding things cannot be developed from less advanced (or less complex) ways of understanding them. And as said previously, his argument is that induction cannot explain how such a transition could take place and that there is no alternative account available.

We Do Have to Learn to Discern Features Whether or Not They Are Innate

Induction does not explain how we can find novel meanings and make them our own. In other words, it does not explain how we can learn to discern novel aspects and features. Fodor got this right, no doubt. But I want to show that we, nevertheless, do learn to discern novel aspects and novel features, regardless of whether they are innate or not.

I am going to use a thought experiment to illustrate that we might not necessarily be able to discern, see, sense a quality which is a necessary feature of a phenomenon, even if we are genetically endowed with the capability of doing so. We have *to learn* to discern every feature, every quality, every new meaning, innate or not. Let us continue with the example of the color green. Being able to see it is an example of a capability that is obviously innate, but which we still have to learn to use. Quite simply, how can we see that the cucumber is green, or the lawn, for instance? Do we have to learn to see the greenness of the green? As it happens, Stefan Einhorn, Professor in Molecular Oncology at the Karolinska Institute in Stockholm, has addressed this very question in his book *A Hidden God*:

> This experience of color comes into being in our awareness as a consequence of light waves with certain wavelengths being reflected by a certain surface, such as a lawn, for instance. This reflected radiation activates nerve cells in the eye. The nerve impulses go to the brain and they are "translated" into an experience of green color.
>
> (1998, p. 45, translation mine)

This is a straightforward enough answer, implying that we do *not* have to learn to see the greenness of the lawn at all. We are just equipped for doing so. But this answer can be challenged. It may be that light, lawn, eyes, brain, sensitivity to a certain wavelength are necessary conditions for discerning the greenness of the grass, but they are not sufficient. Something is missing.

This may sound odd, because reacting to a certain wavelength in a certain way is absolutely one of those innate capabilities of ours, believed by Fodor to be the only kind of relevant capability that we possess. Most of us are equipped by birth to see green. Still, I claim that we have to learn to see it, and in order to do so we need certain experiences. And here is the thought experiment that I want to use as a tool. Imagine that you live in an entirely green world! Everything is equally green and is always green. Exactly the same nuance, no difference at all. Do you think that you would notice the greenness of the grass in that world, and would you know what "green" is at all? And would you have an idea of color? Would it be possible for you to learn to see greenness if a teacher coming from another world tried to help you by pointing to all kind of green things (to anything, as everything is green), saying "green" each time. No, you could not learn to see green in the inductive way (by inspecting different instances of the same green color).

But there is no entirely green world! Should we really be impressed by a thought experiment involving a fictive and impossible situation? Moreover, this experiment involves envisaging something relatively rare: an ever-present aspect of the world. Still, there are other examples, however, of aspects of the world around us that are always present and hence invisible.[2]

You do not sense the quality of the air, a particular scent, or a certain sound if they are present all the time, and present in the same way. You do not even notice the pain in your stomach if you have had it for your entire life, all the time (Sachs, 1983), nor your way of living, if you have never come across other options (Magnér & Magnér, 1976).

The point is that when something (a color, a sound, a scent, a pain, a way of living, etc.) is present all the time and present in the same way, the information is received by the organism without any awareness on the part of the person. In terms of information impinging on the organism, the individual sees, hears, feels. But in another sense, she does not. Why this seeing without seeing, hearing without hearing, feeling without feeling? What does it take to see what you see, hear what you hear, feel what you feel? If you see something all the time, if you hear something all the time, if you feel something all the time, you will not be able to discern that which is seen, heard or felt.

So what is always present cannot be discerned, regardless of whether the capability of discerning it is innate or not. Actually, nothing can be discerned by simply receiving sense data from it. The reason is, as will be shown, that the meaning of something does not rest in that thing but transcends its boundaries. This is why we have to learn to discern novel meanings. And this is how we learn to discern novel meanings.

Learning to Discern Novel Features and Aspects

What would be needed in an entirely green world to enable its inhabitants to see (in the sense of becoming aware of) the greenness of their world and to develop a concept of color? As has been pointed out again and again in this book, most people think that we can make novel meanings our own by engaging with instances that have that meaning in common, though differing otherwise. And as has been pointed out again and again, it just does not work. But even if most people emphasize sameness, there are others who emphasize difference as the origin of meaning. According to de Saussure (1916/1983) language is a system and the whole is present in each and every one of its parts. A single word in itself does not mean anything, not even through linkage to its referent (see the word *green* and the green plant pointed at in the example earlier in this chapter); its meaning originates from its relation to (difference from) other words, other color terms in this case (from the differences between colors, I would say). A similar idea was presented in the context of concept formation in mathematics and science by Cassirer (1923), who argues, for instance, that the meaning of a number does not derive from the number itself but from the position of that number in a system of numbers to which it belongs, and that a higher order concept in mathematics and science refers to how lower-order concepts vary and not so much to what they have in common.[3]

The information theorist Garner (1974) expresses a similar idea when he says

> the single stimulus has no meaning except in the context of alternatives. When somebody uses the term circle, they infer that it could have been another form, such as square or triangle. . . . Each descriptive term used defines what the alternatives are, by defining what the stimulus is not. Thus the organism infers sets of stimulus alternatives, and without these inferred sets, no one can describe the single stimulus.
>
> (p. 185)

In his book, he shows how the meaning of the same entity keeps changing, depending on what it is compared with. And as anything can be compared to anything, all things and all beings are in principle inexhaustible.[4] The role of differences, variations in our perception of the world, has attracted interest in many other cases, also.[5]

In accordance with what has just been said, it is another color that the inhabitants of the green world need in order to become able to see its greenness. Preferably, they need something that exists in their world already (and is green, of course), and they need something completely like that thing, except with regard to color, such as a green ball and a red ball, for example.

Let us continue the thought experiment, and let us compare two randomly selected groups of the inhabitants of that green world. Let us try to teach one of the groups what green is by means of induction and encourage the participants to try to see what three different green things (a ball, a cube and a prism) have in common (depicted on the left side of Figure 3.4). This is the principle of sameness embedded in the pattern of *induction*.

46 Sameness and Difference in Learning

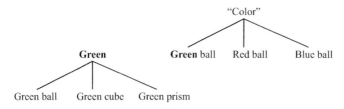

FIGURE 3.4 Two patterns of variation and invariance for learning (discerning) what "green" is.

The participants are supposed to notice the sameness of the three concrete, perceptible instances of green and to become aware of the green color (feature), thanks to the simultaneous experience of three things having the green color in common but differing otherwise. According to the previous line of reasoning, however, this will not happen. As pointed out previously, the arrangement does not work and cannot work, for the simple reason that if you cannot see the greenness of any of three green, though otherwise different, things, you cannot see what they have in common, either. This is the case if you have never discerned the feature "green" previously.

The alternative pattern of variation and invariance, graphically depicted on the right side of Figure 3.4, is called *contrast,* and in that pattern the principle of variation is embedded. In this case the other group of participants, equally ignorant of what green is, as well as of the meaning of *color,* is assumed to notice difference, instead of sameness, and become aware of what green (feature) is, as well as what color (aspect) is, as a result of the simultaneous experience of things that differ in color but are the same otherwise. In the case of induction, the super-ordinate category (green) refers to what different instances have in common; in the case of contrast, the super-ordinate category (color) refers to how the different instances vary (differ from each other), resembling Cassirer's (1923) alternative to induction (see note 3).

Induction and contrast are two ways of grouping instances. In the first case they have the same color (green) but differ otherwise (as to form, for instance). In the second case they differ in color but are the same otherwise (have the same form: ball, for instance). These two ways of grouping instances seem structurally similar: one thing is the same, the other varies. Why are they depicted as structurally different in Figure 3.4 (as located at different levels in the system of categories)?

The thing is that we have to see this question from the point of view of what is to be learned (i.e., from the point of view of the object of learning). We are dealing with pedagogical contexts, and the pattern of variation and invariance must be seen in relation to what we hope that the students will learn. In our example, for instance, the object of learning is discerning green; green is thus the focused feature and has to be contrasted with at least one other feature of the same kind (i.e., another value in the same dimension of variation, which is color in this case). This is why we talk about contrast when color varies, and about induction when something else (form, for example) varies.

We might imagine two teachers who choose to juxtapose two different sets of three objects, both in order to afford the learners the experience necessary for becoming aware of what green is. One is betting on induction, the other on contrast. The latter wins.

Dimensions of Variation and Values

As argued previously, when someone notices the color green, she does so because it differs from at least one other color. We should also remember that two colors are also required to define the aspect "color." Individual colors and "color" must be experienced simultaneously, because one cannot exist without the other (in the learner's awareness). The meaning of features originates from how they differ from each other. The aspect (color) is the experience of difference, and the features (colors) are those things that differ. Color is a *dimension of variation* and different colors are *values* in that dimension.[6]

Values correspond to features, and dimension of variation corresponds to aspect in this book. A critical aspect is thus a critical dimension of variation and a critical feature is a critical value.

In accordance with the distinction between dimensions of variation, on the one hand, and values within a dimension of variation, on the other hand, we can also distinguish between two kinds of learning: in one case a new dimension is opened up; in the other case new values in a dimension already opened up are encountered and appropriated. For instance, if a dart has always been thrown from the same distance, trying another distance means opening up the dimension of distance, and hence this is an example of the first kind of learning, while throwing it from yet another new distance is learning of the second kind. The same applies to colors. The second color that we come across in the imaginary green world enables us to open a new dimension of variation. As long as we are aware of that dimension, each further color we encounter enables us to learn a new value in that dimension. Watson and Mason (2005, 2006) would call the former "opening possible dimensions of variation" and the latter (the learning of new values) "expanding the permissible range of change" (see also Goldenberg & Mason, 2008). In this book, the focus is on the former kind of learning, on the opening up of new dimensions of variation. The systematic introduction of new values in the learning situation is, however, a cornerstone in Montessori pedagogy.[7]

Is it then the case that color is always a dimension of variation and green is always a feature? No, this is not how things are. Green is green (a feature) in relation to red or blue (other features), and color is a dimension of variation in relation to green, red, blue (features). But color is a feature in relation to form or size (other features) and blue is a dimension of variation in relation to light blue or dark blue (features). The same word obviously indicates different meanings in the different cases, in accordance with its position in the system of categories.

Neither From the Specific to the General, Nor the Other Way Around

The thesis that the learner must simultaneously be aware of at least two features and the difference between them, in order to discern any of them, is in agreement with the idea that no new meaning can be found by means of induction: you cannot start with what is specific and find what is general. You cannot start with two green things and thus become aware of the color green. Nor can you understand what truth is by inspecting true statements only. But it does not work the other way around, either. You cannot start with what is general and find what is specific. We cannot start with a general explanation of what color is in order to help someone who has never been exposed to different colors. Nor can you help someone to understand the idea of numbers without the learner having experienced different numbers. Learning will not arise from a general explanation of a novel meaning that does not refer to anything that the learner is experiencing at the time or has encountered previously.

According to the present line of argument, learning, development does not go from features (what is specific) to aspects (what is general), nor the other way around. What is general and what is specific are discerned simultaneously when a new meaning is appropriated. There cannot be any features experienced without the awareness of the aspect that unites them, nor can there be any aspect experienced without the awareness of features that belong to it. Differences and features that differ cannot exist without each other.[8]

The basic conjecture in this book is that the experience of differences is necessary for learning to perceive the world as we perceive it, or to perceive it at all, for that matter. I am not saying that invariance is irrelevant for perception or for learning to perceive. I am just saying that in this book I will primarily deal with differences and variation (although I will certainly deal with sameness and invariance, too). Seeing something (in this case the greenness of the grass) amounts to seeing how it differs from other things (in this case, from other colors). The meaning of colors, of words, of anything, originates from differences. Without differences there can be no meaning at all.[9]

The present theory, however, contradicts Davydov's (1990) theory of theoretical generalization, according to which learning goes—or should go—from the general to the specific.[10]

Patterns of Variation and Invariance

While the main focus of this chapter is the way in which the experience of difference against a background of sameness enables learners to discern critical aspects of objects of learning and critical features of tasks, the main focus of Chapter 6 is the learner's actual experience as a function of the experiences that are made possible, and hence the learning that is made possible, in the classroom. And the experiences that are made possible are described in terms of patterns of variation and invariance, as seen by an observer. Let us now look at the patterns of variation and invariance as seen by the learners.

Let us juxtapose two (or more) objects that differ in one respect, and are the same otherwise (e.g., a sunny landscape in the summer and the same landscape— also sunny—in the winter). The learner will then most likely notice the difference between the two features that differ (the color of the sunlight).

We should observe, however, that there are two necessary conditions for discerning and noticing a particular feature for the first time. First, the learner has to discern at least two features that differ in a certain respect. Second, she must *not* discern features that differ in other respects. The learner should experience variation (differences) in one respect, but not in others. In order to distinguish two aspects that have not been distinguished previously, a difference between them has to be created by letting one vary, while the other remains invariant. If both varied together, the learner would not be able to separate them. These are the two necessary (and sufficient) conditions for the learner to be able to experience a certain aspect of an object of learning and certain features that she has not discerned before.

Contrast

The minimal pattern of variation and invariance involves two aspects, at least one of them focused (considered to be critical and highlighted, therefore), each one varying or being invariant. Contrast was introduced above through a comparison with induction, in Figure 3.4. Another way of representing the difference between induction and contrast is shown in Figure 3.6. Just like Figure 3.4, it can be envisaged as representing two tasks. In the case of induction the learners are exposed to things that have the same color (green), hence color is invariant (i), and different forms (ball, cube, prism), hence form varies (v). The task is to determine what those things have in common. In the case of contrast the learners are exposed to things that have different colors (green, red, blue), hence color varies (v), and the same form (ball), hence form is invariant (i). The task is to determine how those things differ from each other.

color	form	**color**	form
i	*v*	*v*	*i*
induction		contrast	

FIGURE 3.6. Induction and contrast (focused aspect, to be discerned, in bold, v = varies, i = invariant in this and in other similar figures). "*i*" (in italics), implies "not opened up" (by the learner) and "*v*" implies "opened up," in this figure and those that follow.

Discerning green (a feature or a value in the color dimension of variation) is the object of learning, but according to the previous line of reasoning, the idea of green presupposes the idea of color (a focused aspect or a dimension of variation). According to the basic conjecture of the theory presented in this book, through contrast (perception of difference) the learner becomes aware of a quality (meaning) that she has never been aware of before. This amounts to separating (in the sense of making visible) the green color from what it is the color of: the green ball, in our example.

Generalization

The learner has to realize, however, that it is not only the ball that is green (or red), but also all kinds of other things, having other forms. In other words, she has to generalize the particular color that has been separated. This happens by keeping that color invariant, but varying the objects that have that color, in other respects, as to form, for instance (see Figure 3.7). But this is exactly the pattern of induction in Figure 3.6, which has been said not to work for making a new meaning one's own. It works, however, for generalizing a meaning (across form, for instance), once the meaning is found through contrast. As was pointed out above, induction works when the meaning is not new. In Vygotsky's experiment, described in note 1, for instance, the meanings corresponding to the artificial words refer to combinations of features already known to the learners (big, small, high, flat). The participants in the experiment just had to work out which combinations of features the artificial words denoted. And this can be done, of course, by seeing what the instances that were labelled in certain ways had in common. But generalization can also be seen from another perspective. By discerning aspects that vary independently from the focused aspect, the learners generalize the focused aspects over the non-focused aspects. The latter should simply not be taken into consideration when discerning the focused aspects. Green is green, regardless of whether the green thing is a prism, a ball or a cube, or whether it is small or big, or flat, or wooden, or made of cloth.

In this way, form is opened up and separated from color, or—in other words—color is generalized across form. In the same way, we can generalize color across all kinds of entities, by systematically varying their different aspects, while keeping color invariant. Assume that the learners have discerned triangle as a feature, to take another example (by juxtaposing a triangle to a square and a circle, for instance, of the same size and color). By subsequently juxtaposing the same triangle to triangles of varying sizes, angles, rotational positions, the geometric form

color	form
i	*v*

FIGURE 3.7 Generalization (focused aspect in bold).

of triangle is generalized across size, angle and rotational position. Triangles can be small or large, of any size, can have any angles which sum to 180 and they can be rotated in any way, while still remaining triangles. This process of generalization, can be seen as an example of the Hegelian principle of ascending from the abstract to the concrete, mentioned in Chapter 2. Through contrast, color (green, red) is abstracted. By generalizing color over different instances, the abstract meaning expands and becomes more and more concrete (as color becomes the color of many concrete things). This means also that in contrast, dimensions are opened up to enable the learner to take values in those dimensions into consideration, while in generalization dimensions are opened up to enable the learner to disregard values in those dimensions, just as pointed out in Chapter 2, in the section "Aspects Critical for Making Distinctions and Aspects Critical for Generalizing."

Generalization that follows contrast might happen spontaneously, brought about by the learner herself. Or it can be pedagogically constituted, through someone else creating the pattern as a condition for learning. While the experienced pattern of variation and invariance is a necessary and sufficient condition for generalization to take place (actually, the experience of the pattern *is* generalization), the presence of the pattern that the learners are expected to experience is a necessary but not sufficient condition for learning. In order to generalize green, there must be different green things, but the fact that there are different green things present is no guarantee of their color being generalized by the learner.

The pattern of generalization seems to be the same as that of induction, but there is an important difference: *generalization is preceded by contrast*. In the case of generalization, when it is pedagogically constituted, we are not trying to find out what the different cases have in common but how they vary, and the conclusion we draw is something like, "So this can be green, and also this and . . . this" and not so much "See, they are all green!" Both contrast and generalization separate aspects (in our case color and form) from what they are aspects of and from each other. Through contrast, we are trying to find necessary aspects of the object of learning, those that define it. Through generalization, we want to separate the optional aspects from the necessary aspects.

Fusion

But after it has been taken apart, the whole has to be put together again. "Putting together" refers to the learner experiencing the different aspects simultaneously, after having separated them. This happens through the experience of simultaneous variation in all relevant aspects. This pattern is called fusion, and it defines the relation between two (or more) aspects by means of their simultaneous variation. In our specific case the two aspects are independent: any color might appear with any form (see Figure 3.8). In this case all the aspects being fused are focused

color   form

v   *v*

FIGURE 3.8 Fusion between two aspects (both focused).

aspects. (The object of learning being to experience the different aspects simultaneously.) But letting different aspects vary simultaneously might serve a purpose other than bringing them together. The pattern may be instrumental to practicing the discernment of a particular aspect when other aspects are also varying. For instance, when learning to estimate the density of different materials, the students learn to distinguish between varying volumes while mass is invariant, and the other way around: they learn to distinguish between varying masses when volume is invariant. Usually, however, both (and also other) aspects vary at the same time; nevertheless the various aspects have to be estimated independently from each other.

Yet another distinction, relevant for fusion, has to be made with regard to relationships between different aspects. So far, aspects that are independent from each other have been dealt with. But there are aspects that are functionally or logically related to each other. In such cases, we cannot keep one invariant while the other varies. Let us assume, for instance, that the object of learning is to see price as a function of demand and supply. Price, demand and supply are thus necessary aspects. There is also commodity, but it is functionally independent of the other three aspects. In order to develop the capability of seeing the three defining aspects simultaneously, the corresponding features have to vary against a background of other invariant aspects (such as commodity, for instance; see Figure 3.11).

The object of learning is, however, to be able to see price as a function of demand and supply under freely varying conditions. In order to practice that, we have to let demand and supply vary randomly at the same time and let price vary as a function of the relation between them for an invariant commodity. The procedure has to be repeated with different commodities.

The Path of Learning

The central thesis advocated in this book is that appropriating a new meaning (i.e., learning to discern a new aspect, or a new feature) is a function of an experienced pattern of variation and invariance. A minimal pattern consists of two aspects of two instances, both of which might vary or remain invariant (see Figure 3.9). There must be an object of learning that the learners are supposed to appropriate and there must be a number of tasks that are meant to aid the learners to do so. Such tasks are pedagogical tasks, the purpose of which is learning and not very much else (see the discussion in Chapter 1 about learning as an aim and learning as a by-product).

	x	y	
(1)	*i*	*i*	(repetition)
(2)	*v*	*i*	(contrast)
(3)	*i*	*v*	(generalization)
(4)	*v*	*v*	(fusion)

FIGURE 3.9 Four basic patterns of variation and invariance. Focused aspect in bold.

These minimal patterns are the building blocks of more complex ones. The first one refers to the absence of variation. In this particular framework, no distinction is made been one exposure and several exposures. The other patterns have been described briefly above. It should be possible to embed all the patterns in pedagogical tasks. Actually, the patterns are relations of sameness and difference between tasks (or such changes within tasks).

In spite of the distinction made in this book between focusing on sameness and focusing on difference, the two have something fundamental in common. In both cases it is assumed that the learner's simultaneous experience of different instances is of decisive importance. But what is simultaneous is either the experience of how the different cases differ or the experience of what they have in common. Linked to the former alternative is the idea of the cycle of learning, moving the experience from an undifferentiated whole, through differentiation and integration, towards a differentiated and integrated whole. On the one hand, things have to be distinguished (separation), on the other, they have to be brought together (fusion). Separation is again of two kinds. If we have two aspects, of which one varies while the other is invariant, the varying aspect may be a necessary aspect (in the case of contrast) or it may be an optional aspect (in the case of generalization). In the latter case the focused aspect[11] is invariant, much like in induction. The main difference is, however, that the variation is not there to highlight an invariant feature, but to show how the features differ from each other.

The relationships between these patterns are illustrated in Figure 3.10.

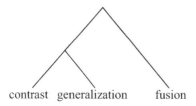

FIGURE 3.10 Relationships between different patterns of variation and invariance.

We should remember that the various patterns refer to the structure of the learner's awareness (i.e., in what respect she experiences differences and in what respects she does not). Patterns of variation and invariance, in terms of how instances are juxtaposed "objectively" (as seen from the observer's perspective), will be dealt with in Chapter 6, the topic of which is how teaching is performed.

In learning, the stages necessarily occur in a certain sequence:

CONTRAST → GENERALIZATION → FUSION

Interestingly, Vygotsky (1986) referred to Piaget, quoting Claparede's (1919) law of awareness, according to which "awareness of difference precedes awareness of likeness" (p. 163). This principle is thus in accordance with the principle that generalization follows contrast.

The basic patterns of variation and invariance (2–4) in Figure 3.9 can obviously be seen to form a temporal sequence. Furthermore, as mentioned previously, those patterns constitute the building blocks for representing more complex patterns. In the examples so far, only two independent aspects (one focused and one not focused) have appeared together. But there might be more aspects (both focused and not focused) that have to be taken into consideration (or not) simultaneously, and they might be functionally or logically related to each other. Let us look at an example that is dealt with more in detail in Chapter 6. The tasks involve bidding for commodities at an auction, in relation to demand for and supply of the commodity. The sequence of patterns created in the study is shown in Figure 3.11. Both demand and supply are focused aspects and price is related to both (it varies with them). The commodity varies or remains invariant independently of demand and supply.

demand	**supply**	price	commodity
v	*i*	*v*	*i*
i	*v*	*v*	*i*
v	*v*	*v*	*i*

FIGURE 3.11 Pattern of variation and invariance for learning to discern price as a function of demand and supply. Focused aspects in bold.

Critical Aspects and Critical Features, Again

Let us use the same example from the end of the previous section to briefly summarize possible ways of answering the question What is to be learned? In accordance with what was said in Chapter 2, the answer in this specific case might be pricing (in terms of the content of learning). It might also be to see (distinguish) the price of a commodity in terms of the relationship between demand and supply (in terms of the educational objective). The preferred answer in this book is, however, discerning demand and supply and the relationship between them (in terms of critical aspects). The latter means distinguishing between price as a function of attributes of the commodity, on the one hand, and price as a function of facets of the market: demand and supply, on the other hand. This also implies that the learner has to learn to distinguish between levels of demand and to distinguish between levels of supply.

The last answer to the question What is to be learned? (formulated in terms of critical aspects) cannot—as pointed out previously—be formulated in general terms. It is relative, not only to the object of learning, but also to the learners. The answer must take the specific learners into consideration. Here, I had fairly typical students, of 10 to 12 years of age, in mind.

In Figure 3.11 it is assumed that the students have not appropriated the meaning of demand and supply previously. At the same time it is hoped that they will relate the price of a commodity to the relationship between demand and supply in novel situations in the future. Hence, they must learn to discern demand and supply and the relationship between them. This might happen through the experience of the pattern of variation and invariance in Figure 3.11. What the students are supposed to learn is to discern the critical aspects. This cannot be done without discerning critical features, but which particular features are chosen is arbitrary, as the role they play in the learning situation is merely instrumental. In novel situations, in which the students are expected to make use of what they have learned (which might also be called application[12]), the students have to find some particular critical features—those applying in the specific situations.

Both the focused and the unfocused aspects may be critical, as may the relationship between them. As far as the focused aspects are concerned, they must be separated through contrast (demand varies, supply invariant and the other way around). As regards unfocused aspects (the commodity in this case) they have to be separated through generalization. Focused aspects have to be discerned in order to be taken into account; unfocused aspects have to be discerned in order to not to be taken into account (the relationship between demand, supply and price is independent of the nature of the commodity). It is assumed that the students become able to discern the relationship between demand, supply and price through the experience of fusion in Figure 3.11.

As mentioned previously in this chapter, critical aspects are dimensions of variation, and critical features are critical values. Discerning an aspect that has not been discerned (i.e., opening up a dimension of variation) amounts to making distinctions (between that dimension and others, as well as between different values in the same dimension). Discerning a particular value within a certain dimension of variation amounts to making distinctions too (between values). The kind of learning dealt with here is very much about telling things apart (making distinctions). In order to make a distinction, the learner has to be aware of the two features distinguished between, simultaneously. Discerning a critical aspect means that the learner is simultaneously aware of differences between different features in that aspect, and that each feature is experienced against a background of a horizon of possibilities (of other features).

Why Is the Experience of Difference, Against a Background of the Experience of Sameness, Necessary for Learning to Discern Novel Features and Novel Aspects?

How can we possibly grasp, experience, notice, perceive a particular feature? Why would this require the experience of difference against a background of invariance, instead of the other way around?

Thinking Apart

In order to perceive anything, it has to be perceptible. In order to be perceptible, it has to be separated (in the learner's awareness) from other things. Why would we not be able to see the green color in an entirely green world? The reason is that in order to see the green color of a cucumber, for instance, we must be able to separate the greenness (the feature) from the cucumber (the whole). But if everything is green, we cannot think apart the greenness and the green things. In order to do that, we need an alternative to green. And that we do not have in a green world.

How can you see your own near-sightedness, for instance, given that you are near-sighted? In order to do that, you have to separate your sight from that which is seen. Although you can see different things, you have only one sense of sight (just as in the green world, there are different things but only one color). Then, for the first time in your life, you try a pair of glasses, and everything looks different, sharper. You take off the glasses, and all of a sudden things are back to normal. Thanks to the differences in your sight when looking with and without glasses (and the sameness of what you are looking at), your near-sightedness can be separated from what is seen, and it becomes perceptible! How can we perceive the height of someone? The height has to be separated from the person (by seeing a shorter or a taller person). There are thus certain necessary conditions for discernment to take place. In order to separate something from something else, you must experience variation in the former, against a background of invariance in the latter. Either you have to see one thing, changing in one respect, remaining the same in others, or you have to see two things, different in one respect, the same in others. You must experience variation against a background of invariance.

Let us imagine a little child who has only come across one language, say, Chinese. She cannot separate "language" and "Chinese": they are one and the same. This means that she cannot have the same understanding of language as someone who is aware of the fact that there are different languages. Nor does she have an understanding of Chinese other than it is what humans speak.

Let us imagine another child who has not seen any animals other than dogs. "Animal" and "dog" are the same thing for her; which word she uses does not make any difference to the meaning it has for her. Similarly, a child who calls different animals "vow-vow" is usually said to over-generalize "dog." But "vow-vow" means as much animal as dog and we can equally well say that she has not differentiated "dog" from other animals.

Vygotsky (1986) commented on exactly this phenomenon:

> The first words of a child already play the role of generalizations. The word "flower" appears in the child's vocabulary much earlier than the names of concrete flowers. And even if by some accident the child learns the word "rose" prior to that of "flower", he uses "rose" as a general name, calling all flowers he sees "rose."
>
> (p. 143)

But if the first flower the child sees is a rose, whether she will call it "rose" or "flower" depends on the word that happens to be used by the adult whom she has been listening to. Regardless of which word the child uses, the meaning would, however, be the same: an undifferentiated rose-flower. Not because of generalization, but because of insufficient differentiation.

The undifferentiated use of sub- and super-ordinate categories functionally resembles Vygotsky's pseudo-concepts (see note 1). The same word (e.g., "dog," or "vow-vow") is used by both the adult and the child in different senses (e.g., as referring to dog or to dog/animal) none of them being aware of the differences. When children recognize two yellow blocks as similar, without being able to tell in what way they are similar, in Vygotsky's card-sorting experiment (earlier in this chapter; see note 1), it is very likely that they see the blocks as wholes, without being able to separate out and refer to their different features (e.g., their color). Pseudo-concepts link the adult and the child to each other. They are using the same word with different meanings, but with the same referent. This opens up the way for the child to learn from the adult and to acquire at last the canonical meanings of words.

Scientific and Spontaneous Concepts

Vygotsky (1986) emphasizes the distinction between scientific and spontaneous (everyday) concepts. The need for discerning—and thus separating—aspects defining the former is easier to recognize than the need for discerning (separating) aspects of the latter. It is easier to see that something specific has to be done in order to separate acceleration from velocity or elasticity from demand and supply, for instance, than to see that color must be separated from objects or that "twoness" must be separated from pairs of things. The reason is that in the case of spontaneous concepts, the environment usually provides the learners with the pattern of variation and invariance necessary for discerning (separating) the defining aspects.

Nonetheless, new concepts are introduced in school all the time without differentiating between conceptual levels. Children use natural numbers (1, 2, 3 . . .) without differentiating numbers from the specific kind of numbers that natural numbers are. Students are introduced to geometry without it being differentiated from the specific kind of geometry that they are dealing with, Euclidian geometry. Lénárt (1993) carried out a series of studies in which spherical geometry was introduced in parallel with plane geometry. Students, between 10 and 15 years of age, dealt with various geometric entities (such as squares, triangles, etc.), on curved surfaces as opposed to plane surfaces, and found out, for instance, that the rule that the sum of angles in a triangle is 180 is only true if the triangle is in a plane. By introducing spherical geometry, the taken-for-granted nature of plane geometry is suspended and a new meaning, "geometries," is opened up, alongside new ideas of plane and spherical geometries. Actually, this is how plane geometry becomes plane geometry for the students.

Also, Galili and Hazan (2000) demonstrated empirically the power of alternatives. They compared students' understanding of optics in two 1-year-long secondary school courses in physics. One course was conventional, insofar as it focused on the received wisdom of today's science: the students were taught what they were supposed to learn. In the other course, the canonical ideas of modern science were contrasted with the historically varying ideas of science in the past. In addition to the particular ways of seeing certain phenomena that the students were expected to develop, they were also taught alternative ways of seeing the same phenomena. In addition to teaching them what is considered right today, they were also taught what is not considered right today. And thanks to this, they developed a far better understanding of what is considered right than those who were not exposed to alternative ways of seeing.

The same is true of the decimal system and positional number systems in general. The two usually remain undifferentiated for many years in school. One could argue that the decimal system cannot be understood without another number system being introduced. Vygotsky (1986) suggested that the decimal system should be dealt with together with another number system for this very reason.

Having access to only one account of historical events in some part of the world, during a certain period of time, is likely to leave the account and the events intertwined in the learners' awareness (they cannot separate the two and thus read the account as if they were watching the event itself). They do not feel that they are being exposed to a particular account, but that they have direct access to what actually happened (Patrick, 1998, 2002).

Unseeing the World

The point I want to make is that a feature is not visible unless it is, in some sense, separated. This is a central idea in this book but also one that is hard to go along with. The thing is that it is very difficult—and frequently impossible—to see something in a way in which we have seen it earlier if we now see it in a different way. The reason is that we cannot "unsee" our current way of seeing that thing. We cannot imagine seeing a ball without being able to see its roundness, its color or to feel its texture as a child who has not yet discerned those features.

Discernment implies separation. Features are thus separated from the instances they are features of, and from each other. When throwing the same ball from different distances, the thrower separates the particular distance, from which she happens to throw, from the throwing, and separates variation in distance from variation in throwing and can thus adjust to different distances in different situations.

This line of reasoning might strike the reader as slightly—or perhaps more than slightly—strange and redundant. I am suggesting that in order to become aware of something, we have to separate it from something else and that there are necessary conditions for this separation to take place. To the extent that learning amounts to experientially separating two things from each other, helping others to learn amounts to bringing about the conditions necessary for this separation to happen. Being visible amounts to being separated, for the simple reason that what is not separated cannot be seen.

We cannot see the greenness of the cucumber without separating it from the cucumber; we cannot hear the tone without separating it from the Chinese word; we cannot see the elegance of the actor's movement in Cantonese opera without separating the elegance from the movements; we cannot see the frame of reference without separating it from our perception of moving objects. In order to separate tones from words, we need to hear words that differ in tone but are the same as far as the sound and speaker are concerned, and we have to experience those words simultaneously (even if we must necessarily hear them one at a time). In order to separate the elegance of movements from the movements, we need to experience the same movements with varying degrees of elegance. And there is no way of separating the frame of reference from the seeing, without seeing the same thing from another frame of reference.

The idea of separating a feature from that which it is a feature of, and by doing so making it visible, is vividly captured by the quote (from the 19th-century British philosopher and theologian James Martineau) chosen by Eleanor Gibson as the first lines of her book on differentiation theory:

> When a red ivory ball, seen for the first time, has been withdrawn, it will leave a mental representation of itself, in which all that it simultaneously gave us will indistinguishably co-exist. Let a white ball succeed to it; now and not before, will an attribute detach itself, and the color, by force of contrast, be shaken out into the foreground. Let the white ball be replaced by an egg, and this new difference will bring the form into notice from its slumber. And thus, that which began by being simply an object cut out from the surrounding scene becomes for us first a red object, and then a red round object; and so on.
>
> (Martineau, *Essays Philosophical and Theological,* as quoted by E. J. Gibson, 1969, p. 95)

A corollary of the previous line of reasoning is that people may see the world differently, simply because things—or certain aspects of things—that are visible to some people are invisible to others.

Delimitation

In order to experience difference (or sameness, for that matter), we must experience entities that differ from each other (or are similar) in certain respects (or the same entity that changes in certain respects while it remains the same in others). Where an entity begins and where it ends is, however, not always self-evident. Every comparison actually rests on particular ways of constituting those entities: choosing them, taking them apart, bringing them together, separating them from other entities and from the context in which they appear. They have to be delimited and this must be done by the learner. Just as de Saussure (1916/1983) says about language:

> Language does not present itself to us as a set of signs already delimited, requiring us merely to study their meanings and organization. It is an indistinct mass, in which attention and habit alone enable us to distinguish particular elements.
>
> (p. 145)

Entities are delimited and separated from their contexts; parts are delimited and separated from wholes. In order to understand what a nut is, you have to be able to see the limits of the nut, the dividing lines between it and the world. The same with the anvil. And with the stone used to hit the nut. You have to be able to see them as separate objects with boundaries, occupying a certain space. Marton and Booth (1997) illustrated delimitation by asking the question What does it take to see a motionless deer among the dark trees and bushes of the night woods? and answering it thus: To see it at all, we have to discern it from the surrounding trees and bushes; we have to see its contours, its outline, the limits that distinguish it from what surrounds it. We have to see, at least partially, where it starts and where it ends. Furthermore, you have to be able to grasp qualities of objects, their attributes. Marton and Booth continue: "But seeing its contours *as* contours and as the contours of a *deer* implies that we have already identified it as a deer standing there. . . ." (p. 86). And being a deer is certainly an attribute of the deer. Marton and Booth (1997) call delimitation discernment and thus talk about the discernment of features (and aspects) and also about the discernment of entities (from their context) and the parts from the wholes. To avoid confusion, I will talk about *discernment* of features (and aspects) and *delimitation* of entities from contexts, and parts from wholes (following Svensson, 1976, 1977), with regard to the latter).

"Separation" is obviously used in one sense in the context of discernment and in another in the context of delimitation. In the former case, aspects are separated; in the latter, parts are separated.

Discernment and delimitation are not independent of each other. On the contrary: they mutually constitute each other. You have to delimit entities and identify their boundaries (you have to parse the world), on the one hand, and you have to discern their features, on the other hand, by comparing them with each other, or by comparing different appearances of the same entity.

A striking illustration of this relationship is found in Katona's (1940) book *Organizing and Memorizing,* in which he reports on studies of how people handle various tasks and how their ways of handling those tasks affect their understanding and their memory. In one of the tasks the participants were asked to read the following series three times and try to remember it:

581215192226

All those who managed to recall the series partitioned it somehow (delimited component parts). There were three different ways of doing this:

581 215 192 226
58 12 15 19 22 26
5 8 12 15 19 22 26.

(Katona, 1940, pp. 9–22)

The third way of partitioning the series, which results in much better retention, is interesting. In this case, the participants discovered a pattern in the series: the difference between the groups alternates between 3 and 4. Remembering the first number and the pattern of the two kinds of differences, is sufficient for remembering the whole series. But how could the participants discover the pattern? It can only be seen if the series is partitioned in accordance with the pattern. The only reason for partitioning the series in this particular way is, however, that you can see the pattern. In accordance with what was said above, the partitioning and the pattern of differences between the parts mutually constitute each other. This is true for the relationship between the two kinds of differences in general (differences between the entities and their context, in relation to which they are discerned and delimited, on the one hand, and differences between features of separate entities, on the other hand).

Partitioning the series in the first or second way means opening up (or becoming aware of) the possibility of partitioning the series by keeping a certain number of elements together (e.g., in pairs, in triads) without taking the relationship between the elements into consideration. The third way of partitioning means opening up (becoming aware of) the possibility of another way of partitioning the series, one based on the relationships between elements.

Accordingly, delimitation and discernment are closely related. When using the same data for characterizing different ways of dealing with the same task, Svensson (1976, 1977) used delimitation as "figure" and discernment as "ground," while Marton (1974, 1975; Marton & Säljö, 1976a, 1976b) did it the other way around. The latter approach is adopted in this book as well.

Grouping

Delimiting amounts to taking apart. Once entities are seen as separate entities, they can be united, grouped together in various ways.

In most of the learning tasks in this book, the learners deal with certain instances of an object of learning in order to become capable of dealing with other, novel instances of the same object of learning. They have to discern certain features and aspects of the instances dealt with and to handle novel instances in terms of the aspects discerned. In order to discern a certain aspect or a certain feature, the learner must experience certain variation (make certain distinctions) against a background of invariance in other respects. The pedagogy implied by the present theory is very much about creating patterns of variation and invariance. Patterns of variation and invariance are brought about by combinations of instances (e.g., tasks, examples, illustrations) that are there for the learners to experience. Sometimes we find fundamental differences in learning, simply because the very same instances are grouped together in different ways and thus constitute different patterns of variation and invariance. In Chapter 6, further examples will be presented and discussed, but in the present context, a study of the learning of Cantonese tones by speakers of non-tonal languages carried out by Ki and Marton (2003; see also Ki, 2007) will be used as an example of learning as a function of the grouping of instances. In Cantonese, which is a complex dialect of Chinese, word meanings in spoken language are differentiated by both sounds (more correctly: segments, i.e., discrete sequential units of sound) and tones. Differences in pitch (of which tones make up a special case) also have an important function in non-tonal languages (such as English), for making distinctions at the level of sentences (between imperative and interrogative moods, for instance), but not at the level of words. It thus turns out to be spectacularly difficult for speakers of non-tonal languages to focus on sound, tone and meaning simultaneously at the word level. To do so takes a reorganization of the attentional field (i.e., what is attended to, discerned, focused on, at the same time).

There are six different tones in Cantonese: high-level, high-rising, mid-level, low-level, low-falling, and low-rising. Let assume that we are designing an exercise aimed at helping beginners to learn to discern and recognize tones and to relate them to differences in meaning. How should we proceed? Let us take one of the tones, say low-level. Were we to follow the logic of induction, we would let the learners practice on the same tone (low-level), letting the other aspects of the words (the sound and meaning) vary. The focused feature, the tone, is thus invariant, while the unfocused features, the sound and the meaning, vary. Then we could continue with another tone, high-rising, perhaps, and let the learners practice words that all have this tone in common, but differ in other respects (i.e., as far as sound and meaning are concerned).

Following the logic of contrast, on the other hand, we would group the very same words the other way around: we would let that which is focused on (the tone) vary, while keeping that which is not focused on (the sound) invariant. The meaning varies in any case, because the words are different (see Figure 3.12). These two different ways of grouping the same set of nine words (representing three different tones and three different sounds) were compared as alternative

Group A
tone-invariant
Sound variant treatment

Group B
tone-variant
Sound invariant

	Tone55	Tone33	Tone21
JIM	Flood	Dislike	Salt
CE	Car	Sleep	Evil
FAN	Share	Sleep	Tomb

	Tone55	Tone33	Tone21
JIM	Flood	Dislike	Salt
CE	Car	Sleep	Evil
FAN	Share	Sleep	Tomb

FIGURE 3.12 Learning Cantonese tones using two patterns of variation and invariance (Ki & Marton, 2003).

techniques for learning the words, in the sense of identifying the meaning upon hearing the words (sound and tone). The learners following the contrast design clearly outperformed those following the induction design. Our interpretation was that the learners discerned that which varied (the sound and meaning in the induction design; the tone and meaning in the contrast design) and linked those aspects together (sound and meaning in the induction design, and tone and meaning in the contrast design). There was a clear indication that the latter significantly contributed to the restructuring of the learners' attentional field.

As already mentioned, the necessary features of these nine words are the tone, the sound and the meaning. Furthermore, when the task is completed the learner is expected be able to give the meaning upon hearing the word (the tone and the sound together), by pointing to the appropriate picture. The experiment demonstrated that learners discern tones much better when the tone varies and the sound is invariant, as compared to the sound varying and the tone being invariant.

Learning to link meaning and tone—as in the experiment—is, however, not good enough for word learning, because there are words (lots of them, actually) with the same tone but with differing sounds and differing meanings. In order to discern the sounds as well and link them to meanings, the learners have to do another exercise. In the next experiment, the two patterns of variation and invariance that were compared in the first experiment, were now used as parts of a sequence. First tone varied, while sound was invariant (contrast), followed by the tone remaining invariant, while sound varied (generalization). The meaning varied all the time.

In this way, we helped the learners to discern the two critical aspects, by letting them vary one at a time, while the other was invariant.

The two patterns of variation and invariance described here are, however, still not sufficient for learning Cantonese words. Doing this amounts to learning to discern tone, sound, meaning, one at a time and to focus on them simultaneously, once they have been discerned. In order to achieve that, we have to let all necessary aspects vary at the same time (Ki, Ahlberg & Marton, 2006).

Differences and Experienced Differences

As mentioned previously, several times in fact, no new meanings can be appropriated through induction or sameness. New meanings are appropriated through contrast or differences. Still, as was also mentioned above, most adults use induction as their approach to helping children to learn the meanings of "green," "three," "democracy," "virtue," "quadratic equation." Nonetheless, most children seem to learn those things. But how can they learn what is impossible to learn (due to the failure of induction)? The same could be asked in relation to Ki and Marton's (2003) study: Should we not expect all the participants in the contrast group (learning the tone-meaning relations) and none of the participants in the induction group to succeed? Although the former learned decidedly better, the difference was definitely not all or nothing. Is the basic conjecture of this book wrong?

Well, we should remember that even if adults use induction, sameness, as their main pedagogical device, there are plenty of differences, variations, in the world around us. So even if the adult keeps pointing to three mice saying only "three," or three apples saying only "three," it is likely that the child has previously come across things one at a time, or in pairs. To the extent that the child remembers and is aware of other quantities simultaneously, she will learn, seemingly thanks to the experience of sameness but in reality thanks to the experience of differences. When children learn what words, such as *mummy, dad, lamp, red, dog, car, yammi,* for instance, mean, they have probably already discerned and noticed the corresponding aspects of the world around them. In that case, they are structurally in the same situation as the linguist hearing "*gavagai*." They do not need to discern a novel meaning, they have to select one (by means of induction). They have noticed the features, but they do not know what they are called. Probably this is why differences have not frequently been singled out as a necessary condition for learning. They are there, even if no one notices them, and they work whether or not they are noticed (in many cases, at least). As they are mostly present in the learner's awareness, invisible to the observer, their role has not often been noticed.

On the other hand, it is a common experience for us to discover similarities between different cases. How would we otherwise manage to get around and handle our world in comparatively reasonable ways? Yes, we frequently find similarities and it is important for us to do so, but we should remember that we find the similarities, because we are at least marginally aware of cases that differ. I can carry out an experiment in one of the lecture halls in my university in Sweden.

I invite my 10 visiting colleagues from Shanghai to join me on the stage, and I ask the audience "Can you suggest something that our friends here have in common?" The first thought of most people in the audience would very likely be: "They are Chinese, of course!" Let us replicate the experiment in Shanghai with the same actors, but with a local audience. Do you not think that it is less likely that they would come up with the same idea as their fellow students in Sweden? (I am assuming that the audience's awareness of the difference between the visitors' facial features and their own is vital for their seeing the similarity between the visitors.)

This explains the fact that students can learn from a method of teaching that does not actually provide them with the pattern of variation and invariance necessary for appropriating a particular object of learning. For some students it might indeed be impossible to learn, while others might have previous experiences that are sufficient in themselves for learning, or sufficient together with what they experience in class. This is one of the reasons why it is *not* the case that everyone learns when the necessary pattern of variation and invariance is present, and nobody when this pattern is absent. The other reason is that students do not necessarily learn even if it is possible for them to do so. For example, they have to be trying, at the very least. This is why there is a probabilistic advantage to the necessary patterns of variation and invariance: when they are present, the likelihood of learning taking place is higher. When they are absent, the likelihood of learning is lower.

In other words, as mentioned in the previous section, our way of representing patterns of variation and invariance refers to which pattern is available for the learner to experience, on the one hand, and what pattern is actually experienced by her, on the other hand. Mason (2011) makes the same distinction—using different terms—between implicit (observable) and explicit (experienced) variation.

The fact that learners might experience the necessary differences and appropriate novel meanings, even if the teacher has not supplied them with the seemingly necessary conditions, does not make it less important to pay attention to the pattern of variation and invariance that the learners encounter. Actually, an overwhelming majority of failures to understand derive from patterns of variation and invariance that make it less likely, but not impossible, to experience the necessary differences. Students are frequently taught about the nature of subordinate categories of a higher-order category: different forms of governance, of music, of painting; different genres, architectures, diagnostic categories related to the same organ or part of the human body, political ideologies, and so on. Mostly, one kind of thing is described, exemplified, and then another kind is described, exemplified and so forth. For example, first a narrative style of writing is characterized and exemplified by texts with different contents, but all in a narrative style, followed by a non-fictional style being characterized and exemplified by texts with different contents, followed by a third genre, and a fourth and so on. In such a case the differences between genres are available to the students; it is not impossible to experience them simultaneously and hence experience the differences between them. Not impossible, no, but pretty hard. In such a case the different genres are separated by the focus on what is common to the examples within each sub-category. The things that differ are taken apart and the differences are implicit at best. We might compare this way of structuring teaching with one that has a primary focus on differences, and a secondary focus on sameness. In this case, the teacher might present what the same content might look like in one genre, and a second and a third. Conclusions about the differences can be made, and the specific features of different genres might be generalized to other content.

This line of reasoning applies also to Ki and Marton's (2003) study described in the previous section. First of all, although there may not be tonal differences at the word level in a certain language, it does not mean that people cannot hear differences between words pronounced with varying pitch, and second, even if there was just one tone focused on in each exercise for the induction group, the participants—or at least some of them—could remember and compare across different exercises. This point may reasonably be applied to other studies with similar designs.

This book is about necessary conditions of learning, and the conditions are truly necessary in many cases. It is impossible to notice something that is always present and it is impossible to distinguish between a category and one of its sub-categories if the learner has not encountered at least one other sub-category (e.g., governance/democracy, flower/rose, animal/dog). In other cases, such as with Cantonese tones, we expect the differences to be stochastic (i.e., they can be in terms of probabilities).

Discernment, Difference, Simultaneity

In the previous section, the distinction between differences and experienced (lived) differences was elaborated. The former refers to the observer's perspective, something that we can point to and explain to other people. The latter refers to the learner's experience. But why would what the observer is seeing (experiencing) differ from what the learner is seeing (experiencing) if they are inspecting the same things arranged in the same way? The reason is that the experience of sameness and difference is not only a function of what is there to be experienced but of what things are experienced simultaneously. The structure of our awareness, what is experienced in relation to what, originates from simultaneity. There is a circular relationship between discernment, variation and simultaneity. As argued, again and again, no discernment (of features or aspects) can happen without the experience of difference. But no difference can be experienced without the simultaneous experience of the things that differ. And two things cannot be experienced simultaneously—as two things—without being discerned. Discernment, difference and simultaneity are necessarily related to each other. None of them can exist without the others; they presuppose each other and hence cannot be temporally ordered. Nevertheless, the teacher can contribute to bringing them about. As was pointed out previously, there are two necessary conditions: first, in order to experience a difference, there must be a difference (as seen by an observer) to be experienced and second, in order to experience that difference, other things should remain invariant.

Discerning and Learning to Discern[13]

There are many different objects of learning that appear in the various examples used in this book. But all these objects have certain things in common. They are all aimed at increasing the likelihood that the learners will handle novel situations in powerful ways. Handling a novel situation in a powerful way originates from seeing it in a powerful way. Seeing a novel situation in a powerful way amounts to discerning the aspects and features that it is necessary to take into consideration in order to successfully solve the task and to focus on those aspects and features simultaneously. Our hope is thus that the students will get better at discerning what has to be discerned in novel situations. But how can we get better at discerning something?

The present model of description builds on the distinction between dimensions of variation and values in those dimensions. Being able to handle a novel situation in a powerful way amounts to being able to discern those features of the object of learning in that particular situation that it is necessary to take into consideration. But the situation is novel, which means that the learner cannot have learned what features of the object of learning it is necessary to take into consideration in that situation. What she can have learned is to discern the necessary aspects or dimensions of variation. And that can be learned by learning to discern different features or values in the same dimension of variation. So by learning to discern some values in one situation, the learner learns to discern other values in the same dimension of variation in another situation. In the next section this will be illustrated by means of some examples.

Using the Known to Prepare for the Unknown

As the future is considered to be unknown to an increasing extent, preparing students for an unknown future is increasingly seen as one of the major ambitions of the educational system. But how can the educational system, which is supposed to promote what is known, achieve that aim? How can the students be prepared for the unknown by means of the known? Could the development of the ability to discern relevant dimensions of variation (the known) help the students to discern the critical features of novel situations (the unknown)?

In this section two studies will be summarized briefly. Both are experimental studies of motor learning in young children. The tasks are typical experimental tasks, the mastery of which is hardly relevant outside the specific experimental context. The objects of learning in these studies are probably not very representative of objects of learning in schools. Moreover, neither of the studies was based on the theory promoted in this book. As a matter of fact, both studies pre-date the theory by about two decades. Nevertheless, they are about the relationship between learning and the conditions of learning (i.e., both studies look at the effects on learning of differences in patterns of variation and invariance). In actual fact, in both studies, principles that could have been derived from this theory are put to the test.

As was pointed out in the previous chapter, if you want to prepare learners to handle future, novel, situations in powerful ways, you have to help them to learn to see those situations in powerful ways. Let us look at a study of learning among young children where the future, novel situation is simply a new experimental condition, differing from previous experimental conditions (Moxley, 1979). Eighty children, between 6 and 8 years, participated in the experiment and were divided into two groups. The task was to try to hit a target (a carpet) with a shuttlecock. In one of the groups (A) the children threw 20 times from five different angles, from the same distance, sitting on the floor with their feet pointing towards the opposite wall. In the other group (B) the children had to throw shuttlecocks 100 times from the same angle. Afterwards, both groups tried to hit the target with shuttlecocks from an angle new to everyone. The group who initially encountered varied conditions (A) succeeded best with the criterion task. So in this case children who experienced varied conditions were prepared to handle a throwing task in which the angle of throwing was one that they had never tried before. This was because through experiencing variation in the angle they learned to discern the angle as an important aspect of the situation, even when the specific angle (the feature or the value) was completely new to them. The reason is—according to my interpretation—that although they did not learn to throw from every single angle, they learned to discern the dimension of variation and values in it. The necessary condition for this to happen was that they could experience the different angles simultaneously, even if these experiences were distributed in time. This is a case of *diachronic simultaneity,* which means that events that happen at different points in time are experienced at the same time. When events occurring—or aspects being present—at the same time are experienced simultaneously, we talk about *synchronic simultaneity.* In any case, by discerning a particular critical feature (the angle of throwing in this case), the learner can take the particular value into consideration and adjust her actions (here: throwing) to it.

Let us now imagine a child who keeps throwing from the same place, from the same (horizontal) angle, with the same shuttlecock (i.e., a child practicing under the second set of experimental conditions, B). The child can feel the weight of the shuttlecock, can see the distance to the target, can see and feel the (horizontal) angle of the throwing. She throws, sees how far from the target the shuttlecock lands; throws again, trying to get closer to the target, sees the result and so on. She adjusts her throwing, but she adjusts to the whole situation without being able to distinguish between its different aspects. This adjustment happens as she sees the different results of her throwing, and as she tries to do better she changes her way of throwing. When the distance to the target, the (horizontal) angle of throwing and the weight of the shuttlecock are invariant, it is neither possible nor necessary to discern them. But the children still have to adjust and improve their throwing by getting the shuttlecock closer and closer to the target. What are the critical aspects, then, in this situation? What is it that the children have to discern and take into consideration? There are two such critical aspects: the direction or the angle of the throw on the one hand and the force by which the shuttlecock is thrown on the other hand. The children can—and have to—discern these two aspects and see how they co-vary with the precision of throwing (i.e., how far from the target the shuttlecock lands). Children improve their performance by discerning these two critical aspects, taking them into consideration simultaneously in accordance with how differences in these aspects correlate with differences in precision. In a way the children adjust to the specific angle and the specific distance they throw from. But they adjust to invariant aspects of the situation by means of varying what can be varied in this situation: the force and the angle of the throw. The invariant aspects of the situation can be adjusted to (and mostly *are* adjusted to), but they cannot be discerned. The invariant aspects are holistic constraints on the activity and the adjustment to them takes place without awareness. Such adjustment is common in environments with certain invariant features. For instance, this is why students adjust to the specific patterns of communication in school, or to the hidden curriculum (mentioned in Chapter 1) without being aware of doing so.

Compare this with the children throwing from different angles. As the distance from which they throw is the same and the shuttlecock is the same but the angle varies, they need to learn to adjust to differences in the angle of throwing. As they throw from different angles (which they see and feel) they can discern the effect of the differences on their throwing or in the way they have to adjust the two other critical features (which are the same as in group B, of course: the direction of throwing, the vertical angle.) and the force by which the shuttlecock is thrown) to the differences in the (horizontal) angle of throwing. This means that the situation is more complex than when simply throwing from the same angle, as another aspect of the situation is discerned and adjusted to. Accordingly, when they throw, the perceived (horizontal) angle of throwing is also taken into account. When throwing from a novel angle, children from condition A adjust to the perceived (horizontal) angle, while children from condition B cannot do so, at least not initially because they have not discerned the (horizontal) angle of throwing. It has simply not existed for them.

The difference between the two groups in this experiment was that children in situation A opened up an additional dimension of variation (in horizontal angle) as compared to children in situation B. Hence they were better able to handle situations that were novel in this particular respect. They have not so much learned to throw from five different places with five different (horizontal) angles as they have learned to pay attention to (discern) the angle in the situations they have encountered, or will encounter in the future. They have appropriated the dimension of variation (angle) rather than specific values in that dimension (the specific angles from which they practiced throwing during the experiment).

In the same way, if students are working with systems of linear equations in two unknowns and the unknowns are not called x and y in every problem but sometimes a and b or d and v, the students are not so much supposed to learn that the unknowns may be called a and b or d and v, as that they can be called anything and not only x and y (Häggström, 2008). Similarly, as mentioned earlier, triangles are usually presented with the base line in a horizontal position on the page. If you include some examples where the triangles are rotated to different positions, you do not do it in order to help the students to learn to handle triangles in those positions that appear in the examples, but to separate any triangle from its location and generalize over position. The student will then be expected to be capable of handling any triangle independently of its location (Guo & Pang, 2011).

We might also refer to the learning of Cantonese tones, or more generally, Cantonese words. If you want to learn to make sense of spoken language, the greater number of varied cases (varying between male and female, young and old, more and less distinct, soft and hard, low and high, etc.) you encounter, the greater likelihood that you will be able to make sense of a pronunciation that you have never come across previously.

Kerr and Booth (1978) carried out a study similar to Moxley's (1979) above, in which the task was again to hit an object, but the difference between conditions had to do with the distance to the target. The task was to hit a target with miniature beanbags. Thirty-six children with an average age of 8.3 years and 28 children with an average age of 12.5 years participated in the experiment. Both age groups were randomly assigned to "specificity" and "schema" groups. All children were tested at the beginning and at the end of the experiment, the younger group throwing from three feet and the older from four feet. The deviation from the target was measured after each throw, and the difference between the average error at the beginning and at the end of the experiment was used to measure the effect of the practice between the two tests.

The practice for the specificity group consisted of a great number of throws, all from the criterion distance of three feet for the younger children and four feet for the older children. Children in the schema group practiced at two different distances, none of which were the criterion distance. Interestingly, the children in the schema groups outperformed the children in specificity groups when throwing from the criterion distances (i.e., from the distances from which all of the practice of the specificity group was carried out, and none of the practice of the schema group was carried out). Hence, practicing something other than what was tested was more effective than practicing exactly what was tested.

In this case the dimension of variation opened up in the schema group was the distance between the throwing child and the target. In line with what was suggested by the experiment with the shuttlecock described previously, we would expect the schema group to outperform the specificity group when the throwing was from a distance novel to both. The reason is that, due to variation in distance, distance is separated from the very act of throwing. If it were not a separated aspect of the task, throwing could not be adjusted to variation in distance. Once experientially separated, the way of throwing and the distance are supposed to vary in a coordinated way, forming a functional dependency, or a function. What is not supposed to vary is the distance between the place where the beanbag lands and the place where the target is. This distance is supposed to be zero all the time (even if it rarely is). Having formed the relationship between the distance and the way of throwing, estimating the novel distance influences the way of throwing. This is why the schema group outperforms the specificity group when the throwing is done at distances novel to both. But how could the schema group outperform the specificity group at the distance from which the latter group did all its practice and the former group did not do any of its practice? This would imply that learning to discern and open up a dimension of variation is a more powerful approach to learning than simply learning a particular value.

Interestingly, in their description of students' ways of handling an entirely different learning task (about Native Americans), Newman, Griffin and Cole (1989, p. 122) made a distinction between two kinds of wrong answers in a pre- and a post-test in their intervention study. Some students' answers already fell in the right category in the pre-test, even if they were wrong. If the answer was supposed to be *tribe*, they wrote "state" or "band," for example. Other students' gave wrong answers that were not constrained by any conceptual boundaries (i.e., they fell outside the correct category). So when the expected answer was *tribe*, they could write basically anything, such as "trade," "movable small," "farming," or "permanent large." There was no improvement in the first group as far as categories were concerned on the post-test after teaching: for these students, all the categories were correct from the beginning. The main improvement in the other group was in terms of categories: almost all the students got them right in the post-test, though they failed to come up with the correct answers quite a few times. The distinction made by Newman et al. resembles the distinction between dimensions of variation (corresponding to "categories") and values in the dimensions (corresponding to specific words or concepts). Their results, as well as those of Kerr and Booth (1978) seem to support the distinction between two kinds of learning, one related to dimensions of variation and one to values in those dimensions. These results also seem to support the focus on the former in this book.

The Transfer of Learning

According to the line of reasoning in this book, in order to become capable of handling certain situations or tasks in powerful ways, we have to learn to see those situations or tasks in powerful ways. We have to learn to discern the features that are critical in relation to what we are trying to achieve and take them into consideration simultaneously. For this to happen, we have to encounter and experience certain necessary patterns of variation and invariance. From this it follows that what we need to discern depends on what we are trying to achieve, on the nature of the situations or tasks and on the nature of the critical features. The idea is thus that while it might be necessary and possible to discern a particular feature in order to master a certain task, it might be irrelevant and impossible to discern the same feature in order to master another task. Furthermore, what novel and unknown situations we will be able to handle in powerful ways in the future depends on what features we are able to discern, and what features we will be able to discern in the future depends (in part) on what aspects or dimensions of variation are being opened up in our awareness.

If you have tried to hit a target from different distances, it is more likely that you will adjust to a new distance as a necessary feature of a new situation than if you have thrown from only one distance previously—however many times you have done it. If you have tried to hit a target with small balls of differing weights, it is more likely that you will adjust to the weight of a new ball in a new situation than if you always have practiced hitting the target with balls of the same weight.

If we learn to master a task and handle another situation in a more powerful way than we would have done without this learning, we talk about *transfer* (referring to the effect of learning to handle one task on our ability to handle another task). Transfer is usually seen as a function of experienced similarity between the two tasks. If the learner can see how the two tasks are alike, she is thought to be able to profit from her learning from the first task. The idea of transfer is closely associated with the idea of sameness. But against the background of the current line of reasoning, transfer appears in a somewhat different light, seen as a function of difference and not of sameness (only; see Marton, 2006). Let us consider the example of experiencing the elegance of the artists' movements in Cantonese opera, mentioned earlier. If we have only seen the movements performed by professional artists with the same level of elegance, we will never be able to separate the elegance of the movements from the movements themselves. But if we have seen the same movements performed with less elegance previously, then we will be able to see the elegance of the artists' movements (Lo, 2012; Lo & Marton, 2012).

Let us take another example: asking people to describe something (a book they have read, a house in which they live, the environment surrounding it, etc.). On the whole, the more different books, houses, environments people have come across, the more can they tell about the book that they have read, the house in which they live, and the environment surrounding it, because the more differences they have had the opportunity to notice. They can see and tell more, not because they have seen the same thing before, but because they have seen other—and different—things of the same sort.

Similarly, in the experiment described previously, with toddlers throwing shuttlecocks at a target, those who have experienced throwing from different angles have an important advantage over those who have kept throwing from the same angle. This effect is thus not due to sameness of the instances but due to differences. In this case—just as was pointed out previously—it is not so much (or not only) that the children seem to learn to throw from the five specific angles they have practiced throwing from but that a dimension of variation (angle) is opened for them, alerting them to this particular aspect of novel situations.

In the example just mentioned, we obtain an answer to one of the most important questions about the system of education: How can we prepare our students for the unknown by means of the known? If they throw from five different angles (the known), they become able to handle any angles (the unknown). If the students deal with many different cases (of EEC patterns, mathematics problems, different pronunciations of English, etc.), they do not so much learn to deal with the specific types of instances as learn to discern the particular dimensions of variation, hence they will most likely get better at handling cases that they have never seen before. This follows from what was said previously about discernment always happening at two levels simultaneously: specific values are discerned and the corresponding dimension of variation is opened. It is also important to notice that variation among instances in these cases does not have the function of drawing attention to what is common among the instances but to how they vary.

Notes

1. In Vygotsky's experiment, carried out in the early 1930s, four different pairs of features defined the meaning of four artificial words.

   There were 22 wooden blocks of five different colors, six shapes, two heights (tall and flat), two sizes of horizontal surface (large and small). On the underside of each block there was a nonsense word, invisible to the participants, corresponding to the combination of two features of the blocks, in accordance with the following system:

lag	tall, large
bik	flat, large
mur	tall, small
cev	flat, small

   Height and size were thus aspects of the blocks, necessary for defining what the words meant. In sessions carried out individually, the experimenter started by spreading out the blocks on the table with the words facing down; he picked up one of the blocks, turned it around and read the word on the other side aloud. Then he put the block down again with the word facing up and asked the participant to pick another block of the same kind. After the participant had made several choices, the experimenter turned one of the blocks with a different word underneath upside down, telling the participant that the two blocks turned up were not of the same kind (if indeed they were not) and encouraged the participant to continue looking for blocks belonging together. Another block was turned upside down again, and so on. The number of blocks with the words visible thus kept increasing, making it easier and easier for the participants to find the groups as defined by the experimenter.

The aim of the whole procedure was to study how the participants went about bringing the blocks together, and there were three qualitatively different strategies found. The first one of these was *syncretic grouping*. In this case, the participants' lumped together a number of blocks as a consequence of some vague feeling. The forming of the "heap" could be the result of guessing, or of simply picking blocks lying close to each other. The second category was *complexes*. In this case blocks were grouped together in accordance with factual, but varying, relations between blocks. There could be one kind of relation between one block and another (they might, for instance, have the same color), while a third block could be included in the heap on the ground because of another relation to the second block (both were flat, perhaps). This is very much like Wittgenstein's *family relationships* (members of a family having the same surname have different kinds of relationships to each other).

There are several kinds of complexes, the most advanced of which is the *pseudo-concept*. In this case, the participants seem to act as if they had a concept in mind (i.e., a concept defined by a certain feature—or by certain features—applying to all instances). They may, for instance, pick all triangles, acting as if they were thinking of the concept of a triangle. But the blocks are actually brought together in pairs: the first with the second, the second with the third, but what links the blocks within each pair together happens to be the same feature, without the learner being able to make this explicit.

Bringing all the blocks together in terms of the same defining features (tall–large, flat–small, etc.) represents the third—and most advanced—level of handling the experimental task.

It does not seem likely, however, that tall, flat, large and small are really novel features for the participants. (The experimental task actually presupposes that they can be noticed). Accordingly, Vygotsky's study is not a study of how people acquire new meanings but rather of how people make sense of words that are new for them, in terms of combinations of meanings discerned previously. Furthermore, by asking the participants to look for blocks of the same kind, meaning is identified in terms of sameness. As argued in the following section, this is a reasonable thing to do given that the meanings are not new to the participant.

2. "Seeing" and "visible" are used metaphorically, as synonyms of "experiencing" and "can be experienced."
3. The German-Swedish philosopher Ernst Cassirer presented an alternative to induction as a model for concept formation in mathematics and science about 100 years ago. After Einstein had published the general theory of relativity, it was included in Cassirer's (1923) analysis.

The idea of lumping things together and finding out what they have in common (as you do in induction) does not provide us with a powerful account of the origin of concepts, Cassirer says. It implies a hierarchy of concepts, with less and less content and meaning the higher we proceed. Conceptual development would, in this view, take place by lumping together instances, finding what is common to them, then lumping together lower-order concepts to form higher-order concepts, by finding out what is common among the lower-order concepts and so on, until we can no longer find anything in common.

Cassirer remarks that concept formation in mathematics and science is not at all like induction. Instead of disregarding what is particular, a scientific concept offers "a universal *rule* (italics in original) for the connection of particulars" (p. 20). The formula $(x - x_0)^2 + (y - y_0)^2 = r^2$ (where x and y are the co-ordinates of any point on a circle in the system of Cartesian co-ordinates, x_0 and y_0 the co-ordinates of the center and r stands for the radius) applies to all circles. The relationship between the terms is valid for all cases and by inserting specific values in the formula, we can identify any specific case. In a scientific concept what is general and what is specific are interconnected. The meaning of every specific instance does not derive from any real essence (substance) of that specific instance (corresponding to the concept which it is an instance of), but from the position of that instance in a system of instances and from the position of the concept it is an instance of, in a system of concepts. The meaning of a number does not derive from the number itself but from the position of that number in a system of numbers to which it belongs.

Previously, I referred to the formula for a circle that is applicable to all circles and captures what is invariant across (common to all) circles, namely the relationship between their constituent parts. In the same way, we can define the natural numbers $(1, 2, 3 \ldots)$ in terms of the relationship between them such as $x_i + 1 = x_{i+1}$. This rule specifies the relationship between all and any natural numbers: we can substitute any natural number for x. In these cases, we are using the mathematical concept of function to characterize mathematical concepts, and not the Aristotelian concept of sameness, neglecting how various instances differ and focusing only on that which is the same; but Cassirer argues for using the mathematical concept of a function as a model for concepts in general (at least for mathematical and scientific concepts). When forming the concept of metal, for instance, we cannot include any particular color, density or hardness as descriptors because all metals do not have the same color, density or hardness. But all metals have *some* color, density, hardness. Instead of thinking in terms of particular *values*, called "marks" by Cassirer (p. 22; such as red, blue, yellow, for instance) we should think in terms of variables (e.g., color) that can take different values (e.g. red, blue, yellow). In terms of the previous distinction between *dimension of variation* and *values* in that dimension, color is the former and different colors are the latter. In the same way, to take another of Cassirer's examples (p. 22), we cannot include a special form of procreation, movement or respiration in our concept of animal, because none of them is common to all animals. But all animals engage in *some* form of procreation, movement and respiration. Hence we have to include these (and other) variables in our definition of animals. These variables take different values for different animals, of course. What is specific for different animals is not simply neglected, when we move from specific animals to animals in general. By moving to more and more general conceptual levels, the meaning of the concepts is not impoverished (as in the case of Aristotelian logic) but is enriched instead.

4. We initially notice features of things not because they are alike but because they differ from each other. Experiencing difference is a necessary condition for discerning a feature of a phenomenon. But there are infinitely many features that can be discerned by means of infinitely many differences.

 Depending on what you compare with what, you can discern and notice completely different features. Furthermore, even when the different features have been discovered and discerned previously, juxtaposing one thing with another accentuates the difference between them. As there is no end to what comparisons can be made, every object (or person) is basically inexhaustible.

 Let us look at a simple example from Garner (1974). Consider the geometric object in Figure 3.1. What would you say you see? Look at the same object in Figure 3.2. How would you describe it? And look at Figure 3.3. What would you say this time?

 When looking at Figure 3.1 only, most people say that they see a circle, a ring, two circles or perhaps two concentric circles. Very few people would mention the size of the object and probably nobody would mention its location. But people certainly do so

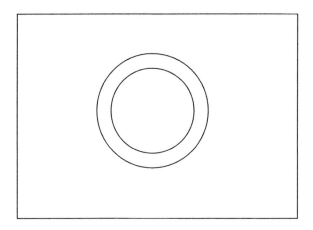

FIGURE 3.1 A single geometric figure (Garner, 1974, p. 184).

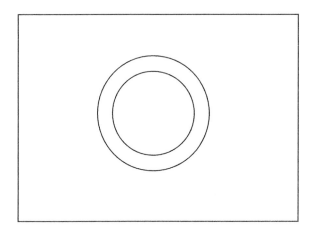

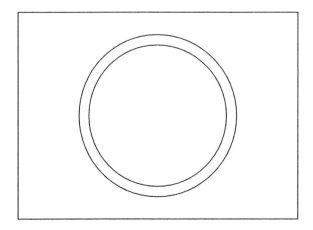

FIGURE 3.2 Two geometric figures juxtaposed (Garner, 1974, p. 184).

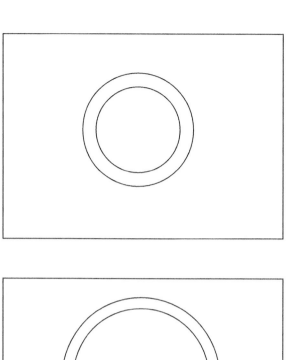
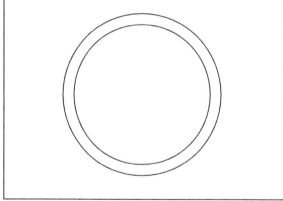
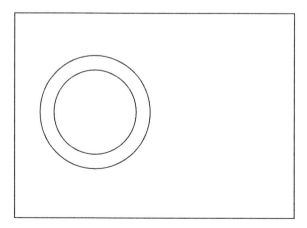

FIGURE 3.3 Three geometric figures juxtaposed (Garner, 1974, p. 184).

when they look at Figures 3.2 and 3.3. They discern the difference between two objects (the size) and between three objects (size and location). By choosing other objects as a contrast, we could encourage people to notice the fact that the lines are solid (not broken); the surface within the smaller circle is white, empty, flat, smooth, of paper; that the ring delimited by the two circles is thin, narrow, thick, wide, white, empty.

There are thus many, in principle infinitely many, features of even a very simple figure. Usually, we do not see these features, because they are not separated from the figure. Still, if they were brought out by means of appropriate differences, we would agree retrospectively that we have actually seen them from the beginning. The mechanism for bringing the separation about is straightforward enough: it takes the particular pattern of variation and invariance that we call *contrast* (see the next paragraph). In this case for every contrast, there is a difference between two figures (or variation between several), while other features are the same. The contrast makes the observer notice the particular features that differ. They are precipitated, so to speak; they are separated (from the figures in Garner's specific examples) and become visible. In order to separate the particular features (in the sense of making them visible), the learner has to experience differences in relevant aspects (such as size, location, etc.).

As pointed out in the previous paragraph, the simultaneous awareness of two colors, of the world seen with or without spectacles or of two geometrical objects, constitute a *contrast*. Contrast is, of course, not always perceptual. "True" and "false" are contrasting *values* in a *dimension of variation* that may be called "truth-value," just as "democracy" and "dictatorship" are contrasting values in a dimension of variation that may be called "governance," and in the same way as two colors are values in a dimension of variation called "color." If you walk into a sauna, among all the naked bathers, you might be painfully aware of the fact that you are dressed; among children, you become aware of the fact that you are an adult. In Sri Lanka, you might become aware of being Swedish, among women that you are a man or among the hungry that you are well fed. Standing next to a basketball player I feel short; standing next to a very young person I feel old; compared with different people, I might feel slow, noble, courageous, healthy or I might feel like a failure. Are these attributes (features) *my* attributes? After all, they originate from the experience of differences. If everyone had the same gender, I would not have any gender at all. If everyone were the same as I am in all respects, I would not have any qualities at all. This is the relativity of experience.

The implication of all of this is that we can never understand how others understand anything without knowing (or guessing, at least) what comparisons they are making and what differences they see (what distinctions they make). In the same way, in order to enable learners to develop a certain understanding of something, we have to ensure that a certain difference can be discerned by them. In order to understand what a dog is, it is necessary to compare it with a cat (or some other animal); in order to understand what an animal is, it has to be compared with a human being, or a plant; in order to understand what a living creature is, a contrast must be made with something that is not a living being.

As should be obvious from the examples the previous paragraph, opening a dimension of variation by juxtaposing two values can give rise to a new meaning. But in the examples given in the paragraph before that, the comparison does not bring about a meaning that the person has never experienced before. Instead, an aspect that is already known to the learner is made to stand out.

5. There are of course many other examples of emphasis on the central role of variation and differences as far as the origin of meanings is concerned, within different fields and with different theoretical orientations. Wittgenstein is mentioned in note 6, Montessori in note 7, Bateson in note 9. There is the anthropologist, Lévi-Strauss, founder of structuralism, describing rich belief systems in terms of fundamental oppositions (Wilcken, 2010, p. 192); the mathematician Spencer Brown (1972), stressing the fundamental role

of distinctions ("a universe comes into being when a space is severed or taken apart." p. v); the sociologist, Luhmann (2002), with strong epistemological interests in second-order observations (i.e., the observation of observations), arguing that meaning ascends from the horizon of possibilities (p.120); the philosophers Derrida (2001) and Deleuze (2004), among others, working with "difference theories . . . the core of postmodern thinking and perhaps the only element of it that will survive" (Baecker, 2002, on the back-cover of Luhmann, 2002). These are but a few remarkable contributions to a discussion about differences and variation as seen from different points of view and in varying ways. We might also recollect Rudyard Kipling's striking wording: "What should they know of England who only England know" (quoted by Laurillard, 2012, p. 75).

So, referring to variation and difference in connection with meaning is far from unique. What is possibly a bit more unusual is relating this discussion to learning and trying to derive implications of practical interest, which is definitely an intention with this book.

6. According to Mulhall's (1993) reading of Wittgenstein's *Philosophical Investigations* (1958, in particular, §209 and §210):

> the capacity to perceive a particular aspect of a given object . . . [presupposes] a grasp of a general dimension of variation in terms of which the object could be located by comparison and contrast with other objects.
>
> (p. 71)

A few pages earlier in the same book, we are offered an example of this:

> Take the concept of facial expression: it could not be acquired by someone who had seen examples of only one facial expression, who had only ever seen sad faces, for that concept has its existence only within a play of features . . . ; teaching the concept to him requires isolating a particular dimension of variation by pointing to samples of different points along that dimension—it involves conveying one particular way in which objects can vary, can differ from and resemble one another.
>
> (p. 62)

A "particular way in which objects can vary" is exactly what an aspect is in Mulhall's interpretation of Wittgenstein (and of Heidegger, by the way). An aspect specifies the kind of object something might be, a holistic characteristic of the object (e.g., facial expression or drawing) that cannot be reduced to material attributes (such as form or color, for instance).

Although Mulhall's interpretation of what Wittgenstein says about seeing aspects is very much in accordance with the views expressed in this chapter, about seeing as a function of experienced differences, the distinction between holistic and material aspects of entities is not made in this book. As argued previously, we cannot discern— much less learn to discern—a particular facial expression, or the concept of "facial expression" without seeing different facial expressions. But neither can we discern the color green, or the concept of "green," if we have never seen any other color.

7. Inspired by the work of two French physicians, Jean Itard (1775–1838) and Eduard Seguin (1812–1880), Maria Montessori developed a pedagogy, in which variation and differences (and invariance and similarities) are used very systematically, especially as far as the training of senses is concerned (e.g., learning to differentiate and order form, color, size, length, weight, sound, number). Much like Itard and Seguin, Montessori focused on the ordering of values within dimensions of variation. Signert and Marton (2008, p. 183; see also Signert, 2012) have identified five principles underlying Montessori's use of variation and invariance:

1) The greater the difference between two characteristics (values), the easier it is to experience the difference.

2) In order to learn to experience small differences (between values), which are hard to discern, greater differences shall precede smaller differences.
3) When values can be ordered in a dimension of variation, children can—and should—learn to do so.
4) Before dealing with two or more dimensions simultaneously, the child should learn to discern one dimension at a time.
5) Children have to learn to separate attributes (features, values) from things, and attributes from attributes.

(see Montessori, 1949/1987, p. 161)

8. The meaning of the dimension of variation is, however, restricted by "the permissible range of change" (Watson & Mason, 2005, p. 5), that is, by the values discerned, hence it is in principle open to change by additional values being discerned.
9. The dividing line between the inanimate and the living world is, according to the biological anthropologist Gregory Bateson, that while in the former we can understand what happens in terms of forces and impacts, in the latter we make sense of what happens in terms the organism's perception of differences, or more precisely, the organism's perception of "differences that make a difference" (Bateson, 1980, pp. 7–8). And perception of differences is all there is to perception (p. 32).
10. In relation to the present theory, this would mean that an aspect precedes the features that define it. But this is not consistent with the assumption that the two must appear simultaneously. In this respect, we are dealing with two mutually exclusive theoretical assumptions, if Hegel's principle is interpreted as meaning going from the general to the specific, which seems to me to be Davydov's (1990) interpretation. But as argued in the section with Hegel's principle as a heading in the previous chapter, Ilyenkov (2008) and Engeström (personal communication, February 14, 2012) have an interpretation of this principle that is much easier to reconcile with the present line of reasoning.

The most radical implications of Davydov's pedagogy of learning concern the ordering of the curriculum. The idea is to go from the abstract to the concrete (in the sense of going from the more to the less general, as pointed out in the previous paragraph) and not the other way around, as basically all educational expertise have advised us to do for many centuries (see, for instance, Kroksmark, 2011). One striking feature of the Davydov curriculum in mathematics is that algebra precedes arithmetic (Schmittau, 2004). The students do not even come across numbers during the first year in school. The rationale is that quantity is more general than number, and algebra is more general than arithmetic. If the learners start with something specific, they need to do a restructuring when subsequently encountering something that is more general. If you work in the reverse order and start with what is more general (abstract), then that which is more specific (concrete), when encountered subsequently, will appear as a special case, within the conceptual framework already developed. Moreover, a deeper understanding of things can only happen within a wider frame of reference (a more advanced conceptual level): "The adolescent who has mastered algebraic concepts has gained a vantage point from which he sees concepts of Arithmetic in broader perspective" (Vygotsky, 1986, p. 202).

Children taught according to the Davydov curriculum start by comparing and contrasting quantities (usually continuous quantities, such as length, volume, mass) and learn to codify relations of equality or difference between them (see Figure 3.5). In the first grade, children might compare two volumes (of water, for instance) and conclude that one is larger than the other. They might also find out that the two volumes can be made equal either by taking away a part from the larger volume (K) or adding something (C) to the smaller (B). With the teacher's help, the children might schematize the relationships between the three quantities (see Figure 3.5).

But from the point of view of the child who has never discerned quantities before, the symbols in Figure 3.5 do not necessarily represent general quantities, more than 7

```
      K
     / \
    B   C
```
$$K = B + C$$
$$B = K - C$$
$$C = K - B$$

FIGURE 3.5 Part–whole relations (Schmittau, 2004, p. 27).

and 2 and 5 necessarily represent general quantities. To begin with, the symbols represent specific volumes of water, just as 7 and 2 and 5 might represent 7 and 2 and 5 buttons. The general part–whole relationship must be discerned from juxtaposed (differing) specific cases. It is true that an understanding of algebra aids the understanding of arithmetic, but quantities must always be some particular quantities, just as there is no positional system in general, but only various actual positional systems. In the same way, green does not exist in general, but green cucumbers do.

What is important in Figure 3.5 is not so much that letters are used instead of numbers, but the fact that addition is dealt together with subtraction and that relationships between parts and whole are brought out. The two theories (Davydov's and the present one) share the view that what is more specific cannot be grasped without grasping what is more general. According to the present theory, however, what is more general cannot be grasped either, without grasping what is more specific.

The view advocated in the present book is that the more and less general levels must appear simultaneously; each assumes the existence of the other. And even if Davydov talks about moving from the general to the specific, he is in actual fact dealing with both at the same time. Interestingly, he quotes Vygotsky:

> The process of concept formation develops from two aspects—from the aspect of the general and from the aspect of the particular—almost simultaneously.
>
> (Quoted by Davydov, p. 188)

Why "almost," one might venture to ask? Is this why the "real process of concept formation was never solved by Vygotsky" (Davydov, p. 181)?

11. A focused aspect is one to be learned or to be learned about. It is an object of learning or a constituent of the object of learning, either a necessary or an optional aspect (one to be discerned and taken into consideration or one to be discerned and not taken into consideration). It is assumed to be a critical aspect for at least some of the learners.
12. There is no sharp distinction to be made between a learning phase and an application phase; both learning and application are involved in every interaction between a learner and an object of learning, but there is a difference in relative emphasis between aspect and features, when the former is newly discerned and when it has already been made one's own. The same difference is dealt with in the section "Discerning and Learning to Discern" in this chapter.
13. This distinction was dealt with in relation to the object of learning, in the section "Critical Aspects and Critical Features, Again," in this chapter.

4

WHAT DOES THE WORLD LOOK LIKE TO OTHERS?

In Chapter 3, it was shown that experiencing certain patterns of variation and invariance is a necessary condition for discerning and learning to discern certain critical aspects. But in order to contribute to bringing those patterns about, we need to know what the critical aspects are. While the previous chapter was about how the learners might discern critical aspects and features by dealing with the tasks, the present chapter is about how the teacher or researcher might discern critical aspects and features by observing the learners' ways of dealing with the tasks. The question asked in this chapter is: How does this take place? As the learners' ways of seeing the object of learning are defined by the aspects discerned and focused on, finding out what they are amounts to finding out how others see something. Or—to say it slightly differently—how something appears to others. But how can we find out what things look like to other people? How can I possibly see what another person is seeing when looking at the same thing that I am? Questions like these have been addressed by a research specialization, phenomenography, defining a domain of inquiry that the theory outlined in the previous chapter is intended to contribute to (Harris, 2011; Marton, 1981).

The Revelation of Jonas Emanuelsson

My former doctoral student, Jonas Emanuelsson, says on the first page of his thesis:

> When I was a child, about 10 years old, I kept contemplating the nature of colors and the question of how other people see the same color as I see. I made a thought experiment where I envisaged something green. How do I know that it is green? I asked myself, disregarding physical and biological explanations. My answer was that I have learnt that this particular nuance is

called green. Other people around me call it green as well. They are making the same distinction as I do. I went on with my questions and concluded that the color we call green does not necessarily look the same to others. What would it look like if I could swap gaze with someone else? Perhaps what is green to me is red to others but we use the same word to refer to it.

(Emanuelsson, 2001, p. 1 [translation mine])

Emanuelsson's conclusion is thus that the only thing that we can observe, as far as other people's ways of seeing the world is concerned, is whether or not they make the same distinctions (between colors, for instance) as we do. But this is true not only for colors, but for everything else. We can never experience others' experiences of anything. We can observe whether or not two people make the same distinction, or whether or not someone else makes the same distinction as we do and does so consistently. It is exactly at this point that we encounter the limits of inter-subjectivity. We can never get closer than this to each other's ways of experiencing the world around us. We cannot share each other's experiences, but we might share the way in which we discern differences in what we experience.

What Is to Be Learned, Again: Ways of Seeing

According to the line of reasoning in the previous section, a way of seeing (or experiencing) something can be defined in terms of the distinctions made. And an object of learning can be defined in terms of the aspects that it is necessary to learn to discern and focus on simultaneously. An aspect that it is necessary to discern corresponds to one or several distinctions that have to be made. An object of learning can thus be defined—in terms of critical aspects—as a way of seeing something.

As argued earlier, we act in accordance with what we see (or experience). Hence, powerful ways of acting go with powerful ways of seeing. There is quite a bit of support for such a conclusion.

The most important difference between experts and novices in different fields has been repeatedly found to be related to the aspects of a situation that are discerned and taken into consideration (i.e., how the situation is seen). Chess masters, for instance, see the chess board in terms of a relatively large number of possible configurations: they are not focusing so much on the position of single chessmen but rather on larger patterns, which they identify in a few seconds. They also easily remember such patterns, while they are no better than average players at remembering chessmen and their positions on the board when they are arranged at random (Chase & Simon, 1973; de Groot, 1965). Chi, Feltovich and Glaser (1981) demonstrated that physicists see problems in terms of conceptual categories of physics, while their students see the same problems in much less powerful ways, namely in terms of the specific objects that appear in the problems. So while the physicists differentiate between concepts and principles that are necessary for solving the problems, making distinctions, for instance, between problems that can be handled in terms of the law of the conservation of energy and problems that can be handled in terms of Newton's second law, novices might make distinctions between, for example, problems in which inclined planes appear and problems in which there are things that rotate. The experts thus see the problems in terms of the features that it is necessary to take into consideration for solving them. The students mainly see the problems in terms of features that are more easily perceptible but less relevant for solving the problems.

In pedagogical contexts, you must assume that one way of seeing a particular situation is more powerful in relation to a certain aim than another. Why would you otherwise try to help others to develop particular ways of seeing and particular ways of acting? Sandberg (1994) carried out a study of professional vision, driven by a pedagogical knowledge interest. He set out to study the question, What makes an excellent motor optimizer in the car industry excellent? The idea was that once we have a good answer to this question, we can help more motor optimizers to become excellent.

The specialists in question are engineers developing car engines with an optimal combination of qualities (fuel consumption, durability, exhaust emission, power, etc.) by means of adjusting the fuel and ignition systems, given a number of legal constraints. Sandberg found three qualitatively different ways in which these engineers saw and handled their task. One way is to monitor one quality at a time, by manipulating the monitoring parameter. When the quality in question is found to be satisfactory, the engineer proceeds to the next quality and works on it until that is alright, then proceeds to the third quality and so forth. But as the adjustment of parameters later in the sequence affects the qualities adjusted in the earlier steps, the work has to move in cycles (i.e., starting again once the sequence is completed, until the combination of qualities deemed optimal is reached). While this first way of handling the task is additive (i.e., the different qualities are taken care of one after the other in a sequence, or rather, in cycles), in the second way of carrying out the task, the engineers try to take the interaction between different qualities into consideration and move in steps in which one quality is seen in relation to the others and to the engine as a whole. Several qualities and parameters are thus attended to simultaneously. In the third way of handling the task the engineers even take the driver's experience into consideration (another critical aspect) in addition to the interaction between different qualities and parameters. These qualitative differences amount to the aspects of the task that the engineers discern and focus on simultaneously, the three different ways of approaching their work representing increasingly complex and efficient modes of operating. Interestingly, the engineers seemed to be aware of differences between themselves in how good they were at doing their job, but without being aware of what they did differently. They had an agreed rank order and that order seemed to correlate highly with the qualitative differences found in their way of handling and seeing their work. Some are better at it than others. That can be seen by inspecting the motors they develop: some work better than others.

Sandberg has thus come up with a conjecture about why some are better at motor optimizing than others: when developing the motor, those who are better optimizers take the various qualities (together with the parameters that control them) and the drivability of the motor into consideration simultaneously. Why do some do it, but not others? Because their experiences with motors have made it possible for them to discern the necessary aspects of the motor to be developed, including its drivability, and to focus on them simultaneously. This is as far as our *why* questions take us. The next move is to put the conjecture to the test by creating the conditions that make it possible to discern the necessary features and to focus on them simultaneously, and see to what extent those conditions help motor optimizers to become better motor optimizers.

Sandberg's study illustrates something else as well. As said previously, the engineers are aware of the fact that some are better at their work than others. But what they do differently is simply not visible to them. The reason is that the differences between them have more to do with differences in how they see their task than what they actually do. But differences in what the task looks like to the others are simply not visible to them because there is only one way of seeing the task that is available to them: their own.

In conclusion, what you can possibly do in a certain situation, how you can possibly solve a certain problem reflects how the situation or the problem appears to you—what you notice, what you attend to. How you handle a phenomenon that you encounter depends on what you see it as, what it means to you and what it appears to be. After all, in a particular situation, we always act according to the way that situation is perceived by us. If you take for granted that there is only one way of solving every problem in mathematics (i.e., if you see mathematical problems in such a way) and you know that you have never learned how to solve a certain kind of problem, if you happen to encounter a problem of this type, you will certainly not try to solve it. On the other hand, if you assume that problems in mathematics can be solved in different ways and that you might very well be able to find a way of solving a particular kind of problem (i.e., you see yourself and problems in mathematics in this way), it is very likely that you will have a go at a problem of a kind that you have not come across earlier.

Finding Critical Aspects

How can the teacher—or the researcher—discern what the learners discern and have to learn to discern? When learning to write, for instance, the child might learn to distinguish between writing and drawing to begin with. Subsequently, she might learn to distinguish between letters and figures, before she can distinguish different letters or different figures. When you look at a literate child, you cannot see those earlier, partial achievements because they have become fused, inseparable aspects of the full-blown act of writing. The answer is that the teacher—or the researcher—can make such discernments to the extent the learners make distinctions differently. In order to discern the distinction between writing and drawing (in terms of linear versus circular movements of the hand holding the pen) as a step in learning to write (for an example, see Figure 2.1 in Chapter 2), you must encounter children who do not make that distinction and children who do, but not more than that. Then you realize that making this distinction is an aspect of learning to read and write. But in order to perceive it as a distinct step towards literacy, you must find some learners who have not made that step.

We can see that the methodological principle used here is one suggested by the theory. The learners discern certain features by experiencing differences between different instances (of what they experience) in certain respects (between drawing and writing, for example), against a background of sameness in other respects (e.g., paper and pen are being used). The researchers discern what the learners have discerned, thanks to the experience of differences between different instances (of the results of the learners' efforts) in certain respects, against a background of sameness in other respects (e.g., trying to produce writing).

Let us consider another example, from Feldman (1980). Children of different ages are asked to draw a map of a toy landscape. In Figure 4.1, we can see a drawing that is supposed to be a projection of a toy landscape into the form of a two-dimensional map. Instead of conventional symbols, there are quasi-realistic pictures of three trees and two houses. The trees are lumped together and placed on the fringe of the landscape, and so are the houses, separate from the trees. Imagine now another map showing better correspondence to the actual toy landscape. In this case, not only the kind of objects (houses and trees) but also their spatial arrangement in reality is captured on the map: the two houses are located at some distance from each other, two trees are placed in front of one of houses, the third tree is placed in front of the other house (just as they are in the toy landscape). We cannot see any critical features in this case; a map of the landscape is all that we can see. But let us contrast this imaginary drawing with the map in Figure 4.1. Now we can see what the two have in common: the things and the number of things represented (two houses and three trees). And we can also see what differs: the spatial relationship between the things represented (while in Figure 4.1 we can see what objects and how many of them appear in the toy landscape, in the second (imaginary) map that is not shown here, we can also see how those objects are placed in relation to each other. We can thus identify two necessary aspects of drawing a map: the things represented (and their numbers) on the one hand and their spatial relationships on the other hand. These two aspects have been identified by Piaget and Inhelder (1967) as necessarily invariant during the transformation from landscape to map. As far as the drawing in Figure 4.1 is concerned, the second necessary aspect is a critical aspect (in relation to the imaginary map) in that case: it is missing, and the constructor of the map has to learn to discern it in order to become able to draw more useful maps. According to Mathews (1992, p. 106), attempts to draw maps structurally similar to this one are frequent among 6-year-olds. At this stage the child discerns one aspect

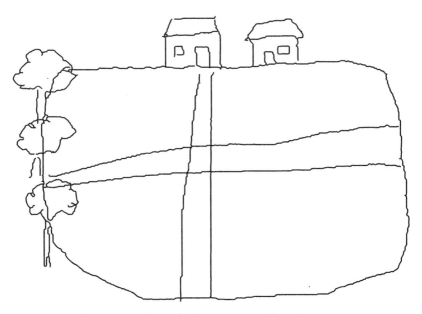

FIGURE 4.1 A fictive map of a toy landscape (inspired by Feldman, 1980, p. 52).

without attending to others. Discerning an aspect (what objects and how many) amounts to making distinctions in that respect. This is one of the learners' ways of seeing map drawing. In the second way of seeing map drawing, one more aspect is discerned: distinctions are made also in another respect (the spatial arrangement of objects). Subsequently, all the critical aspects (including symbolic, instead of quasi-naturalistic representation of various entities) are discerned and brought together (i.e., focused on simultaneously), and a map more in accordance with the canons of map drawing is produced.

We can see that unlike some of the studies referred to in the previous chapter, in which the learners are assisted in opening up certain dimensions of variation by means of introducing variation in those dimensions, while other dimensions are kept invariant (see, for instance, Ki & Marton, 2003), this time the procedure is reversed. We are trying to find out which dimensions are opened up by the learners themselves, through our (i.e., the researcher's) observation of the pattern of variation and invariance in the learners' ways of handling the task.

The Learner's Perspective and the Observer's Perspective

We should remember one thing, however. Even if children discern and focus on the logical–mathematical or on the spatial aspect, as seen by the researchers, they do not see any "aspects." What they see are trees, houses, roads and, perhaps, also that the trees are close to the house but far away from the road. So the children see the concrete things, specific to the landscape they are trying to depict.

They see them against a background of other concrete things, present in the actual landscape, or familiar to them from before. The observer looks at the drawings against the background of other drawings produced by other children, or by the same children at another point in time, and makes sense of them in terms of aspects and features discerned and focused on.[1]

In the same way, in Hannula and Lehtinen's (2005) study, quoted in Chapter 2, the children say "one" or "two" or "three," seeing one, two, or three sweets while the observer is seeing the children discerning the quantitative aspects of the situation.

We are thus dealing with two different perspectives: the participants' (the children involved in the study in the case just mentioned) on the one hand and the observers' (the researchers carrying out the study) on the other hand (see the previous section, for example). The set of alternatives (different numbers of sweets, for the children, and children paying or not paying attention to quantities, for the observer), in relation to which the actual case is seen, defines the perspective from which one thing or another becomes visible.

Logic and Understanding

The Norwegian psychologist Jan Smedslund made a highly important observation after having followed and scrutinized Piaget's research in Geneva. If someone says something odd about a situation that we are also experiencing, there are two options available to us. We might assume that this shared situation appears in the same way to the other person as it does to us. The reason for her to say things that strike us as odd is that she is simply not logical, at least not in the same way as we are. The other option is what we frequently do in everyday life: we give the other person the benefit of the doubt, at least to begin with. We assume that she is just as logical as we are, but that we do not see what she sees. The situation appears differently to her. In that case we have to try to find out how it looks to her and thus clarify the misunderstanding.

There is a circular relation between logic and understanding, Smedslund (1970) argued. We have to take one for granted in order to probe the other. Assuming that the children in his investigations were reacting to the same situation as was perceived by him, Piaget took understanding for granted and studied how their logic differs from adult logic, Smedslund said. But we should follow the practice of everyday life, he continued. We should take logic for granted and try to find out how things appear to other people. Actually, such a stance follows from considering acts and ways of seeing as being intertwined, being two aspects of the same whole. Such a stance implies that what people do is consistent with what they see (the two are logically related).

Let us consider an example from Neuman's (1987) study, mentioned in Chapter 2. Some 6-year-old children said that they have 5 fingers on their left hand and 10 fingers on their right hand. It was shown that if we assume that their answers are logical, as Smedslund advises us to do, we can find the meaning that "five" and "ten" have for them, which makes their statements about "five fingers on the left hand" and "ten fingers on the right hand" appear completely logical. They are using numbers as names—of their fingers—the first one is called "one," the second "two" and so forth. The name of the last finger is the name of all fingers together on the same hand. The last finger on one hand is called "five," hence the fingers on this hand together are called "five." The last finger on the other hand is called "ten," hence all the fingers on that hand are called "ten" together. By discovering the meaning numbers have for children, we can help them to discover the meaning numbers have for us.

Asking Questions

Having "ways of seeing" as objects of learning means that the students are expected to become good at discerning certain necessary aspects and focusing on them simultaneously. If we want to find out to what extent they have learned to do so, we should not point out those aspects for them but let the students discern them by themselves. Only then might we be able to find out how they deal with novel situations, how they handle the unknown by means of the known.

Variation theory (see, for instance, Marton & Trigwell, 2000) builds on a research specialization called phenomenography (Bowden & Walsh, 2000; Marton, 1981; Marton & Booth, 1997). It is about different ways of seeing situations and phenomena—about different ways in which the world around us appears to us. Some questions and some tasks are obviously more useful for finding out others' ways of seeing the world than other questions and other tasks. First of all, the tasks have to be novel and open-ended. This means that it is left to the learner to open up dimensions of variation as she finds it necessary. Emanuelsson (2001) carried out a study about how teachers' questions enable them to find out how things appear to their students. If the teacher asks the question, Can the octopus change its color? for instance, the space of possible answers is restricted to yes or no. The question does not require the students to open up other dimensions of variation (p. 235). Similarly, they do not have to open a dimension of variation in order to answer the question, Can you mention an animal that can change its color? The dimension of variation is *animals* and it is given by the question. You only need to pick a value in that dimension (i.e., one animal that changes color). Had the teacher asked the question, Why does the octopus change its color? the students would need to open a dimension of variation, for instance, "mechanisms for survival." In this case, they might see the octopus's ability to change its color, the size of the whale shark and the lugworm's burrowing into the sand as three different ways of protecting oneself from enemies, three different mechanisms for survival. In the first case, a fact is proposed and the learner has to remember it in order to decide whether or not the statement is correct; in the second case, the fact is given and the learner has to remember an animal to which it applies; in the third case, a fact is stated and an explanation is asked for. (In the case where this is a novel question, the explanation has to be created by the learner herself.) In a similar way, the question, "How much is 3 × 4?" is about a specific number, while the question "How can two numbers make 12?" (p. 236) calls for students to open the dimension of variation operations with values (such as addition, subtraction, multiplication, division, etc.), and also to open each one of these values as dimensions of variation with an infinite number of values. In the former example, the mathematical operation is given and the outcome (one answer) is asked for; in the latter case, the operation itself has to be chosen and the set of answers is unbounded.

Let us examine a pair of tasks from the point of view of constraints and possibilities—one not very conducive to finding out what aspects of the problem the students discern, the other much more so. Here is a problem aimed at probing students' insights into Newtonian mechanics. The task appeared in a Swedish nationwide test in physics for year 11 (upper secondary, year 2) students:

> In an experiment with a ball, it is found that when the ball falls, it is affected by the air with a braking force F, which is proportional to the velocity of the ball, v,
> that is, F = kv where k in this case is 0.32 Ns/m. What would the final velocity of the ball be if it were dropped from a high altitude? The ball's mass is 0.20 kg.

In order to solve the problem, the learner has to realize that there are two opposite forces acting on the ball: the gravitational force and the breaking force (mentioned in the problem) and that when the two reach equilibrium state, the ball continues with constant velocity. An equation can thus be set up representing this equilibrium state:

kv = mg,

where   k = 0.32Ns/m
        m = 0.20 kg
        g = 9.81m/sec^2

The learners do not have to discern what aspects of the event have to be taken into consideration: they all are pointed out in the question. But they have to know that the gravitational force acting on the falling body is *mg* and that if you drop something from a high enough altitude, the gravitational force and the breaking force will eventually balance each other and the body will continue falling at constant speed.

In order to explore the different ways in which students see novel situations, and to find out if they have developed more powerful ways of seeing in everyday life as a result of their studies, the questions asked have to be rather simple and straightforward, and neutral, with regard to the difference between everyday and scientific conceptualizations (it should be possible to answer them from either perspective). And above all, the questions should not point out the relevant aspects of the problem to be solved, as this is exactly what the students are supposed to find out (discern).

Another way of asking questions aimed at exploring whether or not—or how—the students have made Newton's first law their own is to present a situation with a body in movement and explore to what extent the students see the situation in terms of that law (i.e., to what extent they discern aspects of the situation that must be taken into account when using this law). We might, for instance, ask the following question, as did Johansson, Marton and Svensson (1985):

> A car is driven at a high constant speed on a motorway. What forces act on the car?
>
> (p. 237)

Analyzing Answers

Ways of handling tasks (answering questions, solving problems, etc.) are the primary units of analysis. Identifying the units is the first step. The second step is to identify the differences between units. The third step is to describe the different kinds of units. The fourth step is to clarify the logical relations between units.

The procedure follows the theoretically defined path of learning described in the previous chapter. The identification of the units is followed by contrast (focus on differences), generalization (focus on similarities) and fusion (focus on both differences and similarities). In this chapter, the second step is highlighted most. The method of analysis is elaborated on in greater detail by Marton and Pang (2008).

Example 1: Newtonian Mechanics

The question about forces acting on a car moving at a constant high speed is related to a highly popular topic in studies of conceptual understanding of classical mechanics, namely, Newton's first law:

> A body will rigidly maintain its state of uniform motion in a straight line, or its state of rest, unless it is acted upon by an impressed force.
>
> (Roche, 1988, p. 50)

In other words, a body at rest or moving with the same speed straight ahead will continue to do so unless a force affects it.

One student says the following during the interview dialogue:

> And then a force which is directed forward has to be greater than those there. Number 3 [pointing to arrow representing force in the direction of

movement] thus has to be larger than number 1 and number 2 [pointing to arrows representing forces opposite to the direction of movement], otherwise it wouldn't move forward.

(Johansson et al., 1985, p. 238)

What the student says, together with his drawing, represents a way of dealing with the task, which is a unit of analysis for this kind of study.

Another student says the following in the course of the same kind of dialogue:

When he drives at a constant speed, all the forces counterbalance each other.

(Johansson et al., 1985, p. 239)

This is another way of dealing with the same task.

All of the students discerned two kinds of forces: one in the direction of the movement (and related to the driving force of the motor) and the other in the opposite direction (friction between the tires and the road surface, and air resistance operating on the car). But there was a clear dividing line between two kinds of answers. Some of the students (actually, a majority of them) argued that the force in the direction of the movement must be greater than the sum of the forces in the opposite direction (otherwise the car would not move), while the other students said that forces in both directions must be equal (otherwise the car would accelerate or decelerate). The first kind of answers represents one of the most widely known misconceptions running counter to Newton's first law (see, for instance, Thornton & Sokoloff, 1998). In this case, the students discern that the car is moving (a car is driven *at a high constant speed* on the motorway). Their distinction is between moving and being at rest, and it calls for something that accounts for the difference. Most people do indeed think that movement implies force: (there must be a force pushing the car, otherwise it wouldn't be moving. It would be at rest). In the other case, the students discern that the car is travelling at an even speed (car is driven at a high *constant speed* on the motorway). Distinction is made between uniform speed (or rest) and changing speed: we have rest and movement at constant speed on the one hand and movement with changing speed on the other hand. The two ways of seeing the problem represent two ways of making distinctions. The second way of seeing includes (builds on) the first. The distinction between rest and movement is presupposed: we cannot speak of speed without there being movement. The necessary aspects are identified through the comparison of the two ways of seeing: forces and movement are discerned in both cases, speed only in the second.

Example 2: Arithmetic

Let us once more return to Neuman's (1987) study, referred to in Chapter 2, this time as an example of identifying qualitative differences. Insights into differences in how simple arithmetic tasks are seen and handled could contribute to preventing a substantial portion of the mathematical difficulties that about 15% of the students in each age cohort from 10 years and onwards suffer from in Sweden, Neuman (1987, 2013) and I believe (see, for instance, Marton & Neuman, 1989).

I would like to illustrate these differences in terms of different ways of dealing with one particular problem, but the same differences can be found in handling (and seeing) any simple arithmetic problem.

The qualitative differences in ways of seeing the object of learning discussed in this chapter are frequently found in learners' answers to the problems presented to them. But in order to formulate a question, a problem, you must have some idea of what kind of differences you (as the author of the question) are interested in. Before Neuman even started her study, she suspected that part–whole relationships between numbers (i.e., how numbers are divided up) are fundamentally important for how arithmetic problems are mastered. Accordingly the first question she asked, in her study of 105 6-year-old children before they started school, was as follows:

> Look, here are nine marbles, can you count them? *Yes, 1, 2, 3, 4, 5, 6, 7, 8, and 9.*
>
> Now I will hide some of them in my left hand and the others in my right hand.
>
> Can you guess how many I have in my left hand and how many I have in my right hand? *Yes, that's fine. . . .* Can you make another guess?

The interviewer did indeed hide the marbles in her two hands and did not show them while the child made five guesses (giving pairs of numbers).[2]

Numbers as Words

A few children's guesses were pairs of numbers of which one or both were larger than 9, such as "9 and 13." In these answers the principle of saying number words was honored; these children made a correct distinction between number words (asked for by the question) and other words (not asked for). Within number words, distinctions were made between different (natural) numbers. We could say that these answers reflected an understanding of the task that differed from what was intended. Children felt in this case that they were supposed to come up with two (different) number words.

Numbers as Names

When looking at the rest of answers, one difference between the guesses was striking. In some cases, one of the numbers was 9 every time, such as, for instance

> 2 and 9 . . . 4 and 9 . . . 8 and 9 . . .[3]

How did children see numbers and the task in this case? We have to recall how "5 fingers on the left hand and 10 fingers on the right hand" was found to be completely logical if numbers are seen—and used—as names. In relation to the present question, we might assume that children who make guesses in this particular way (the second guess always being 9) somehow imagine the 9 marbles lying in a row, with the first one being 1, the next one being 2, where these two are in one of the interviewer's hands. The second marble is the last one among the marbles there. It is called 2, hence the marbles in that hand are called "2" together. (As was pointed out earlier, children learn that if the counting of objects is seen as labeling them, or giving them names, the name of the last object counted is the name of all the objects together.) The next marble is 3, it is the first one in the interviewer's other hand, then 4 and 5 and so on to 9. The last one is always called 9, so the marbles in that hand are always called 9 together, and, accordingly, the child says that there are 9 in the second hand every time, regardless of her guess for the first hand. This is the same way of seeing numbers as was the case with "5 fingers on one hand, 10 fingers on the other." These cases involve seeing and handling numbers as names. The numbers differ from each other in terms of their position in the sequence, but they lack a cardinal sense, or "manyness." Each number represents one object only.

Numbers as Magnitudes

In other cases, some of the numbers in the five pairs of guesses added up to 9, or added up to something close to 9. For instance: 2 and 7 . . . 4 and 6 . . . 1 and 7. How can we make sense of such answers? What do the children see in these cases?

Well, we might assume that in these cases the "manyness" of numbers is discerned, but not the sequential order (the 1st, the 2nd, the 3rd . . .).

Children frequently make distinctions between "small numbers" (1, 2, 3), "mid-sized numbers" (4, 5, 6) and "large numbers" (7, 8, 9) along with making distinctions between parts and wholes. Assuming that they have come to the conclusion that a small number and a mid-sized number add up to a large number, and possibly also that two mid-sized numbers may add up to a large number, a mixed series of right and almost right guesses appears perfectly logical. This approximate grasp reflects the children's sense of numbers as magnitudes.

Numbers as Patterns

At this point we might ask, If these two ways of seeing numbers are considered to be necessary steps in the development of seeing and handling arithmetic problems, how can children advance further and master operations by which numbers are combined in canonical ways? In order to find an answer, we must go beyond noticing children's answers to problems. We have to observe and analyze their ways of arriving at those answers. Neuman (2013) makes a very strong point here.

She says that there are two main ways of learning to handle simple arithmetical tasks, one of which most likely results in difficulties with mathematics. What then are the qualitative differences in seeing and handling numbers that are of such dramatic importance? Let us look at a specific case to begin with.

Consider a child participating in Neuman's study being asked to guess how many of nine marbles the interviewer holds in her left hand and how many in her right hand. Let us also assume that the child does not know the possible combinations of numbers making up 9 (such as 1 and 8, 2 and 7, 3 and 6, etc.), but having mastered both numbers as names and numbers as magnitudes is looking for two parts making 9 together. So what can the child do? A little girl guesses "2 in the left hand" and is aware of the fact that the two numbers guessed should make 9 together. How many marbles does the interviewer have in her right hand if she has 2 in her left hand?

This is a so-called missing addend problem that can be written as $2 + \_ = 9$. The little girl puts 9 fingers on the table (first her open left hand, then 2 fingers on her right hand, then 2 more. After that she folds the last two fingers out of the nine: right middle finger and right ring finger. At last she touches her lips with each one of seven unfolded fingers, counting them one at a time and concluding "seven" (marbles in the interviewer's right hand).

The same missing addend problem appeared also in another word problem (I have 2 kronor and I want to buy an ice cream for 9. How many more kronor do I need?). It was solved in the same way by some children, while others solved it in a similar way, but without counting the remaining 7 fingers, or even folding any fingers. In this case, they just put up nine fingers, looked at them and said "seven." All these slightly different ways had several things in common. First of all, these children are using their fingers to *represent* numbers, to make numbers and relations between numbers visible.

Second, they turn a problem that appears additive to them (2 + something is 9) into a subtraction (taking away 2 from 9). Third, they open up for swapping two addends (2 and 7 in this case), making use of the commutative law of addition ($a + b = b + a$). By opening up two dimensions of variation (operations and sequential order), they focus on the relations between numbers, the part–whole structure, instead of the specific operations. By doing so they can choose the operation that is easiest to carry out, in the way that is easiest.

The opening of these two dimensions of variation is partly driven by the children's attempts to make the numbers and the relationships between them visible, by using their fingers, and by having the undivided 5, the whole hand, as the first part of numbers larger than 5. In the actual example, for instance, the child starts with putting the whole, 9, on the table. Within this whole, the given part, 2, has to be placed. As the five cannot be broken, the two marbles cannot be envisaged at the beginning of the 1, 2 . . . 9 sequence. They have to be put in the end of it and then taken away in order to find the remaining part. Then either you see that there are 7 fingers—corresponding to 7 marbles—left, or you have to count them. You can also subtract 2 from 9, saying "one goes away—8 (left). 2 go away—7 (left) . . . 7 are missing."

By handling various tasks in this way, in terms of the relationships between numbers, the learners become able to see the first ten natural numbers (1 to 10) in terms of the 25 possible combinations into which they can be split (**2/1/1**; **3/2/1**; **4/3/1, 4/2/2** . . .).[4]

Using fingers for making the numbers, and the relationships between them, visible by creating "finger numbers" is the most common way that children become able to see numbers as patterns and by doing so enter the world of arithmetic.

Numbers as Counted Number Words

According to Neuman (1987, 2013), this decisive step is taken by most children (about 80%) before they start school (at 7 years of age in Sweden, at the time when she carried out her study). What happens to the children who have not done so before starting school? They could very well receive help to develop the necessary prerequisites for learning simple arithmetic. But if these prerequisites are not generally recognized, it is most likely that the students will have to practice and learn addition and subtraction tables to begin with. And as Neuman (2013) points out, in those tables, 2 + 7 is presented as one fact, 7 + 2 another, 9 − 7 a third and 9 − 2 a fourth, instead of presenting number 9 seen as the pattern **9/7/2**, as one number divided into two parts, that can be presented in many ways, not only the four mentioned above but in at least four in addition and eight in subtraction.

More specifically, let us return to the guessing game and envisage a child who has guessed "2 in one hand" and is aware of the fact that there are 9 marbles all together but has never developed the finger-numbers approach nor opened up the operation or the sequential order dimensions of variation, and this child is facing the question: "How can I possibly figure out how many marbles the teacher has in her other hand?" Well, the strategy that some children might use is to imagine two marbles lying in a row, the first one and the second one. These are the marbles in the interviewer's left hand. Then there are the marbles in her other hand: the third one, the fourth one, and so on to the ninth marble, the last one. The image is very much the same as in the category "numbers as names", but in this case the learner wants to find out how many marbles there are in the interviewer's other hand. If you do not know how many there are, you have to count them. But what can you count? You might utter the number words and count them: you call the third marble "three" and count one (referring to the first marble in the interviewer's right hand), then you say "four," counting two and so on: five[three], six[four] and so on up to nine[seven]. As you have said "nine," you have to stop, as that was the last number word referring to the last marble in the interviewer's other hand. As you have kept track of the number words that you have said and, as the last one (9) was the seventh, you know that if there are two marbles in the interviewer's left hand, there must be seven in her right hand. This is a double-counting procedure that can be carried out in another way, too, by using your fingers to keep track of the number words uttered. So you might say "three," set up one finger (your left thumb, perhaps) to indicate that you have said one number word, say "four," set up another finger and so on until you have said "nine" and set up the seventh finger. Now, either you see the "sevenness" of your seven fingers (a full hand + two), or you have to count them—by touching your lips (as in a previous example) or your nose with one finger at a time and counting the touches. In either case the number words used for counting are counted. This actually amounts to opening the counted number words as a dimension of variation. Accordingly, we can say the children in this case see numbers as counted number words.

It may appear improbable that such seemingly subtle differences as we find between numbers as patterns and numbers as counted numbers would make the difference between becoming able and not becoming able to do sums. After all, in both ways of seeing and dealing with numbers, fingers are used as tools.

But in the case of numbers as patterns, fingers are used for making numbers visible, by using numbers for counting the fingers, while when numbers are seen as counted number words, fingers are used for counting numbers. Furthermore, in the former case, the whole and its two parts are represented in every problem, while in the latter case, only one part—that which is sought—is represented.

What you do not learn through double counting is to split the first 10 natural numbers into different pairs or parts, to swap those parts when it makes life easier for you and to choose between addition and subtraction depending on which is easiest. You are stuck with double counting: it is a cul-de-sac. Through the other path, through seeing and handling numbers as patterns, the learners become capable of experiencing the first 10 natural numbers as wholes and as parts that can be combined flexibly in many different ways. This is the true sense of mastering number facts.

If you do not grasp numbers in such a way, it is impossible to advance further in arithmetic. "Repeated addition is neither the easiest, nor the most common way of carrying out multiplication," Neuman (2013) says. "But it is the only way to find the answer, if you do not know the multiplication table. If you engage in double counting for addition and subtraction, you must engage in triple counting for multiplication. You must count the number words that you utter again and again, and you must count how many times you have counted those words" (pp. 21–22). And this just does not work. On the other hand, Neuman continues:

> For pupils who have developed the capability [of experiencing the first 10 natural numbers as wholes and parts], repeated addition is comparatively straightforward. Let us take the table of 6 as an example. Most children know that 6 + 6 = 12 long before they have started multiplying. And they know immediately that if we add 6 to the "2" in 12 we get 8, i.e. that **12 + 6 = 18**, if they can see the pattern 6/2/8. Which can be seen as easily as 2/6/8, of course. Nor will it be especially difficult, after 18, to split

the number 6 at the 20-boundary to think 18 . . . 20, 24 for someone who knows that 6 can be split into the parts 4 and 2, or 2 and 4. Then you can go on adding in the same way.

(p. 23, translation mine)

We can now summarize the qualitative differences in how numbers are seen and handled, in terms of different conceptions and different critical aspects (see Figure 4.2). Through the critical aspects, the conceptions (or ways of seeing) are logically related to each other, together constituting the outcome space of the different conceptions. This is one of the examples of qualitative differences in how the world around us is seen. But it is also an example of the pedagogical model of explanation argued for in this book. The question of why a pupil does not know how much 4×9 is can be answered as because she does not know that $9 = 1 + 8 = 2 + 7 = 3 + 6$, nor that $1 + 8 = 8 + 1, 2 + 7 = 7 + 2$ or $3 + 6 = 6 + 3$.

Example 3: Understanding Texts

In the two previous examples used in this chapter, the participants are dealing with problems, and the researchers try to find out what aspects the participants discern and take into consideration. Different ways of seeing the problem ("conceptions," in phenomenographic literature) are identified and found to be hierarchically related to each other (they can be ordered in terms of increasing number of critical aspects opened). Interestingly, we get a similar picture when exploring the differing understandings of texts that the participants are invited to read. The main point of a text can, as a rule, be empirically broken down into constituent critical aspects and/or features just as can be done with other abilities. The group of participants is serving as a prism, as it were, if we consider the text to be the white light and the different ways of seeing it the spectrum of different constituent colors. Actually, this is how the research approach of phenomenography started in the early 1970s. In a typical study from that period, we invited the participants to read a text, in the context of individually run interviews. After reading, the participants were asked about their understanding of the main point or about what

	part-whole	manyness	position in sequence
number words	*i*	*i*	*i*
names	*i*	*i*	*v*
magnitudes	*v*	*v*	*i*
patterns	*v*	*v*	*v*
counted numbers	*i*	*i*	*v*

FIGURE 4.2 Different ways of seeing numbers, in terms of dimensions of variation.

they thought the author wanted to say with the text. We were thus not so much interested in finding out what details the participants could or could not recall but wanted to study how the text appeared to them. We found that we could distinguish between a limited number of qualitatively different ways of making sense of the text in each case. Furthermore, those qualitatively different ways were found to be logically related to each other, in terms of distinctions made, and could thus be ordered in relation to each other in terms of their complexity and precision. To put it in another way: understandings of the text differed in terms of what parts and aspects were discerned and focused on simultaneously (i.e., how complete or partial the understandings were; Marton & Säljö, 1976a, 1976b; Marton, Hounsell, & Entwistle, 1997). Each system of categories of description, depicting different ways of seeing the message of the text could be rewritten in terms of a limited number of aspects that might vary, be invariant or not present in the participants awareness at all, very much in the same way as in the previous examples in this section. Categories of description depicting different ways of seeing the same object of learning, logically related to each other, and which can be rewritten in terms of a limited number of necessary aspects, is the empirically based foundation and the study object of the research specialization we call phenomenography.

Let us consider a study in which secondary school students read a short story by Franz Kafka, "Before the law." This is how Marton & Booth (1997, p. 150) summarized it:

> The story concerns a man who tries many times to get admittance to the Law, the door to which is open but fiercely guarded by a man who refuses him entry, saying that he is not allowed in but that he should wait and see. However many times and in however many ways he tries to get in, he is unsuccessful. As the old man makes a final attempt, asking why nobody else has ever tried to go through the door, only to be told by the guard that the door was only for him, and now that his life was coming to an end, the door was to be closed.

Four qualitatively different ways of understanding Kafka's parable were found. In one of them the participants saw the reason that the man failed to get into the Law (which again was interpreted in different ways) as being that he did not try hard enough. It was not the Law (whatever it was) that made a difference. The distinction was between how the man had acted (not forcefully enough) and how he should have acted (more forcefully; A_1). In the second way of understanding what the author had meant, the man's way of acting was taken for granted. Actually, it did not make much of a difference. It was the Law (whatever it was) that did not let him in. Had the Law been different (more generous, more democratic), the man would certainly have gone through (A_2).

According to the third way of understanding, the first and second ways of seeing the story have to be combined: the tragic end of the story had to do with either the nature of the Law, or the nature of the man, or a combination of the two (B). According to the fourth way of understanding what the author was trying to tell us, the story is a paradox: there is no way of finding out what actually happened, why it happened or what should have happened. Whatever conclusion you arrive at, it can be refuted. And this is how it was meant to be (C).

These four ways of understanding Kafka's story are logically related to each other. The third understanding combines the first and the second one, and the fourth understanding builds on the third but adds the paradox as the message. The logical relationships between the four different meanings of the story constitute its outcome space, graphically represented in Figure 4.3.

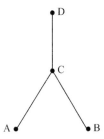

FIGURE 4.3 Relationships between four ways of understanding Kafka's "Before the Law" (adapted from Marton, Asplund-Carlsson, & Halász, 1992, p. 6).

This study is elaborated on in the next chapter, from the point of view of how the learners went about reading Kafka's parable.

Example 4: Price and Pricing

One of the most popular examples in the research tradition to which this book belongs is the "price of the bun." Dahlgren asked young children (1979) and students at a business school (1978) questions about price and pricing.

One of the questions was "Why does a bun cost one krona?" The question assumed that those answering it would try to explain why the bun was as expensive as one krona (which was indeed expensive in the late 1970s). This interpretation was shared by all participants, and many of them seemed to compare the bun with things that cost less. The explanation was then phrased in terms of attributes of the bun, especially in terms of its appeal to the customers: "Because it is so good!" "Because it tastes great!" (A). Other ways of seeing the price of the bun were in stark contrast to this. These other ways were not phrased in terms of attributes of the bun but in terms of market mechanisms, and were hence much closer to models of explanation in economics. According to Pong's (2000) retrospective interpretation, the participants probably said something like "the bun could cost that much, because there are many people who want buns" (demand; B_1) or "because there are not so many bakeries around" (supply; B_2) or its price depends on "how many people want to buy buns and how many buns there are to buy" (demand and supply; C). The last way of seeing is the most complex among those found. (Just as Category C represents the most complex way of understanding Kafka's parable in the previous example.)[5]

These four conceptions (or ways of seeing) have been found again and again in subsequent studies with the *same* object of learning. As an example, let us consider a study by Pang and Chik (2005). Ten-year-old year-4 students answered the following question in individually run interviews:

> Have you ever tried the hot dogs [or "biscuit sticks" in the parallel version of the question] sold in our school tuck shop?[6] Do you know how much they are sold for? Maybe you know or you don't know. Anyway, just for your information, hot dogs are now sold for HK $4.50. Suppose that you are the new owner of the shop. What price would you set for a hot dog? Would you set the current price, or a different price? What would you consider when you set the price?

Differences in meaning similar to those found by Dahlgren (1978) were also found in this study, although the specific examples differed, of course:

A. Price Depends on Attributes of the Commodity

> No, I would sell hot dogs for $3.50 each. I would consider the size of the hot dog.
>
> (S 63)

The explanation is phrased in terms of attributes of the hot dog, namely its size. Bigger hot dogs cost more than smaller ones. As we can see, this kind of answer is by no means wrong. Differences in price are related to differences in attributes of the same kind of commodity. The sausages that have to be sold are compared with other sausages, bigger and smaller. This is a perfectly reasonable explanation in the context of sausages varying in size. In other contexts other explanations might be more powerful.

B_1. The Price Depends on People's Willingness to Buy

> $4.50, because hot dogs in my school are sold for $ 4.50 and they are always sold out. Even though you may charge a higher price, I think many students would still buy it. As you know, there are quite a number of students who do not have their breakfast at home and they would go back to the school to buy hot dogs.
>
> (S 87)

In this case, the focus is not on the sausage but on the potential buyers. Possible differences in price are set in relation to possible differences in people's willingness to buy. If all the hot dogs are sold out at a given price, you can even charge a higher price.

B₂. The Price Depends on How Much There Is to Buy

> I would sell it for $15 because I could earn more money. As you know, a box of soft drink is sold for $3.00 in the tuck shop. The biscuit stick is a new product on the market. If I reduced the supply by 30 boxes, that means I would just supply 10 boxes a day, then the students would rush for it. If I increased the supply by 50 boxes, then the students might not go for it. So, I would reduce the supply so that I would earn more.
>
> (S 26)

Now the focus is not on the potential buyers but on the stock of the commodity (biscuit sticks in this case) available. The student opens up a dimension of variation in supply, comparing different cases varying from large to small (supply). The less there is of something, the more can you charge for it. The focus is on the selling part and on the seller's way of acting in relation to the availability of the product in question.

C. The Price as a Function of Willingness to Buy and How Much There Is to Buy

> During recess, I used to go to the tuck shop to buy the biscuit sticks, but I think the price is too low. If I were the owner, I would sell it at $7.50, because this tuck shop is the only food shop within this school. Also I would consider whether the students could afford to buy the biscuit sticks at this price.
>
> (S 102)

Unlike the previous cases shown, the student discerns and focuses on not only one aspect but two, simultaneously. Both the demand and supply dimensions of variation are opened up, although the latter does not so much refers to the size of stock in the owner's own shop but refers to the availability, or rather the lack of it, in other potentially competing shops.

Thus, four different ways of seeing (conceptions of) price and pricing were identified. These ways of seeing differ from each other—and can be described in terms of—dimensions of variation that were opened up. They are characterized by means of the possible differences discerned—and focused on—by the learners, as shown in Figure 4.4. The different ways of seeing the same phenomenon (price and pricing in this case) define the variation between conceptions of the

Category	Attributes of product	**Demand**	**Supply**	Price
A	*v*	*i*	*i*	*v*
B₁	*i*	*v*	*i*	*v*
B₂	*i*	*i*	*v*	*v*
C	*i*	*v*	*v*	*v*

FIGURE 4.4 Patterns of experienced variation and invariance that correspond to different ways of seeing price.

phenomenon, and the dimensions of variation opened up define the relationships between conceptions, constituting the outcome space.

We can see that the relations between conceptions are depicted in terms of which dimensions of variation that are opened. For instance, if dimension a (attributes of the commodity) is opened in conception A, dimension b (people's willingness to buy) is opened in conception B_1, dimension c (how much there is to buy) in conception B_2 and both b and c are opened in conception C, then C is superordinate to B_1 and B_2, while the latter two are parallel in relation to each other. This is another example of the hierarchical organization of conceptions.

Example 5: Relative Magnitude

Marton and Pang (2006) have studied how secondary school students in Hong Kong made sense—and could be helped to make sense—of changes in the price of a commodity as a function of the relative magnitude of changes in supply and demand. Seven classes participated in the study, some under experimental conditions and some under control conditions. Each class was divided randomly into two groups, one of which received one question aimed at finding out the students' ways of handling this problem, before the teaching sequence, and another, which received a different but structurally identical problem. After the teaching sequence was completed, the two questions were swapped between the two groups within each class. In this way, all the classes did the same problems before and after the teaching sequence, yet none of the students handled the same question more than once.

The two questions were as follows:

Question 1

In 1997, a new bird flu virus H5Nl was found in humans in Hong Kong. A total of 18 cases were reported and six people died. To stop the spread of the bird flu, the government immediately killed about 1.2 million chickens in the territory. However, it was surprising to find that after this move, the price of live chickens in the market did not increase but instead fell. Why? Please explain.

Question 2

Some years ago, original video compact discs (VCDs) were rather expensive, and many people turned to buying pirated VCDs. There were many shops that sold pirated VCDs. Over the past few years, the Customs and Excise Department of the Hong Kong government has put a lot of effort into stopping the illegal trade in pirated VCDs, and we can now find fewer shops that sell pirated VCDs. However, it is interesting to note that the price of pirated VCDs has not increased but has remained more or less the same as it was in the past. Why? Can you explain this?

Let us, as an example, consider the first question. To begin with, the learner is supposed to pay attention to supply and demand when it comes to prices and changes in supply and demand when it comes to changes in price. What the problem suggests is that the supply of chickens has gone down. Now, if supply goes down, the price should go up, unless there is a change in demand. But if the demand goes down, price should go down as well. We understand, of course, that demand is supposed to go down if people have become afraid of eating chicken. If both supply and demand go down at the same rate, the price remains the same. But the price did not remain the same in the actual case: it dropped. And the fact that it did suggests that the demand *dropped more* than the supply. A line of reasoning of this kind is supposed to lead to the intended object of learning (i.e., seeing change in price as a function of the relative magnitude of change in demand when compared to change in supply). The different ways of seeing the two problems (illustrated here with reference to the second question) were the following:

> A. Attributes of the commodity (e.g., changes in the quality of the pirated VCDs; market mechanisms—demand, supply—not discerned).
>
> B_1. Changes in demand (e.g., changes in the number of people that want to buy pirated VCDs; supply not discerned).
>
> B_2. Changes in supply (e.g., changes in how many pirated VCDs are available; demand not discerned).
>
> C. Changes in demand and supply (e.g., changes in how many pirated VCDs are available and how many people want to buy them; magnitude of change not discerned).
>
> D. The relative magnitude of changes in demand and supply (e.g., change in how many pirated VCDs are available compared to change in how many people want to buy them).

Actually, the difference between category C and D seemed to be critical for most students. This is about *change of change,* a second-degree (quadratic) relationship, to be compared with *change,* which is a first-degree (linear) relationship.

We actually find the same distinction between the two ways of seeing the physics problem (the car on the highway) previously in Example 1: Newtonian Mechanics. In that case also, there is a distinction between a first- and a second-degree relationship (between change in position, i.e., movement, on the one hand and change in the rate of change in position, i.e., velocity, on the other hand).[7]

Example 6: Understanding Understanding

The hierarchical organization of the outcome space implies that more complex ways of seeing (conceptions) represent wider variation or wider space (more dimensions of variation are opened up). But these kinds of relationships are not just empirical findings. Learning is actually conceptualized in the current theory as a widening of the space of the object of learning.[8] The conjecture is empirically supported by findings showing just such a widening space. But there is also empirical support of another kind: as should be obvious from the present example, the learners might conceptualize learning in terms of a widening space. This example is taken from a study of Hong Kong high-school students' views of learning and understanding (Marton, Watkins & Tang, 1997). Quite a few students did not distinguish between memorizing and understanding, while among other students distinctions were found between different views of understanding. Here are three examples of what the students said about learning as understanding (as referred to by Marton & Booth, 1997, p. 41):

Being Able to Do It (What You Have Learned in Another Situation

> After understanding certain things, to be able to apply them, the knowledge, in answering questions and in other situations, not just in situation A where I learned it, but also applying it in situation B and C.
>
> (S 5)

Being Able to Do It Differently

> You will have to understand very clearly the meaning of the whole passage, and then answer in your own words. If you just copy, you will not be able to get good results.
>
> (S 6)

Being Able to Do Something Different

> If you are taught that two plus four equals six and if people then ask you what is four plus two and you do not know the answer, that means that you have not understood. You only know two plus four but not four plus two.
>
> (S 7)

We can see how the three quotes illustrate a gradual widening of the space of learning, from variation in situations only, to variation in situations and in ways of doing something, to variation in situations, in ways of doing something and in what is being done.

The Idea of Phenomenography

Most descriptions in this book are phrased in terms of different ways of seeing something, or different ways in which something appears or, simply, meanings. We can also add conceptions, different ways of experiencing something as well as the lived (experienced) objects of learning. These different labels do not refer to different kinds of things; they are used as synonyms and they refer to the basic unit of phenomenography (see Marton & Pong, 2005). The reason that many terms are used is that none of them is perfect for the purpose (they are words or expressions that have many other connotations and point to different aspects of what is meant to be the basic unit of phenomenography). The latter is a research specialization concerned with qualitative differences in how we see the world and how it shows itself to us. All the six examples in this chapter are phenomenographic descriptions.

What I just called "the basic unit of phenomenography" is not necessarily the same thing as a concept (although the two may correspond to each other in many cases). This unit is defined in terms of the necessary aspects of the object of learning discerned by the learner.

There is a basic distinction that separates phenomenography from what it is not, and this distinction is between first- and second-order perspectives. A statement made from a first-order perspective is a statement about what things are like (e.g. The Sun revolves around the Earth). A statement made from a second-order perspective is a statement about what things appear to be (to someone), such as, for instance, Elmer sees the Sun revolving around the Earth. The distinction between the two perspectives is a pragmatic one: arguments about the first kind of statement are about what the Sun and the Earth are doing, and astronomical information is highly relevant; arguments about the second kind of statement are not so much about what the Sun and the Earth are doing, but more about what Elmer is doing (perceptually) with the Sun and the Earth; astronomical information is less relevant than information about what Elmer is saying and doing (see Marton 1978, 1981).

Phenomenography is about the different meanings of the same things (or about ways of seeing, experiencing and conceptualizing them), where "things" refers to anything that might have different meanings. We can learn about meanings by reading, by solving problems, by seeing, by hearing, by feeling, by moving and so forth. Research findings about different meanings might be grouped together in terms of how these meanings are learned (through perception, communication, immediate experience, conceptual engagement, etc.). In phenomenography, however, different meanings are grouped together in terms of what they are meanings of: price, quadratic equations, Cantonese opera, democracy, matter, wines from Eger and so on. The different meanings are captured in terms of categories of description that can then be broken down into critical aspects of the act of learning, which allows the logical relations between the categories to be made explicit.

Where Are "Ways of Seeing?"

If we are interested in describing what things or beings look like to others, the question might be raised: What is the location of the thing we are describing? A point made by Trankell (1973) is relevant here. In a study, carried out methodologically long before this kind of study was done by others, he tried to describe the world of a single mother of Finnish–Romany extraction, living in Sweden. He said: "I am not so much trying to see with her eyes; instead I am trying to see what she sees." And we may then ask: Where did Trankell's heroine see what Trankell was trying to see? Well, where could the world she saw be located? A reasonable answer is that it was surrounding her and not in her head, as some would argue.

Subject and Object

According to the most frequent view of the relationship between subject and object, between person and world, the two are separate. The person obtains sensory information from the world (light waves, sound waves, heat, pressure, etc.). This information is in itself meaningless, but it is put together somehow in the person's mind to form an inner representation of the world out there. So when we see the world "out there," we actually see the inner representation of that world, with our inner eyes. This is the enrichment view of perception (and learning, etc.) mentioned in Chapter 2, with reference to Gibson and Gibson (1955). A powerful counter-argument to this idea is the one presented by Ryle (1949) and others: the infinite regress. How can those meaningless bits of sensory information be put together to form something meaningful? It would presuppose an entity that already has access to the meaningful whole. How could the bits be assembled otherwise? We could imagine a little guy residing in the person's head, a template person, perhaps. But then the little guy must have representation in his head, and where would he have got it from? Perhaps from a yet smaller guy, and so on . . . ad infinitum. Arguably, this paradox is an inner version of Meno's paradox, discussed earlier. You cannot create more meaning from less meaning.

According to Marton and Booth (1997), the problem originates from treating the person and the world as separate entities that have to be connected to each other. This is called the subject–object dualism, where the subject is the person and the object is the world.

What then is the alternative? The assumption underlying this book, as well as many other theoreticians' work (Gibson's ecological psychology, versions of the Gestalt school of psychology, the socio-historical school of activity theory, etc.) is that we learn to see meaningful wholes, features, patterns and structures of the environment. It may be that this happens by means of receiving information through our senses, but, nevertheless, we perceive persons, cars, bridges, triangles, threats or beauty and not meaningless sensory information that is used subsequently to form internal representation of cars, bridges, triangles, threats or beauty.[9]

We do so because the meanings are there, and we are afforded the opportunity to experience them. And because we have learned to experience them. The meanings emerge as relationships between person and world. It is in this sense that subject and object are not separate. Person and world are related to begin with. There are not two worlds, a subjective one and an objective one; there is one world only, and that is both subjective and objective. The world we live in is an experienced world, a world that we are dealing with, that we try to understand, that we make sense of in many different ways. (Hence experience is conceptualized broadly here, including all the ways in which the world around us is sensed and grasped by us.) Even the world described by science is obviously a world described by humans. There is no description without someone doing the describing.

Where Is the Greenness of the Cucumber?

We may ask: What is the ontological status of the statement "We cannot see an aspect of something unless that aspect is separated from other aspects," argued in Chapter 3? And we may ask: Where does this separation take place?

As far as the second question is concerned, it is obviously not the case that greenness is physically separated from the green cucumber, nor can we physically separate the elegance of movements from the movements themselves or the frame of reference from seeing something from that frame of reference. The separation is obviously taking place in someone's experience, in someone's awareness (or—to use a synonym—in the world that she is aware of). The latter is important. Saying that something is taking place in another person's experience does not necessarily mean that it is taking place in her mind, or in her head. As seen from her own perspective, as seen through her own eyes, it is taking place in the world that she is experiencing. The greenness of the cucumber appears where the cucumber is: on the kitchen table and not in the head of the learner. The statements are statements about how something is experienced. They are experiential statements, referring to our understanding of what things look like to other people.

Awareness and Variation

When we talk about a certain dimension of variation being opened up, where is this dimension opened? The answer is that it is opened in the learner's awareness. What then is awareness, and where can we find it?

The point was made in the previous chapter that even if we point to similarities instead of differences when trying to teach a child a word, *yellow*, for instance, and therefore in that situation it is impossible for the child to understand what yellow is (by inspecting a yellow chicken, a yellow melon and a yellow scarf, for instance), she may still experience the yellowness of those things, thanks to her earlier experience of other colors.

In order to experience difference or variation, the learner must experience different things or qualities simultaneously. As mentioned earlier, the different things or qualities may be present at the same time (synchronic simultaneity) or may have appeared at different points in time but are experienced simultaneously (diachronic simultaneity). The medium of experiences of simultaneity is awareness. It is simply all that which is experienced as differing or being the same and experienced simultaneously. There is an individual awareness that keeps changing constantly. Some things are focal, others are experienced peripherally. Some things are in the foreground, others in the background. According to Gurwitsch (1964), we are aware of everything all the time, although in widely different ways and to widely different degrees. I may keep listening to a fascinating lecture about the latest findings from research on the ability of primates to master simple arithmetic. I may be completely focused on the content of the presentation but still aware of being a man, living in Sweden, loving my wife, having four grandchildren (soon, five). I am aware of that it is a Monday in winter, late afternoon, that our country is being governed by a liberal–conservative government and an endless number of other things. But I focus on certain things, and, therefore, certain other, related, things come to the fore, while other things are again at rest. Thanks to the continuity and simultaneity of the awareness of things, events and qualities, they may be juxtaposed immediately. This is why I may have an instant experience of sameness and difference when I see someone whom I have not seen for 20 years. I notice the difference in this person's appearance against a background of sameness. And of course, without noticing the sameness, I could never see how this person has changed.

Finding the Force

It probably seems fairly reasonable that the same problem might appear differently to different people, that some manage to see the key features, while others fail to do so. People may view the same scenery differently, structure the same situation in different ways. But it might seem a bit odd to argue that learning to crack nuts is about seeing something in a certain way. Let us therefore go back to our favorite example in Chapter 1, just once more. Take the force with which the nut is hit, for instance. The chimpanzees must discover that the force used matters for the success of the attempt. They must learn to modulate the force, hitting harder or hitting softer. They must discover (i.e., discern) this particular aspect (dimension of variation), and they have to take it into consideration. And taking it into consideration involves being able to differentiate between using more and less force. When they do so, I say that they have learnt to see the situation in a different way.[10]

The conjecture about how this happens is as follows: In order to discover the right amount of force to be used, the learner must discover that the force used might vary, and so does its effect. Imagine that the learner has advanced to the point that she can grab a rock and hit the nut with it. Most likely, the first time she will fail, using too much or too little force. Perhaps she tries again and fails . . . several times. Then, after having used too little force, she might by chance use too much force, with a different outcome (instead of failing to crack the nut, it will be mashed). The idea of variable force, in some sense, may occur to her, and a dimension of variation (of force) is opened up. Let us assume that during the first 14 attempts the learner used more or less the same force (at least with the same effect). When the learner happens to create a contrast, she becomes aware (somehow) of possible variations in force. The force used during the first 14 attempts are values (or just one value, if it was the same every time) in that dimension; the force used during the 15th attempt is another value. The force required to successfully crack the nut might be yet another.

Actually, the whole thing is more complicated than this: you might have to use different amounts of force for different kind of nuts. Some are harder than others, and what the learner has to learn is to use the right (and variable) amount of force in different cases.

Doing as Way of Seeing

One of the arguments behind the educational objectives movement is that goals should be defined as clearly as possible, and in this way all those involved should have more of a shared understanding of the goals than otherwise. Ways of seeing does not seem an attractive option from this point of view. How can we possibly see other people's ways of seeing? In accordance with what was said previously, I do not think that I can see what other people see, but I can see what other people do and I can "read" what they do in terms of how things must appear to them (how they must see things) if they do what they do and if we assume that there is a logical relationship between what they see and what they do. For instance, someone is aiming at a fish in clear, shallow water with a harpoon angling towards where the fish seems to be, while someone else is aiming the harpoon towards the point where the fish probably is but where it does not seem to be, because of the refraction of light at the surface of the water. When comparing the two fishermen we can conclude that one has not taken one of the critical features of the task (the refraction of light) into consideration while the other has, or that one has not made the critical distinction between the apparent and the real position of the fish, while the other has done so. What the observer sees is what the participants do, but the observer reads what the participants do in terms of what they most likely see. A way of seeing is described in terms of critical aspects that are discerned (and taken into consideration i.e., in terms of the distinctions made and focused on simultaneously).[11]

Studying Learning or Studying Communication

Recent studies of learning have to a great extent been studies of communication (Runesson, 2005). One of the merits of this approach, it has been claimed, is that when you study how people interact, how they communicate with each other, you study something that is visible, unlike, for example, when you study what the world looks like to others:

> communication is at the nexus of thinking, individual action and collective and social practices, and, unlike individual consciousness, it is accessible for study.
> (Säljö, 2001, p. 115; for the alleged visibility of communication, see also Nishizaka, 2006)

However you do not actually see *turn taking, repairs, dominance* and *coordination* (terms used to describe communication, referring to some of its component parts) any more than you see the meanings of the things that I describe here as expressions of what the world looks like to others, which you might call individual consciousnesses. You see something as something in relation to other things. Depending on what you choose to compare a particular scenario with, you see it differently, or, if you prefer, you could say that you see different things. You might delimit a situation and compare it to other instances of communication. In that case, you describe communication. Or you may compare the very same situation with other instances of making distinctions (because in the very same situation, people both communicate and make distinctions). In that case, you describe how that situation appears to someone (the person making the distinctions) or you describe individual consciousness.

Acts and Experiences

As argued previously, how something is seen or how something appears to someone is dealt with in this book in terms of distinctions made by the learner. But what does making a distinction mean? Is it about seeing differences between things or about acting differently in relation to different things? How do perceiving differences and acting differently relate to each other? The former is usually seen as a necessary condition—or as a cause—of the latter. Certain acts presuppose certain perceptions, or certain perceptions are thought to trigger certain acts.

The difference was pointed out previously between what is observable, what the learners say and what they do (how they act) on the one hand and what is not observable, how they see things or how things appear to them on the other hand. In the beginning of this chapter I mentioned, however, that we can observe how people make distinctions between things, and this is the sense in which we use these two expressions. In some of the studies referred to in the last section of Chapter 2, how people see things or how things appear to people are supposed to explain what they do or what they are capable of doing. Seeing and doing are thought to be causally related. Seeing, in those cases, refers to internal representations of the world. Those internal representations are supposed to control what the person is doing (see, for instance, Stilling et al., 1995). But *seeing,* as I use the term here, means making distinctions, and making a distinction is an act (i.e., it is "doing"). In this case, there is no seeing separate from doing, where the former explains the latter. There is one thing only: making distinctions (i.e., "doing," which is read by the teacher or the researcher as expressing "seeing"). If a young chimpanzee nut-cracker apprentice is looking for a suitable stone to hit nuts with and picks up a small stone, drops it, picks up a big stone, drops it, picks up a middle-sized stone and tries to use it, we could say that it seems that the young learner is looking at (or seeing) stones in terms of size. (She is apparently making such distinctions.) The chimp's way of handling stones is thus "read" by the observer as an expression of the way she sees (or is capable of seeing) stones, or how stones appear to her. If we wish to understand—or to explain—why some chimpanzee apprentices manage to see stones in terms of their size and are hence capable of picking stones that they can use, we could consider their previous experiences from the point of view of whether these experiences have made it possible for the learners to develop the ability to make distinctions between stones in terms of size (i.e., see them in that particular way).

People frequently assume that first there is a thought and then an action follows. The former controls the latter, so to speak. Libet (2004) has, however, demonstrated, in a series of fascinating experiments, that our conscious decisions to act in one way or in another are preceded by processes in the nervous system, of which we are not conscious at all, and which actually seem to produce the conscious decisions.

Libet's experiments raise interesting questions about free will, our responsibility for our own acts and so forth. The present context is pedagogical and more modest: the focus is on the relationship between understanding/experiencing/seeing on the one hand and acting/doing on the other. No temporal ordering or hierarchical relationship between the two is assumed. Understanding/experiencing/seeing are here considered from the point of view of abilities. By saying something or by doing something, the person demonstrates that she can say it or do it. It is not the mind or the brain that understands (experiences/sees), but the person. Or to put it slightly differently, we do not have to worry about the distinction between the person and her mind.

The methodological implication of this line of reasoning and of Smedslund's principle, which assumes that other people's way of acting is consistent with their way of seeing/understanding things (see the section "Logic and Understanding" in this chapter), is that understanding does not cause acts; instead, acts express understanding. The relationship between acts and understanding is not causal but logical.

Describing How the World Appears to Others

In phenomenography we try to describe how the world around us might be seen or experienced. We try to capture ways of seeing and ways of experiencing in terms of dimensions of variation, values and instances. But what can we experience? Can we experience a dimension of variation or a value in a dimension? Clearly, we can experience an instance, a concrete phenomenon, located in a situation, located in space and time. We can experience a rose or a circle, for example. But the circle is actually a circle that has been drawn, not a mathematical circle in a two-dimensional plane. A two-dimensional plane cannot be experienced, because it cannot be realized in our three-dimensional world. But we cannot even experience a general drawing of a circle; we can only experience a specific drawing. Or specific roses, whether drawn or alive. Still, somehow, we must be able experience variation, both between different instances of the same value and between different values in the same dimension of variation. Otherwise, we would be locked into each single instance, and we would not be able to separate aspects of the instance, either from the instance or from each other. But the experience of such variation is mostly tacit. It is hard to capture it in words. It is even hard to bring it to the forefront of one's awareness. Sometimes, however, it happens that we become consciously aware of variation and can even tell others about it. Entwistle and Marton (1994) carried out a study of university students' ways of preparing for exams. They found a biology student giving a most vivid description of how she had learned about the human skull:

> [What I visualize] it's the general shape, and once I get that general shape on paper the rest will follow.... [draws] ... At the moment I'm visualizing a head there, and that's basically what l see. I know there're muscles in various places, but I'm not going into that sort of detail when I first think of it. I just have the rough shape.... I've learned two dimensional on that plane and two dimensional on that plane, and then I've seen a real skull. So basically I've got these two which are put together.... I could visualize a square skull in three dimensions by just turning it, and then I'd go to a real skull and see what bones were in the same position, but of course it's a very, very different object. Yet you can sort of, transpose those ideas, so that once you do that and you're given a real skull in the exam it's much easier to go through. So you don't actually have a picture of either a square, non-realistic skull or a real skull, you just know where everything is.
>
> (Entwistle & Marton, 1994, p. 168)

Experience can obviously transcend the senses and variation might be experienced, as well as invariance.

Two Kinds of Results

Phenomenography asks: What are the qualitatively different ways in which this particular phenomenon might be seen? However, each phenomenographic study also asks the question: What are the qualitatively different ways in which this particular phenomenon is seen by those participating in this study (or by people in the population represented by those participating in the study)? Thus, we mostly receive two kinds of results in such studies. On the one hand, when we find a new way in which someone sees something, it is a discovery of a particular way of seeing that particular phenomenon: "Oh, this is a way in which this phenomenon might be seen!" This is a universal finding, an answer to the question asked by phenomenography as a research specialization and constitutes a novel category of description. On the other hand we also find that this particular participant expressed this particular way of seeing a particular phenomenon. We can thus conclude that this person has been able to see that phenomenon in this particular way on that particular occasion.

Let us consider an example. In the previous section I referred to Neuman's (1987) study. One of the ways in which some of the participants saw numbers was "numbers as names". Numbers in this case refer to the sequential position of numbers, where, for example, 7 is the seventh number (and only that). If nobody had ever had found this particular meaning of numbers previously, it would be a highly interesting finding, with potentially universal generalizability (that numbers can be seen in this way). On the other hand, we cannot make such a discovery without someone expressing this particular way of seeing numbers. And this is an answer to the second question described previously; this particular person has expressed this particular way of seeing numbers in a specific situation. And if she has expressed it, this means that she has been able to express it. While the answer in the first case is a category of description, the answer in the second case is a statement about an empirical fact.

On the Validity of Experiential Descriptions

Research on what the world looks like to others can be found within many specializations (hermeneutics, empirical phenomenology, anthropology, history of ideas, etc.). Much of what is discovered about people's ways of seeing the world around them originates from what the participants say that they see. There is always some uncertainty with the analyses of what people say, as their validity is contingent on the intentions of the people observed: Perhaps they meant something completely different from what the researcher thought they meant, perhaps they were just pretending, perhaps they just had stomach problems during the interview, perhaps they wanted to please the interviewer or they wanted to appear in a certain way. In our case, we are not studying attitudes or preferences, we are studying abilities, in the sense of what people can learn to do. We are interested in how we can help others to learn, in the sense of contributing to enabling them to see and deal with something in a certain way. They can, of course, deceive us, pretending not to be able when they are, but they cannot possibly pretend to be able when they are not.

Performance implies ability. By doing something, the learners show that they can do it (then and there at least), and they show that they can have an understanding that is consistent with the performance. If I ask a 6-year-old "How much is 2 + 7?" and she says "7, 8, 9 . . . *nine*" I can see that she is acting in accordance with the commutative law of addition, 2 + 7 = 7 + 2, and I can draw the conclusion that she has opened the dimension of variation of ordering addends, because, in effect, she has.

Qualitative Differences in Learning, Specific to Specific Objects of Learning

Phenomenography thus offers a way to find out and describe qualitative differences in learning. This is not done in terms of universal qualitative differences, neutral with regard to the content of learning and thus applicable to any learning task, such as the SOLO taxonomy, for instance. Inspired by Piagetian descriptions of qualitative differences in handling the same tasks, the SOLO taxonomy was developed by Biggs and Collis (1982) for analyzing students' responses to open-ended questions in school. The different categories refer to different ways of handling the same task, but they are expected to be applicable to different tasks, in fact, to any tasks. There are five different levels (simplified here):

Prestructural (No crucial aspects of the task are mastered)
Unistructural (One crucial aspect of the task is mastered)
Multistructural (Several crucial aspects are mastered)
Relational (Several crucial aspects are related to each other)
Extended (In addition to the previous level, a new level of conceptualization is introduced in terms of an integrating theme).

The so-called van Hiele levels refer to qualitatively different ways of handling tasks in geometry. Although the system is limited to geometry, within it, the levels are assumed to be applicable to any tasks. Putting it very simply, the different ways of seeing and handling geometry are as follows:

Level 0: Geometric objects identified visually and holistically
Level 1: Geometric objects dealt with in terms of their properties
Level 2: Geometric objects dealt with in terms of their logically ordered properties
Level 3: Geometric objects dealt with in the context of mathematical systems
Level 4: Geometric objects dealt with in the context of alternative mathematical systems (Burger & Shaughnessy, 1986; van Hiele, 1986).

The most widespread system for describing qualitative differences in the context of educational measurement is the Bloom taxonomy. As explained in Chapter 2, it distinguishes between six different levels:

Remembering
Understanding
Applying
Analyzing
Evaluating
Creating (Anderson, Krathwohl, Airasian & Cruikshank, 2000; Biggs & Tang, 2007, p. 81).

The SOLO taxonomy is theoretically inspired and based on empirical research, and it can be used for characterizing qualitative differences in ways of dealing with the same tasks, much like the system of van Hiele levels in geometry. Bloom's taxonomy, on the other hand, originates from a common-sense classification of questions in achievement tests. In one case (SOLO and van Hiele) we are supposed to distinguish between different ways of dealing with the same task, while in the other case (Bloom) we are supposed to distinguish between different tasks. The distinction between different ways of dealing with the same thing on the one hand and dealing with different things on the other hand is something that, in my understanding, frequently goes unnoticed, and this contributes to the confusion about learning targets, intended learning outcomes or educational objectives in curricula and course descriptions.

The model of description argued for in this book is assumed to apply to any tasks, though it has a specific form for every task. The intended, the enacted and the lived object of learning (what is to be learned, the learning that is made possible and what *is* learned) are described in terms of dimensions of variation, both dimensions of variation that need to be opened, corresponding to critical aspects of the object of learning, and dimensions of variation that are actually opened.

The model of description inherent in phenomenography is, however, content specific. Every description is unique to the object of learning in question, even if we might find structural similarities between different ways of seeing one object of learning and another. This means that when, for example, students are learning about pricing, we describe different ways of seeing pricing. When students learn about bodies in motion, we describe different ways of seeing bodies in motion. The dimensions of variation are different for different objects of learning, and so are the values in those dimensions.[12]

Describing Qualitative Differences in Learning

So what does the methodological proposal put forward in this chapter boil down to? First of all, it is a counterpart of the theoretical proposal present in the book as a whole. While the theory presents patterns of variation experienced by the learners as the driving force and the outcome of learning, the methodology presents patterns of variation and invariance experienced by the researcher as tools and objects of description. The whole thing is about characterizing variation and describing differences.

The methodological question dealt with in this chapter is about qualitative differences in the relation between the learners and the object of learning, or to put it differently, qualitative differences in the lived object of learning. What is to be described is simply the lived object of learning. Other labels have been used to refer to the same thing (ways of seeing, ways of experiencing, meanings, etc.). In the past the term *conceptions* has been used most frequently (Marton, 1981; Marton et al., 1997). Whatever we call it, it is a complex of aspects or dimensions of variation. It is characterized in terms of the dimensions of variation being opened (in the learner's awareness on that particular occasion). In every dimension of variation there are values that vary. Furthermore, the different ways of seeing (or conceptions) are logically related to each other in a hierarchically organized outcome space, relative to the specific object of learning and to the specific group of learners participating in the study.

The different appearances of the lived objects of learning (i.e., ways of seeing, meanings, etc.) are different appearances in relation to each other. (In order to see a way of seeing as a way of seeing, we must encounter at least one other way of seeing the same object of learning.) An aspect or a feature is critical if it must be opened in order to achieve a learning target (appropriate the object of learning) but has not been opened yet. Learning in this case amounts to acquiring a novel meaning. This is the kind of learning dealt with in this book.

Although the object of learning is specific, it is general relative to the tasks, instances, examples, problems and illustrations that the learners have to deal with. In dealing with these tasks, we expect reasonably similar outcomes, and mostly "reasonably similar" is what they are.

But there are still additional sources of variation (in all likelihood many, many more). What is described is described from the vantage point of a specific theory. Can we imagine that the same thing could be described from the vantage point of another theory?

Rewriting Qualitative Differences

When I was an undergraduate student, in the 1960s, Fred Kerlinger's book *Foundations of Behavioral Research* was the methodological bible in Swedish educational research. Its epistemological position was nicely captured in these words: "All the theorists accept all the facts," Kerlinger (1964) said. "But they interpret them differently," he added.

Subsequently (from 1968 and onwards) this formulation was fiercely challenged. According to the alternative position, all facts are theory and value drenched; they cannot be separated from the perspective from which they are seen and from the interests they are serving. According to this line of reasoning, qualitative differences in learning and development, those described by Piaget and those described by Vygotsky, for instance, are incommensurable (i.e. they cannot be compared to each other). At best, we can understand why they are incommensurable and we can analyze the theoretical foundations from which they originate.

I agree fully with the point that we cannot describe "facts" (such as a particular kind of qualitative difference) in a neutral way. Doing so would imply having access to a completely theory- and perspective-free description, capturing "the naked truth", capturing "things as they are". No, there is no such thing. But I do believe that we should be able to relate one description of something to another description of the same thing. Otherwise we become locked into our own theoretical perspectives, and no cumulative development can take place other than within the confines of the same theoretical and value system. Actually, this discussion resembles the question of platonic ideals. Let us think of a word, such as *love,* for example. You cannot name it without using some particular language, and you cannot point to it other than through a particular instance. Still, the different words in different languages and the different particular cases have something to do with each other. The question boils down to this: Are there different ways of seeing the same thing, or are there different things only? Your answer depends presumably on your epistemological position. If you see facts, principles and theories primarily as social constructions, it is reasonable to say that they are different social constructions (Hacking, 1999; cf. Kuhn, 1970). If you think that scientific research is about the study of a reality independent of us (as Kerlinger thought), it is reasonable to assume that there are true facts that are interpreted in different ways. The third way, which I subscribe to, is to realize that there are no facts, principles or concepts, neutral with regard to how the phenomena that they refer to are seen and how they are named. But there are different ways of seeing and talking about the same things. Their meaning is embedded in the system of distinctions and in the variation in ways of seeing and naming them. We cannot describe anything without doing so from a certain perspective, and we cannot present a certain perspective without applying it to something. But we can nonetheless separate the perspective from what is being seen from that perspective. Qualitative differences arrived at in one research tradition can be rewritten and aligned with another tradition. Even if we cannot prove one model of description to be superior to another, by rewriting these differences we might be able to exemplify how two descriptions of the same phenomenon could be made commensurable.[13 14]

As we have seen in this chapter, phenomenography was initially a descriptive research specialization, aiming at finding powerful categories for characterizing qualitative differences in how the world around us is seen. Its pedagogical potential was first pointed out by Kroksmark (1987). The theory elaborated in this book is meant to be an instrument for realizing this potential.

Notes

1. We can identify the two critical aspects because one of them varies between the two drawings while the other is invariant. Hence, we can separate them from each other. If we find a third drawing that shows the same objects in the same spatial arrangement as the imaginary map but uses conventional symbols, we can identify yet another critical aspect: the dimension of realism–conventionalism in the choice of symbols.
2. In all the cases, after the child made a guess by saying two number words, the interviewer uttered some words of encouragement and asked the child to make another guess, up to five guesses.
3. These guesses reflect the same way of seeing numbers as the one underlying the little girl's reasoning in Chapter 2, where she claimed that she had 5 fingers on one hand and 10 on the other.
4. We find the same way of categorizing relations between numbers, in terms of parts and wholes instead of arithmetic operations, in the Davydov curriculum (as described by Schmittau, 2004), referred to in Chapter 3 (see note 3:10). We also find a similar approach to the teaching of arithmetic in Sun's (2011) reference to some Chinese textbooks in elementary arithmetic, in Chapter 6.
5. We should observe that even if the same letters are used to refer to ways of seeing of varying complexity in different cases, no similarity is assumed between categories of description labelled in the same way. In other words, although C is used to refer to the most complex way of seeing the object of learning in cases that differ as far as the object of learning is concerned, C in one case and C in another case are not comparable, except in terms of relative complexity (because of the difference in the object of learning).
6. Small shops in Hong Kong schools where the students can buy snacks and soft drinks.
7. In relation to note 5, it has to be said that even if no similarity is assumed between certain ways of seeing different objects of learning, such similarities can be found, just as in this case.
8. "Widening space" has to be understood, in relation to contrasts, as making more distinctions between more narrowly defined instances of the object of learning and in relation to generalizations as making fewer distinctions between more widely defined instances.
9. As an example of differences between the theoretical orientations mentioned, in spite of similarity in this respect, a dividing line between Gibson and Gibson's (1955) account of perceptual learning and the present theoretical approach can be pointed out. Memory does not seem to play any role in Gibson and Gibson's account (what is perceived is in the world, waiting to be picked up by the right kind of organism), while the present line of reasoning presupposes that we can simultaneously experience things that occur at different points in time (diachronic simultaneity). In more general terms, we actually see the world not so much through our eyes but through everything that we have experienced previously. To do so certainly requires memory, even if the focus of the research presented here is on how we learn new ways of seeing things, through the discernment of critical aspects. The assumption that makes this enterprise pedagogically meaningful is that it is more likely that people will be able to see something in a certain way in the future if they have already learned to see it in that way rather than if they have not, given that they have memory.
10. *Seeing* thus refers to a particular aspect of what the learners do (or say). And if the seeing is expressed in words, it is not a question of reporting "This is what I see" but demonstrating that "I am able to discern those features (to make those distinctions) and focus on them simultaneously." And being able to see something in a certain way is the kind of ability that we should help students to develop. We cannot tell the students how to handle an unknown situation, but we can assist them in learning to discern certain aspects of any situation.

11. But a way of seeing is also described in terms of what differences are neglected or not taken into consideration (and perhaps should be neglected or should not be taken into consideration). This is the case with generalization—in order to generalize, certain aspects should not be taken into consideration.
12. We have to distinguish seeing the same thing in different ways from seeing different things. There is a methodological distinction to be made between two kinds of studies, both referred to as phenomenographic studies. In the first kind of study, there is a task shared by all the participants, and there is an intended object of learning, a way of seeing that the participants might develop when dealing with the task. This object of learning is, as a rule, not defined entirely in advance in terms of aspects or dimensions of variation; those are found in the course of the research. This simply means that the researchers might develop a better understanding of the object of learning than they had at the beginning. As mentioned earlier, in the first studies in the research tradition to which this book belongs, the participants were asked to read a text (non-fiction), and they were told that after reading the text they would be asked to tell the interviewer what the text was about (e.g., Marton & Säljö, 1976a, 1976b; Svensson, 1977). After the reading, the interviewer (in the individually administered interview) asked an open question, such as "What do you think the author of this text wanted to say?" Further questions followed, based on what the participant said. The interviewer tried to explore the participant's understanding of the text in an interactive manner, as fully as possible. The object of research in these studies was the varying meanings that the texts turned out to have for the participants. The object of learning was to make sense of the text, and this was supposed to happen through reading the text and describing it. By comparing the participants' differing understandings of the text with each other, as well as with the researchers' own understanding, differences in meaning appeared in terms of what parts of the text had been delimited and what aspects of it had been discerned. The dimensions of variation opened up and focused on simultaneously characterized the outcome space, the system of logically related categories of description.

These kinds of studies were followed by studies in which the tasks were problems of various sorts, for instance, in mathematics (e.g., Ahlberg, 1992; Neuman, 1987), physics (Bowden et al., 1992; Ingerman, Linder & Marshall, 2009; Prosser, 1994), computer science (Booth, 1992), history (Patrick, 1998), religion (Hella & Wright, 2009), economics (Dahlgren, 1985), accounting (Rovio-Johansson & Lumsden, 2012) and in other subjects. All these studies belong to the first type of phenomenographic study described previously.

In the second kind of study, the participants were simply asked "What does X mean to you?" and their answers were followed up, usually in individually run interviews, in order to explore the various meanings of X, more or less in the same way as the participants' understanding of texts were explored in the first kind of study. "X" could be basically any phenomenon, such as political power (Theman, 1983), death (Wenestam & Wass, 1987), the meaning of life (Marton & Månsson, 1984), understanding (Helmstad, 1999), learning (e.g., Marton, Beaty & Dall'Alba, 1993; Pramling, 1983; Säljö, 1979; Van Rossum & Schenk, 1984), being an academic (Åkerlind, 2003), teaching at university (McKenzie, 2003), etc. There is an important difference between the two kinds of studies. When the question "What does X mean to you?" is asked, there is no shared example or instance that the participants can discern different aspects of. No distinction can be made by the researcher between what they talk about and how they talk about it (as both vary). In order for the researcher to determine what the participants discern, a necessary condition is that there is something that is common to all participants as well as something that varies between them. In the second type of study, this necessary condition is mostly absent. If I ask a participant "What does happiness mean to you?" I am asking about the meaning of a concept, of a word, instead of asking about an instance. If an instance is shared, I can see what aspects the participants discern.

But if I ask about the meaning of a general concept, the participants frequently provide their own examples or instances. Now as both the instances and the participants' ways of talking about them vary, I cannot isolate my research object, that is, the participants' ways of dealing with and seeing the specific instances.

You could say that at least we discover which examples the participants select. If we ask the question "What does *animal* mean to you?" and find that children in some countries say "dog," "cat" or "horse" while others say "cow," "bull," "goat" or "lamb" and others again say "wombat," "koala" or "kangaroo" we can argue that such a study depicts the different ways in which animals are seen by children in different places in the world? Yes, in a way we can. The word *animal* refers to different things in different places. In this sense the meaning of "animal" does indeed vary. But at the same time it means that we can hardly say that participants in different places are looking at the same thing or at the same situation. No, the differences in meaning have to do with the very fact that participants are seeing different things to which the same word refers. At the same time, such questions are deductive, in the sense of introducing a super-ordinate level (which might be considered a dimension of variation), where the participants are asked to "fill in" values in the dimension given.

Let us look at a study of this kind. Szklarski (1996) investigated how conflicts appear in Swedish and Polish children's awareness. Some of the questions he used (in written and/or oral form) were 1) What does "conflict" mean to you? 2) Describe a conflict that you have been involved in and how it ended. The results were framed in terms of categories on different levels, for example, *Causes of conflicts:* Causes related to principles; Causes related to objects; Causes related to individuals; Causes related to situations (p. 108) and *Handling of conflicts:* Offensive handling of conflicts; Defensive handling of conflicts; Unifying handling of conflicts (p. 133). The labels in this case refer to the categories into which the researcher divided the different examples introduced by the participants. You could say that the distribution of Swedish and Polish children over the different categories does indeed tell us about differences in how conflicts are experienced by them. But it does not tell us anything about how they view a particular conflict. In order to find that out, we would need to present the same conflict to all of them.

In the first methodological option, the participants bring in conceptual tools (opening up dimensions of variation) for dealing with the example presented by the researcher, while in the second methodological option the participants bring in examples in order to deal with the concept presented by the researcher, just as was pointed out previously.

What is referred to here as the second methodological option in phenomenography thus yields accounts of what people choose to talk about, rather than what they discern. In this respect it resembles content analysis, thematic analysis or grounded theory (Glaser & Strauss, 1967). In contrast to the first methodological option, the second methodological option is a hybrid form of phenomenography. Having said that, I must add that there is no way to argue that one form is better than another. It depends entirely on the purpose of the research. If you want to find out about differences in how animals are seen by children and find that children in different places see different animals, the latter difference is one of the differences in their life–worlds as far as animals are concerned. On the other hand, if you want to find out about qualitative differences in how students handle certain problems in biology, it would be preferable to let them all handle the same problems.

It has to be said, however, that this methodological distinction is far less clear cut than I might have implied. A general concept might be embodied in a concrete situation which is shared by most participants. In a study about ways of seeing learning among high-school students in Hong Kong, the students project the general concept onto their everyday reality in school, the basic structure of which is experienced by most students. So when they talk about learning, they talk about a shared reality (see Marton,

Watkins & Tang, 1997). This is also illustrated by the last example of the analysis of the participants' answers in phenomenographic studies, given earlier in this chapter, the example of different ways of seeing understanding (Example 6: Understanding Understanding).

The best example of a general question being answered through a detailed account of a concrete reality is Sandberg's previously mentioned study of motor optimizers' ways of seeing their work, referred to earlier in this chapter. The reality of the work place is so much a shared experience that there is no need for the researcher to introduce something (a case) that can be experienced by all the participants: it is already there.

If the participants do not share such an experience (whether in their lives or introduced by means of a task or a scenario), we will not arrive at a description in accordance with the way of describing qualitative differences in learning proposed in the next section. The unit of description is there said to be a category of description referring to the aspects of the object of learning discerned and focused on simultaneously. If there is no shared object of learning, we will find that the participants see different things, rather than seeing the same thing differently. These different things will then appear as values in a dimension of variation made up of instances brought about by the participants.

13. One of Piaget's and Inhelder's (1974) most well-known discoveries was that young children (those who have not yet advanced to the stage of "concrete operations," between 7 and 11 years old, Piaget thought) believe that if we change the shape of a lump of matter (e.g., clay), the substance (amount of matter), the weight and the volume will change as well. Gradually, they realize that the "amount of stuff" remains the same even if the shape of the lump changes (from "sausage" to "pancake," for example), and subsequently they discover the invariance of weight across transformations of shape, and at last the invariance of volume is established. There are thus four distinctly different levels of understanding (ways of seeing) changes in the shape of matter:

   1) When the shape is changed, substance, weight and volume is assumed to change as well.
   2) When shape is changed, substance is assumed to be invariant, but weight and volume are supposed to change.
   3) When shape is changed, substance and weight are assumed to be invariant, but volume is supposed to change.
   4) When shape is changed, substance, weight and volume are assumed to remain invariant.

   What the child can see is the change in shape, and Piaget and Inhelder (1974) assumed that the actual perception remains the same, regardless of what is conserved or not. When the shape of the clay lump changes, conservers and non-conversers alike *see* substance, weight and volume changing as well. Conservation is achieved, Piaget and Inhelder assume, by means of the child mentally correcting the erroneous understanding, although perception remains the same. The child's emerging operational thinking co-ordinates relations ("the pancake is thinner but bigger; the sausage is smaller but thicker") and incorporates reversibility ("you can make a sausage of the pancake or a pancake of the sausage"). The operational thought thus corrects the erroneous understanding. This is a move from intuition to operationality, driven by the child's discovery of the reversibility of operations (e.g., flattening, rolling into a ball): whatever is done can be undone. "True reversibility is . . . the discovery of the inverse operation *qua* operation, and that is why the mental approach accompanying the transition from intuition to operationality leads quite automatically to a grasp of conservation" (Piaget & Inhelder, 1974, p. 12). Other researchers, such as Gibson and Gibson (1955), Kuhn (1970), Hanson (1958), and myself, for instance, believe otherwise, however: when the meaning of the situation changes, when we learn to see something in a new way, the very perception is changing.

Piaget and Inhelder point out (p. 8) that consecutive differentiation of matter, weight and volume is an important part of what is happening. According to the theory advocated in this book, it is not only an important part, but it is the main issue. When children learn that substance, weight and volume are conserved, they learn to separate substance from shape, weight from substance and shape, and volume from shape, substance and weight. In the transition from the state of not having opened the dimension of variation of shape—or established the invariance of substance, weight or volume—the first impression (perceptual) might be corrected (by logical thought). But once the shape dimension of variation is opened up and the invariance of matter, weight or volume is appropriated, this dimension becomes a part of the learner's perception: she *sees* the changing shape and the invariant substance, weight and volume.

What is critical, for instance, for separating shape and matter *and* for conserving the latter, is to see that the amount of matter does not change when shape changes. The child has to discern and focus on this particular aspect of the situation (that nothing is added, nothing is taken away). According to the present line of reasoning, this takes a simultaneous experience of adding or taking away something and not adding or taking away anything. Once the child has discerned and paid attention to this aspect, shape and substance will become separated and the latter becomes conserved. Interestingly, Smedslund (1961) introduced exactly this kind of variation in an experiment carried out with a different purpose (investigating the role of conflict as compared to external reinforcement in developing conservation of substance) and many of the participating—and initially non-conserving—children gave answers indicating an awareness of the conservation of substance.

What is, in my view, critical in relation to the question "Was there more before?" (turning a lump of clay into another shape or pouring liquid from one glass to another) is whether or not the child has noticed that nothing has been added and nothing has been taken away. This proposition logically implies that the amount of clay or the volume of liquid remains the same. While Piaget and Inhelder seem to assume that whether or not such an observation has been made, the child might fail to conserve unless they have developed operational reversibility (through their actions), I believe that the question is whether or not the child has discerned the critical feature of the situation (i.e., nothing added, nothing taken away). The whole thing then boils down to two empirically comparable conjectures. Should children keep practicing turning the clay sausage into a pancake and vice versa, or should they be encouraged to deal with the question of whether there was more before than after when something is added or something is taken away, as compared to when nothing is added nor taken away.

The conclusion is that the same differences in making sense of changes in the form of a lump of matter can be identified both in the Piagetian and the current theoretical framework, but the meaning of what happens differs, as does the pedagogical conclusion with regard to how such changes can be brought about. The differences encountered with a certain theory as the point of departure can thus be rewritten in the model of description originating from another theory. By doing so, we can conclude that in a sense the same thing is seen in both cases but also that it is seen differently in each of those cases. And a new understanding of the phenomenon may originate from that difference in seeing.

14. Probably the best known in-depth exploration of what was learned in specific cases—and of what could have been learned in those cases—appears in the seminal work of Max Wertheimer (1961), a book called *Productive Thinking*. The first chapter starts with the author watching a teacher showing a class of students (whose ages are unknown to the reader) how to compute the area of a parallelogram by multiplying s by h when s is the length of one of its sides and h is the altitude (i.e., the perpendicular distance between side s and the side which is parallel to it; see Figure 4.5). In order to prove the theorem (that the area of the parallelogram equals the area of the rectangle with side

lengths *s* and *h*), the teacher draws the parallelogram in Figure 4.5 on the blackboard, names the four different corners *a, b, c* and *d,* and says:

> I drop one perpendicular from the upper left corner and another perpendicular from the upper right corner.
> I extend the base line to the right.
> I label the two new points *e* and *f*
> The teacher then demonstrates with help of the figure that the area of the parallelogram is indeed the base times the altitude.

(p. 14)

FIGURE 4.5 The area of the parallelogram: The first task. Adapted from Wertheimer (1961).

Next day Wertheimer visits the class again, and he asks the pupils if they can find the area of the parallelogram in Figure 4.6. He can then conclude that the pupils handle this new task in two distinctively different ways (in addition to the answers "I can't do it. We haven't done this"). Here we thus have a qualitative difference in learning, which would not have appeared if the same figure that was used during the initial lesson had been presented to the class again. One of the ways that the students handle the new task can be seen in Figure 4.7. Here the pupils follow the instructions of the teacher and do exactly as they were told in the previous case, disregarding the difference between the two cases. Wertheimer calls it a *blind solution*: although it is mathematically correct, it is basically impossible for the pupils to see that the area of the rectangle thus created equals the area of the parallelogram. The alternative is the *sensible solution*, reflecting better understanding in Wertheimer's view (see Figure 4.8). This solution originates from seeing how the parallelogram can be transformed into a rectangle (by drawing the lines, orthogonal to the base of the parallelogram, or by first turning their papers 45 degrees and then drawing those lines). If the learning target was being able to compute the area of a parallelogram and to prove the theorem used, some students have achieved it (those producing Figure 4.8, or the same figure rotated to another position) and others have failed (those producing Figure 4.7). What is it, then, that the latter should have learned but did not? Well, it is exactly that which separates the two solutions from each other. There is something in the problem that they should learn to discern—that which is the critical feature.

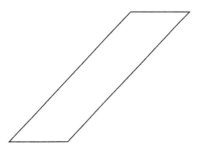

FIGURE 4.6 The area of the parallelogram: The new task. Adapted from Wertheimer (1961).

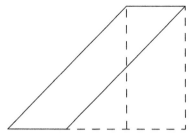

FIGURE 4.7 The area of the parallelogram: "Blind solution" of the new task. Adapted from Wertheimer (1961).

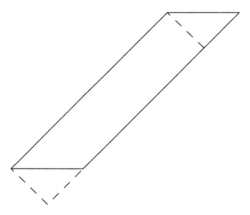

FIGURE 4.8 The area of the parallelogram: "Sensible solution" of the new task. Adapted from Wertheimer (1961).

Wertheimer actually points out what he thinks this is. In accordance with the Gestalt theory (of which he was, by the way, a founder), what it takes to solve this problem is to be open to the structural requirements of the situation and trying to transform a less good gestalt (the parallelogram) to a better gestalt (a rectangle). This means noticing that on one side there is too much while on the other side there is too little, delimiting the part of the parallelogram where it is too big (i.e., where something should be taken away) and where it is too little (i.e., where something is missing), and seeing that the excess fits exactly into the space where there is something missing. This means simply observing the difference between the two short sides and seeing the nature of the relationship between them.

This relationship could be seen through the teacher's demonstration. (The alternative being just to follow the teacher's instructions without seeing this relationship.) But in addition to that, though not actually mentioned (and presumably taken for granted by Wertheimer), the learner has to discern two aspects of the parallelogram: its form and its rotational position (if they can separate the two and see that in Situation 2 the rotational position has changed but the form is invariant). Hence, they can deal with the same form in the same way as they did previously and end up with Figure 4.8.

Accordingly, we can see that Wertheimer singled out a critical insight (something that distinguishes between the two ways of dealing with the second problem), and it is the transformation of a not-so-good gestalt to a better gestalt. Even this critical insight can be further broken down into composite parts, like the partitioning of the parallelogram into a triangle and the remainder, envisaging the missing triangle and fitting the cut-off triangle into the place of the missing triangle. So there is a partitioning of the parallelogram and a transfer of a triangle. As Wertheimer points out, these two moves are based on certain insights that adults take for granted but children have to master. And if they do not, they will fail this particular task. They have to realize

> that in shifting the triangle from the left to the right no change occurs in the size or the form of the triangle;
>
> that in doing so no changes occur elsewhere in the figure, no contraction or expansion in other parts;
>
> that objects like the parallelogram, etc., have their constancy, are not changed in size by drawing lines in them;
>
> that stated equality of some separate lines or angles secures equality of whole figures in distant places;
>
> that cutting into parts and rearranging them in an actual operation does not change the area;
>
> even that mere thinking operations—stating equalities, etc.—in no sense change the material;
>
> and so on.
>
> (Wertheimer, 1961, pp. 62–63)

There are probably many more potentially necessary insights. I just want to add one more:

> The form of the parallelogram remains the same when you rotate it.

What does it take to have these insights in terms of the present theory?

You have to separate (distinguish) the form (and size) of the triangle from its transposition;

you have to separate the constancy of the remaining figure from the transposition of the triangle;

you have to separate the form of the parallelogram from lines drawn within it;

you have to separate the partitioning and rearranging of the parallelogram from its area;

you have to separate your thoughts from the object of your thinking;

you have to separate the form of the parallelogram from its rotational position.

In each case you have to discern two or more aspects and separate them from each other. If you cannot discern any of those aspects, you have to learn how to discern them, in order to master the task. In that case they are critical aspects, critical for you and the task.

Wertheimer's previous list identifies a number of potentially critical aspects of the task. These are worded in terms of invariances of the size and form of the triangle, parts of the triangle, size of the parallelogram, of whole figures, area and material. My rewrite is worded in terms of the separations necessary for the experience of invariance, implying the experience of variation in relevant aspects.

But there is an interesting twist to this, however. The area of the parallelogram appears as the first chapter in Wertheimer's posthumously published book and is probably the most well-known analysis of a case of learning in classroom. But in the same volume we find a far less known piece of writing: suggestions for teaching about area appearing as Appendix 4 (pp. 272–285) that was not included in the original edition from 1945. The object of learning is finding the area of a figure. In case the idea of size of area is not clear to the pupils, Wertheimer suggests that it be introduced through "the problem of being 'bigger' or 'smaller'" (i.e., by means of varying the size; p. 277).

He starts with two rectangles with the same base but with different heights, asking the question: How can we find out how much larger one is than the other? (Figure 171 in Wertheimer's book). By comparing rectangles that differ with regard to the length of both sides, the idea of measurement, the formula area = $side_1 \times side_2$ and the commutative aspect of the formula are introduced. The distinction between figures that can be turned into rectangles (Figure 176 in Wertheimer's book) and those that cannot (Figure 178 in Wertheimer's book) is made through a contrast which highlights the fact that some figures can be converted into much simpler figures while the area remains invariant. Wertheimer even suggests that volume and area be contrasted, thus opening up what I would call the dimension of variation of dimensionality. This is basically the same as the idea that a base-10 positional system cannot be understood without encountering at least one other positional system, or the idea that linear equations cannot be understood without encountering at least one system of equations of higher order. Once a solution to a certain kind of problem is found, Wertheimer suggests that the pupils handle a few more problems of the same kind (generalization), but not too many, he says. Tasks that are as interestingly different as possible should be introduced instead. This is another contrast, in the parlance of variation theory, in this case with regard to the solution of area problems. By means of this contrast, the pupils become more clearly aware of the nature of the different figures and to the extent that different methods of solution are used for the same kind of figures, method of solution and kind of figure become separated, and hence the former becomes visible to the pupils. Wertheimer comments on his approach in the following way:

> One might suppose that to mix such varied tasks would be too much for the brain of a child. Some would say that the child should stick for a time to the area of the rectangle alone, then for a considerable time to the parallelogram alone. And they would regard the procedure of interspersing other, even "impossible," tasks as psychologically dangerous, on the ground that one should stick to a thing and give it much repetition, before turning to a new task.
>
> (Wertheimer, 1961, p. 283)

Actually, Wertheimer's choice of the object of learning is as radical today as it was almost 70 years ago, just as the Davydov curriculum is radical, partly for similar reasons. Instead of dealing with rectangles, parallelograms, triangles and irregular forms one at a time, he is delimiting area as the topic and deals with the different forms together. The reason may have been that the meaning of these forms originates from the differences between them, and these differences are necessary conditions for understanding their nature. Wertheimer did not say so, however. He was referring to the risk of the pupils getting bored with too many tasks of a similar kind. Of course, the point may have been well taken, but the interesting fact is that Wertheimer's pedagogical approach does not follow from his theory. (The gestalt view has never been a theory of learning, even less of teaching). No, his way of reasoning here is intuitive, just like the methods of millions of excellent teachers.

In the last two notes, I have referred to two cases (Piaget and Wertheimer) in which potentially critical aspects were originally identified in terms of invariances but were then rewritten in terms of experienced variation, of which experienced invariance is a function. In order to experience something as invariant—actually in order to experiencing something at all—it has to be discerned. And in order to discern it, the learner must experience variation.

5
THE ART OF LEARNING

The purpose of Chapter 4 was to reveal how we can find the critical aspects of a certain object of learning for a certain group of learners. But the learners themselves are not, as a rule, aware of these critical aspects when they are learning by themselves. How can the learners possibly increase their chances of finding these critical aspects? Is there an art of learning?

Learners Generating Patterns of Variation and Invariance

A necessary condition for finding and experiencing a certain aspect of the object of learning is that the learner has the opportunity to encounter differences in the relevant dimension of variation. This might happen by accident or thanks to someone's efforts. Such efforts can be made by the learner or by others. In this chapter, the former will be dealt with; in the next chapter, the latter. This chapter is thus about how learners make learning possible for themselves. Or try to do so, anyway.

The kind of learning dealt with in this book is—as has been pointed out several times—not the only kind of learning there is. But it is probably the most fundamental form of learning. We act in relation to tasks, situations and problems in accordance with the different meanings they have for us. Differences in meaning are the most important differences in young children's widening of their understanding of the world around them as well as in scientists' widening of the frontiers of human knowledge. The thesis here is that there are important similarities between the least and the most complex cases of human learning.

Opening Dimensions of Variation

In the previous chapter, it was shown that different ways of seeing something can be depicted in terms of dimensions of variation being opened up and discerned.

Accordingly, children might develop more powerful ways of seeing by bringing about variation in critical respects. Well, do children do this? Yes, indeed they do.

Piaget (1952) described how children, even in the first year of life, are involved in "experimenting in order to see" (p. 275). The child happens to notice a certain feature of the world around her, for instance, the "dropability," "throwability" or "rollability" of things, and then she engages in acts aimed at bringing out that particular aspect of things by repeating and varying these acts:

> Even in repeating his movements to seek and find an interesting result, the child varies and gradates them. So it is that, when throwing objects from a distance or rolling them, tilting up a box or making it slide, etc. he drops these objects from increasingly high altitudes . . . shakes his bassinet more or less, pulls harder or less hard on the hanging strings . . . , etc.
>
> (pp. 273–274)

From the point of view of this book, the most interesting thing in Piaget's observation is that children introduce variation in a certain dimension of their acts. By doing so, they open up that dimension, separate it and subsequently fuse it with variation in another dimension. Children investigate how variation in one dimension is related to variation in another dimension. This is an example of children exploring and testing the effect of variation in one respect on variation in another respect. Lindahl (1996) studied learning in very young children in pre-school, and made observations similar to Piaget's. Here are two examples of children generating variation and studying its effects.

Some children are interested in distinguishing and assessing the different effects of physical strength, first, as a factor affecting motion and second, as a means of applying different tools with varying effect. Physical strength as a factor in movement is something that is experienced directly, for example, children can test the effect of strength when moving on an incline, when running, or cycling up or down slopes or ramps.

Tor exemplified this:

> Aged 19 months, he ran up and down the wooden ramp leading from the outer door of the day home to the playground. He varied his speed, depending on whether he was running down or up the ramp. Tor tested this activity over and over again, for many days in a row.

The slope of the ramp was designed in such a way that it was possible to push prams or bicycles on it. Since Tor's home was adapted to the needs of disabled persons (in other words, it had neither door sills nor stairs), this activity possibly provided him with extra stimulus. His consciousness appeared, however, to be focused on testing the effect of strength on movements on an incline.

The intensity of the strength (i.e., the varying effect that children experience when wielding different tools against other persons or other objects) is also experienced directly.

Fia was 21 months old when the following occurred:

> Fia was playing with the preschool teacher and pretending to feed a teddy. She pressed the teddy's mouth firmly with the fork and then gave him a hug. Then Fia fed herself gently, after which she fed the preschool teacher and a playmate till they protested loudly.
>
> The teddy had to put up with being fed firmly, but when Fia fed herself, she regulated the strength intensity because then she knew how much strength was required. The other people regulated her feeding by protesting when it hurt. This was the way Fia learned to test and adjust her own strength.
>
> (Lindahl, 1996, p. 134, Trans.)

Lindahl and Pramling Samuelsson (2002) described the case of a little Japanese boy who happened to notice that you can make things rotate by spinning them. In other words, he noticed or discerned the "spinnability" of things, and he kept practicing with all kinds of objects to become an expert spinner over the next few days. While in the examples from Piaget and Lindahl the children introduce variation into the act of doing something, seemingly in order to explore the effect of the variation on something else, in Lindahl and Pramling Samuelsson's example, the child is repeating the same act with different objects. In the former case, Piaget tells us about the focused aspect (the height, the intensity, etc.) varying and so does Lindahl: Tor varied his effort to run fast, Fia varied how hard something is pressed against someone. These are examples of *contrast*. In the latter case, Lindahl and Pramling Samuelsson tell us about the focused aspect (the act of spinning) being invariant, while the unfocused aspect (the object being spun) varies. This is an example of *generalization*.

Also, Athey (1990) and Nutbrown (1994), whose main focus was on children age 3 to 5 years, pointed to how children in pre-school, during play or otherwise, suddenly notice particular aspects of the physical world around them, such as, for instance, the vertical extension of things (height), how things might contain other things, the roundness of things and so on, and then they keep looking for—or bringing about—instances of that aspect. They then engage in discerning and focusing on that aspect for a period of time, while bracketing other aspects. There are many more such aspects (e.g., spatial order, size, shape, tessellation, angles, perimeter, circumference, numbers, sorting, time, matching, quantity, position, estimation, transformation, addition, length, equivalence, distance, symmetry, properties of natural materials, cause, effect and functional relationships, centrifugal force, rotation, color, magnetism, gravity, trajectory, change, speed). Nutbrown (1994, p. 63) called such aspects "ideas," but they seem to correspond to dimensions of variation. Several aspects are organized into frequently appearing patterns of attention and behavior, usually dominated by one of those aspects. Three schemas are used as examples: dynamic vertical, dominated by the aspect *height,* dynamic circular, dominated by *rotation* and *roundness,* and containing/enveloping, dominated by *capacity* (how much it contains).

The first one of these is illustrated by the case of Gary, who in the seventh and eighth month of his fifth year showed a disproportionately great interest in acts of increasing and decreasing height, manifested in his initial fascination with workers moving up and down the roof of his home, replacing roof tiles; having small figures moving up to the top of the doll house; drawing ladders; using the climbing frame in the nursery garden, again and again, exploring different routes; using his body to extend and explore height when jumping, bouncing and climbing three logs, "often launching himself into the air with the cry and gestures of a current television super-hero" (Nutbrown, 1994, p. 41).

Athey's (1990) and Nutbrown's (1994) results are in agreement with Piaget's finding, mentioned previously, that children discover (discern) certain aspects of the world around them, one at a time, and, once they are discovered, the children keep focusing on them for a period of time. This way of describing learning and development is also in agreement with the theory described in this book, as well as with the studies mentioned in the section "Discerning Aspects of the World Around Us" in Chapter 2.

Play and Creativity

In another example of how patterns of variation and invariance might be created spontaneously, Jensen (2007) refers to Pellegrini and Gustafson (2005), pointing out that humans (and some animals) use objects in investigative ways: How does it work? or What can I do with it? (cf. *inverse teleology* in the use of tools mentioned in Chapter 1). Exploring how something can be done in different ways is, according to Calvin (1996, 2004), specifically human. It can be called "creativity."

Sutton-Smith (1979) considered play with objects (or signs) as an opening up of new options. The first step towards general functional freedom occurs at 18 months of age, when the child explores how the same thing can be used in different ways (object invariant, function varies) and how different things can be used in the same way (function invariant, object varies; Jensen 2007, p. 107).

Being Good at Learning

Runesson (2005) analyzed footage of a 10-year-old girl learning about the graphic representation of motion by using a motion detector, measuring the distance between the learner and the instrument. (The experiment was carried out by Nemirovsky, Tierney and Wright, 1998, and the data have also been further analyzed by Nemirovsky, 2011.) The object of learning was to gain control over the time–distance graph shown on the screen. The learner had to find out that the graph depicted the change over time of the distance between a transmitter (the *button*) held by the child and a sensor (the motion detector connected to a computer equipped with the relevant software), so changes in a time–distance (or time–velocity, or distance–velocity) system of co-ordinates could be displayed on the computer screen. In this particular case, a time–distance graph was depicted. As the girl was holding a transmitter in her hand, and when she moved closer to the sensor, the distance decreased and the graph went down (see Figure 5.1). An adult present at the site encouraged her to find out how she could control the graph, something that she seemed to be keen on learning in any case.

The main difficulty that has to be overcome is that the time co-ordinate is moving all the time. This means that when the child is moving away from the sensor, there is change in two dimensions (both the time co-ordinate and the distance co-ordinate are increasing, yielding a positively sloped line of increasing length (see Figure 5.1). When the child is moving closer to the sensor, the distance co-ordinate is decreasing and the time co-ordinate is increasing, yielding a negatively sloped line that keeps decreasing (see Figure 5.1). The slope of the line is proportional to the speed of the child's movement: the faster she moves, the steeper the lines are. The little girl started by systematically exploring the relationship between her own movements and the graph on the computer screen. She moved closer to the sensor, keeping the button in front of her and walking more or less at the same rate. Then she moved away from the sensor, holding the button in the same way, walking seemingly at the same rate (exploring the dimension of variation, *direction of movement in relation to the sensor*). She could

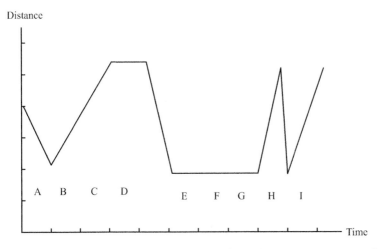

FIGURE 5.1 Fictitious graphic representation of the relation between time and distance aspects of the learner's movement (inspired by Runesson, 2006, p. 168).

then conclude that the direction of the line on the computer screen changed in accordance with how she changed the direction of her movement, upwards when walking away and downwards when coming closer (dimension of variation, *vertical direction of the graph*). Then she walked away as far as she could and discovered that the line became horizontal beyond the distance of three meters (the reach of the sensor was three meters). The *permissible range of variation* (Watson & Mason, 2005) was exceeded. Similarly, the line became horizontal every time she stopped, the distance being constant while time moved on (dimension of variation, *speed of her movement back and forth*). Then she stopped and moved the button vertically, without any visible effect—the line was horizontal as the distance to the sensor was constant (dimension of variation, *vertical movement of the button*). The same thing happened when she moved the button horizontally while she was standing still and the distance to the sensor was roughly the same (dimension of variation, *horizontal movement of the button*). After this, she wanted to study the effect of the speed of her movement on the graph. She made a mark on the floor to enable herself to walk the same distance several times—at the same speed or at differing speeds (see Figure 5.1; dimension of variation *speed of her movement*). In this way she managed to create various zigzag patterns as she wished (dimension of variation, *direction of the graph*). Then she came up with a question: Can I make the line completely vertical? She was aware of the fact that the faster she moved, the more vertical the line became, but after thinking about it for a short while she realized that the line can never be completely vertical, because however fast you move it always takes *some* time to move (focusing on the dimension of variation, *time* and *horizontal change in the graph*). This conclusion shows that she managed to discern distance, time and speed, and she managed to bring them together as well. The whole exercise took 12 minutes, a period during which she managed to create the necessary conditions for learning to master the system which she was a part of.

Forming Patterns of Variation Together

When children are with other children or with adults, they produce patterns of variation together, thus, possibly contributing to bringing about necessary conditions of learning. Björklund (2007) offered an example from a Swedish language pre-school in Finland.[1]

> The children are sitting at the table and eating cornflakes as a mid-morning snack.
> Elisa (2:7) says "you have a little, I've got a lot" and she points first to Adam's plate then to her own.
> Adam (3:1) measures a couple of centimetres between his first finger and thumb and says "this little", then spreads his fingers and says "I've got this much."

Elisa replies "look here, I've got lots, lots, lots" and circles around her dish of cornflakes.

Adam says "then I want to have a lot, I want a lot, this much" and puts up all the fingers of one hand.

When Adam gets more cornflakes he says "I got a lot, Elisa!"

Elisa says "I want more too, much, much more, this much," and she spreads out all ten fingers.

Julia (3:9) raises her hands in the air and shows ten fingers "I've got this much."

Adam and Teo (3:5) also show all ten fingers.

Adam stretches up one of his arms as high as he can reach, "this much."

Elisa gets more cornflakes and Adam says "Elisa, you got a lot."

(pp. 126–127)

What makes this episode interesting is that the group of children maintains a focus on a quantitative aspect of the world around them, or more precisely on eating corn-flakes, and vary their comments in various dimensions. First, quantity is represented (and varied) as a distance between two fingers (Adam), then as an actual amount of something (Elisa), then as five fingers (Adam), ten fingers (Elisa) meaning *more,* then ten fingers again (Adam, Teo), an arm reaching as high as possible (Adam), an actual amount again (Adam).

There are a few things that we may notice here. Quantity is referred to—or is represented—in many different ways, cutting across distinctions between continuous and discrete, distance and amount as well as different scales. We can see this as generalization or as the absence of distinctions. We can make a comparison to Davydov's (1990) idea of starting the teaching of mathematics with general aspects such as quantities, equalities, differences and so on, before dealing with numbers (see note 3:10). Actually, this is exactly what the children do in this episode, although the general aspects appear to be of necessity embedded in specific objects and parts of the children's bodies.

Later, different children show 10 fingers each, and by doing so they generalize the quantity "10 fingers" across children and separate it from each particular instance (I am assuming that children initially experience *10 fingers* as their own fingers, then subsequently separate their own fingers, as parts of their body, from *10 fingers* as a measure used by everyone).

Separating Aspects and Relating Them to Each Other

In addition to questions about how single dimensions of variation are discerned and how attention to them is maintained, there are many important questions about relations between different aspects of situations—notably, causal relations. In this case, there is a dependent variable, the one that is affected, and there are independent variables that might affect the dependent variable. This is actually the fundamental structure of scientific experiments and one of the major tools of humanity for advancing our knowledge of the world (Crombie, 1953). But this way of thinking is also a potential individual capability, by means of which many problems can be handled. The basic idea is simple enough: keep all but one of the potential independent variables invariant and see whether or not the dependent variable varies with the independent variable. If the question is answered in the affirmative, we have found the effective independent variable, otherwise we continue our search with another potential independent variables, while keeping the others invariant.[2]

Piaget and Inhelder (1969) considered the mastery of separating variables and varying them one at a time in order to study the effect of that variation on variation in another (dependent) variable, as a defining feature of formal reasoning. In particular, he has studied the development of this ability by using such tasks as elasticity and the pendulum. In the first case, the children have to find out what factors affect the flexibility of metal rods that vary in length, thickness, cross section and material (steel or brass). They also have to explain their conclusions. The 9- or 10-year-olds choose a particular dimension of variation (usually length) and inspect the flexibility of longer and shorter rods without worrying about the other dimensions. Then they might investigate another dimension of variation (such as thickness), again without worrying about the other dimensions. In this case, they do not start with an overview of the different dimensions, nor do they make any attempt to keep all of the dimensions invariant but one. When asked about proving their claims, they usually select a long, thin rod and short, thick one to show the role of length, because "you can see the difference better." Children from 11 years onwards to an increasing extent start by making a list of all the potentially relevant factors and varying these one at a time, while keeping the others invariant. Among 14-year-olds, this approach is fairly general, in spite of the fact that it has never been taught in school, as Piaget and Inhelder (1969) remark (p. 147).

Another task used for studying children's ability to dissociate different factors is the *pendulum* problem. The question is what makes the pendulum swing faster. There are different aspects that the child may vary: the length of the string, the attached weight, the height from which the weight is dropped and the initial force by which the pendulum is made to swing. Actually, it is only the first factor that affects the speed. In order to arrive at this conclusion, you have to vary one factor at a time, while keeping the others invariant. Younger children (on the level of concrete operations, according to Piaget and Inhelder) vary all the factors at the same time. They have particular difficulties with handling the weight (which does not affect the speed of the pendulum). They usually vary both the length of the string and the weight simultaneously. As the former actually affects the speed of the pendulum, the children's assumption that the weight does so as well is reinforced. The only way to transcend this is to vary the weight while other factors remain invariant, allowing you to conclude that the weight does not affect the speed (p. 148).

Variation and Invariance in Problem Solving

When the learner encounters a task which she cannot solve to begin with, she has run into a problem that has to be solved. This is why we call such situations "problem solving." She must do something with the problem, something productive that will lead to a solution. The problem has to be rewritten. If you cannot solve it, you must find another way of seeing it in order to succeed.

Wertheimer

This book is about learning, as changing our way of seeing things, and it is assumed that problems can be solved if we manage to see them in fruitful ways. Let us consider an example, also taken from Wertheimer's (1961) *Productive Thinking*. He calls it "the famous story of young Gauss." This is a well-known story that exists in different versions. According to Wertheimer, the famous mathematician (Gauss) was 6 years old when the teacher in his class gave the pupils the task of adding the first 10 numbers. Just like the other pupils, Gauss would have been able to carry out the addition by adding the numbers one at a time: $1 + 2 + 3 + 4 + \ldots$, but he wanted to do it in an easier way. In this way the task was turned into a problem, which he solved without too much effort. Instead of adding one number at a time, one after another, he said, "I add the first number and the last one and then get 11. Then I add the second number and the second last number and get 11 again. In fact the first ten numbers form five pairs, the sum of each being 11. The sum of the first 10 numbers is thus 5×11."[3] Writing the numbers on paper, as in Figure 5.2, makes it easier to see this. We do not know if little Gauss did so, but it is always easier to find a new way of seeing something, if you see it somehow to begin with.

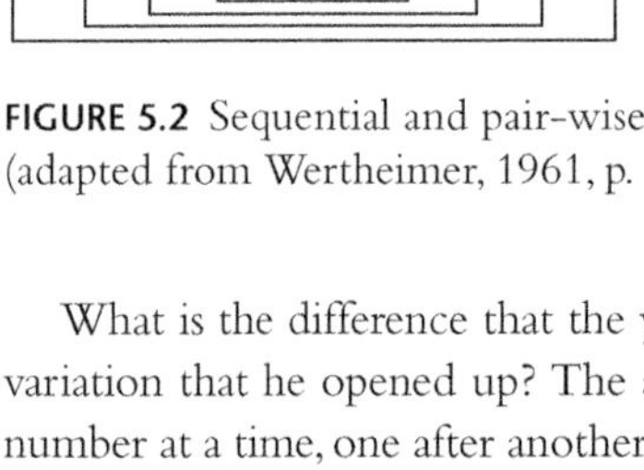

$$1 + 2 + 3 + 4 + \ldots$$
$$3 + 3$$
$$6 + 4$$
$$10 \ldots$$

$$1 + 2 + 3 + 4 + 5 + 6 + 7 + 8 + 9 + 10$$

FIGURE 5.2 Sequential and pair-wise grouping of the first 10 natural numbers (adapted from Wertheimer, 1961, p. 109).

What is the difference that the young boy found, and what is the dimension of variation that he opened up? The aspect was that of ordering, namely, adding one number at a time, one after another, in the same order as they were presented in the task. By coming up with an alternative (adding the numbers in pairs starting from the beginning and the end) there was a difference between two features (the two ways of ordering the addends) and the dimension of variation was opened. A necessary condition for finding this way of solving the problem is that the learner has made the commutative law of addition (that the ordering of addends is discretionary) his own already, or if not, that he does so while solving the problem.

Wertheimer carried out a series of experiments with children, using different versions of the same problem. He found that several children developed insights that were similar or identical to that of young Gauss. He also found some differences in the solving procedure. In certain cases, the compensatory relationship (as one number increases by a certain amount, another decreases by the same amount) within the pairs of numbers was discovered by seeing the series from left to right and then discovering the alternative direction: seeing it from right to left. Here again is the discovery of a difference between two features, which allows a dimension of variation (direction) to be opened up. And it was probably opened up because the learner explored the problem, perhaps simply writing it down before starting to add the numbers, and looking at it from different perspectives, from left to right and from right to left.

Davydov

As mentioned in Chapter 3, Davydov (1990) made a distinction between empirical and theoretical generalization, the former referring to what in this book is called induction and the latter to generalization by revealing the fundamental (and generalizable) structure of singular cases. According to the line of reasoning in this book, in order to bring about such generalization, the learner must create variation and invariance within a single instance. Davydov (1990) argued that empirical examples of theoretical generalization can be found in Krutetskii's (1976) studies of learning and problem solving in mathematics. One of the main results of these studies is that while most children "generalize the solutions to mathematical problems only through gradual and protracted comparisons," a few of them "found a generalized solution when breaking down one problem and applied it to all problems in a class 'on the spot'" (p. 204). Davydov considered these findings to illustrate empirically the distinction between the two kinds of generalizations. At the same time, he argued that Krutetskii had not tried, much less managed, to reveal the sources of the two types of generalizations, and theoretical generalization was related mainly to the person, in his presentation, lending it an innate character, as it were (p. 205).

This idea of theoretical generalization entails—in my understanding—learner-generated, within-task variation and invariance.

Let us look at one of the problems specially designed by Krutetskii to illuminate this phenomenon:

> Three fishermen were spending the night on the riverbank. All were smokers, but only one had an open pack of cigarettes. They divided the cigarettes

equally. By the morning each one had smoked 4 cigarettes, and they left altogether as many cigarettes as each one had had at first. How many cigarettes did each fisherman get when the cigarettes were divided equally?

(p. 126)

Now, this problem can be easily solved by setting up an equation[4]:

$x = 3(x - 4)$, where x is the quantity asked for, which gives $x = 6$.

From Krutetskii's reporting, we cannot know how many students had actually set up an equation, but they were also asked to construct novel problems of the same kind. This certainly put serious demands on their qualitative understanding of the nature of the problem. The following quote shows the line of reasoning of a seventh grader who was asked to solve the problem and invent others of the same kind (and by doing so demonstrated the capacity for generalization):

> Compose a problem like this one—means to compose one of the same type. . . . What is the essence of this problem? Fishermen, cigarettes—that's unimportant. There are three identical unknown numbers. They are decreased by a single known number after which the remainders equal each unknown number before it was decreased. If all the remainders together are equal to the whole, then each constitutes 1/3 of this whole. The number was decreased by 2/3. **Then the known decrease is 2/3 of the number** [emphasis mine]. Each had 6 cigarettes. . . . So . . . that there were originally three numbers is also unimportant. There could be four or five. Then there are some equal unknown numbers from which equal amounts were taken away, after which the sum of the remainders was equal to each original number. Well, now I can compose a hundred of these problems. For example: four friends had equal amounts of money. After each had spent 60 kopeks, together they had as much as they as each one had at first. That's a problem. And here's another: five hunters had equal number of bullets. When each one had fired 12 times, they all had left as many bullets as each one had at first. How many bullets were there?

(p. 258)

Quite obviously, this student has mastered the task and managed to generalize it. But how did he transform the task and thus revealed its essential structure? Well, how did the learner see the problem? It seems to me that he tried to make a distinction between aspects of the problem that are accidental on the one hand and aspects that are necessary on the other hand by means of the pattern of variation and invariance called generalization. The fact that there are fishermen in the problem and that they smoke cigarettes is mathematically irrelevant. And not even the number of members involved matters: there were three, but there could have been four or five, or any number, actually. Nor is the known amount critical. It was four in the problem, but it could be anything. What is critical, what matters, what has to be present in any problem of this kind is that there are some equal unknown numbers from which equal amounts were taken away, after which the sum of the remainders was equal to each of the original numbers. This relationship has to apply to any problems of this type. In order to construct new problems of the same type, you simply vary aspects that are free to vary: What kind of members? (fishermen, friends, hunters); what did they share? (cigarettes, money, bullets); how many members? (3, 4, 5); how much (how many) was (were) taken away? (4, 60, 12). The given problem is solved immediately if you discern its basic structure, recognizing that 1/3 (of the unknown number) + 4 = the unknown number, and realizing that 4 is 2/3 of the unknown number. Hence, the unknown number must be 6. What does it take to see this? You must open up the dimension of variation of the meaning of 4 through the contrast between the quantity of the cigarettes smoked and 2/3 of the unknown number. You have to see the two as alternative meanings of the same number, by means of the pattern of variation and invariance called "contrast."

As far as I can see, the problem is solved through contrast and by generalization (the basic structure being the focused aspect, which is invariant; the various component parts being the unfocused aspects, which are varied). The single initial problem is thus turned into what Watson and Mason (2005) called an "example space"—an infinite set of examples defined by the dimensions of variation opened up through generalization. The move from a single example and the grasp of its fundamental structural meaning can be seen as an example of the Hegelian idea of ascending from the abstract to the concrete, mentioned in Chapter 3, the fundamental meaning of the initial problem being "the abstract" and the problems in the example space being "the concrete."

Krutetskii (1976) also wrote about highly gifted children in mathematics. One of them is Sonya, who was 8 years old. As it happens, she was given a problem that was structurally similar to the previous one: How much does a fish weigh if its tail weighs 4 kg, its head weighs as much as its tail and half of its body, and its body weighs as much as its head and tail together? Sonya solves this problem in the following way:

> Its body is equal in weight to its head and tail. But its head is equal in weight to its tail and half of its body, and the tail weighs 4 kg. Then the body weighs as much as 2 tails and half of the body—that is, 8 kg and half of the body. Then 8 kg is another half of the body, and the whole body is 16 kg.
>
> (p. 198)

Just as in the case of the previous task, the trick is to see that 4 is the weight of the tail, but also 1/4 of the fish, or as Sonya sees it, that 8 is the weight of two tails but also 1/2 of the fish. This is just yet another case of contrast—the opening up a dimension of variation—namely, that of the meaning of 4 in the problem (or of 8).

Let us look at another case of what Davydov would consider theoretical generalization in Krutetskii's study. A pupil, considered mathematically apt (by Krutetskii), who has just solved a task using the formula $(a + b)^2 = a^2 + 2ab + b^2$ is facing the example $(C + D + E) (E + C + D)$.

"There will be 9 terms," the pupil says, "but we can use the $(a + b)^2$" and he rewrites the example $(C + D + E)^2$. "Now any two terms can be combined," he says and rewrites again $(C + [D + E])^2$. He uses the formula and gets $C^2 + 2C (D + E) + (D + E)^2$, uses the formula again for the last quadratic term, and obtains at last $C^2 + D^2 + E^2 + 2CD + 2CE + 2DE$.

For Krutetskii, this is an example of generalizing from one example only, and for Davydov this is an example of theoretical generalization. Krutetskii comments as follows:

> Mathematically able pupils easily found the generality hidden behind various particular details, saw the deep inner essence of phenomena behind an external design, "grasped" what was main, basic, general in the externally different and distinctive, found elements of the familiar in the new.
>
> (p. 240)

There are two questions to be asked about this statement. First of all, how does such generalization come about? Second, what is the "inner essence of phenomena"?

Let us look at two of the examples from Krutetskii's study. As far as the first example is concerned, I argued that the key to solving the problems is to see the two names of the same thing: "2/3 of the unknown number" and "the number of cigarettes smoked per head," both referring to 4. Their meaning in a specific context results from juxtaposing the two. Neither of the two is more essential than the other. The key is the difference (and the equality), and not the sameness. Neither can be reduced to the other.

In the last example you have to juxtapose b in the formula and [C + D]. Any two terms in a trinomial can be combined into one term in a binomial. The key to solving the second task is to see the relation between the two, or—to express it differently—the learner must have the dimension of variation of grouping terms in a sum opened up.

Let us go back to the first question raised: How is the generalization taking place? Obviously, the learner has to do something with the problem. In this case, he rewrites it, and rewrites it again.

The important difference in Krutetskii's study, which Davydov refers to, is between empirical and theoretical generalization. But in a way the distinction is built into the design. He starts by giving the participant a novel problem considered to be rather difficult (like the one above). Some of the participants solve it right away (like the boy did in the example). They are considered to have made use of theoretical generalization: they succeeded in revealing the essential structure of the problem only by trying to solve that very problem. Other participants who failed to do the same were offered easier problems that gradually led up to the solution of the first, difficult problem. These participants were considered having used what Davydov calls "empirical generalization," as they solved the target problem (the difficult one) by means of working through (and supposedly comparing it with) other, easier problems.

This means that differences between the participants show up as differences between solving a problem without first dealing with other and easier problems on the one hand and solving it after having first solved other and easier problems on the other hand. But it does not necessarily imply that the participants who solve the problem right away do so without help from their previous experiences. What is it that makes them see the novel problem in a powerful way? When dealing with that problem are they not simultaneously aware of other problems that they have encountered earlier? Are they not aware of parts and wholes, of sums, of fractions, of the fact that although there were three fishermen, there could have been any other number? Well, this is exactly what the boy says: "That there were originally 3 numbers is also unimportant. There could be 4 or 5." It is hardly likely that this knowledge results from his experience of the problem itself; more probably, he was already aware of the fact that word problems can have different structures (may be of different types), that numbers differentiate between problems of the same type but not between different types. Saying that some students solve a problem on their first attempt while others have to work on other, easier problems first does not reveal why some do the former, while others do the latter. It seems reasonable that the former involves experiencing patterns of variation and invariance generated by the students themselves, while the latter involves experiencing patterns of variation and invariance supplied by others.

Some learners might simply be able to generate the necessary patterns of variation and invariance by themselves, thanks to their previous experiences of math problems.

"Theoretical generalization" is mentioned by Davydov mostly in the context of taking the scientific view (the deep structure) of the phenomenon dealt with as the point of departure in teaching (see also Engeström, 1991, for example). But the reference to Krutetskii's work presents theoretical generalization as an act of the learner. As far as I can see, the distinction between theoretical and empirical generalization—as illustrated by Krutetskii's work—corresponds to the distinction between the learners creating the necessary conditions for learning and those conditions being created through teaching. This is, of course, something other than the distinction suggested by the terms *theoretical* and *empirical*.

Learning by Reading

Several of the examples given earlier in this chapter demonstrated that learners create necessary conditions for their own learning when they interact with physical objects. This is done by generating variation in certain respects while maintaining invariance in others respects. In these cases, what the learners do is visible to the observer, and the dimensions of variation are comparatively easy to identify. But what about the use of linguistically mediated information—learning by reading, for instance? If the learners do the same in this situation (i.e., create variation in certain respects while maintaining invariance in others), what they do is not directly observable. We have to rely on inspecting their account of how they approached the task, and their account of the text itself, to get an indication of how they have gone about the task.

Reinterpreting Approaches to Learning

Marton (1974, 1975) and Marton and Säljö (1976a, 1976b, 1997) made a distinction between two ways of going about learning: the deep approach and the surface approach. The former refers to the learner focusing on the meaning of the text being read (the signified); the latter refers to the learner focusing on the text itself (the sign). In the first case, the learner is primarily trying to understand the text in order to be able to explain it to someone else; in the second the learner is primarily trying to commit the text to memory in order to be able to recall it. The distinction was based on the learners' own accounts of how they went about learning (i.e., how they experienced their own attempts to learn). These experiences seemed to differ also in terms of variation and invariance. Those adopting a deep approach tried to find the main point in the text, and the words for capturing it, by trying alternatives. Those adopting a surface approach tried to make sure that they would remember what they had read.

Deep and Varied Approach to Learning

Silén (2000) investigated medical students' ways of learning in the context of a problem-based learning program, from the point of view of the students' responsibility for, and independence in, their own learning. She concluded the following:

> Challenging one's own perspective, looking for alternative explanations, comparing different ways of seeing the same thing, searching for novel angles and trying out understanding and doing things in different ways, are acts that the students take the initiative in themselves. This implies that this is an important and fundamental constituent part of learning. It is interesting that in the present context (the students' own responsibility for their

learning), seeking variation becomes to a great extent something that the students have to do.

(p. 265, translation mine)

This study was followed up a few years later, in the same context, with the same kind of students, by Fyrenius, Wirell and Silén (2007). In this case, 16 medical students were interviewed about their understanding of certain physiological phenomena and about their approach to learning about those phenomena. In 10 of the 16 cases, the researchers found that the students strived for changes in perspectives and to deliberately create situations or actions rich in variation (p. 156). This is often expressed metaphorically—talking about turning around, twisting, looking at the object of knowledge from different perspectives:

It [the tutorial] contributes what you should use the knowledge for, it is like the clinical, "Why is that treatment better than this one? Why doesn't it work? The same kind but it ought to work" . . . then you have more, like, applied it, even more like twisted and turned it, and applied it more and dissected it even more, so to say.

(S11, p. 157)

In the next quote, we can see the same "turning and twisting" metaphor in the context of "repetition with variation":

If you work through one thought several times so that you sort of get familiar with it in a way, it sort of, that you can twist and turn it in various ways and then it sticks better.

(S12, p. 157)

The need for coming up with different options (or perhaps opening up a dimension of variation) was expressed by another student in the following way:

[Facts] are tested against other facts and there's questioning work in progress all the time, how can this potentially be related to this? And then maybe you come up with some alternatives, some of which are more likely than others, some feel as if they have potential.

(S7, p. 157)

The quote from S12 resembles a way of going about learning found by Marton, Wen and Wong (2005) among Chinese students. It turned out that they frequently combined learning for understanding and learning for remembering (variation and repetition). They read different accounts of the same thing, and they read the same account several times but in different ways. Comparing studies of high school students with their own study of university students, Marton et al. (2005)

argued that while understanding and memorization are not differentiated in young high-school students' accounts, they are frequently separated and even contrasted by older high-school students, to be brought together in a complementary relationship by many university students. Changing ways of seeing what "understanding" means appears to contribute to the differentiation between understanding and memorization. The different meanings of understanding are voiced in terms of the opening up of consecutively wider dimensions of variation, as was pointed out in the previous chapter, in the account of Marton, Watkins and Tang's (1997) study of Chinese high-school students' views of learning, understanding and memorization. In Chapter 3 it was argued that the necessary conditions for learning, in the sense of understanding, could also be formulated in terms of patterns of variation and invariance. Actually, many of the university students in Marton et al.'s (2005) study seemed to gain the same insight. Twenty students from various fields of study, at an elite Chinese University, were followed during the first one and half years of their courses. Many of them referred to the importance of variation in gaining understanding and, to an increasing extent, to the central role of differences.

Some students pointed to the pattern of variation and invariance, previously called "generalization." The focused aspect of the object of learning is invariant, while other aspects vary:

> Extracting what is general from different cases.
>
> (S20–97)

> You and the thing are in the same world. It has already been in your mind. I might not be able to speak it out, but if I encounter this word, a picture will appear in my mind and I know the general idea
>
> (S3–99)

> . . . you know something about what you have learned, extend this knowing and draw inferences about other cases from one instance
>
> (S6–97)

> . . . getting deeper and deeper, from the superficial to the essence
>
> (S7–99)

> . . . you cannot stay on the surface of what you learn. You should mix in your own ideas while you learn it. So you can further digest what you learned . . . to have your own idea after you learned it.
>
> (S5–97)

Other students referred to the pattern of variation and invariance, previously called "contrast." The focused aspect of the object of learning varies, while other aspects are invariant:

> . . . to change to another point of view, or another side, and try to think from that person's point of view
>
> (S6–99)
>
> I will first grasp its intention and extension, then grasp its characterization, find the difference between it and other things.
> The difference is of great importance . . .
> Through comparison, for example when I get a concept, I will first read through it to find its general idea and its key points. Then compare the key points with the difference between this concept and others
>
> (S20–99)
>
> For example, I need to understand three kinds of knowledge, A, B, C. A is the learned knowledge while B and C are the unknown knowledge. Then I will use A to analyze B. After understanding B and comparing A and B, I have got knowledge AB. Then I can use AB to analyze C and thus get the knowledge ABC. In this continuous process, there is neither a clear end, nor the clear starting point. Understanding and memorization are mixed and this enlarges our knowledge
>
> (S20–99)
>
> Try to think from other people's perspectives
>
> (S8–97)
>
> . . . knowledge becomes deeper . . . If I want to understand something, at first I should generate interest in it. Then I will seek for its features and why it has such features that makes it different from others
>
> (S18–99)
>
> (If you want to understand something, what would you do?) I will first think, look up references, and then discuss with classmates, comparing my opinion with theirs (S15–99).
>
> (Marton et al., 2005, p. 310)

Experiencing patterns of variation and invariance in learning illuminates what a deep approach to learning is like. In order to develop a powerful way of seeing something, the learner must decompose the object of learning and bring it together again. Such decomposition happens in two ways: through delimiting parts and wholes and through the discernment of critical aspects. Towards such an end, the learner has to create the necessary patterns of variation and invariance. This is the deep approach to learning in terms of the theory of variation.

Surface—and Less Varied—Approach to Learning

What is the alternative to the deep approach, in such terms? Marton et al. (2005) found three students who demonstrated an alternative approach at the beginning of the study, with one of them also representing such an alternative at the end of the study. The most common answer this student gave to questions about his way of studying was "I will read it over and over again" (S12–99). When he was asked whether he had a particular method of preparing for argumentative (as opposed to short answer) questions, he said:

> I will memorize the key points, such as those beginning with "First," "Second," and discussion and exposition.
> (Do you think you have some special methods to memorize things?)
> No, I only read them many times.
> (For example, if you read something three times, is it the same every time? Does the meaning change?)
> The same. I just repeat it until I can memorize it.
> (No difference?)
> No.
> (S12–99)
>
> (Marton et al., 2005, p. 300)

The repetitive (invariant) way of handling the learning task can also be illustrated by some interview excerpts from a study by Boulton-Lewis, Marton, Lewis and Wilss (2004), who looked at how a group of Australian students with comparatively weak academic backgrounds tried to cope with the demands of university:

I: So what does study actually mean to you?
S: Probably just actually learning the material. Actually sitting there for an exam . . . if I have to study for an exam I'll be copying out the sheet and rereading it over and over, you know, start doing that a week before the exam or something so I can be familiar with that.
I: So after you rewrite what you are actually studying, what's the process after that?
S: I find the easiest way for me to do it is probably writing it out again and reading it to myself and then reading it, reading it, reading it. (1:97)
I: Did you try and memorize them?
S: Yes. I wrote them over and over again on a piece of paper, the science word for it and the meaning for it. I used to write out a whole sheet before I'd get it in my head. I used to try that method before as well, just getting there and saying the bold words and the definition and read it over, I used to do both, like read the other ones and the ones I don't get through I write over and over until I get it. (2:97)

I: How do you actually memorize it?
S: Read it over and over, then I come back and then I cover it up and I see if I remember it then I'll have a look at it, if I'm right I'll keep going but if I'm not I'll read it again and again and again until I get it. (10:97)

(Boulton-Lewis et al., 2004)

These quotes illustrate Brousseau's (1997) thesis about the paradoxical nature of the didactic contract, mentioned in Chapter 1, from the learner's perspective: by trying hard to fulfill the didactic contract, in the sense of becoming able to answer the teacher's questions, the students make it impossible for themselves to fulfill the didactic contract in the sense of making the ideas taught or read about their own.

As mentioned in Chapter 1, the distinction between deep and surface approaches to learning resembles the distinction between two ways of fulfilling the didactic contract, mentioned in the previous paragraph, as well as Skemp's (1976) distinction between relational and instrumental understanding. All these differences have one difference in common. The learner may try to learn *to see* (and do) certain things, her focus being on the things to be seen (the situation, the text, the problem), or she may try instead to learn *to do* certain things, her focus being on the things she is doing. In the former case, in future situations, she will probably focus on the situations themselves and do more or less different things in different situations. In the latter case, in future situations, she will likely focus on what she is doing and hence try to do more or less the same thing in different situations.

Acts and Outcomes of Learning

When we want to characterize the relationship between the act and outcome of learning (i.e., the relationship between its "how" and "what" aspects), we may start by describing the two separately, one at a time, and try to find the relationship between them. With the philosophy of internal relations (see Bradley, 2008, for instance) as support, Svensson (1976) argued, however, that how we learn and what we learn are fundamentally intertwined. There is an internal relationship between the two: neither of them can be as it is without the other. In order to make a particular object of learning her own, a certain learner has to do certain things. What a particular student has learned tells us something about how she must have gone about learning it, and the other way around. We should not therefore try to define the "how" and the "what" of learning, one at a time, independently from each other. We have to start with the assumption that two are related and then describe them accordingly. Svensson (1997) called this way of going about research on learning "contextual analysis." What has been said about critical aspects in Chapters 2 and 3 is clearly aligned with this line of reasoning. A critical aspect is something that the learner has to learn to discern. This implies a dimension of variation being opened up through a contrast. Learning to discern a critical aspect thus amounts to opening up a dimension of variation, and having learned to discern that aspect amounts to having opened up that dimension of variation. Let us look at an example of learners discerning critical aspects—in this case, critical aspects of a text that they are reading.

BEFORE THE LAW

In Marton, Asplund-Carlsson and Halász's (1992) study, referred to in the previous chapter as an example of phenomenographic analysis of qualitative differences, a group of Swedish and a group of Hungarian secondary school students read Franz Kafka's famous parable "Before the Law" on four occasions and then answered questions about what the story was about and what the author wanted to say. Let us have another look at that study, this time from the point of view of how the learners approached their task and to what kind of understanding they arrived. Here once again is the summary of the short story read by the participants:

> The story concerns a man who tries many times to get admittance to the Law, the door to which is open but fiercely guarded by a man who refuses him entry, saying that he is not allowed in but that he should wait and see. However many times and in however many ways he tries to get in, he is unsuccessful. As the old man makes a final attempt, asking why nobody else has ever tried to go through the door, only to be told by the guard that the door was only for him, and now that his life was coming to an end, the door was to be closed.
>
> (Marton & Booth, 1997, p. 150)

When responding to the question "What did the author want to say with the story?" after reading the story, the students gave varying answers, among which the researchers identified four distinctively different ways of seeing the gist of the story, ordered in terms of complexity and logically related to each other in a hierarchical structure, characterized by differences in what was discerned and focused on in the story and what was not.

These categories build on answers to the experimenter's question ("What was this story about?/What did the author want to say?"). Hence, they represent outcomes of learning. At the same time the participants' answers differ as to the pattern of variation and invariance inherent in them.

A_1 The participants may have a definite, clear view of what Kafka wants to tell us:

> He makes protest against our bureaucratic society. We have too little democracy. The law and the upholders, "the elite" govern us. We have nothing to say, no power. If we try to object, they only ask us to wait.
>
> (S 15:3, Marton, Asplund-Carlsson, & Halász, 1992)

In this case, the man cannot get through the gate because of the Law and not because of what he does or what he does not do. The point of departure is thus the question: What is the Law? This question corresponds to a dimension of variation that is opened up. This opening up is even more explicit in some other interview excerpts belonging to the same category, such as the following, for instance:

> The author constructed this in such a way, I believe, so that everyone should understand it in accordance with his own thoughts, his own personality. Thus it means different things for everyone. The Law could mean absolute knowledge, the laws of nature, our own essence itself, the goal of life or the meaning of life. If the author (or whoever who reads it) is religious, you can interpret the door to the law as the gate to Heaven, to which everyone should find his own way. Of course, we can accept the law as it is, law. It would then mean that the law is not equal for all. But this solution puts too much aside, simplifies and is therefore less acceptable.
> (H 27:3, Marton, Asplund-Carlsson, & Halász, 1992, p. 10–11)

A_2 Or the learners may have a different, but equally definite view of what the story is about:

> The gate of the Law: the gate of truth. He who wants to enter seeks the truth, wants to stand up for his rights. That he dare not do it means that he dare not stand up for what he himself thinks is right; he escaped from the difficulties, dared not take the responsibility.
> (H4:1, Marton, Asplund-Carlsson, & Halász, 1992)

Here the man cannot get through the gate because of his way of acting (or rather, not acting) and not because of what the Law does or does not do. So the variation experienced by the students whose answers have been thus categorized is a variation in the man's possible actions. (What he did or did not do, or what he could have done.)

B In some cases the participants end up with alternative solutions:

> The first time it seemed a bit more simple. Now I don't understand any more. I'm thinking of everything possible, but faults creep in every time. What is the door of the law? The first time I wrote that it is the goal of life or the meaning of life. Not until life's end do you find out what you haven't found out and maybe only then do you understand the meaning of life (if you ever do). The door of the law could also mean law in the concrete sense. The laws which a simple man is not capable of understanding. The laws seem simple but they can be easily twisted and misunderstood. Who is that guard protecting the door of the law? Maybe man's inner sense keeping him away from (unconscious) things.

> The text can be understood in many ways. Maybe it should merge into a picture. This has not happened for me. Maybe only the author can tell what it means. Yes, for sure. We cannot know what the author wants to say. The work of art could mean different things to each and every one.
>
> (H19: 3, Marton & Booth, 1997, p. 11)

This answer includes the two main interpretations of the story: that the man cannot get in through the door because there is something that he does not do, or does not understand, on the one hand and that he cannot get in because he is not let in on the other hand. This combination of the first and second interpretations represents the third, and next most complex, way of understanding the story. As it is defined by the juxtaposition of two alternative interpretations, it must contain variation in the explanation of what the story is telling us. The answer is still short of the insight that it was actually the author's intention to create a parable that nobody can solve (this is the "highest" category of understanding). Accordingly, this reader feels utterly confused. In order to come up with the most complex understanding, the reader must have found alternative interpretations, between which she cannot choose. The way in which the learner has gone about learning (by generating variation) and the kind of understanding she has arrived at (juxtaposed alternatives) are thus logically related to each other.

C In addition, the most complex way of understanding the story reflects the close relationship between the meaning of the story arrived at and the pattern of variation and invariance brought about by the learner. In this case, the dimension of variation of "the author's intention with regard to the reader's understanding" is opened up, such as in the following case, for instance:

> I cannot find out the ideas behind, I keep running into contradictions. It was the author's purpose, I believe, to make people think, and make them to arrive at many different solutions when trying "to solve" the story. Any solution can, however, be contradicted by some detail that does not fit. There is no perfect solution, the author solved his task perfectly.
>
> (H2:2, Marton & Booth, 1997, p. 7)

The point is that there are alternative interpretations of the story, and it is impossible to choose between them. And this is exactly what the author wanted: the reader is stuck in the story—locked into it.

The quotes given are answers to the experimenter's questions about the participants' understanding of the story that they have read. They thus represent outcomes of learning. At the same time they are examples of how the learners themselves can bring about the variation necessary for their learning. The same data—the students' answers—can therefore be seen both as acts and outcomes of learning. They are truly two different aspects of the very same event: what the students have learned and how they have learned it.

As was pointed out in Chapter 3, variation is used in this book in two distinctly different senses: as "variation afforded to the learners" (i.e., variation as seen by the observer—the teacher, the researcher—and frequently created by them) but also as "lived or experienced variation" (i.e., experienced by the learners). Of course, the teacher and the researcher hope that the two categories overlap as much as possible, but it cannot be taken for granted that this is always the case. Now, when the variation (and invariance) is created by the learners themselves, it is necessarily both afforded by them and experienced by them, in some way. The distinction between "afforded variation" and "experienced variation" thus breaks down in this case, and the two categories collapse into each other. This idea is empirically supported by the study involving Kafka's parable, in that all of the 8 students (out of 60 participating), who managed to voice one, or both, of the two most complex ways of understanding the parable, had engaged in systematically generating variation.

The results of this study are in agreement with Marton and Wenestam's (1988) previous results, which showed that repeated readings did not improve the understanding of a conceptually difficult text unless the reader varied the focus adopted with regard to the text and the perspective from which the text was seen. By varying the meaning (the signified) against a background of invariant words (the sign) and by varying the words against a background of invariant meaning (i.e., the reader is playing around with alternative meanings in the first case and with alternative expressions in the second case), meaning and words get separated and thus become visible to the learner. In the same way, varying the perspective from which the same text is seen separates text and perspectives and thus makes them visible.

Approaches to Learning, and Variation

In the three previous sections, three main ideas were elaborated. First, it was argued that the more powerful, deep approach to learning is more varied. Second, it was argued that the less powerful, surface approach to learning is less varied. Third, it was argued that the way in which the learner goes about learning (i.e., the approach she adopts), and the outcome of learning (i.e., what she learns) are logically related. The relationship is an internal one, but this is an axiom that cannot be proved empirically; it has to be assumed, and we have to explore whether or not our observations are in accordance with its implications. What follows from this axiom in the present theoretical context is that the variation brought about through the act of learning and the variation experienced as the outcome of learning are the same thing. The pattern of variation inherent in the act and in the outcome of learning are identical—although when it comes to the former, a single case at a single point in time is seen in relation to the same case at other points in time (dynamically), while when it comes to the latter, the single case at a point in time is seen in relation to other cases at the same point in time (statically).

Differences in the Structure of the Text Being Read

In the previous section, differences in the learners' ways of going about reading a text were described in terms of what they could possibly discern as a function of the pattern of variation and invariance generated by them during reading.

In Chapter 3 the relationship between discernment and delimitation was dealt with. In order to discern a difference between two things, they have to be delimited (must have boundaries), and they cannot be delimited without discerning differences between them. Discernment and delimitation mutually pre-suppose each other.

A fundamentally important aspect of understanding texts is the delimitation of their part–whole structure and the corresponding discernment of the dimension of depth within a text. In addition to recognizing variation in possible referents of the words (sentences, paragraphs, etc.) in the text, the reader can also open up variation between different levels of the text (such as words, sentences, paragraphs, etc.). The reader might, for instance, focus on the meaning of a word, as the word itself, but also on its meaning in the context of the sentence or of the paragraph, preferably seeing all of these simultaneously. But this can be done only if the word is seen as the word itself, and as part of the sentence, and if the sentence is seen as a part of the paragraph and the paragraph as a part of the text. The delimitation of parts and wholes must not, of course, follow formally definable units, but without a "lived" part–whole structure the text cannot be experienced as a meaningful entity. Structure and meaning are inextricably intertwined.

The relationship between delimitation and discernment, and between structure and meaning, can be illustrated by Säljö's (1982) study of different ways of reading the same text in relation to different understandings of what it takes to read a text. In this investigation, 90 participants, ages 15 to 73 years, read a text of 3,750 words in individually run interview situations. Afterwards they told the interviewer about their understanding of what the text was about, answered questions relating to the text and explained their own ideas about learning and understanding. The text was about different forms of learning; the main point was actually that there are widely different forms of learning. It started with an autobiographical account of torture using electricity in one of the Greek military junta's prisons in the early 1970s. After having been tortured with electrodes, the prisoner begins to feel electric shock at the mere sight of the electrodes, to his great surprise and of his torturers as well. It was pointed out in the text that what is described is an example of classical conditioning, which means that an innate reaction, such as feeling pain on being touched by an electrode, comes, through a learning process, to be triggered by something that originally did not cause that reaction, such as the sight of the electrode. The text then offered another example of classical conditioning, describing the observation that led to the discovery of this phenomenon. Pavlov's dogs learned to salivate at sight of the men in white coats who used to feed them. The unconditional (innate) reaction is salivating at the smell and taste of food, and the conditional (learned) reaction is salivating at the sight of those who come with the food. After these two examples, and the explanation of the first form of learning, classical conditioning, another form of learning, instrumental conditioning, was described and exemplified by an experiment involving a rat in a Skinner box. The rat is moving around in the box and happens to press a lever, which releases a pellet. The next time the rat happens to press the lever, a pellet is released again. Eventually, the rat learns to press the lever and get pellets. This an example of instrumental conditioning, that is, learning to do—or not do—things as a function of reward and/or punishment. After that, a third form of learning, verbal learning, was described, which I do not include here.

Säljö (1982) found two dramatically different ways of making sense of the text. In one case, the readers said that the text was about different forms of learning, and then they described classical conditioning, giving the two examples offered in the text (torture in Greece and Pavlov's dogs), then they described instrumental conditioning and the example offered (rat in the Skinner box) and so forth (see Figure 5.3).

In the other case, they responded to the question "What was the text about?" by saying something like "Well, it was about a man who was tortured with electricity

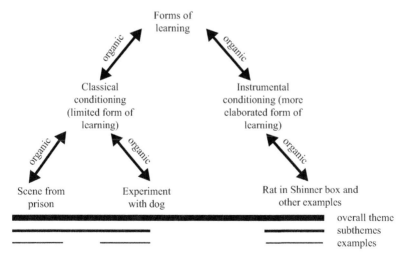

FIGURE 5.3 Text read in terms of a hierarchical structure by readers (adapted from Säljö, 1982, p. 166).

154 The Art of Learning

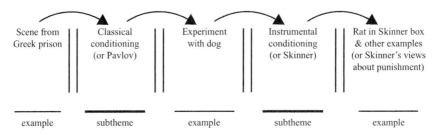

FIGURE 5.4 Text read in terms of sequential structure by some readers (adapted from Säljö, 1982, p. 167).

in a Greek prison . . . then it was about classical conditioning . . . then there were dogs salivating when they saw men in white coats . . . then they talked about instrumental conditioning . . . then again about a rat in a box pressing a lever and getting pellets . . . and so on" (see Figure 5.4).

Interestingly, in both ways of reading it, the participants described the same parts of the text, but in one case the participants identified different structural levels, having part–whole relations to each other; in the other case, participants saw the parts as elements in a sequence. In the latter case, the point holding the text together was invisible to the readers. If asked again what the text was about, they started listing the different parts again (it was about torture . . . classical conditioning . . . dogs salivating . . . etc.).

This study illustrates the fundamental importance of identifying variation in structural levels as well as in relation to aspects of the content. Actually—as was pointed out previously—the two go together. The pattern, evident in the text used by Säljö (1982), of stating a principle and following it with examples, is probably the most common structural relationship found in argumentative texts. Wenestam (1978, 1980) studied how such texts are read, and he found that the two main ways of making sense of the text were those identified by Säljö. Wenestam called the absence of variation in structural levels "horizontalization," to emphasize the difference between hierarchical and sequential structuring.

Discoveries as Discernments

Bowden and Marton (2004) made a distinction between learning on the individual and on the collective level. The former is described very much in the same terms as those used in this book: as changes between different ways of seeing the same thing. However, if a new way of seeing something is new in the absolute sense (i.e., nobody else has introduced that particular meaning of that particular phenomenon before), then we can argue that not only does the individual's "pool of meanings" expand but that of humankind does so as well. The latter is called "learning on the collective level."

As collective learning (which is studied, for example, in the history of science) is driven by individual (or team) learning that is novel in the absolute sense, it should be possible to characterize shifts in fields of knowledge that are similar to the shifts that occur on the individual level, as seen in the examples that have been used to illustrate qualitative differences in learning so far in this chapter, involving discernment of critical aspects and hence changes in ways of seeing things. The following two examples are intended to show that this is a reasonable idea.

Copernicus and Kepler

A prototypical example of such an event is the Copernican revolution in our view of the solar system. As we know, Copernicus questioned the taken-for-granted view that the Sun and the planets (Venus, Mars, etc.) revolve around the Earth. He put forward the alternative view that the Earth and the other planets revolve around the Sun. These two alternatives are two ways of viewing the solar system, where the same parts are thought to be arranged in one way or in the other. So there is a structural difference between the two views. But by introducing an alternative, Copernicus opened up a dimension of variation with two values: "geo-centered" (the taken-for-granted view) and "helio-centered" (the new view). The dimension is *centricity* and refers to what is in the middle, what is fixed in relation to the other parts of the system and what is revolving around what. We should notice that the solar system was not geo-centered before Copernicus. The solar system just *was* in a certain way, and its geo-centricity could not be separated from the solar system as such. Hence, this attribute was taken for granted; it was invisible (quite apart from the fact that objectively it did not exist at all). As mentioned previously, a dimension of variation can only be opened if the learner becomes aware of at least two values in the dimension and becomes aware of the dimension itself at the same time. Helio-centricity is an aspect of one view of the solar system, geo-centricity is an aspect of another view of the solar system. Before the Copernican revolution, no *view* of the solar system existed. The solar system existed, and people believed that they saw it as it was. Their view was not seen as a view (as no other views existed).

Centricity is thus a new dimension in our way of seeing the world. It can be separated from the solar system, and we can perceive the world in terms of it. After all, the entire universe was thought to be geo-centric. Or rather, its geo-centric nature was taken for granted, hence it was invisible (as a *view*). After Copernicus, we can reflect over the centricity of the whole universe or parts of it, and we may end up with the conclusion that the universe is not centered at all: everything is as peripheral and as central as everything else. Copernicus's discovery has provided humanity with another distinction that can be made—about the solar system, about the universe or, basically, about any mechanical system in motion.[5]

The difference between two ways of seeing the solar system is, for instance, logically related to differences in the frame of reference from which the solar system is seen. When seen from a geo-centric perspective, the frame of reference is the Earth itself. Of course, if we are not aware of at least one other frame of reference, we cannot possibly be aware of the fact that we see the solar system from a particular frame of reference. We can never be aware of only one frame of reference. Just as we cannot be aware of only one color, one sex, one form of government.

Copernicus's idea of a fixed sun with the planets moving around it, as opposed to the Earth being fixed with the Sun and the planets moving around it, was a revolution in humans' perception of the world. Still, it did not solve the problem of how the planets move around the sun. Solving that problem took another two revolutions (in the present terminology, it took the opening of two new dimensions of variation). Building on Hanson's (1958) account, Bowden and Marton (2004) described Kepler's discovery of the elliptic orbits of planets—in particular, that of Mars. When studying planetary movements, he felt forced to open up for variation in the nature of the orbit.

This opening up for variation is what Hanson calls "pulling the pattern away from all the astronomical thinking there had ever been." He adds, "before Kepler, circular motion was to the concept of planet as 'tangibility' is to our concept of 'physical object'" (p. 74). Taking Brahe's observations as the point of departure when considering the orbit of Mars around the Sun, Kepler came to the conclusion that the observations could not be reconciled with a circular orbit. The question he was facing was, How can the orbit of Mars be described in such a way that all the observations would follow logically from it? Kepler came up with the idea that Mars followed an oviform (ovoid) orbit around the sun. This is a curve, similar to an ellipse, but with one focus only. Historians of science have always believed that Kepler went from a circle to an ellipse (in fact, he called the oviform "ellipse"). According to Hanson, Kepler used the ellipse (i.e., the real ellipse) as a mathematical model for which the oviform was seen as an approximation: The move of treating observed physical phenomena as approximations to mathematically "clean" conceptions developed after Kepler into a defining property of physical inquiry (Hanson, 1958). In this way, he took one major step and opened one dimension of variation (for orbits that were other than circular), but he refrained from taking another step and opening another dimension of variation. In accordance with his predecessors as far as theories about Mars go—whether using a geocentric or a heliocentric model—he used one focus for the orbit.

But the data did not square with this idea. The oviform orbit was impossible to reconcile with the observations. Kepler understood that what he needed was something between a circle and an ovoid. Eventually, the insight dawned on him: the orbit is an ellipse! Now he opened up a new dimension of variation (from one focus to two foci) and made a move in a dimension of variation established earlier (between a mathematical and a physical hypothesis). This was a profound figure–ground reversal: what was there to begin with as a mathematical instrument was now seen as depicting the physical reality. In this way, Kepler could account for all of Brahe's observations as to the various positions of Mars at different points in time.

In these examples (centricity of the solar system, planet orbits and their foci), new dimensions of variation were opened up, creating scientific revolutions. The discoveries of Uranus (1781), Neptune (1846) and Pluto (1930) were scientific achievements of another kind. In the dimension of variation "planets," which had already been constituted, new values were added to those that were already known.

On the Origin of The Origin of Species

The creation of the theory of evolution is another example of a revolutionary change, namely, in our view of the origin of species. Also in this case, the process can be characterized in terms of opening up new dimensions of variation. (Again, I am using Bowden and Marton's, 2004, account.)

Acts of studying and acts of revolutionary research are different, of course. This is made inevitable by differences in complexity, timescale and driving forces. But in order to make one's own a discovery made by someone else, and to use it as a tool for seeing relevant phenomena in more powerful ways, it is necessary to discern the same aspects of those phenomena as were discerned in the discovery of this tool and to focus on these aspects simultaneously.

Brumby (1979) showed that university students of biology might well come up with reasonable wordings of the theory of evolution, but very few of them appropriate it and are able to use it as a tool when they encounter problems, such as in the following example:

A patchwork picture of human skin-color variation was placed in front of each student participating in the investigation, and the question was asked: "If we suppose that man originally arose in one place, say in Africa, where some of the oldest human skulls have been found, then how do you account for the different skin colors that exist in the different races round the world today?"

After the students had given their explanation, two further questions were asked:

> "What would you predict to happen to this couple's skin (dark-skinned), if they went and lived permanently in Norway?" and "If they had children born in Norway, what would their children's skin look like?" Further: "What would you predict to happen to the skin of this little girl (very light-skinned) if she went and lived in Africa for the rest of her life? If she married someone of her own race, they lived in Africa, and had children there, what would their children look like, at birth?"
>
> (Brumby, 1979)

Only 15% of the students gave accounts in accordance with evolutionary theory. The rest of the group interpreted the question in Lamarckian terms (i.e., in terms of change on the basis of need). They thus failed to appreciate the difference between changes acquired during the lifetime of an individual and changes in the proportions of individuals with certain characteristics in a population occurring over many generations. They did not realize that changes occur in a population as a result of more and more individuals having a certain characteristic. They thought instead that changes were a consequence of single individuals having more and more of a characteristic (and then genetically passing it on to their offspring). A substantial number of the students believed, for instance, that the baby of the white couple moving to Africa would be born with darker skin (darker than the parents had at birth). Far fewer thought that the black couple moving to Norway would have a baby born with lighter skin. These responses can be understood in terms of the difference between the natural gain of pigment within a lifetime (sun tanning) being familiar, and loss of pigment within a single lifetime not being familiar.

Appropriating the theory of evolution and using it as a tool for making sense of the world—something that most of the students failed to do—involves being able to identify a number of critical aspects. Being able to discern them and focus on them simultaneously would amount to seeing something of what Darwin saw.[6]

Let us now look briefly at how Darwin's way of seeing the relationship between species developed.

There is no way we could do justice to the subtle and complex process through which Darwin arrived at his formulation. Gruber (1974) and Mayr (1982) are excellent sources and I use them to draw attention to just three necessary aspects of the theory of evolution, which is the second example of learning on the collective level appearing in this chapter.

The first volume of Lyell's *Principles of Geology,* which instantly became Darwin's bible, appeared in 1830. Lyell started with two fundamental observations: first, that species are extremely well adapted to their environment; second, that they live in a constantly (but slowly) changing world. As Lyell believed that species are constant and cannot change, his conclusion—in agreement with almost all geologists in the 1820s—was that species must become extinct and be replaced by new species, but how the latter can happen he could not tell. By the end of 1831, Darwin sailed from England on the HMS *Beagle*. Half a year after his return home, in March 1837, the well-known ornithologist, John Gould, when working with Darwin's bird collection, alerted him to the distinctness of the mockingbirds (*Mimus*) collected on three different islands in the Galapagos. The remark had a profound effect on Darwin's thinking. To begin with, geographically distributed variation within a species contradicted Lyell's idea of invariant species. It also directed Darwin to consider geographic speciation (i.e., instead of comparing populations and species in time, as most of Darwin's forerunners did, he opted for comparing species and populations geographically).

A few months later, Darwin was convinced that species are modifiable and that they multiply by natural processes. He was still unclear about what factors could account for the transformation of species. Another year later, he was reading Malthus's famous book:

> In October (actually September 28) 1838, that is, fifteen months after I had begun my systematic inquiry, I happened to read for amusement, Malthus on Population, and being well prepared to appreciate the struggle for existence which everywhere goes on, from long-continued observation of the habits of animals and plants, it at once struck me that under these circumstances favorable variations would tend to be preserved, and unfavorable ones to be destroyed. The result of this would be the formation of new species. Here, then, I had at last got a theory by which to work.
> (from Darwin's autobiography, quoted by Mayr, 1982, p. 478)

From Darwin's notebook, we learn about the particular passage that made such an impression on him: "It may safely be pronounced that population, when unchecked, goes on doubling itself every 25 years, or increases in a geometrical ratio" (quoted by Mayr, 1982). In the contest for scarce resources "the survival of the fittest" hampers, however, the uninhibited growth of the population. There is thus the mechanism for the adjustment of the species to varying environmental conditions. In order to see things as Darwin saw them, it is necessary to discern and be simultaneously aware of the same aspects of the phenomenon that he discerned and focused on. As it happens, this is exactly what Alfred Russell Wallace (1823–1913) did, completely independently from Darwin, who did not publish his findings for some 20 years. Wallace set out, in the beginning, to search for an answer to the question Lyell was unable to answer, about the introduction of new species. He left England in April 1848 for the Amazon valley and was struck by the variation within the very same species that he found there. Thus, by focusing on geographical distribution of species instead of variation in time, he came to reject Lyell's idea of invariant species, as had Darwin more than 10 years earlier. At last Wallace, too, read Malthus' *Essay on Population*. As was the case with Darwin, the reading sparked off a sudden illumination, and he could formulate his version of a theory of the origin of species, which closely resembled Darwin's.

Another matter of interest is the stepwise manner in which the theory developed, opening up for one dimension of variation at a time, as it were, in accordance with the remark made earlier about the stepwise path of learning.

My intention here is simply to give some examples of what was of decisive importance in the Darwin–Wallace discovery. Both Darwin and Wallace discerned three critical aspects or dimensions of variation (at least): the adjustment of species to changing environmental conditions, the heterogeneity and geographical distribution of the very same species and the uninhibited exponential growth of populations in conjunction with limited food supplies. Both Darwin and Wallace saw the same pattern and arrived at the seed of the theory of evolution independently from each other. And—it might be added—this is exactly what most students in Brumby's (1979) study failed to do.

Opening Up Dimensions of Variation and Finding New Values in Them

The history of science is full of revolutionary changes as well as of the activities of "normal science" (ongoing collection of findings, the building of different areas, in terms of specialization, the mapping of various domains, etc.).

Opening up new dimensions of variation on the one hand and finding new values or more exact values in dimensions of variation, constituted already, on the other hand are two necessary kinds of knowledge formation, both on the individual (see the section "Dimensions of Variation and Values" in Chapter 3) and on the collective level. The discoveries of Copernicus, Kepler and Darwin are examples of the former; the discovery of Uranus, Neptune and Pluto, mentioned a few pages earlier, are examples of the latter.

Innovations and the Opening Up of New Dimensions of Variation

The difference between opening up new dimensions of variation on the one hand and finding new values in dimensions that exist already on the other can be observed in many different fields. As mentioned several times previously, the kind of learning that is focused on here is learning that amounts to appropriating a new meaning, a new way of seeing (i.e., making distinctions). There are many spectacular examples in sports. In the 1968 Olympic games, a young American, participating in the high jump did something extraordinary: he turned his back to the bar while jumping. He won the gold medal and his "Fosbury Flop" has now conquered the world (at least the world of high jumping). A Swedish ski jumper, Jan Boklöv, introduced a new technique in ski jumping in the 1980s. Instead of keeping his skis in parallel when flying through the air, he made a "V" with them, jumping much further that the other competitors. In judging a jump, the length of the jump is combined with an assessment of style, and even if his jumps were the longest, they were judged to be the worst as far as style was concerned. But that has changed and nowadays the V style is standard. This is an excellent example of opening a new dimension of variation, in this case the angle between the skis in a ski jump. Previously, it was taken for granted that they should be kept parallel during the jump. Boklöv introduced an alternative, a different angle between them, and by doing so opened up the angle dimension of variation.

There was also a revolution of a similar kind in cross-country skiing in the same decade. Up until then, skis were kept in parallel when moving across the snow in competitions. A new style was then introduced, called "skating," in which the skis are kept at an angle. It turned out to be a faster way of using the skis. Nowadays, there are two kinds of races in cross-country skiing: traditional (skis in parallel) and free-style (skating). Prior to the introduction of skating there was no "traditional style," simply because it was the only style that existed and hence it could not be separated from skiing. "Skating" opened up the dimension of styles in cross-country skiing, because after its appearance there were two styles instead of only one (and one that was invisible as a style).

We find examples of this kind of learning on the collective level—the ascent of new meanings, new ways of seeing—through the opening of dimensions of variation, not only in sciences and sports but also in every field of human activities. While in medieval paintings adults and children have the same bodily proportions, after a certain point in the history of art, adults and children are painted having different bodily proportions, just as they do in reality (Bogdan, 1999, p. 22). Another example is the introduction of spatial perspective in paintings, an innovation introduced by the Florentine Leone Battista Alberti, in 1435 (Buck-Morss, 1975, p. 37).

I would like to add a local example of how new ways of seeing can be introduced into our everyday life. The home town of my university is Gothenburg (in Swedish, Göteborg). Now, in this time of electronic communications, letters outside the English alphabet can cause trouble: "ö" is exactly such a letter. As a sign of the ingenuity of people of the Swedish West Coast, someone introduced "Go:teborg," which can easily be typed on an English keyboard and at the same time retains the unique link between letter and sound. What must it have taken to come up with this brilliant idea? First of all, you have to see the letter "ö" as a whole consisting of two parts, the "o" and the two dots. Secondly, you have to imagine various locations for the two dots around the "o." to open a dimension of variation. In other words,

1) Break the unity of the original letter'
2) let the two dots revolve around the "o";
3) let them stop to the right of the "o."

Finding Novel Meanings

In order to handle a situation in a powerful way, there are certain features of that situation that you must be able to discern and take into consideration simultaneously.

To discern a certain feature, and in order to learn to discern that feature, you must experience a certain pattern of variation and invariance. You might come across such a pattern by sheer luck or thanks to other people arranging it for you. If not, you have to generate that pattern by yourself. The more novel the situation, the more important it is to do so.

To discern a certain feature you must open a certain dimension of variation. If you have never opened that dimension previously, opening it introduces a new meaning. This is true for the little child learning what color is, and it was true for Darwin addressing the question of the origin of species. A basic idea in this book is that meanings are brought into being by the opening of dimensions of variation, and that making meanings your own is the most fundamental form of learning. But how can you possibly aim at discerning a feature, opening a dimension of variation that you do not know? Well, you cannot.

But still you can enhance the likelihood of finding the critical feature, opening up the critical dimension of variation. You have to explore the task and the situation as freely and as systematically as possible. You have to create variation in some respects while maintaining invariance in others. Then you change what varies and what is invariant.

You may change the point of view, or the perspective from which you look at the task, or problem. You can expand the task into an example space, by varying its different parts and aspects. You might use different ways of representing the task, using different tools to handle it. You might compare it with other tasks and with different ways of solving them. You keep asking "What if?": "What if this part was different?" "What if this is not true?" "What if everything was the other way around?" You have to question what is taken for granted, you have to let ideas come to the fore and you have to put them to the test.

You have to remember that the solution to the task is always in the task itself, but in order to find it you have to go outside the task. You have to study it vigorously and in depth. You study the task by juxtaposing it with other things, both similar and different. The more you know, the more you find to compare the task with.

This is how you find novel meanings.

Notes

1. There is a Swedish-speaking minority in Finland, and Swedish is an official language there.
2. Similarly, in many studies referred to in this book, all aspects of a situation but one are kept invariant. In those cases, however, this is done in order to enable the learner to discern the varying aspect and not in order to judge its status as a cause.
3. The general case is captured in the theorem that the sum of the first n natural numbers (s_n) is given by $s_n = n(n + 1)/2$.
4. As we can see in this example, there are standard ways of solving tasks in mathematics and rewriting a task in terms of an equation is a powerful method. If you use it, you may not need to engage in problem-solving, as it was defined above.
5. It can be questioned, of course, whether Copernicus was first to open up centricity as an aspect of the solar system, of the universe or of other mechanical systems in motion.

The point is, however, that when it was introduced the first time (whoever introduced it), humanity was provided with another tool for seeing the world; hence, the space of alternative ways of seeing the world was widened and enriched.
6. This is not entirely true, of course. A theory, or a way of seeing something, always has a more-or-less unique personal, cultural and social context as well, and the meaning of the theory derives from these, too.

6
MAKING LEARNING POSSIBLE

In Chapter 5 it was shown how learners make it possible for themselves to learn, by creating the patterns of variation and invariance necessary for learning what they are trying to learn. But as was pointed out earlier, the learning of most things (all words of all languages, for instance) requires the help of others. This chapter deals with how learning can be made possible by others (frequently teachers) who contribute to creating patterns of variation and invariance that are necessary for learning what is to be learned. The conditions thus created may be necessary, but sufficient they are not. Still, it is more likely that learning will occur when these conditions are present than when they are not.

Three Faces of the Object of Learning

In Chapter 2, different senses of the object of learning were mentioned, in the form of three ways of answering the question, What is to be learned? These are three ways in which the answer is given:

1) In terms of content (e.g., "photosynthesis"),
2) in terms of educational objectives (e.g., "the students should be able to discuss in writing how energy is stored through photosynthesis"),
3) in terms of critical aspects (e.g., "discerning what happens to the energy from the Sun that reaches the Earth," opening the dimension of variation containing the values "leaving the Earth again" and "being stored").

It is the third way of characterizing the object of learning that is the focus of this book. It appears, again, in three forms: the intended, the enacted and the lived object of learning. The first one is the object of learning as an aim, as seen by the teacher; the second is the object of learning in terms of what it is possible to learn, as seen by the observer. The third form is the outcome, the object of learning as seen by the learners. The first and the third form are described from a second-order perspective (the observer is trying to depict how the object of learning appears to others, to the teacher and to the learners, respectively). The second is described from a first-order perspective (how the object of learning appears to the observer).[1] This is the topic of the present chapter.

Necessary Conditions of Necessary Conditions of Learning

Necessary conditions of learning were described in Chapter 3, in terms of the learners' experience: in order to discern a certain feature and a certain aspect, the learner must experience a certain difference (variation) against a background of sameness in other respects; in order to bring together two different aspects, the learner must experience variation in both, simultaneously. But what does it take to bring those experiences about? In order to experience something, there must be something to be experienced. In the previous chapter it was shown how learners produce variation—and maintain invariance—in order to obtain such experience. By turning around an object, for instance, the learner can experience the different facets of that object and be aware of them simultaneously, which are necessary conditions for having a three-dimensional image of that object (see Örnkloo, 2007). The learner's experience is a necessary condition for learning about the shape of the object, and turning it around is a necessary condition for the experience. There are thus necessary conditions (primary), and there are necessary conditions (secondary) of the necessary conditions. By bringing about the latter, the learner may achieve the former. And it is also by bringing about the latter that another person can make it possible for the learner to achieve the former. This is also the theme of this chapter.

This means that that there are necessary conditions that are specific for the experience of every pattern of variation and invariance described in Chapter 3. In order to experience the pattern called "contrast" (i.e., variation in the focused aspect and invariance in other aspects), for instance, there must be variation in the focused aspect against a background of invariance in other aspects. Such a to-be-experienced pattern can be brought about by the learner, by grouping instances together that differ in the focused aspect but are the same in other aspects, by concentrating on possible changes in the focused dimension and neglecting other dimensions or by creating variation in the focused dimension while not doing so in other dimensions. But the same pattern can also be afforded to the learners by someone else, by providing them with instances differing in the focused dimension and being alike in other dimensions, by directing the learner's attention to variation in a focused aspect against a background of invariance in other respects or by changing the same instance in one respect but not in others. Most of the examples in this book are about different ways of juxtaposing different instances, while—as pointed out in Chapter 3 and Chapter 5—Davydov's idea of theoretical generalizations means transformations of (changes in) the same instance. Similarly, other patterns, such as generalization, for instance, can also be brought about, either by the learner or by someone else. This means that each pattern can be a pattern experienced by the learner (a necessary condition for learning) and a pattern that can be experienced both by the learner and by the observer (the necessary condition for the necessary condition). The reason to why the latter is not always available for the observer to experience is that the learner might experience instances that are not actually present but are remembered (she may, for instance, notice that someone whom she has previously only heard to speak Dialect A, is now speaking Dialect B, while the observer having only heard that person speaking Dialect B is unable to understand the learner's perplexed looks).

In the same way, an experience that is necessary for one student may not be necessary for another student (because she might have experienced it before).

The Origin of Differences

In the previous section, a distinction was made between necessary conditions of learning, in terms of the learner's experience (primary) and necessary conditions of the necessary conditions, in terms of that which is experienced by the learner (secondary).[2]

It was also argued that the secondary conditions could be brought about in three different ways: through the way instances (examples, problems, illustrations, etc.) are combined, through the way the learner's attention is focused on certain aspects of certain instances, but not on others and through the way certain aspects of the same instance are changed or remain unchanged. All of this can be done by the learner or with the help of others.

Patterns of Variation and Invariance Through the Combination of Instances

The first of the three ways of creating patterns of variation and invariance is by far the most frequent in the examples appearing in this book. The particular pattern of variation and invariance that the learners experience is assumed to be related to how different cases (instances, examples, etc.) are organized: what is lumped together with what (see the section on "Grouping" in Chapter 3). In many of the cases described in this book, differences are expected to originate from the juxtaposition of instances that differ in one respect and are the same in others: Cantonese words with the same segments, for example, uttered by the same person but differing in tone (so that the contrast between tones separates the tones from the words); trying to hit the same target with the same ball from the same distance but from different angles (so that the contrast between angles separates the angles from the throws).

But how does this bringing together different things to be learned (e.g., tones, angles) relate to the much-embraced pedagogical principle of "one thing at a time"? In order to make learning easier for the students, teachers often divide the content into portions that small enough for the students to deal with. Let us have a quick look at a study of the teaching of punctuation marks (Gustavsson, 2008). If you want to teach 10-year-old children to use punctuation marks (full stop, question mark, exclamation mark), would you teach one at a time or all three together?

In a study, three teachers planned a lesson about punctuation marks together with a researcher. The researcher, subscribing to principles advocated in this book, argued for dealing with all three at the same time. The teachers thought that this would be too difficult for the students, and a compromise was arrived at: one of the teachers taught full stop and question mark (but not exclamation mark) in her class. A comparison of a pre- and a post-test showed very moderate improvements (15%). The teachers and the researcher then planned a new lesson in which all three punctuation marks were dealt with, to be taught by one of the other teachers in her own class. This time the gains were much higher (63%). A third lesson, similar to the second one, was carried out by the third teacher, in her class. The results were similar to the results of the second study. The relationship between the results in the three classes was found to be the same when a delayed test was carried out after 4 weeks.

The effect of dealing with one thing at a time, as compared to dealing with several alternatives together, was also studied by Hatala, Brooks and Norman (2003) in another context, with another content. Two randomly selected groups of medical students listened first to the same lecture about patterns of ECG outputs, reflecting three different kinds of heart failures (myocardial infarction, ventricular hypertrophy and bundle branch blocks). After the lecture (which included illustrative cases, two for each category), the students practiced on 12 further cases. In one situation they were dealing with four cases, which illustrated one category at a time, and in the other situation they were dealing with all 12 cases together. The lecture they had listened to, the cases they worked on and the time spent on the cases were the same. What differed was the focus of the students' attention during their practice of the interpretation of ECG outputs. In the first situation, they primarily attended to the similarities between the four cases within each diagnostic category, while in the other situation they primarily attended to the differences between the three categories, as reflected by the 12 specific cases. All the study materials were the same in both situations, only the way of grouping them together differed. After the learning session, all the students participated in a test of diagnostic accuracy, in which they had to allocate ECG outputs to the three categories. The accuracy of the group that had dealt with mixed cases reached a level that was more than 50% higher than that reached by the students who had dealt with the categories separately.

When settling on a diagnosis by means of interpreting an ECG output, the student obviously makes a choice between a limited number of options (three in the study referred to). Focusing on differences between options (categories), when learning, is obviously a more powerful approach than focusing on the similarities within one option at a time. Again, the results support the thesis that meaning derives from differences.

How can we reconcile the principle "look at things together rather than one at a time" with the principle "let one dimension vary at a time and keep the others invariant"? The answer is that the "one at a time" principle applies to the opening of dimensions of variation or aspects, while the "let's deal with them together" principle applies (with certain limitations) to dealing with values or features within the same dimension of variation ("punctuation marks" being a dimension of variation and "full stop," "question mark" and "exclamation mark" being values; "heart failure" being a dimension of variation and "myocardial infarction," "ventricular hypertrophy" and "bundle branch blocks" being values).[3]

But as I have already mentioned, the way in which different cases are organized is just one of the ways in which the learners' experience of variation and invariance is molded. There are two other ways, described as follows.

The Shifting Focus of Attention

In Chapter 5 I referred to Nutbrown's (1994) research, which indicates that children might focus on one particular aspect of beings or things at a time, such as their height or texture, and keeping that focus for a while before shifting to another aspect. This is something that children do spontaneously, and by doing so they learn to discern the same aspects in future, novel situations. But as the following study shows, this pattern of behavior (focusing on one particular aspect at a time) might also be brought about by others (such as a teacher).

Kwan, Ng and Chik (2002) describe a lesson in Chinese, in a year-2 class in Hong Kong, in which the learning target (what the students were expected to be able to do after the lesson) had two intertwined components: 1) describing animals, and 2) using the four language skills in an integrative manner. The lesson was aimed at contributing to the development of some generic skills: observing things and describing them in words. It built on a previous lesson in which the students were learning how to describe a panda, in terms of its characteristics and its way of moving. In the actual lesson they were learning how to describe a sloth, by watching a 3-minute-long video. It showed a young sloth, who had lost his mother, climbing down from a tree, swimming over a narrow river, climbing up into another tree and there meeting another sloth, luckily one with a friendly attitude.

The teacher, together with the students, brought about a very elaborate pattern of variation and invariance. Among other things, the video was used again and again, but in different ways every time. To begin with, it was used simply to show and narrate the story (the learning process started with the "whole": the entire movie with the narration). The students formed groups and discussed within each group how to describe the appearance and movements of the sloth. Afterwards, the video was shown again, without narration (that aspect was blocked out), and the students were asked to focus on the sloth's appearance, such as its color and form (i.e., they had to focus on one single dimension at a time). The third time, the video was played without narration again (once again blocking out the same aspect), but the students were asked to focus on the sloth's movements when swimming in the water (i.e., focusing on one part of the episode and one aspect of it). After that the video was shown once more, without narration. This time the students were supposed to focus on the sloth's movements, when climbing down from one tree and climbing up into the other (focusing on another part and another aspect). To the extent that the students experienced the pattern brought about by the teacher, "same sloth, different movements":

    sloth   **movement**
     i v

the movements were separated from the sloth (in the learners' awareness) and were hence made visible to the learners.

This pattern of repetition and variation is similar to the one found in two studies, Marton, Aslund-Carlsson, & Halász (1992) and Marton, Wen and Wong (2005), in which some (successful) students spontaneously read the same text again and again but in different ways (from different perspectives, for instance). In the present case the teacher had the students watch the same video again and again, but in a different way (i.e., focusing on different things) every time.

After this, the students were asked to revise their accounts of the sloth's appearance and its movements. Subsequently, one representative for each group read the group's account while the film was played with the narration muted. The teacher gave feedback to each group and gave homework to the class: to describe another animal (a spider monkey).

We can say that there were many things that varied, but this is not the main point. More important is the systematic pattern of variation: one aspect varied at a time against a background of other invariant aspects. When the different aspects and parts of the object of observation were discerned and separated, they had to be brought together. This was done by groups of students who were asked to narrate the video when the sound was deleted. The different groups did it differently, of course, and they received feedback from the teacher, and to a lesser extent from the other students. After discussion in the groups, they were supposed to hand in a written description of the video.

In this lesson, we can see how a space of learning for observing and describing was constituted. Through this and through the comparison with similar work done on another animal (panda) and also similar homework on a third animal (spider monkey), the students were afforded the possibility of learning to pay attention to different aspects and different parts of what was to be described, doing so by listening and by watching, then bringing the different aspects and parts together and expressing the whole in spoken and in written form.

We might compare this pedagogical design with how the same topic is habitually dealt with in Hong Kong schools. There are basically two ways of doing this:

Practice 1:

- Teacher shows video (with images and sound);
- Pupils form groups to discuss what they see in the video;
- Group representative reports the results of their discussion;
- Teacher gives comments on the group work.

Practice 2:

- Teacher shows video (with images and sound);
- Pupils complete worksheets with questions on what they see in the video;
- Teacher corrects pupils' answers. (Kwan et al., 2002, p. 47)

In the present case the teacher did something different: he tried to teach the students to see certain things, and he did so by being very conscious of how the techniques he used would affect the students:

> I suggested that the video tapes should be "used" by the teachers so that they can control when to play or stop the video. I objected to the current practice of using Educational Television Videos (ETVs) in which pupils just sat there and observed for about 10 or 15 minutes and that was the end of it. Instead I put forward the view that the videotape should be seen as a teaching resource, where teachers can use this resource to teach and interact with pupils. I had in mind the recording of certain segments such that teachers could use these segments to teach by pausing at the appropriate point, to conduct further questioning or elaboration or discussion. If you look at the lesson that the HKU research team recorded last time (early March 1999), I used a video in which I have included segments of different animals. I did that myself. From there, I taught my pupils how to write about different animals. So the point I want to make is that I want the teachers to use the resource in a lively and sensible way. I do not want to see teachers just sitting there and playing the video to the pupils without any real teaching. So there is an expectation upon the teachers. The video has to be of good quality as well and should have good tasks to follow.
> (Kwan et al., 2002, pp. 47–48)

No comparison was made between the teaching in this class and teaching in other classes, and no outcome data were collected. It seems reasonable, however, that by focusing on one dimension of variation at a time, the learner will be able to notice rather subtle differences between values in that dimension. We can thus expect a more differentiated perception, and a more differentiated perception manifested in words, depicting more varied values in the dimensions of variation in question. Ng, Kwan and Chik (2000) have analyzed what was said during the lesson by the students and what was written in their homework about the spider monkey. The analysis revealed a striking richness, supporting the conjecture about the effect of a highly systematic pattern of variation and invariance.

In this study, the object of learning was more generic than in most other examples in this book—and it was not defined in terms of any specific content. As mentioned previously, the lesson was expected to contribute to some generic capabilities: 1) becoming good at describing animals (and not just describing sloths) and 2) becoming good at using the four language skills in an integrative manner (and not only for describing animals). What might seem a bit paradoxical is that the teacher helped the students to pay very close attention to the very specific details of the sloth's appearance and movement. The thing is that generic capabilities like expressing yourself, grasping the message of a text, solving problems in physics and exercising your critical judgment in analyzing argumentative reasoning demand great openness towards, and concentrated attention to, the specifics of single cases. So the generic skill involved is being good at varying, and closely attending to, the specifics.

Differences as Changes

In Chapter 5 there are several examples of the third way in which patterns of variation and invariance are brought about. In these cases it is not different instances that are compared but the same instance that is changed by the learner. This is frequently the case with learner-generated differences: a mathematical problem is transformed into another form; the same ball is dropped from different heights.

But the learner might also be able to observe how one instance is transformed into another, as a result of changes (against a background of invariance) brought about by someone else (the teacher, for example).

On the Effects of Dynamic Visualization

Marton and Pang (2006) carried out a study about learning to see changes in price as a function of changes in the relative magnitude of changes in demand and supply. "Relative magnitude" refers, in this case, to how much demand changes, compared to supply. Prices will go up if demand goes up more than supply (or if supply goes down more than demand); prices will go down if supply goes up more than demand (or if demand goes down more than supply) and prices will remain the same if both supply and demand go up (or down) to the same extent.

In the target group, two teachers designed the lesson, in accordance with principles derived from variation theory. They varied demand and supply, one at a time, then they varied the magnitude of change (how much they changed) in demand and supply, again, one at a time. At last they brought the two together by means of simultaneous variation. The price of the commodity varied as a function of all these changes, so in this case the variation was at no point limited to one respect (because price is not independent of demand and supply). The three teachers in the comparison group designed their lessons in less powerful ways, as seen from a theoretical perspective. By the end of the series of the three lessons used for dealing with the topic, more than three times as many of the students in the target group as in the comparison group had reached the understanding aimed at (89.6% versus 28.3%).

The two classes in the target group started the three lessons on the same level in relevant respects, as judged from the pre-test. The pattern of variation and invariance was the same, as a result of the two teachers' joint planning, based on the same theory. We would thus expect the students in the two classes to develop the understanding aimed at to the same extent. But this is not what happened. In one class, 97.4% (all but one student) and in the other 81.6% reached the criterion of understanding. This is a statistically significant difference ($\chi^2 = 5.2, p < .05$), and we are obliged to come up with a reasonable explanation that goes beyond one given in terms of the patterns of variation and invariance, which were the same in both classes. Can we then find a difference between what happened in the two classes that might explain the difference in outcome? In the series of three lessons, reflections on an everyday course of events (changes in the price of face masks in Hong Kong during the SARS epidemic, as a function of changes in demand for and supply of face masks) were succeeded by formal treatment (with graphs) of the same relations between variables. For instance, in one class, the teacher demonstrated a graph in which the demand and the supply curves were shown in different positions by means of different lines (see Figure 6.1).

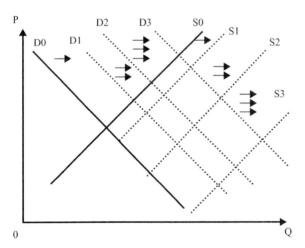

FIGURE 6.1 Demand and supply curves in different positions (Marton & Pang, 2006, p. 213).

The teacher of the other class, who would later have his lessons on the same topic, observed the lessons in the first class and when doing so came up with an idea. After watching the lesson, he wrote a program for visualizing the relationships between the variables. In his class, the students saw only two lines, one being the demand curve, the other the supply curve. By moving them to the right (increasing the value of the variable) or to the left (decreasing the value of the variable), the point of intersection between them, representing the price (as defined theoretically), changed (see Figure 6.2)

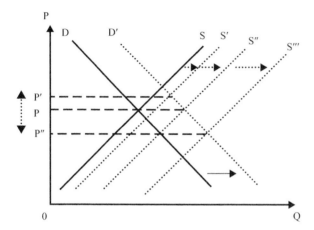

FIGURE 6.2 Demand and supply curves moving to different positions (Marton & Pang, 2006, p. 213).

It seems reasonable to assume that this visualization made the difference between the two classes. The lines are supposed to be moving. In one case they do, in the other you have to imagine that they do. The static picture shows a few positions of the lines and a few points of intersection representing price; in the visualization unlimited sets of positions (of lines and of points) are inherent.[4]

Deriving the Formula

Olteanu (2007) compared the teaching of quadratic equations in two Swedish secondary school classes and found that the students in one class developed a much better understanding of—and proficiency with—the topic than the students in the other class. She found a decisive difference between the teaching in the two classes that in all likelihood contributed to the differences in learning.

The formula for solving a quadratic equation was derived in the more successful class, but not in the other, and it was derived in relation to a specific problem, where the equation in the problem was changed to a form that was the same as that of the formula. In this way it was shown that the formula is simply a specific way of writing a quadratic equation. When we insert the values from a specific equation into the formula, we simply obtain the equation in question in a specific, more easily computable form. Accordingly, it is made possible for the learner to see the relationship between the parameters in the original equation and the value inserted in the formula. (Olteanu's study is presented in more detail later in this chapter.)

In the class in which the formula was derived, the problem "Solve the equation $x^2 + 12x + 35 = 0$" was presented and the teacher showed how this can be done (by means of quadratic completion; see Figure 6.3). The next problem was "Solve the equation $x^2 + px + q = 0$" (the standard algebraic form of quadratic equations). It was then shown that this equation can be solved in the same way as the previous one (see Figure 6.4), yielding the formula for solving quadratic equations).

$x^2 + 12x + 35 = 0$
$x^2 + 12x = -35$
$x^2 + 12x + \left(\dfrac{12}{2}\right)^2 = \left(\dfrac{12}{2}\right)^2 - 35$
$\left(x + \dfrac{12}{2}\right)^2 = \left(\dfrac{12}{2}\right)^2 - 35$
$x + \dfrac{12}{2} = \pm\sqrt{\left(\dfrac{12}{2}\right)^2 - 35}$

$x = -\dfrac{12}{2} \pm \sqrt{\left(\dfrac{12}{2}\right)^2 - 35}$
$x = -6 \pm \sqrt{36 - 35}$
$x_1 = -6 + 1 \qquad x_2 = -6 - 1$
$x_1 = -5 \qquad x_2 = -7$

FIGURE 6.3 Quadratic completion (numerical; adapted from Olteanu, 2007, p. 239).

Allmänt
$x^2 + px + q = 0$
$x^2 + px = -q$
$x^2 + px + \left(\dfrac{p}{2}\right)^2 = \left(\dfrac{p}{2}\right)^2 - q$

$\left(x + \dfrac{p}{2}\right)^2 = \left(\dfrac{p}{2}\right)^2 - q$
$x + \dfrac{p}{2} = \pm\sqrt{\left(\dfrac{p}{2}\right)^2 - q}$
$x = \dfrac{p}{2} \pm \sqrt{\left(\dfrac{p}{2}\right)^2 - q}$

FIGURE 6.4 Quadratic completion (generalization; adapted from Olteanu, 2007, p. 240).

In this way, the teacher made it clear how you get from the standard form to the formula for solution in general (in the algebraic form) and in specific cases. In the other class the general form and the formula were given, but as the latter was not derived from the former, it was not made evident to the students how you get from one to the other (i.e., how the two are related).

In other words, the equation remains invariant through the transformation, although its form and computability change. This is about "conserving" the equation through the changes, a bit like the clay lump being turned into a pancake from a sausage in Piaget's experiment. The form changes, but the amount of substance (and weight and volume) remains invariant.

Comparisons and Changes

Marton and Pang's (2006) and Olteanu's (2007) studies differ in several respects, and not only as regards the content. In the former the pattern of variation and invariance, called "fusion" (three aspects vary at the same time), is brought out in two ways, one of which is a dynamic visualization. In the latter the pattern is a "contrast": one aspect (the form of the equation) varies while another (the equality) remains invariant. In both studies, however, the very same pattern of variation and invariance is brought about either through comparison or through change (transformation). In both cases the transformation appears to be more powerful. The reason is probably that by showing how you get from one form to another, the learner perceives more easily how the two are the same, and also how they differ.

Analyzing Lessons

This chapter is about how the theory presented here can be used in the context of teaching. In this section, there are examples and a discussion of how the theory can be employed for analyzing single lessons—or series of lessons—without making comparisons to other lessons or to other series of lessons.

Using the Object of Learning as a Lens Through Which Lessons Are Seen

Quite obviously, the patterns of variation and invariance that are necessary for learning are created by the teachers and the students in the class, all the time, in addition to being created by authors of textbooks and exercise books, or of other pedagogical resources. Whenever and wherever learning is taking place, there are patterns of variation and invariance. Actually, this follows from the theory: As learning, to a great extent, is about separating and bringing together aspects, and parts and wholes, of the world around us, and as the experience of certain patterns of variation and invariance is a necessary condition for that to happen, the fact that learning is taking place implies that the learners are experiencing certain patterns of variation and invariance. This, in turn, implies that there are patterns of variation and invariance to be experienced. My intention with this book is to make teachers and learners aware of this, so they can more systematically use the concepts and principles made explicit through the theory. But as was shown in the previous chapter, learners create necessary patterns of variation and invariance to various extents. Actually, the conjecture was advanced that the more they do so, the more powerful the resulting learning is. Of course, this conjecture also follows from the theory.

Now, here is a suggestion: just like learners, teachers create necessary patterns of variation to varying extents, and the extent to which they do so co-varies with the powerfulness of the learning that they contribute to. This means that, in addition to planning teaching, the theory can be used for analyzing teaching that is not at all based on the theory. In addition to the theory, however, you need an object of learning, providing a perspective from which the actual teaching is seen. This means that the object of learning that is used as a lens for inspecting the teaching may or may not be identical with the intended object of learning (i.e., the learning that the teacher had hoped to contribute to). The idea of looking at teaching from the point of view of an object of learning that the teacher has not tried to bring about probably sounds somewhat odd, but in such a case the object of learning is just used as an analytic tool for addressing the question, To what extent has it been made possible for the students to learn this or that? Our analysis is thus relative to a particular object of learning, whether or not it is identical with the teacher's intention. At the same time, the analysis is also relative to our assumptions about the students. In order to make conjectures about what it is possible to learn during a specific lesson, we must make assumptions about what the students know and are able to do already before the lesson starts.

Learning, in the present context, means discerning, separating and fusing aspects and features of the object of learning. Assuming that there are necessary conditions of learning that can be defined in terms of patterns of variation and invariance, we can in every single case determine what varies and what is invariant, and hence also state what can be learned and what cannot, if the object of learning is novel to the students. If the students have not previously come across equations that are not linear, we can observe a lesson and conclude whether or not it is possible for the students to learn to understand what a linear equation is during a particular lesson (i.e., we have to see whether or not both linear and non-linear equations appear during the lesson).

Investigating a Single Lesson

A single lesson (about the sloth) was described. According to the theory advocated in this book, it is differences that we notice. Can we then use these theoretical tools for studying single cases? Do we not always need comparisons? Yes, we always need comparisons, but we have seen lessons before, and they are the background against which we see the single lesson. If we had never seen another lesson, we could not possibly separate the entity *lesson* and *the way of conducting the lesson*. But if we have seen other lessons, we can see the way in which this particular lesson is conducted in contrast to an idea of how it could have been conducted (i.e., our image derived from previous experiences).

Acting in Accordance With a Script That You Have Never Seen

Let us look at an example. A double lesson was described and analyzed by Ko (2002; see also Ko & Marton, 2004). It was conducted by a so-called Special Rank Teacher in China (i.e., an expert teacher who had received a prestigious state-granted award and whose work was closely followed by other teachers). Ko (2002) had analyzed the teaching of several excellent and influential teachers and interviewed them. The basic idea was that even if it is very difficult, or even impossible, to characterize what typical Chinese teaching is, it is possible to characterize what is currently considered to be good teaching in China. This lesson illustrates that a systematically planned and conducted lesson does not necessarily imply a lack of activity and engagement among the students. Although Paine (1990) described the Chinese teacher as a virtuoso—an actor or actress performing excellently for a rather passive audience (of students), Ko challenged this characterization and argued that the Chinese teacher is more like a director and that it is actually the students who are the actors acting in accordance with a script that they have never seen. This means that the students have to be active, and they feel that they are thinking on their own, without being aware of the fact that what they are thinking about and the ways in which they are thinking is, to an important extent, shaped by the teacher.

The object of learning in the lesson was to appropriate some related conceptual tools of semantics, such as the scope of meaning of words, the level of generality of words, and homonyms, synonyms and antonyms. What is especially interesting is how these concepts were introduced mainly through contrasts with other ideas on the same level. The practice of the teacher observed here is thus very much in accordance with the current theory, in spite of the fact that there is no concrete relationship whatsoever between the two. As should be obvious from the section on Chinese pedagogy later in this chapter, some of the principles made explicit by the theory have been used for centuries in China and, less frequently, in Europe, too (Mason & Watson, 2005).

First, the meaning of words was focused on by showing that the very same word might have different meanings (if it is a homonym). Meaning 1 is contrasted with Meaning 2, while the word remains invariant. The difference opened the dimension of variation "word meaning" and separated meaning$_1$ and the word (and actually also meaning$_2$ and the word). The pattern was thus

> word   **meaning**
> *i*   *v*

and it was brought about in the context of a short story:

> Afanti was a hairdresser. There was one customer, who always went to Afanti's place to have his hair cut but never paid for the service. It made Afanti very

angry. He wanted to play a trick on the customer. One day he came to Afanti's again. Afanti first cut his hair. Then he began to shave the customer's face, and asked, "Do you want your eyebrows?" The customer replied, "Of course! Why ask?" Then, quick as a flash, Afanti shaved off the customer's eyebrows and said, "You wanted your eyebrows, so I will give them to you!" The customer was too mad to say anything; because he had indeed said he "wanted" his eyebrows. Meanwhile Afanti asked, "Do you want your beard?" The customer had a beautiful beard, and he immediately said, "My beard? No, no! I don't want my beard!" But again Afanti proceeded to shave off his beard. The customer stood up and saw an egg-like head in the mirror. [Both the teacher and students laugh.] Furiously, the customer reproved Afanti, "Why did you shave off my eyebrows and beard?" "I was only following your orders, sir!" Afanti answered calmly. There was nothing the customer could say to that!

(Ko, 2002; Ko & Marton, 2004)

Through the ambiguous nature of the Chinese word *yao* (in Putonghua), meaning both "to keep" and "to give," the concept of homonym was introduced, against the background of all other words, mostly less ambiguous, that the students were familiar with. Subsequently, a contrast with the mirror image of the concept synonym (e.g., see, look at, glance at, etc.) was brought out (see Figure 6.5)

By means of these two patterns (illustrating the concept of homonym and synonym), meaning is separated from word—and made visible to the learners—and word (in the sense of sound) is separated from meaning—and made visible to the learners. In this way the frequently taken-for-granted direct relationship between word and meaning is brought into question.[5]

Throughout the lesson, the teacher introduced concepts by means of appropriate patterns of variation and invariance, frequently contrast. For instance, the meaning of "book" was not brought out by means of many similar examples of books but through comparison with things that are not books (such as magazines, reports, etc.). Directly afterwards, differentiations were made within the class of books (Marton & Tsui, 2004, pp. 49–50).

Postman's Walk

Runesson and Mok (2004) analyzed another lesson, also taught by a widely recognized, excellent teacher in China. This was a demonstration lesson conducted in

Homonym		Synonym	
word	**meaning**	**word**	meaning
i	v	v	i

FIGURE 6.5 Contrast between homonym and synonym, in terms of patterns of variation and invariance.

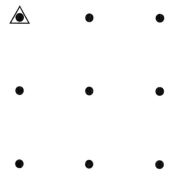

FIGURE 6.6 Problem given in a public lesson (adapted from Runesson & Mok, 2004, p. 76).

Shanghai, in November 1998, with 28 year-4 students, working in seven groups in front of about 50 adult participants in a conference about open-ended tasks. The seven groups of students, with four in each group, were invited to come up with as many solutions as possible to the problem in Figure 6.6.

There are nine dots on the paper. The dot surrounded by a triangle in the left upper corner represents the post office. The postman needs to start at the post office to deliver a letter to each of the eight places, and return to the post office. What could the postman's route be?

During the 10 minutes that followed, one of the groups produced 18 different solutions. The class checked the solutions, and they were found to be correct. The teacher then showed a solution from another group, which was not correct. By choosing the shortest routes only and by neglecting the direction of the postman when leaving the post office, the number of solutions was reduced to eight (see Figure 6.7).

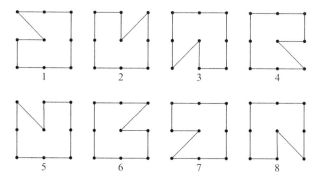

FIGURE 6.7 Eight solutions of the problem given in a public lesson (adapted from Runesson & Mok, 2004, p. 78).

After that the students were asked to group the patterns of the routes in terms of similarities and differences. They discovered that four patterns (1–4) could be turned into each other by rotating them clockwise and that the other four (5–8) could be turned into each other by rotating them counterclockwise. Even the remaining two patterns could be turned into each other by flipping them either horizontally or vertically. This classificatory exercise meant that the patterns were not considered in terms of the everyday context of a postman coming with letters. They were dealt with as mathematical entities in the context of geometry. In this way all the patterns representing the shortest route could be produced through transformations of one pattern, by four rotations and one of two reflections (flipping).

At last the teacher asked the question, "How many best solution were there to the problem?" There was a lively discussion among the students: was it 1, 2, 8 or 16? Then the problem was moved back to the context of everyday life. A postman walking from house to house, and then back to the post office, must necessarily walk in one direction or the other, and must go to one house or another. There are actually 16 different ways of doing this, ways which cannot be rotated or reflected (though in mathematics they can, for sure).

What was it possible to learn during this lesson? Many things actually, some of which follow:

1) By keeping the problem invariant and varying the solution, the students could learn that there might be different solutions to the same problem.
2) By keeping the problem invariant and varying its context (everyday and mathematical), the students could learn that how many solutions there are and which ones are better than others depends on the context in which you deal with the problem.
3) By keeping the pattern invariant, but varying the rotational position, the students could make the idea of rotation their own.
4) By keeping the pattern invariant, but varying the reflections, the students could make the idea of reflection their own.
5) By keeping the set of patterns invariant, but varying how it is described, the students could learn that a set can be understood in terms of its elements or in terms of the transformations (in this case rotation and reflection) that generate it.

Comparing Teaching

In this section some studies comparing ways of teaching are analyzed. As there are no data about what the students actually learn, these comparisons must once again be made in terms of the learning that is made possible. And again, in addition to the particular theoretical perspective used, possible objects of learning are adopted as lenses through which the possibilities for learning are seen, whether or not they are in agreement with the intended object of learning (i.e., with what the teachers were planning to help their students to learn).

"The Teaching Gap"

The main thesis in this book is that what varies and what is invariant is of decisive importance for what can be learned. One of the best-known examples that can be used to illustrate such a perspective on learning is to be found in Stigler and Hiebert's bestselling book from 1999, *The Teaching Gap*. This book is a popular summary of a most ambitious study called TIMSS video. TIMSS stands for Trends in International Mathematics and Science Study, and it refers to comparative studies of achievement in mathematics that have been run since 1995. Students from the United States, a country that invests more money in education than any other country in the world and is the sole superpower in educational research, have not succeeded particularly well. (For instance, in eighth-grade mathematics, 20 of the 41 countries participating in the 1995 TIMSS scored significantly higher than the US, and only seven scored significantly lower according to Stigler and Hiebert (1999, p. 6).[6]

The TIMSS video was supposed to bring some clarity to the situation: Why are American students not doing better in math? The researchers chose 100 classes at random in the United States, Germany (students with achievement similar to American students) and Japan (students with achievement much higher than American students) and recorded one math lesson in each class. By comparing what happened during the lessons in those three countries, the researchers hoped to gain a better understanding of the differences in achievement among them. One of the most interesting findings was the differences between the United States and Japan as far as the pattern of the math lessons was concerned. In most lessons in the United States, the teacher introduced a particular method for solving a certain class of problems. After the demonstration, the teacher gave the students a number of different problems of the same kind, which they had to solve by using the method introduced by the teacher, the assumption being that by practicing the method over and over, the students should in the future be capable of solving problems of the same type.

In a typical Japanese lesson, on the other hand, the teacher introduced a rather complex problem and invited the students to have a go at it—individually or together in small groups. After a while the teacher asked the students to show their solutions, their attempts were compared and teacher and students might conclude that one way of solving the problem is more powerful than the others, and in such a case the students could practice that particular way of solving this kind of problem on some other, but related, problems.

As the Japanese students had outperformed the American students in TIMSS, Stigler and Hiebert assumed that the Japanese pattern was pedagogically more powerful than the American pattern. In spite of these labels, both patterns are actually used to varying extents in most countries. In fact, the Chinese lesson on the postman's route is very much like a Japanese lesson in mathematics, as it is characterized here, and the difference between the Japanese pattern and the

American pattern also appears in Runesson's (1999) comparison of different ways of dealing with the same content in Swedish classrooms. You can probably find the same difference between teachers in any culture, and probably even within the teachers themselves: the same teacher might use one pattern on one occasion and the other on another occasion.

But why would one pattern work better than the other? There are two major differences between the lessons in mathematics observed in Japan and in the United States.

One Difference Between American and Japanese Classes: Method Invariant, Problems Vary or Methods Vary, Problem Invariant

One difference (particularly relevant for the discussion in this book) is that in the American case the method of solution is the same while the problems differ (somewhat at least); however, in the Japanese case the solutions differ while the problem is the same. The difference between the most frequent pattern in American and Japanese classes can be illustrated in the following way

method	**problem**	**method**	problem
i	v	v	i

where *i* stands for "invariant" and *v* stands for "varies," just as in previous cases (although here from the observer's perspective).

As mentioned, the American pattern may actually follow in the Japanese classrooms, once teacher and students have agreed that certain ways of solving the actual (or similar) problems are better than others. In that case the students might keep practicing the most powerful method of solution.

Now, what is it possible to learn in lessons like these? In the American case the students are supposed to become capable of solving a particular kind of problem in a particular way. How "particular kind" is defined depends on the variation in the problems that students keep practicing. The teaching of mathematics is frequently structured like this. Hence, during another lesson the students are supposed to learn another particular method for solving another particular kind of problem, and during a third lesson another and so on. Having been taught mathematics in this way, the students will be able to solve problems that they have solved before, assuming that they remember how they have solved these problems previously. But when they encounter a novel problem that they have never seen before, or if they do not recognize it as belonging to a kind of problem that they have learned to solve, they will be at a loss, precisely because they have not learned to solve problems that they have not learned to solve.

But this is exactly what they have to try to do in the Japanese case. You have to learn to do something with the problem, to change it, to transform it in such a way that it can be solved. You have to explore it, by doing different things, and by doing different things you become aware of how those things and what they lead to differ. Subsequently, by comparing different solutions, the students learn about solutions, about solving the problem given during a particular lesson. But the Japanese students work in similar ways during other lessons, and thus they get confronted with a great variety of "novel problems" and a great variety of methods to solve them. According to the basic principle of learning advocated previously, the learners pay attention to that which varies. If this is true, the Japanese students will focus primarily on ways of solving problems, while the American students will primarily focus on how problems among certain kinds of problems differ from each other, mostly in terms of numerical values.

The distinction discussed here also exemplifies the distinction mentioned earlier between induction and contrast and is hardly unique to mathematics. It actually relates to the central question introduced in Chapter 3, namely, that of the use of induction as the primary way of searching for knowledge. In the first case (induction), that which is focused is the same, kept invariant, repeated, while what is unfocused varies. In the second case (contrast), it is the other way around: that which is focused varies and what is unfocused is invariant. As the object of learning here is to become able to solve certain kinds of problems; according to one theory of teaching, the method of solution (that which is to be learned and that is thus focused on) should be kept invariant, while according to the other theory of teaching, it is primarily the method of solution that should vary.

Another Difference Between American and Japanese Classes: Being Told How to Do It or Finding Out Yourself

The other difference is that while the American students are *told* how to solve a certain kind of problem, the Japanese students have to try to *find* a way of solving a particular problem themselves. Even this difference can be formulated in terms of differences in the pattern of variation and invariance. When you are told how to solve a problem, the one who tells you makes all the distinctions that have to be made. In the best case you learn to recognize what has been discerned. You might learn how to solve that particular kind of problem, but you cannot possibly see the solution as *a* way of solving that kind of problem. In fact, there is no way of separating that kind of problem and the solution presented by the teacher unless you come across another way of solving the same kind of problem. When trying to solve a problem on your own—if you really try to solve it—there is probably a change (difference) in how the problem appears to you. You develop a way of seeing it. This is true whether or not you actually manage to solve it. If you do not and you eventually see how it is solved by someone else (the teacher or a classmate), there will be a contrast between the canonical way of solving it and your own. Your own, perhaps less elegant or even failed attempt, will enable you to see the solution much more clearly. It will have a particular meaning for you.[7]

Different Ways of Handling the Same Content by Different Teachers

Runesson (1999) studied how the same content (fractions) was handled in five Swedish teachers' classrooms. As her observations were not related to student outcomes, she could only present differences in the enacted objects of learning in the different classes (i.e., the different things that was made possible for the students to learn in the different classes). But even the conclusions she drew about the enacted objects of learning rested on the assumption that the aspects of the object of learning that she had observed were indeed critical. I want to use an example of such differences from Runesson's study, as this was the first time that the theory of learning discussed in this book was used as a tool for analyzing differences in how the same content was handled in different classrooms.

One of the differences found resembled the difference that Stigler and Hiebert (1999) found between (what they saw as) typical Japanese and American classrooms. It was the difference between introducing a method and using it for solving different problems on the one hand and introducing a problem and using different methods to solve it on the other hand.

When introducing fractions, one teacher demonstrated a method for computing a fraction of an integer (dividing the integer by the denominator and multiplying the quotient by the nominator). This strategy was then applied to three different, but similar, problems (How much is 2/3 of a string that is 90 cm long? How much is 1/5 of a string that is 40 cm long? How much is 3/5 of a string that is 60 cm long?).

Another teacher asked the students in her class to mark 3/7 of a 7 × 8 squared rectangle. Some students divided the small squares into groups of seven and marked three squares out of the seven in each group. Other students divided the small squares into seven groups and marked three out of those seven groups. These are two different interpretations of fractions, identified in the research literature (see Behr et al., 1993). By contrasting the two alternatives, the interpretation of fractions as a dimension of variation is opened up, and the students probably become able to discern this (meaning) aspect of fractions.

The difference in how the same content (computing fractions) was handled in the two classes can be written in general form as follows:

	method	problem
Class A	i	v
Class B	v	i

Different Ways of Handling the Same Content in Different Cultures

Let us look at another example. If you always call the unknowns in systems of linear equations in two unknowns x and y, learners might not know what to do if the unknowns are called f and g. So the object of learning could be to recognize the unknowns in a system of linear equations regardless of what letters (or other symbols) are used to denote them. In order to make it possible for the students to discern this critical aspect, they must encounter different symbols, to alert them to the fact that any symbols would do.[8]

This example is taken from Häggström's (2008) analytic comparison of how the topic "linear equations in two unknowns" was dealt with in some classes in Sweden, Hong Kong and Shanghai, in a sequence of 10 or more consecutive lessons.

The main focus of the comparison was finding the dimensions of variation opened up during the lessons and thus identifying what aspects of the content dealt with had been made available for the students to discern. On the whole, he found that among the classes participating in the study, most dimensions of variation were opened up in the classes from Shanghai, the next most in those from Hong Kong and the least number in the only participating Swedish class. One would think that the students who were best in mathematics would need the least number of dimensions of variation to be opened (because they had already managed to discern more aspects than the students who were less proficient in mathematics). But actually, on an achievement test in algebra, the students from Shanghai were best, then the students from Hong Kong and lastly the Swedish students. The correlation between achievement in relevant parts of mathematics and the number of dimensions of variation opened during the lessons (or the "size" of the space of learning) was thus actually positive. I just would like to use one example from the Swedish class and one from one of the classes in Shanghai to illustrate how two sets of problems contributed to constituting the space of (possible) learning in two different classes.

During one of the lessons in the Swedish class the students worked on 18 problems in their textbook. As we can see in Figure 6.8, they are rather similar.

920a)	$\begin{cases} y = x + 2 \\ 3x + y = 6 \end{cases}$	b)	$\begin{cases} y = 2x - 1 \\ x + y = 5 \end{cases}$	c)	$\begin{cases} y = 4x - 3 \\ 2x + y = 6 \end{cases}$	
921a)	$\begin{cases} y = 2x \\ 9x - 2y = 15 \end{cases}$	b)	$\begin{cases} y = x + 1 \\ x + 2y = 11 \end{cases}$	c)	$\begin{cases} y = 3x - 2 \\ 2y - 5x = 0 \end{cases}$	
922a)	$\begin{cases} y = 3x \\ 4x - y = 1 \end{cases}$	b)	$\begin{cases} y = 5x - 3 \\ 7x - y - 6 \end{cases}$	c)	$\begin{cases} y = 4 - x \\ 5x - y = 5 \end{cases}$	
923a)	$\begin{cases} y = x + 4 \\ 5x - 2y = 1 \end{cases}$	b)	$\begin{cases} y = 2 - x \\ 4x - 3y = 8 \end{cases}$	c)	$\begin{cases} y = 2x + 5 \\ 6x - 2y = 5 \end{cases}$	
924a)	$\begin{cases} y = 7 \\ 8x - 3y = -1 \end{cases}$	b)	$\begin{cases} y = 2.5x - 4 \\ 6x - 2y = 12 \end{cases}$	c)	$\begin{cases} 16x - 2y = 9 \\ y = 7x - 2 \end{cases}$	
925a)	$\begin{cases} x = 4y - 2 \\ 3x - 10y = 3 \end{cases}$	b)	$\begin{cases} x = 9 - 2y \\ 5y - 3x = 6 \end{cases}$	c)	$\begin{cases} x = 0.5y + 10 \\ 2y - x = 5 \end{cases}$	

FIGURE 6.8 Systems of equation tasks in a Swedish textbook (adapted from Häggström, 2008, p. 90).

In what ways do the 18 problems differ from each other (apart from the different numbers appearing in them)?

The set of problems can be described in terms of the following patterns of variation and invariance:

- In all the problems we find an equation either in the form "$y = f(x)$" or in the form "$x = f(y)$," together with an equation in the form "$ax + by = c$" or "$ay + bx = c$."
- In 924c the two forms are switched. The two different forms of the first equation constitute a dimension of variation, with the two forms as values.
- The two different forms of the second equation are additional values in the same dimension of variation.
- In all but one task, both equations contain both unknowns. Equation (1) in task 924a is "$y = 7$." There is thus a dimension of variation "number of unknowns in the equation" constituted by the values "2" and "1."
- Integers are used for all coefficients, except in 924b ($y = 2.5x - 4$) and 925c ($x = 0.5y + 10$). There is a dimension of variation "kinds of numbers" with "natural numbers" and "rational numbers" as values.
- Integers are used for the constant "c" in all second equations, except in 924a ($8x - 3y = -1$). There is thus a dimension of variation, let us call it "constant," with "positive whole numbers" and "negative whole numbers" as values.

It may be noted that all these patterns of variation and invariance are generalizations, that they are supposed to tell the learners that a system of linear equations in two unknowns might look like this . . . and this . . . and this.

Let us compare this with a set of problems the students had to work on in one of the classes in Shanghai (see Figure 6.9; Häggström, 2008, p. 142).

1   What is a "System of equations"?
2   How can you tell whether a system of equation is a
    system of linear equations in two unknowns?
3   Identifiy whether the given is a system of linear equations
    in two unknowns.

1) $\begin{cases} x + y = 3 \\ x - y = 1 \end{cases}$ 2) $\begin{cases} (x + y)^2 = 1 \\ x - y = 0 \end{cases}$ 3) $\begin{cases} x = 1 \\ y = 1 \end{cases}$

4) $\begin{cases} x/2 + y/2 = 0 \\ x = y \end{cases}$ 5) $\begin{cases} xy = 2 \\ x = 1 \end{cases}$ 6) $\begin{cases} x + 1/y = 1 \\ y = 2 \end{cases}$

7) $u = v = 0$ 8) $\begin{cases} x + y = 4 \\ x - m = 1 \end{cases}$

FIGURE 6.9 Systems of equations tasks, presented by a Chinese teacher in his class (adapted from Häggström, 2008, p. 142).

The most striking difference between the tasks set for the Swedish and the Chinese students is that the former were supposed to solve 18 problems involving systems of linear equations in two unknowns, while the latter were invited to reflect on and make statements about what a system of linear equations in two unknowns. While the former were supposed to develop and demonstrate proficiency with doing something (solving problems of a certain kind), the latter were supposed to develop and demonstrate proficiency with a way of seeing something (distinguishing one kind of problems from other kinds of problems).

This difference between what was done with the same topic corresponded to another important difference. In the Swedish class the students only dealt with linear equations, their meaning was thus presupposed. In the Shanghai class there were several problems that were non-linear equations, hence a contrast between what linear equations are (first degree) and what they are not (e.g., quadratic, second degree, was afforded to the students). The tasks in the Shanghai class could be described in terms of the following patterns of variation and invariance:

- The contrast just mentioned was inherent in three of the problems (2, 5, 6). The dimension of variation index was thus presented by means of two values: "linear" and "quadratic."
- Another case of calling attention to contrast would be to emphasize a potentially critical feature "in *two* unknowns and not in three" (8). The dimension of variation "number of unknowns" was introduced by means of two values: "2" and "3."
- The remaining four cases illustrate that the equations might be of different forms (1, 3, 4, 7),[9] some of which are quite unusual. The dimension of variation "form of equation" was introduced, just as in the Swedish class.
- Two problems were also meant to alert the students to the fact that symbols other than x and y can be used to denote the unknowns (7, 8). The dimension of variation "symbols" was thus introduced.
- As in the Swedish class, it was implied that the coefficients might also be rational numbers (4). The dimension of variation "kinds of numbers as coefficients" was thus presented.

The first two patterns are contrasts, and they are supposed to be instrumental in focusing the students' attention on one particular value in both cases. But in order to highlight a certain value (feature), according to the theory, a dimension of variation has to be opened. The assumption is that telling the students "linear equations are of the first degree," for instance, is not as powerful a strategy as making a contrast between equations of the first and of the second degree. Actually neither "linear" nor "first degree" makes any sense if you have never encountered anything that is not linear, not of the first degree. In the Swedish class the students actually raised questions about what the expression "linear equations" means, without the teacher being able to satisfy their curiosity.

We can see from the critical features addressed in these two lessons that they represent features that, in the teacher's opinion, should not be taken for granted. These features might be defining features of the concept in question (e.g., *two* equations, *two* unknowns, index = *1*), which the students might miss out on, or features that the student might take for defining features, but which are not (e.g., that the unknowns must be x and y, that both unknowns have two appear in both equations).

Gu (1991) and Gu et al. (2004) have described these two kinds of critical features (or potential misunderstandings). The first kind, missing out on defining features, is illustrated by the difference between "concept" and "non-concept" versions of adjacent angles, the difference being a contrast. The second kind, taking non-defining features for defining features, is illustrated by the difference between "standard" and "non-standard" versions of geometrical figures, the difference being a generalization in Figure 6.10.

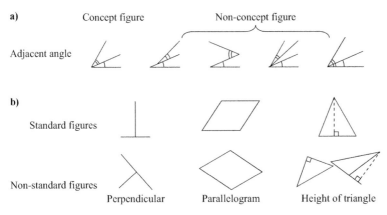

FIGURE 6.10 Taking non-instances for instances (adjacent angles) and instances for non-instances (geometrical figures; adapted from Gu et al., 2004, pp. 317, 319).

We have seen that the teacher in Shanghai opened up a wider space of learning than the Swedish teacher, by dealing with more widely varying mathematical problems. This means that the Shanghai teacher has prepared his students for a greater variety of problems than the Swedish teacher.

As mentioned previously, when using variation theory as a tool for analyzing teaching (in this case, for comparing two ways of teaching the same content), the object of learning, in terms of critical aspects, has the function of a lens through which teaching is examined. In the case of Häggström's study, for instance, he tried to determine whether or not dimensions of variation that have been opened in one class have also been opened in the other classes. In this way he could compare the spaces of learning (i.e., the enacted objects of learning) in different classes, without any assumptions about the correspondence between the intended and the enacted object of learning, and actually even without assuming that all the dimensions investigated represented critical aspects of the object of learning in different classes (see Table 6.1).

TABLE 6.1 Spaces of learning for systems of equations in six different classes (adapted from Häggström, 2008, p. 199).

	SW2	HK1	HK2	SH1	SH2	SH3
DoVs concerning "properties"						
1 Number of equations (two or more equations)						
1a. Two equations, not one	X	X	X	X	X	X
1b. More than one equation		X		X		
2 Number of unknowns (two unknowns)						
2a. Two unknowns not one	X	X	X			
2b. Two unknowns not three (or more)		X		X	X	X
3 Type of equations (linear equations first degree unknowns)						
3a. xy is not first degree				X	X	X
3b. x^2, $(x+y)^2$, is not first degree				X		
3c. $1/y$ is not first degree				X		
4 An unknown represents the same number in both equations						
4a. "Unknowns are the same" is not taken for granted	X	X	X	X		
5 Constants and coefficients can be different types of numbers						
5a. Rational numbers not just natural	X	X		X	X	X
5b. Negative numbers not just natural	X	X	X	X	X	X
5c. Parameters not just specified numbers				X		
DoVs concerning "appearance"						
6 Different letters may be used						
6a. The letters x, y are not taken for granted		X	X	X		X
7 A system of equations can be in different formats						
7a. Format of individual equations not invariant	X	X	X	X	X	X
7b. One expression		X	X	X		
7c. Both unknowns not present in both equations	X			X	X	X
DoV concerning "use"						
8 A way of representing and solving problems						
8a. Alternative to use of equation in one unknown		X				
8b. Alternative to use of guess-and-check method		X				

Note. A gray space indicates that the dimension was opened for variation, and X indicates which alternatives were provided.

Relating Learning and Teaching to Each Other

In the studies in the previous sections attempts were made to describe what the students could possibly learn, but not what they actually learned. In this section, two studies are described in which what the students learned is related to what happened during the lessons observed. In both cases the same content was dealt with by two different teachers in two different classes. Their teaching was not based on the theory argued for in this book but in the analysis of the lessons; the theory was used as a tool, just as in the studies in the previous sections.

Learning Cantonese Words

Much of the research referred to in this chapter originates from a project in Hong Kong about good practice, addressing the question, What makes teaching "good teaching"?[10] For dealing with this rather grandiose question, we (the research group at the University of Hong Kong's Faculty of Education) adopted three principles as our point of departure: 1) We would define good (and less good) teaching in terms of the students' learning. 2) We would focus on student learning in rather specific terms: What do the students learn from specific lessons?[11] 3) We would try to understand possible differences in what the students in different classes learned about the content of a certain lesson in terms of how that content was handled in those classes.

We thus chose a simple—and, for us, very lucky—methodological option: we studied how the same content was dealt with in different classes and what the students learned about that content in those classes, during the lessons observed.

In one of our very first studies we explored two lessons in Chinese, taught in two year-2 classes (Chik, 2006; Chik, Leung & Marton, 2010). The two teachers actually worked together—and had worked together for many years. They planned their lessons together, and they also planned together the lesson studied by us. They agreed on the same learning target, and they used the same text material. As the students in the two classes were on the same achievement level in Chinese, we had every reason to expect similar learning outcomes. But this was not at all what happened. The content of the lesson involved seven Chinese words that the students were expected to learn during the lesson, in the sense of becoming capable of using them in an appropriate way in written and spoken language (in reading, writing, speaking and listening). After the lesson, a cloze test[12] was used for observing the results. In the text in Figure 6.11, words were removed and the students were supposed to fill in the missing words. These words were actually the target words of the lessons. (In Figure 6.11, they are underlined.)

Father wishes to take us <u>as guests</u> to a friend's house. He asks, "What must one do in order to be a <u>polite</u> little guest?" My younger brother says, "We should <u>greet</u> people when we meet them." My younger sister says, "When we are eating, do not <u>pick and choose</u> food in the dish." My elder sister says, "When talking to someone, you should face him. Do not <u>look around</u>. When other people are talking, do not <u>interrupt</u> as you like." I say, "On leaving, we must say goodbye." Father is very pleased on hearing these suggestions. He promises to give us the chance to be polite guests.

FIGURE 6.11 Text used in the study (adapted from Chik et al., 2010, p. 104).

When we compared how the two classes did on the test, we were greatly surprised. One of the classes significantly outperformed the other (see Table 6.2).

TABLE 6.2 The test task (words in bold had to be produced by the pupils) and the results on the post-test (adapted from Chik et al., 2010, p. 118).

Second Part: Complete the following text with appropriate words/phrases you have learnt in the lesson.

Our teacher often tells us to **greet** teachers and classmates when we meet them in school. In the classroom, when the teacher is talking with other classmates, do not **interrupt** as you like; when the teacher talks to you, do not **look around**. After school, we have to say goodbye to our teachers and classmates. Then, we can be counted as good students who are **polite**.

Outcomes/Class (n = total number of responses)	2A (n = 30)	2B (n = 31)
(a) Appropriate use of all words	30	9
(b) One to three blanks missing/inappropriate	—	22

The question is, what was the difference in what happened in the two classrooms?[13]

One of the most striking differences between the two lessons was the way in which they were structured: teaching had a hierarchical (whole–part) structure in class 2A, while the structure was sequential in class 2B (for this distinction, see Chapter 3.) In the former case, the theme of the text (being polite) was situated in the students' everyday reality (e.g., by discussing the question, "Who is polite in this class?"). The story was about the polite guest, who knew how to behave when visiting someone. The theme was dealt with in the context of the text, which was dealt with in the context of the students' everyday world. Sentences were dealt with in the context of the theme, words in the context of sentences and characters in the context of words. All higher-order units were supposed to be simultaneously present in the students' awareness when the teacher moved on to lower-order units (see Figure 6.12)

In class 2B, the lesson was sequentially organized (i.e., one thing at a time was dealt with), in particular, the three basic aspects of words: form, meaning and pronunciation. The seven words constituting the object of learning (in the sense of content) were dealt with in terms of one aspect at a time (see Figure 6.13)

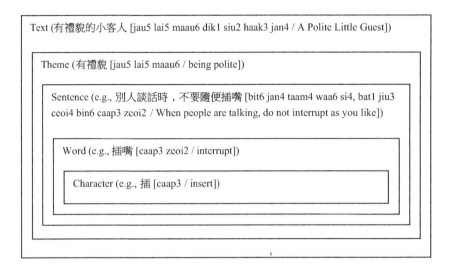

FIGURE 6.12 The part–whole relationships in the lesson in class 2A (adapted from Chik et al., 2010, p. 110).

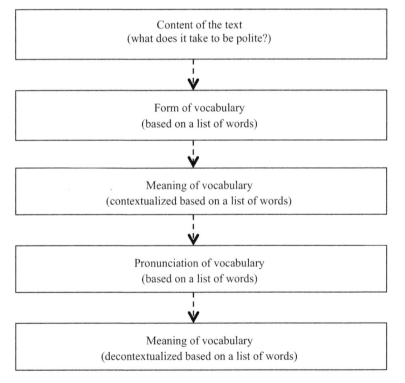

FIGURE 6.13 The sequential structure of the lesson in class 2B (adapted from Chik et al., 2010, p. 113).

Lesson 2A	Lesson 2B
Word 1 →	Word 2 →	Word 3 →...	Attribute 1 →	Attribute 2 →	Attribute 3 →...
attribute 1;	attribute 1;	attribute 1;	word 1;	word 1;	word 1;
attribute 2;	attribute 2;	attribute 2;	word 2;	word 2;	word 2;
attribute 3	attribute 3	attribute 3	word 3;	word 3;	word 3;
			...	...	...

FIGURE 6.14 Comparison of the grouping of the words dealt with in the two classes (adapted from Chik et al., 2010, p. 114).

The difference between a hierarchical and a sequential way of dealing with a text appeared in the previous chapter, with reference to Säljö's (1982) study. In that case, there was a difference between the ways of approaching a text that the learners spontaneously adopted, in terms of which differences in their understanding of the text were accounted for. Chik et al. (2010) thus found the same kind of difference between two teachers' ways of dealing with the text. In both cases, the hierarchical structuring of the text was associated with more powerful learning.

There was a second important difference between the two lessons, linked with the first difference. In class 2A, one word was dealt with at a time, but all three aspects were dealt with together. In class 2B, one aspect was dealt with at a time, but all the seven different words were dealt with together (see Figure 6.14). Had the aspects (form, pronunciation and meaning) been unknown to the students, the latter would have been a better strategy. But as the students were in all likelihood already aware of at least some attribute of every word, it probably worked better to learn the words as wholes, by bringing together the three aspects through fusion. (They did not need to learn to separate the aspects from each other; they needed to bring them together instead.)

Solving Quadratic Equations

As mentioned previously, Olteanu (2007) compared how the solution of quadratic equations was taught in two Swedish secondary school classes. She found that learning was much better in one of those classes. After having worked with quadratic equations over 12 lessons, the students took a test in which they had to solve 20 quadratic equations. In 19 cases out of 20, the same class (class A) succeeded better than the other. As the two classes were on the same level of achievement in mathematics when the sequence of 12 lessons started, Olteanu tried to find the critical differences in the way the same content was dealt with in the two classes, as a possible explanation of the differences between the two classes with regard to solving quadratic equations She actually found two such differences that could be considered keys to the difference in learning in the two classes.

One difference between the two classes that seemed to be important was that while the teacher derived the general formula from a specific task in the "better" class and thus gave the students the opportunity to discern it and its component parts, the teacher in the other class simply stated the formula and had the students practice it in specific cases. This difference was described in more detail earlier in this chapter, in the section "Differences as Changes."

The other important difference between the two classes, which probably contributed to the differences in the final achievement test, was the way in which the two teachers helped the students to use the formula, especially as far the handling of the "minus sign" was concerned. From the students' ways of dealing with the problems in the test, after the sequence of lessons, it can be seen that what made a difference to the students' performance—in addition to their general understanding of the relation between quadratic equations in different forms and the formula—was their handling of the parameters, p and q. The students ought to understand that they have to transform the equations into the form $x^2 + px + q = 0$, where x^2 has to have a positive sign and $-p = + (-p)$ and $-c = + (-c)$; that is, the negative sign indicates a negative number and not subtraction. When there is a minus sign, they have to think of it in terms of adding a negative number instead of subtracting a positive number. Actually, neither of the two teachers had expected the students to have problems with the signs of the coefficients, but teacher A discovered the difficulty and tried to do something about it by bringing out the distinction between the sign denoting (and belonging to or "being part of") a number on the one hand and denoting an operation (subtraction) on the other hand.

The difference between the learning that was made possible for the students in the two classes with regard to handling the "minus sign" originated partly from the differences in the space of variation opened up by the two sets of problems in the two classes (see Tables 6.3 and 6.4) but also from the differences in the ways in which the two teachers dealt with this particular difficulty. In class A it was addressed by the teacher in the following way:

$x^2 + 2x - 15 = 0$:
[1.10] Maria (teacher A): Is it written in the form $x^2 + px + q = 0$?
[2.10] Emilia: No . . .
[3.10] Maria: Isn't it? Yes, it's minus, yes. But if we compare it (the teacher writes above the given equation $x^2 + px + q = 0$), then I say it's the same, but what is q equal to?
[4.10] Emilia: −15
[5.10] Maria: Yes, minus 15, in other words, so the minus sign is part of q, q equals minus 15 and p equals 2, and I must not have any coefficient in front of x^2, and it has to equal 0, so it is in that form. (Lesson 25, 2003–04–03).
(Olteanu, 2007, p. 141)

The same difficulty appeared in class B, too, and was handled by the teacher there in the following (and in all likelihood, less helpful) way:

[19] Anna (teacher B): The formula says then, that the line of symmetry is half the coefficient with reversed signs, so what is it then?

[20] Gun: Three.

[21] Anna: Three, and then it lies symmetrically/it is symmetrical, plus, minus, and what you have to do is to interpret the formula, it says half of *p* squared, and this is half of p (pointing to 3) it . . .

[22] Gun: Mm . . .

[23] Anna: And the (pointing) three squared?

[24] Gun: 9

[25] Anna: 9, and then you have to take this (pointing to *q*) with reversed sign minus 5. (Lesson 27, 2003–04–03).

(Olteanu 2007, p. 151)

Difficulties with the rewriting of any equation in the standard form $x^2 + px + q = 0$ was found to be a primary critical difference between the enacted objects of learning in the two classes. The secondary critical difference, which, no doubt, contributed to the main difficulties, was the frequent absence of the distinction between the negative sign meaning subtraction and meaning negative number. Such difficulties are brought to the fore, and thus can be dealt with, by means of a set of sufficiently varying problems. We can compare the set of problems the students had to deal with in the two classes. In Table 6.3 we can see that in teacher A's class, the signs of both *q* and *c* keep varying, while in teacher B's class there is no variation in sign (see Table 6.4). Also the unknown quantity and the constant term are on different sides in equations 1 through 3 and 8 and on the same side in equations 4 through 7 in teacher A's class, but on the same side in all equations in teacher B's class. Furthermore, in the set of equations, we find that the x^2 coefficient can have a value other than 1 and can be > 0 as well as < 0. The latter can also be found by working through—or simply inspecting—the set of problems chosen by the teacher in class B, but there is no systematic variation in the signs of *p* and *q*, or between the two sides of the equations. This is in spite of the fact that it is by means of introducing sufficiently varying problems that the students' difficulties can be addressed, thus preparing them for dealing with problems that vary along the dimensions that have been opened during the lesson, just as in Häggström's (2008) study, or in any lesson in mathematics, for that matter.

TABLE 6.3 Quadratic equations in teacher A's class (adapted from Olteanu, 2007, p. 133).

	Quadratic Equations				
No.	Type I	No.	Type II	No.	Type III and IV
1.	$x^2 = 144$	5.	$(x + 1)(x - 3) = 0$	8.	$x^2 - 6x + 9 = 0$
2.	$5x^2 = 845$	6.	$x^2 + 4x = 0$	9.	$x^2 + 12x + 35 = 0$
3.	$4x^2 - 13 = 23$	7.	$8x^2 - 4x = 0$	10.	$x^2 + 2x - 15 = 0$
4.	$(x + 14)^2 = 4$			11.	$x^2 - x - 30 = 0$
				12.	$2x - 3x^2 = -1$

TABLE 6.4 Quadratic equations in teacher B's class (adapted from Olteanu, 2007, p. 145).

	Quadratic Equations				
No.	Type I	No.	Type II	No.	Type III and IV
1.	$x^2 - 4 = 0$	3.	$(x + 2)(x - 4) = 0$	4.	$x^2 - 4x - 5 = 0$
2.	$(x - 1)^2 - 9 = 0$			5.	$-0{,}01x^2 + x + 2{,}3 = 0$

Bringing About Learning: Patterns of Variation and Invariance as Tools for Planning and Conducting Teaching

In the last two examples the theory of learning presented in this book was used to analyze cases of teaching in which the teachers were not aware of the theory at all, though one of them in each case acted intuitively, from time to time, in accordance with its principles. It seemed that the theory could be used to explain differences in the students' learning in terms of what happened in the classrooms, as seen through the lens of the theory and the object of learning. In the following studies we tried to explore whether or not—or to what extent—the same theory could be used not only for analyzing teaching but also for enhancing learning, by making teaching more powerful.

Learning About Price

How do people make sense of price and pricing? As was pointed out in Chapter 4, there has been a surprisingly large number of studies on this issue in the research tradition underlying this book. One of those studies was used in that chapter as an example of analyzing interview data to identify qualitative differences in ways of seeing something. In accordance with earlier research, four different ways of seeing price were found:

1) Price as a function of attributes of the commodity
2) Price as a function of the eagerness of the buyers (demand)
3) Price as a function of the availability of the commodity (supply)
4) Price as a function of the relationship between the eagerness of the buyers (demand) on the one hand and of the availability of the commodity (supply) on the other.

In the first case, attributes of the commodity are discerned and focused on (if it is beautiful, big, tastes good, etc., then it is more expensive). In the other cases, market mechanisms involving buyers and sellers are discerned and focused on: in the second, category demand; in the third, supply; in the fourth, the relationship between demand and supply.

As has been shown by Dahlgren (1978), even university students, after 1 year of full-time study in economics, see price and pricing only to a limited extent in terms of the relationship between demand and supply, in concrete, everyday and work-related situations. Can we then enable 10-year-olds to do this? This was the question that Pang and Chik (2005; see also Pang, Linder & Fraser, 2006) set out to study. The investigation was carried out as a learning study (see Chapter 7): using the current theory as resource, five teachers of five year-4 classes in Hong Kong planned a double lesson together, to be taught in each class. The lessons were carried out in parallel, instead of in a sequence, where each lesson was used as a means of designing the next lesson (as is the practice in learning studies, described in the next chapter).

What can we do to enhance the likelihood of enabling the students to see price in terms of the relationship between demand and supply if we take the current theory as our point of departure? We can assume that the learners, who are year-4 students, see differences in price, predominantly in terms of differences in attributes of the commodity in question, and make comparisons between different commodities of the same kind (huge ice-cream/small ice-cream, beautiful doll/ugly doll, pants of high quality/pants of low quality, etc.).

If we want to help the learners to learn to discern the demand aspect of price, comparison has to be made between situations in which the readiness of the potential buyers to buy the same commodity (i.e., demand) varies, as does the price. According to the theory, you discern what varies and link those aspects that vary at the same time to each other. Hence, in this case you have to vary demand and keep the commodity and also supply invariant. You cannot keep the price invariant because it is variation in price that you want to explain (and it must be discerned by the learners, otherwise the question asked does not make sense). The next step is to make it possible for the students to discern supply. In this case demand has to be kept invariant while supply varies, in addition to price. And again, the commodity should be the same in the different cases. Then it will be possible for the learners to discern supply. At last the learners have to discern how the price varies as a function of variation in both demand and supply. The necessary pattern of variation and invariance is shown in Figure 6.15.

This pattern applies in cases where the learners cannot discern demand or supply from the beginning (i.e., they do not discern, and focus on, market mechanisms).

The critical features were identified on the grounds of economic and empirical observations. The previous scheme was derived from the theory and from the results on the pre-test. But the pattern has to be implemented in a real classroom, in a form that can be grasped by the learners. It has to be embedded in some kind

commodity	**demand**	**supply**	price
i	v	i	v
i	i	v	v
i	v	v	v

FIGURE 6.15 Pattern of variation and invariance necessary for discerning the market aspects of price and the relationship between them.

of activities that the students can engage in. The way to do this, however, does not follow from the theory. The next step is left entirely to the teacher or researcher's own ingenuity. In the study discussed here the participating teachers came up with an idea of an auction in which the supply of commodities would change during the auction as would the amount of money they have to spend (purchasing power), which here stands for demand.

The students had to participate in the auction in groups of six. Each group was supposed to buy as many items as possible during the auction, and the different groups were competing with each other in each class. In the first round of the auction, each group was given a certain amount of auction money, again, a measure of purchasing power, representing demand. They were expected to make bids for four different kinds of items, available in varying numbers, representing supply. After all the items had been sold, the teacher helped the students to notice that the final prices were higher than the floor prices that the auction was started off with, and that the final prices were higher because of the keen competition. This conclusion was put to test in the next round, in which the groups received the same amount of auction money (demand, in terms of purchasing power, was invariant), while the number of items available to buy was reduced (supply varied). After having repeated the auction, the students (with the support of the teacher) could see that when demand was the same, but supply went down, the price went up. In the third round the number of items available for buying was the same as in the previous round (supply was invariant), but the groups received less auction money from the teacher than before (demand, in terms of purchasing power, went down). The students could see that in this case the price went down too.

The students were expected to notice that changes both in demand and supply affect the price of a certain item. Capitalizing on these insights, the teachers tried to help the students to discover the interaction between demand and supply and the effect of this interaction on price (what happens to the price of a certain item when both demand and supply change). This was supposed to be done through a discussion with—and between—students, of the probable price of one of the items (a mechanical dinosaur) when both demand and supply changed. Just before the teaching started, the teachers decided, however, to make the question more interesting, and instead of referring to the same mechanical dinosaur as in the previous rounds, they agreed to discuss the price of a limited edition brand new model (of dinosaur) and, by doing so, introduced variation in the commodity in question. This was the question they introduced in the fourth round:

> As you know, the dinosaur machine is now selling for $80 in toyshops. Suppose that you are the owner of a large toyshop, which is the sole supplier of the new model, which has not been publicly released and is issued as a limited version. At the same time, you observe that the Hong Kong economy has been recovering very well over this period of time. Given these conditions, what price will you set for this new model? Why?
>
> (Pang & Chik, 2005, p. 106)

After the auction, the students were asked the same question about pricing as was discussed in Chapter 4, but this time biscuit sticks were replaced by hot dogs. The distribution of the answers to the test questions was significantly different ($p < .001$) across the different ways of seeing price, listed previously, between the before and after tests. If we look at the target understanding (seeing price as a function of the relation between demand and supply) only, we find that 6.3% gave answers that indicated such an understanding before the lesson, and 25.9% did so afterwards. This is a moderate, but not negligible, difference, especially in light of the bleak results Dahlgren (1978) obtained with university students. Still, the most interesting finding in the study had to do with differences between classes. In four of the classes, the proportion of students expressing the target understanding after the lesson was 9.1%, 12.9%, 14.2% and 22.6%, while in the fifth class it was 61.5%. What happened in the fifth class that did not happen in the other classes?

First of all, we have to notice that the course of action adopted by the teachers was not entirely in accordance with the theory. It follows from the theory that first demand (or supply) should vary, while supply (or demand) is kept invariant, in order to enable the students to discern the varying aspect. Then the pattern should be reversed and demand (or supply) should remain invariant, while supply (or demand) varies, in order to enable the students to discern the other aspect. These two strategies were carried out in all the classes. The next step, according to the theory, should be to bring the two aspects (demand and supply) together and by doing so make it possible for the students to see changes in price as a function of the relationship between demand and supply. In order to achieve that, both demand and supply should vary, while the commodity in question should remain invariant. But this principle was not followed in the last step. In the question that the students and the teacher discussed at the end of the lesson, the commodity was changed. The "old" mechanical dinosaur was replaced by a "new model" in a limited edition, thereby creating variation in the commodity that was supposed to remain invariant. Hence, it was more difficult—or in many cases impossible—for the students to separate the effect of changes in the commodity and the effect of changes in demand and supply. In the high-achieving fifth class the students were actually provided with an experience that would allow them to make exactly such a separation, thanks to an unexpected event, handled by the teacher in a swift and powerful way. In the second round of the auction, purchasing power was reduced while supply was kept the same. Hence, the price was expected to fall. But one of the items that cost HK$110 during the first round was all of a sudden sold for a higher price, contrary to expectation. (This was not a very sensible decision on the part of the students who were bidding). At this point—diverting from the lesson plan—the teacher increased the supply and offered two more items of the same kind at a base price of HK$20—to depress the price—and one of the groups actually bought one item for that price. Because of the joint effect of the students running out of money (lower purchasing power) and the increase in supply, the students could observe a highly dramatic lowering of the price. It seems that the teacher's swift, intuitive adjustment to the actual course of events helped the students to develop the target understanding.

Learning About Elasticity

Judging from the previous study, learning to see price as function of the relationship between two market forces, demand and supply, seems to work pretty well, given that the necessary conditions for this are present.

In the next study we tried to enable older and more knowledgeable students to make their own of a more advanced concept in economics, and to use it as a tool for seeing certain situations in more powerful ways.

Buyers are expected to be less keen on buying when the price of something goes up and sellers are expected to be less keen on selling when the price goes down. (Not only do demand and supply affect prices, but prices also affect demand and supply). We see the latter effect most fully when demand and supply are fully "elastic" (i.e., follow changes in price). But the elasticity of commodities differs. Certain things (e.g., medicine, basic food) are essential and people are more or less forced to buy them, even if the price goes up. In such cases, demand does not follow changes in price to the same extent and the commodities in question are said to have low demand elasticity. In other cases the seller does not have any alternative outlets for a commodity, nor can it be stored (e.g., fresh fruit). It must be sold even if the price is going down. Such commodities are said to have low supply elasticity. Obviously, if the demand elasticity is low and the supply elasticity is high, sellers have greater bargaining power than buyers. If demand elasticity is high (the prospective buyers can get along without buying) and supply elasticity is low (the sellers do not have many alternatives to selling), buyers have the upper hand, in terms of bargaining power.

Now imagine that sales tax was introduced in a country for the first time (or raised in a country where it exists already). Do you think that the price of every item will go up by the percentage that the sales tax specifies? Two groups of secondary school students were supposed to become able to deal with questions like these after three lessons about supply and demand elasticity, in a study carried out by Pang (2002; Pang & Marton, 2003). One of the groups was taught by five teachers (in five different classes) who had together planned the lessons on the basis of the present theory; the other group was taught by five teachers (in five classes) also. These teachers had also planned the lessons together but without using the theory as a resource. The object of learning was the same in both groups, namely, to become able to see how the extent to which the sales tax—if introduced (or raised) in a country—would be put on the top of existing prices (and thus paid for by the buyers) or would be partially absorbed by the sellers (and thus paid for by them) depends on the relative elasticity of demand and supply. The distribution of the sales tax between buyers and sellers would in all likelihood vary starkly from one commodity to another. Of the students in the first group, 70% arrived at such an insight after the three lessons, while 30% did so in the other group. But what made the difference? Pang's (2002) conclusion was that the teaching in the two groups differed in one decisive respect. In the five classes in the first group the same commodity was used to illustrate both low and high demand and supply elasticity. It was pointed out that when people started having red wine with their meals in Hong Kong, in the 1970s, its demand elasticity was high—people could easily refrain from having wine—and its supply elasticity low—all the wine imported to Hong Kong, the only market in the region, came from France. However things have changed since then. Wine is expected with "fine dining," making demand less elastic, while wine is being shipped from all parts of the world and to many different places, making it much easier to handle excess quantities (thus making supply more elastic). Accordingly, were sales tax to have been introduced in the 1970s, the sellers would have needed to absorb a substantial part of it, while sales tax on wine, if introduced today, would mostly hit the buyers.

In the other group different commodities were used to exemplify four different cases: water—a "must" (low demand elasticity); jewels—rarely an urgent buy (high demand elasticity); agricultural products—hard to make sudden changes in what is offered (low supply elasticity); mass-produced commodities—easier to alter what is offered (high supply elasticity). In other words, they introduced the idea of elasticity in much the same—not very powerful—way that I did in the introduction of the concept of elasticity in this section.

When demand refers to one commodity and supply to another, you cannot, however, talk about *relative* elasticity; you cannot compare the demand elasticity of one commodity and the supply elasticity of another commodity. The critical feature (the relative elasticity) simply cannot be seen, unlike in the case of the first group, where differences both in demand and supply elasticity refer to the same commodity (red wine). In one case (the first group) the necessary differences in demand and supply elasticity are represented as *changes* in the *same* commodity, thus creating the necessary invariance, while in the other case (group 2) the necessary differences in demand and supply elasticity are represented as *differences* between *different* commodities, thus *not* creating the necessary invariance. Accordingly, the theory predicts the direction, if not the magnitude, of the difference in achievement under the two conditions (group 1 should do better).

The conclusion that follows is that we have managed to identify one critical difference between the conditions of learning created in the two groups. The difference relates to whether the commodity in the main example is invariant or not. This result is, of course, specific to the specific conditions dealt with and for the specific ways in which the conditions were dealt with (expressed in terms of the two different patterns of variation). At the same time, the results and the conclusions were in agreement with the theory as formulated in general terms. It was found to be of decisive importance whether or not the students were able to see (or experience) the object of learning (the relative elasticity of demand and supply). The necessary condition for this to happen is—according to the theory—that there is variation in the critical respects constituting the object of learning, against a background of invariance in other respects. The necessary variation was present in both conditions; the necessary invariance was present in one, but not in the other. The students learning with all the necessary conditions present undoubtedly learned much better than the students learning with one necessary condition present and one absent.

The Effects on Price of the Relative Magnitude of Changes in Demand and Supply

Marton and Pang (2006) carried out another study in Hong Kong, similar to the one just summarized, both as far as the content of learning and the design of the study is concerned. Again, two groups of secondary school teachers in economics participated. There was a target group of two teachers who were already familiar with variation theory and opted to use it (the "learning study group"), while three teachers in the comparison (or "lesson study") group worked together, but without the same theoretical background or input from the researcher (M. F. Pang), who again participated in the planning and discussions in both groups. All the preparation work was carried out during two meetings (per group), amounting to about 5 hours altogether in each case.

The five teachers and the researcher agreed upon the effect of simultaneous change in demand and supply on price as the content for a sequence of three lessons. The reason for this choice was that the relative magnitude of change in demand and supply is a concept as central as it is difficult in economics (Hong Kong Examination Authority, 1992, 1995). It refers to the fact that market prices may change due to supply changes, demand changes or both. When both supply and demand change in the same direction simultaneously, whether the price goes up or down depends on the relative magnitude of the change in demand and supply (i.e., on which one changes most; Marton & Pang, 2006, p. 197).

The Intended Object of Learning (Aims)

In order to find the critical features of situations for which the concept in question here is useful, a pre-test was used in which the students had to approach two problems, both involving open-ended situations. The idea was to explore qualitative differences in the students' ways of seeing the actual problem. This is how the two problems were phrased:

Question 1

Some years ago, original video compact discs (VCDs) were rather expensive, and many people turned to buying pirated VCDs. There were many shops that sold pirated VCDs. Over the past few years, the Customs and Excise

Department of the Hong Kong government has put much effort into stopping the illegal trade in pirated VCDs, and we can now find fewer shops that sell pirated VCDs. However, it is interesting to note that the price of pirated VCDs has not increased but has remained more or less the same as it was in the past. Why? Can you explain this?

Question 2

In 1997, a new bird flu virus H5N1 was found in humans in Hong Kong. A total of 18 cases were reported and 6 people died. To stop the spread of the bird flu, the government immediately killed about 1.2 million chickens in the territory. However, it was surprising to find that after this move, the price of live chickens in the market did not increase but instead fell. Why? Please explain.

Both questions were found to be dealt with by the participating students in four qualitatively different ways, namely in terms of

 A. Changes in demand,
 B. Changes in supply,
 C. Changes in demand and in supply, without relating the two to each other,
 D. The relative magnitude of the changes in supply and demand.
 (Marton & Pang, 2006, p. 204)

The first category refers to the discernment of the extent of change in demand, the second to the discernment of the extent of change in supply, the third to the discernment of both and the fourth to the discernment of the relation between A and B. This last category corresponds to the intended object of learning as exemplified by an answer to Question 1:

Customs and Excise has tried to stop the illegal trade in pirated VCDs, and there are now fewer shops that sell pirated VCDs. Therefore, we can see that the supply of pirated VCDs decreased. However, people's willingness to buy pirated VCDs also decreased because they were afraid of being arrested. It was true that there was still the willingness to buy' pirated VCDs, but it was decreasing. We thus see the demand also decreased. In this case, we have to look at how much the demand and supply decreased. The level of decrease of the demand and supply were almost the same, and therefore the price did not change much. (Class 2, Student 15).
(Marton & Pang, 2006, p. 205)

The critical difference between the last category and the previous one has to do with the rate of change: "demand increases more (less) than supply . . . demand

and supply decrease (increase) at the same rate . . .". The magnitudes of changes are compared.

The Lived Object of Learning (Results)

In this study also there was a pronounced difference found between the two groups (learning study and lesson study), after the sequence of three lessons, even more pronounced, in fact, than in the previous study (see Table 6.5).

TABLE 6.5 Distribution of the ways of understanding the object of learning, as expressed in the written task in the post-test (Marton & Pang, 2006, p. 209).

Conception	Target Group[a]		Comparison Group[b]	
	Occurrence	%	Occurrence	%
A	0	0.0	0	0.0
B	2	2.6	13	14.1
C	0	0.0	1	1.1
D	6	7.8	52	56.5
E	69	89.6	26	28.3

Note. $\chi^2 (3, N = 169) = 64.197, p < .001$.
[a]$n = 77$. [b]$n = 92$.

The Enacted Object of Learning (Teaching)

When trying to account for the differences in results, a critical difference, which had to do with using the same commodity or not across different cases, was found between the two groups.

In both groups, the target concept was introduced through discussion in intuitive terms of some relevant everyday situations. The introduction was followed in all classes by the formal treatment of the concepts and principles, in terms of economics. The major difference appeared in the first part of the lessons, in the informal introduction. The learning study group, acting in accordance with variation theory, varied demand for, and supply of, one commodity. They chose a graph depicting changes in the price of face masks during the SARS epidemic (see Figure 6.16). It illustrated dramatic changes in price due to dramatic changes in demand and supply, from a moderate increase, to an accelerated increase, to a moderate decrease, to an accelerated decrease. Against a background of invariance in the commodity, the teachers could make the differences in the relative magnitude of change in demand and supply visible to the students, by inviting them to inspect strategically chosen instances (parts of the curve), in the light of authentic clips from Hong Kong newspapers, commenting on the face-mask market in Hong Kong, at different points in time, with the graph in Figure 6.16 illustrating

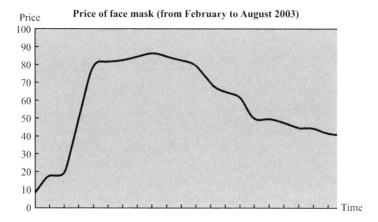

FIGURE 6.16 Fluctuations in the price of face-masks during the SARS epidemic in Hong Kong (adapted from Pang & Marton, 2013).

the fluctuations in the price of face-masks over the same period of time. One aspect varied at a time and the aspects were subsequently brought together, by varying them simultaneously.

In the lesson study group, two different commodities were used: slimming services and bus services. The former was used to illustrate the effect on price of relative increase in demand and supply; the latter was used to illustrate the effect on price of relative decrease in demand and supply. In this way, increase was linked to one commodity, decrease was linked to another. Hence the target concept "relative magnitude of change in demand and supply" could not be separated and hence was not visible to the students. And as changes in the opposite direction (higher demand—lower supply, lower demand—higher supply) were related to different commodities, they could not possibly be illustrated through the examples.

But there was another difference between the two sets of conditions, which probably contributed to the differences in the results. Understanding relative magnitude (that one thing changes more or less than another thing) assumes an understanding of absolute magnitude (i.e., change in how much one thing changes). While the students in the learning study encountered examples of changes in absolute magnitude, the students in the lesson study condition did not come across any examples of that kind.

The choice of the examples was thus of decisive importance. The theory outlined in this book does not suggest which particular examples should be used, but what follows from the theory is the pattern of variation and invariance that has to be created by means of the examples. The conclusion can be drawn that relatively subtle differences in how the content of learning is dealt with, in the sense of the choice and combination of instances (examples) contributed to dramatic differences in learning in this case. The results varied between classes of equally good students taught by equally well-qualified teachers, with 2 of 33 students making the object of learning their own in one class, and only 1 of 39 students in another class failing to do so.

Bringing Learning About: Implementing Patterns of Variation and Invariance

Variation in a certain dimension is a necessary condition for the discernment of the corresponding aspect of the object of learning. But it is certainly not a sufficient condition, as has been pointed out repeatedly. The learner's *experience* of variation is a necessary and sufficient condition. Or even: discernment *means* experience of difference (variation). What the teacher has to do is not only to ensure that the necessary conditions are present, but she also has to try to make it as likely as possible that the necessary conditions are turned into sufficient conditions. It has been found in many studies that the presence of variation, even if it is not confused by variation in other dimensions, does not necessarily imply that the variation is noticed, or experienced. Of course, our common sense, what we know about the world as human beings, would suggest this to be the case. Let us consider an example.

Enhancing the Contrast: Discerning the Elegance of Movements in Cantonese Opera

Cantonese opera is a particular form of entertainment. If you want your young students in Hong Kong, the home of Cantonese opera, to become aware of their own tradition and if you then want, for instance, to enable them to discern and appreciate the elegance of the actors' movements, how would you go about it (Lo, 2012, pp. 120–126)? If you tried to use induction as your pedagogical point of departure, as described in Chapter 3, you would point to different examples of actors moving elegantly and declare that they are examples of the elegance of movements. So you would point to different movements that all have elegance in common. Is it possible that this would work? Hardly. The movements are rather specific (they differ from each other, of course) and they are performed with great elegance in every case. Hence, elegance cannot be separated from the movements (as they go together all the time) and cannot be seen by those who have never seen it before. The children can see certain kinds of movement as separate from movement in general because they differ from other kinds of movement, but they cannot see the elegance of the movements because they have never seen the same movements lacking elegance. Hence, in order to separate the movements and one of their most important attributes (their elegance), the children have to watch the same movements being performed with various degrees of elegance, at the very least through a contrast between elegance and less elegance (or greater clumsiness). In a learning study, the object of learning was to appreciate (notice, discern) the elegance of movements in Cantonese opera. In three lessons, in three consecutive cycles, three groups of students watched a video with a sequence in which four actors enter an imaginary boat, row from one imaginary strand to the other and leave the boat there. Inspired by variation theory, at least four students in each class were asked to make the same performance, in order to provide their classmates with a contrast to the artists' ways of carrying out the same movements, as far as the elegance of movement was concerned. The teacher pointed out the elegance of movement as a characteristic feature of Cantonese opera. We can say that the relevant pattern of variation and invariance (the necessary conditions) was the same in all three cases. But the results differed strikingly: while none of the students discerned elegance as a feature of the artists' performance after the first lesson, 2/3 of the students did so after the second lesson and 4/5 in the third lesson. The three lessons took place in three different classes.

Why did we find such differences when the pattern of variation and invariance did not differ, as seen from the viewpoint of an observer? In the first case the students' and the artists' performances were separated in time and the teacher did not ask the students to compare the two. Instead, the students were divided into three groups, and four students from each group had to perform and the whole class was invited to compare the three performances. Only after that did the teacher show the video with the professional artists, and no comparison was made between the artists' and the students' performances. In the second case the class was asked to compare the performance of a group of students with the performance of the artists in some specified respects. In the third case the lesson was basically the same as in the second case, except that the students were also asked to grade the comparisons.

In all three cases the necessary variation in the elegance of movement was present. But only in the second and the third case did the students make the necessary comparisons between the actors' and their own ways of performing the same movements. In the first case the students' attention was directed to comparisons between their own performances. Although there was, in all likelihood, variation in elegance in that case too, it was not striking enough to be noticed and related to the actors' ways of performing. In order to create a contrast, it is better to start with larger differences before dealing with smaller ones. This is the basic principle advocated by Itard (1801/1962) and Séguin (1866/1977), and also adopted by Maria Montessori, as mentioned in Chapter 3. As a matter of fact, there were differences in elegance even between the actors, but the students could hardly discern those all-too-subtle nuances.

The lesson to be learned from this example is that there are certain necessary conditions that must be present in order to enable the learners to appropriate the object of learning (in this case, in order to be able to discern the elegance of movements there must be variation in the elegance of movements, while the movements themselves should be the same—as seen from the observer's perspective). But in addition there must be conditions that make it likely that the learners do experience the variation. The teacher has to organize the activities in such a way that the experience of variation will be a necessary condition for the students to solve the given task. In terms of the present theory of learning, the implication is that the pattern of variation and invariance cannot remain a feature of the environment only but must be built into the structure of activities.

"The Rate of Chemical Reactions": An Example of Differences in Learning Activities

This line of reasoning indicates that "activities" and "content" have to be brought together, just as in the following study by Lo (2012, pp. 110–113). The topic of the learning study, made up of two cycles only, was "the rate of chemical reactions." The teachers participating had found that many of their (year 10) students erroneously assumed that the initial rate of a chemical reaction is a function of the *volume* of the reactant (instead of realizing that it is a function of the *concentration* of the reactant). The object of learning was to see the rate of a chemical reaction as a function of the concentration of the reactant and independent of its volume.

The experiment employed in the study was the reaction of calcium carbonate with an acid. The idea was to bring out the following two patterns:

1) when the mass of calcium carbonate and the concentration of the acid (the reactant) are invariant, and the volume of the acid varies, the rate of the chemical reaction remains invariant;
2) when the mass of calcium carbonate and the volume of the acid are invariant, and the concentration of the acid varies, the rate of the chemical reaction varies (see Table 6.6).

The class was divided into six groups (A–F). Groups A, B and C had to carry out the same experiment with the same mass of calcium carbonate and the same

TABLE 6.6 Combinations of the six groups of students in the experiment (adapted from Lo, 2012, p. 111).

Group	Mass of $CaCO_3$ (Invariant)	Concentration of acid (Invariant)	Volume of acid (Varied)
1	1 g	0.5 M	5 cm^3
2	1 g	0.5 M	10 cm^3
3	1 g	0.5 M	15 cm^3
Group	Mass of $CaCO_3$ (Invariant)	Concentration of acid (Varied)	Volume of acid (Invariant)
4	1 g	0.5 M	5 cm^3
5	1 g	1 M	5 cm^3
6	1 g	1.5 M	5 cm^3

concentration but different volumes of the acid; the second part of the experiment was carried out by groups D, E and F with the same mass of calcium carbonate and different concentrations but the same volume of the acid. Each group had to plot the rate curve for their own data on a separate transparency. When the whole class got together again, the transparencies were overlaid and the teacher pointed out that the initial rate of the chemical reaction was the same in all three cases (A, B, C) in spite of differences in the volume of the reactant, and was different in the other three cases (D, E, F) when the concentration differed.

Here I want to quote Lo's (2012) description of this first lesson:

> The teacher of the first cycle followed the lesson plan very closely. He was an experienced teacher with a good knowledge of chemistry, and explained the concepts very clearly to the students. The debrief was carried out to help the students to draw a generalization, and the answer was not provided by direct transmission. The lesson had been designed with the best practice of science teaching in mind, in that students were given the opportunity to undertake experiments using an inquiry approach.
>
> (p. 10)

The conditions that were necessary for learning to occur, according to variation theory, were present, and the lesson looked good from the point of view of contemporary ideas of what good lessons look like. Nonetheless, when the results on the pre- and post-tests were compared, it could be concluded to everyone's great surprise, that basically *no learning had taken place* as far as the stated object of learning is concerned. So how could this happen? What the students were supposed to experience simultaneously was on the one hand variation in the volume of the reactant and invariance in the initial rate of the reaction and on the other hand variation in the concentration of the reactant and variation in the initial rate of reaction. But during the largest and most intense part of the lesson, while the students were working in their own group, *both the volume and the concentration of the reactant were invariant in their own part of the experiment, and so was the initial rate of reaction* , of course. It was only when data from the groups were pooled that the teacher tried to draw the students' attention to the variation in volume and invariance in the initial rate of reaction, and the variation in concentration and rate of initial reaction. In the second cycle of the learning study, the design of the lesson was changed in such a way that the students were asked from the beginning to find out the relationship between the volume of the reactant and the initial rate of reaction on the one hand and between the concentration of the reactant and the initial rate of reaction on the other hand. They still had to carry out the same steps as the students in the other class did (i.e., plotting the rate of reaction against time), but having done that, they had to find out what comparisons they had to make with data produced by the other groups in order to answer the two main questions of the lesson. This seemingly rather minor change yielded a major change in how they answered the question used in the first cycle. After the lesson in the second cycle, about 80% of the students answered in a way that indicated that they could see the independence of the initial rate of reaction from the volume of the reactant and its dependence on the concentration of the reactant.

The necessary conditions for learning to occur were present in both lessons, but the structure of the students' activities in the second lesson made it more likely that the students would experience the pattern of variation and invariance necessary for appropriating the object of learning.

The Complexity of Learning and the Inventiveness of Teaching

Consider the fact that learning can be the learning of anything. Whatever exists can be learned or be learned about. So everything can be the content of learning. If we pay close attention to the content of learning, to what is to be learned, as is suggested strongly in this book, we potentially face all the complexity there is in the world. This follows from adopting the current perspective on learning, a perspective in which the different ways in which people learn to see all the different things in the world becomes visible. This is related to how people see what they see, or what they see when they see. It is also related to specific aspects of learning, as was pointed out earlier in this book. But it was also pointed out that there are general aspects of learning. They are not less important than the specific aspects; it is only that the particular theory in this book is not about the general aspects but about the specific aspects (i.e., those related to the content of learning). Most other theories of learning are about the general aspects. This one is not, except when learning is learning to learn (i.e., when learning is its own object, so to speak).

Theories of learning focus, as a rule, on different aspects of learning (behavioral, cognitive, social, neurological, etc.). Although the different theories frequently contradict each other, they are mostly correct, at least as far as the object of research on which they are based is concerned. Problems arise, however, when they are over-generalized. It is true, for instance, that humans, as well as other animals, more frequently do what they have been rewarded for in the past than what they have been punished for, but it is not true that the learning of the mother tongue can be sufficiently explained in those terms (see, for instance, Skinner's 1957 attempt to make such a generalization and Chomsky's 1959 rebuttal). It is true that people master tasks that they find interesting with greater ease than tasks that they do not find interesting, but it is not true that finding a task interesting is a sufficient condition for learning how to master it.

All theories of learning are partial, and so is the present theory. It is about the phenomenal aspects of learning, about how our ways of seeing various aspects of various phenomena change as a result of learning; it is about learning as a change in our way of seeing the world or simply a change in what the world looks like to us. I certainly believe that the present theory focuses on things that are important in many cases, but you cannot plan or carry out a lesson solely based on it.

Pedagogy as a practice is immensely complex and you have to rely on many different sources of insight.

From this it follows that creating a pattern of variation and invariance in line with the principles of variation theory may not in itself be enough to bring about learning. We might not even be able to create a particular pattern of variation. Lo's (2012; see also Lo, Hung & Chik, 2007) study of how an understanding of the electrochemical series can be developed is an excellent example of the need for sheer inventiveness in realizing a particular pattern of variation that is necessary—or favorable—for learning, according to the theory.

This example demonstrates that even if we can use the theory for explaining why a particular pattern of variation works or not, we may still not know how it can be brought about, without the kind of sudden revelation that the teacher (in this case also the author, Lo Mun Ling) experienced.

Electrochemical Series

If two metals are connected in an electrochemical cell, electrons flow from the metal with higher electro-potential to the metal with lower electro-potential. We can then measure the relative electro-potential of the two metals (in voltage). Any metal can be chosen as a reference and be compared with all other metals. The metals can then be ordered in terms of these measurements, to form an electrochemical series. We can choose another metal as reference and obtain another set of measurements, which can again be ordered to form the *same* electrochemical series. The sets of measurements vary when we choose different references, but the relationships between the metals in the series are invariant. This is the pattern of variation and invariance that Lo hoped that the students would experience. In Figure 6.17 we

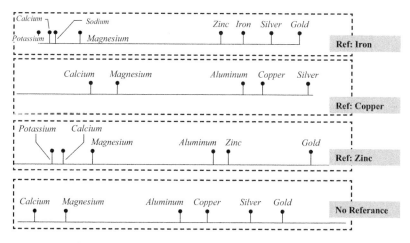

FIGURE 6.17 Electrochemical series of some metals with silver, copper and iron as references (adapted from Lo, 2012, p. 139).

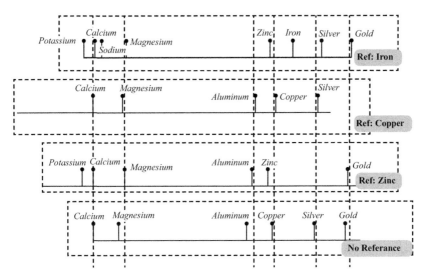

FIGURE 6.18 Student-constructed line graphs using different reference electrodes, lined up with reference to one metal (calcium; Lo, 2012, p. 139).

can see the electrochemical series of some metals using silver, copper and iron as references. The metals are ordered in terms of the relative electro-potentials and the reference metals are put back into the series. Now it is easy to see that the ordering is invariant, but not that the differences between the electro-potentials of metals are also invariant. In order to make it visible, we have to change the way the information is represented. Lo asked the students to represent the measurements in the form of graphs on transparencies as shown in Figure 6.18. The next move is to adjust the transparencies with reference to one metal and then we find that the markings for the same metal are aligned within measurement error for different reference metals.

By adjusting the graphs in relation to each other, the differences originating from using different reference metals disappeared and the invariance of the different relations between metals in the electrochemical series was made visible.

Condensation

Let us consider another example. Even if the theory implies that certain patterns of variation and invariance are necessary for learning it does not indicate how they can be brought about. In this study, described by Lo (2012), the object of learning was condensation: how water turns from gaseous to liquid form when cooled down. In the lesson the teacher compared two cola cans, one standing on a table at room temperature and the other being cold, just having been taken out of the fridge. The students could see how water droplets soon appeared on the cold can but not on the one that was not cold.

The teacher's idea was that the students would see that the droplets had to do with temperature

COLD → WATER DROPLETS
NOT COLD → NO WATER DROPLETS

A discussion followed and the students had problems with deciding where the water came from. Some of them thought that the can from the fridge was leaking somehow and that the drops actually came from inside the can. The teacher responded quickly and emptied the can, dried it and compared it with another cold but full can. Drops appeared on both. The teacher's idea was to demonstrate that the drops did not come from the inside of the can.

COLD (EMPTY) → WATER DROPLETS
COLD (FULL) → WATER DROPLETS

By the end of this first lesson, the students had realized that the droplets did not come from inside the can, but they still could not see that they actually came from the air.

A new move was prepared for the next lesson. This time the teacher took out a cold (full) can from the fridge, wiped the water droplets from its surface, wrapped the can in a layer of tissue, followed by a layer of plastic wrap and then another layer of tissue.

Soon the outmost layer became wet, while the innermost layer (not being in contact with air) remained dry. This outcome was then used as a point of departure for discussing that the droplets must have come from the air. The teacher's idea was obviously

CONTACT WITH AIR → WET
NO CONTACT WITH AIR → DRY

Although the children may not have been entirely convinced that there really is water in the air, the study is a good example of the fact that teachers have to go outside the theory in order to make use of it.

Bringing About Learning: The Order of Things

In Chapter 3 it was argued that learning to see certain things in certain ways proceeds from seeing undivided wholes, to delimiting particular entities, their parts and the relations between the parts, to discerning various features of the entities delimited and subsequently making a whole of the parts and of the features through fusion. We can rarely identify the beginning or the end of this learning process: the differentiation (delimiting and discerning) and the integration (fusion) goes on all the time. But the typical trajectory of learning goes from the undivided whole through separation and fusion towards a new differentiated and integrated whole, just as Heinz Werner says. He calls this principle "the orthogenetic law of development" (Werner, 1948).

In order to delimit, discern or separate, there must be something to delimit, discern or separate *from*. Accordingly, when trying to help others to learn, we should not start with the abstract principle or the solution method but with the entity, the case, the problem—certain aspects or parts of which are highlighted by the principle or by the method of solution. Another way of saying the same thing is to assert that the case, the problem on the one hand and the concept, principle or the solution method in their canonical formulations on the other hand are two different ways of accounting for the same thing, and that the difference between them matters as far as the meaning of the learning task is concerned. Furthermore, the difference is not symmetrical: the solution method being followed by the problem creates a "different difference" from the difference created when the problem is followed by the solution method. Frequently, the teacher starts by talking about the theory, the principles, the concepts and the methods in their canonical form, and these are subsequently applied to concrete cases. To oversimplify things a bit, the alternative way of trying to help others to learn is to let them find the concepts, principles and methods by themselves. Such an approach is frequently called "learning by discovery," or something similar. The two alternatives have been compared again and again with highly varying results (see, for instance, Hattie, 2009, pp. 208–210). These comparisons are comparisons between different ways of organizing learning (i.e., comparisons whose results were declared inevitably inconclusive in Chapter 2). They are inevitably inconclusive because they are comparing two things that are both needed for successful learning. As argued a few lines earlier, the learner must deal with the undivided whole to begin with in order to be able to discern critical parts and critical features. The learner thus has to explore the phenomenon, tinker with it and raise and address questions about it. On the other hand the learners can hardly be expected to find out the canonical formulations and methods by themselves all the time: they must be told. So comparing direct teaching (telling the learners) and learning by discovery (letting the learners find out on their own) is hardly the most useful thing to do.

Being Told and Then Finding Out, or the Other Way Around?

The present line of reasoning is contrary to the received wisdom that first you learn the parts and thereafter you put them together to make the whole. It is also contrary to the received wisdom that the general concept or principle is the whole and that the instances are the parts. According to the view advocated here, each instance, each case is a whole from which aspects, features of a general nature or various parts with features of general nature, are discerned. Let us illustrate this line of reasoning by means of a study carried out many years ago by Székely (1950).

In this study, a puzzling phenomenon (problem A) was presented to one group of participants who were offered a text to read afterwards, explaining what they had just experienced. Another group of participants were asked to read the same text, as they would have done for an exam, and afterwards the puzzling phenomenon was presented to them as an illustration of what was said in the text. After a week, to the participants' surprise, the researcher (Székely) contacted them again and asked them to try to solve another, related problem (problem B), embodying the same physical principle as problem A. The study shows that whether the participants encountered problem A first and read the text afterwards, or read the text first and encountered problem A afterwards, significantly affected the likelihood of solving problem B a week later.

The puzzling phenomenon, here called "problem A," is illustrated in Figure 6.19, which shows a so-called torsion pendulum, which was put in front of each participant individually in the experiment, wound up, and then allowed to unwind with the two weights hanging on the inner hooks. Then the experimenter asked the participants what would happen if the pendulum were wound up again, the two weights were moved to the outer hooks and the pendulum was allowed to unwind again. Some participants said that it would rotate at the same speed as before, others said that it would move faster. The experimenter then demonstrated that the pendulum rotated more slowly with the weights on the outer hooks.

In the text, concepts such as work, angular momentum and moment of inertia, were elaborated and the reader could understand that in the experiment, by moving the weights from the inner to the outer hooks, the mass of the pendulum is re-distributed from center to periphery. The moment of inertia, working counter to the rotation, is thus increased and speed is reduced.

A few days later, when the participants were contacted again, they were asked about the following problem, with the same conditions being used for everyone. Each participant was presented with two metal balls, looking exactly the same and weighing exactly the same. They were told, however, that one of the balls was

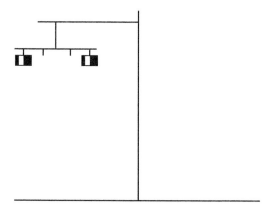

FIGURE 6.19 Torsion pendulum (adapted from Székely, 1955, p. 391).

made of a heavy metal, the other of a light metal. How could they possibly decide which ball was of one kind and which was of the other? Most of the participants figured out that the ball made of heavy metal must be hollow, while the ball of light metal was probably solid. If they did not find this out by themselves, they were told. The problem could be solved by comparing the rotation of the two balls on an inclined plane or on a horizontal surface, or on a combination of both. With the same force bringing them into motion, the solid ball would rotate faster and roll a longer distance, because of the difference in how the mass of the ball was distributed between center and periphery. The moment of inertia, slowing down the movement of the ball, would be greater in the hollow ball, in accordance with the same principle that was in effect in the problem of the torsion pendulum. In Table 6.7 we can see that participants exposed to "problem first" when dealing with the torsion pendulum handled the metal balls problem with greater ease than the "text first" group. Interestingly, most of the successful students were unaware of how they had solved the second problem, and why they were capable of solving it. At the same time they were confident in their solutions.

How should we interpret these results? Participants in the problem-first group were more likely than participants in the text-first group to read the text in order to find a solution to a problem, while participants in the text-first group were more likely than participants in the problem-first group to read the text to remember it. The former way of reading is more likely to generate understanding and hence increases the likelihood of solving a novel problem that can be solved by means of the concepts and principles in the text. This means that the relevance structure of the text differs when it is read in order to understand a problem one has just encountered, as compared to when the text is read in order to be able to recall it (Marton & Booth, 1997, pp. 143–144). Certain things appear relevant in relation to the problem and are thus highlighted, while others recede into the background as the text is read. Those who face problem A first can read the text from the perspective of the problem (in the sense of learning in relation to—or from the perspective of—the object of learning) and discern the critical aspects of the problem retrospectively. To the extent that they do this, they can also see problem B in terms of the same critical aspects. Those who read the text to begin

TABLE 6.7 Frequencies of students solving/not solving the delayed task (adapted from Székely, 1950, p. 394).

	Solved the task	Did not solve the task	
Problem → text	13	7	20
Text → problem	4	16	20
	17	23	

with, read the text without a useful perspective on its content. In consequence, they cannot discern any critical aspects, because there is nothing for which any aspects could be critical. Hence it is more likely that those who start with problem A (and not with reading the text) will solve problem B.

Learning by Trying to Find Out, and Learning by Being Told

In Székely's study, the two different ways of helping the learners ("letting them try to find out" and "telling them") were not compared, but combined (in two different sequences) and it was the two combinations that were compared. Many years later, Bransford and Schwartz (1999), also recognizing the insufficiency of comparing "being told" and "finding out," designed a study of the effects of these two approaches on future learning, rather than on direct outcomes. They could demonstrate that after having tried to solve a problem, students learn much more easily from being told how to solve it than they would in the case where the same total amount of time is used for telling them how to solve it. Schwartz and Martin's (2004) study is a good example of this research paradigm.

The object of learning was to become able to compare scores given in two different scales; for instance, "Which of two students, with a score of X and Y, respectively, who were in different biology classes and took different tests, did better on their respective tests?" Two randomly selected groups of students participated in the experiment. Those in group A, in the "finding out" condition, were asked to try to solve the following problem: "Who broke the world record by the most impressive amount, John in the high jump or Mike in the javelin throw?" (The raw data for the distribution of the best results during the year in the two sports were presented.) The students in group B, in the "being told" condition, were shown a graphical method for standardizing scores by using histograms and a method for comparing the derived standardized scores, which they practiced under the supervision of the teacher. The students in group A thus had to try to solve a problem that was an instance of the object of learning, while the students in group B were shown a method for solving that kind of problem. After these two parallel sessions, lasting equally long, both groups participated in the same "being told" session and worked on the same examples in the same way. In these examples, which were intended to be a learning resource for dealing with the target problem, the students were instructed in how to compute and compare standardized scores (for example, "Is Betty better at assists or steals?"). The raw scores are converted to the same scale by subtracting the mean and dividing by the standard deviation for the scale in which the raw score is given:

> Say that x is the result on one test, with mean m_x and standard deviation s_x, and y is the result on another test, with mean m_y and standard deviation s_y. While x and y are not directly comparable, the standardized scores $z_x = (x - m_x)/s_x$ and $z_y = (y - m_y)/s_y$ are.

Finally, the students were given the aforementioned target problem (comparing the scores of two students in two biology tests). Means and standard deviations for the two tests were given, together with the raw scores for the two students. Over 60% of the participants in group A solved the problem correctly, fewer than 30% did so in group B.

Why would group A fare so much better? The first "being told" session for group B meant just comparing two figures produced by the procedure specified as an algorithm by the task. The students did not have to find out what to compare and what attributes of the two biology tests they had to take into account. But the "finding out" group had to do exactly that: they had to compare the distributions over the best results in both high jump and javelin throw. For someone who is statistically literate, it is obvious that it is necessary to look at central tendency and to look at spread, because these are the two dimensions in which the two distributions differ. If the learner has not developed the idea of relative scale (as opposed to "absolute") previously, she has to do so in order to grasp the problem. She has to realize that she can compare the relation of a raw score to other raw scores in one scale, with the relation of a raw score to other raw scores in another scale. In other words, you cannot compare raw scores directly, but you can compare the *relationships* between raw scores in different scales. In order to do that you have to compare the two sets of raw scores and find out how they differ from each other. The learner must first be able to discern one kind of difference: whether the scores are higher or lower in one set as compared to the other (i.e., comparing some central measure). Second, she has to be able to discern another difference: even if the scores are on average similar (or identical), they may still be more or less spread out (one has to compare some measure of variation in scores).

This is the answer that the "finding out" group were more likely to come up with than the "being told" group. In the parlance of variation theory, the necessary features to be discerned were central tendency and spread (or variation). There could be different measures of both, but in the context referred to, mean and standard deviation are used for producing normalized scores. This is a convention, a historical fact. Even if someone could arrive at the idea of central tendency and variation on their own, they could not possibly know what measures are generally accepted and used for transforming scales to standardized measures. The learners must be told this.

If the students are expected to learn to discern the critical features and solve a certain kind of problem, it seems better to have a go at the problem before being told the answer, instead of being told right away. "Trying to find out" is a better preparation for being told than "being told." The combination of two ways of learning is more powerful than either of them.

Productive Failure

Kapur (2008, 2010, 2012) has recently carried out a series of studies, resembling the Bransford–Schwartz "preparing for future learning" paradigm, but with the main focus on the fact that it can be highly meaningful to invite students to try to solve problems that they have not learned to solve, because even failed attempts to find out things might have positive effects on learning. Let us consider one of these studies by Kapur (2012). In this study, year-9 students were expected to learn the meaning of variability and to be able to compute variance in data sets as a measure of variability. Two groups of students worked under different conditions, but for the same amount of time. Under the "being told" condition, the teacher explained the concept of variance and showed how to compute it in a data set. Subsequently, the student kept practicing on various problems and they received feedback from the teacher. Under the "finding out" condition, the students were asked to compare three data sets showing the number of goals produced by three strikers in the premier league over 20 years. The students had to come up with a formula for calculating the consistency of each player (i.e., the variability of the three distributions). Of the total time allocated for learning, they spent half of it in this way and the second half was spent in the same way as the whole time was spent by the other group (i.e., they listened to the teacher's explanation and kept practicing on various tasks involving computing the variance [s^2] of different data sets; though, of course, they spent only half as much time on this as the other group did). Kapur distinguished between different outcomes. Both groups did equally well on items measuring "procedural fluency" (i.e., in computing the variance). On items measuring data analysis, conceptual insight and transfer, the "finding out" group did better than the "being told" group.

What Makes Learning Better?

The results arrived at by Székely (1950), Bransford and Schwartz (1999), Schwartz and Bransford (1998), and Kapur (2008, 2010, 2012) show that trying to find out (followed by being told) results in better learning than either of these experiences alone, or both in the reverse order.

But what is it that makes learning better? Earlier in this chapter, it was suggested that dealing with a problem before being presented with a method of solution, creates a relevance structure for learning and a perspective from which the principle to be appropriated might be seen. In addition to this, Schwartz and Martin (2004, pp. 134–136) argued that the "finding out" condition is conducive to the discernment of the critical features of the situation—an explanation that is in agreement with the argument presented in this book. But why is that condition conducive to discernment? Their line of reasoning—as well as that of the present book—implies that it has to do with the pattern of variation and invariance in that condition: it is reasonable to assume that contrastive cases play a key role there. By comparing two distributions, or concrete cases in general, we are asking the question: in what important respects do they differ? In other words, we have to find the critical dimensions of variation. The idea of variability (the dimension of variation), for instance, is probably grasped by becoming aware of differences between values in that dimension. Furthermore another dimension of variation, that of the method for measuring variability is opened up, when the learners' own attempts to find such a measure are contrasted with the canonical solution. Two (critical) dimensions are thus opened up, simultaneously with the learners becoming aware of differences in those dimensions, in accordance with what was said in Chapter 3.

The conditions compared in the studies just mentioned, I called "finding out" (by the learners) and "being told" (by the teacher). But what the learner must carry out herself is the act of discernment. She must learn to make distinctions, to experience differences. And nobody can experience difference for someone else.

The Path of Learning

Ki, Ahlberg and Marton's (2006) comparison of learning Cantonese words, by encountering simultaneous variation in both tones and segments—compared with encountering variation first in tones, then in segments, and then simultaneously in both dimensions, as referred to in Chapter 3—suggests a preferred sequence in learning, starting with the undivided whole, separating those of its aspects that are critical for the completion of the learning task and then bringing all them together again into the regained whole. This means that the learner goes from one experienced whole to another experienced whole by first separating and then integrating the different aspects of the whole. The two wholes are, however, different. The first one is undivided; the learner cannot possibly discern its various aspects. The second whole is a whole as well, but as its critical aspects have been separated, the learner can discern them and adjust to variation in any of those. For instance, a child who has learned to hit a target from a certain distance, with a ball of a certain weight, has learned the act of throwing as an undivided whole, as far as distance and weight are concerned. She cannot discern those aspects and hence cannot adjust to changes in them by taking the differences into consideration. If she can separate them, however, she should be able to adjust to any combination of values in those two dimensions of variation.

The learning cycle should thus start with the learners' encounter with the undivided whole. This is how they encounter things and events in daily life. To begin with, there are things, in which aspects like mass, volume and density, for instance, are not separated. The learners thus cannot possibly sort out why things float or sink (see, for instance, Pramling & Pramling Samuelsson, 2001). By enabling them to discern and separate the various aspects, by letting them vary one at a time, they will become capable of solving the problem. They might be able to deal with a specific problem and, by dealing with cases varying in different respects, they can become able to deal with novel problems that have to do with sinking and floating. The preferred sequence of variation and invariance that this line of reasoning suggests—as was stated in Chapter 3—is:

INSTANTIATION → CONTRAST → GENERALIZATION → FUSION

where "instantiation" stands for the learners' initial encounter with the object of learning, in the form of a problem that captures holistic qualities of it, such as, for instance, the specific problems the learner initially encountered in studies by Székely, Schwartz and Martin, Kumar, and so on. In order to discern critical aspects, the learner must engage with the whole from which the aspects have to be discerned (i.e., the object of learning).

Contrast and generalization may imply several loops, one for each dimension of variation, and fusion at the end of the sequence refers to the learners' handling of instances that vary in all of the dimensions opened up through contrast and generalization.

Hierarchical and Sequential Structure in Reading and Writing
Two Ways of Teaching Words

Earlier in this chapter, Chik et al.'s (2010, see also Chik, 2006) comparison of how two teachers taught seven Chinese words was summarized. Two critical differences between what happened in the two classrooms were identified: 1) The aspects of words were grouped in terms of words (the words being super-ordinate to aspects) in one class (A), while words were grouped together in terms of aspects (aspects being super-ordinate to words) in the other class (B); 2) the text used for teaching the seven words was structured hierarchically in class A and sequentially in class B. It is primarily the second difference that is relevant here.

In teacher A's way of dealing with the text, its theme, "being polite," was present all the time, and for every paragraph the text as a whole was present, and for every sentence the paragraph to which it belongs was present, and for every word the sentence in which it appears was present. This means that every word was present on different levels simultaneously: as a word as such, as a part of a sentence, a part of a paragraph, a part of the whole text. In class B the whole text was dealt with to begin with, then left aside, followed by one aspect at a time, without linking them to each other as aspects of the same words.

Clearly, not only was the fusion of aspects more enhanced in class A, but also the words obtained richer meanings by being there simultaneously on different levels.

But how could this happen? An entity (a text, for instance) appears through features; the whole consists of parts. Words follow words in a linear succession in written as well as in spoken language. In the previous chapter an example of two different ways of reading the same text was presented (from Säljö, 1982). In one case, the reader did not see any whole: one thing appeared after another, all on the same level. We can call this a sequential reading of the text. In the other case, which was much more successful, the text was read on two (or more) levels, as it were. There was an ever-present and ever-changing whole, and there were the different parts. But both the whole and the parts appeared through the same words.

Hence every word was read both as itself, so to speak, and as a part of a greater whole (or of several greater and greater wholes). We can call this a hierarchical reading of the text. We could also say that in the hierarchical reading of the text, an additional dimension of variation was discerned by the readers, corresponding to structural differences between different levels of the text. This difference was found between the ways in which the readers read the same text. But—as we see in Chik et al.'s (2010) study—similar kinds of differences can be found between the ways in which the same text is taught by different teachers.

This means that while students may adopt one or the other way of reading and structuring a text that they are studying, and accordingly learn differently from the same text, teachers may adopt one way or another to teach their students, producing differential effects of the same kind that we find among students who spontaneously handle their task in different ways.

Two Ways of Boosting Creativity in Writing

Cheung (2005; see also Cheung, Marton & Tse, 2010) carried out a study in which the object of learning was a so-called generic attribute, namely, the creative aspect of Chinese writing, measured in terms of the variability of written compositions and of the students' ways of behaving in the classroom. Eight year-3 classes participated, divided into a target group and a comparison group. In the target group the four teachers carried out four learning studies (see Chapter 7) of a modified form during a school year, while in the comparison group the topic of each learning study was dealt with according to four lesson plans developed by one teacher but taught by all four teachers. As an important part of the learning study, the teachers in the target group used variation theory as a conceptual tool in their teaching. This did not happen in the comparison group. Each learning study (and the corresponding lessons in the comparison group) was supposed to contribute to the advancement of the object of learning. In the four learning studies, it was intended that this would take place by increasing the students' awareness of causal sequences in real-life stories (what leads to what), by enhancing their ability to find solutions to problems in imaginary tales, by increasing their skill at ordering events in a relatively long temporal sequence in real-life stories (a school cleaning day, for instance), by helping them to become better at depicting characters in imaginative tales and by developing their sensitivity to the relationship between characters and events (for instance, being aware that by having different strengths, different animals can contribute to solving different kinds of problems).

The target group showed significantly higher values both in measures of variability derived from the students' writings (e.g., using more words, using a greater variety of words) and variability in the students' behavior as observed by using the Williams rating scale (Williams, 1993). Furthermore, the difference between the target and the comparison group increased during the school year (there was a significant interaction between time and difference).

There was also a completely unexpected, serendipitous finding, highly relevant to the topic of the present section. It was noticed that in addition to the major differences in outcome measures between the target and the comparison group, there were significant differences *within* the target group as well, especially between two of the classes, 3A and 3D. As we can see in Figures 6.20 and 6.21, the two classes differed both in terms of the variability of compositions (the "creative aspect" of them) and the variability of their behavior in the classroom (the Williams scale). The interaction with time may also be noted: the rates of development differ.

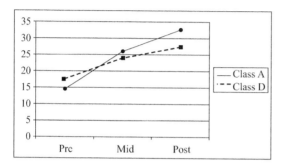

FIGURE 6.20 Total scores on the Chinese creative writing scale of class A and class D participants (adapted from Cheung et al., 2010, p. 154).

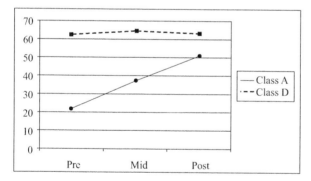

FIGURE 6.21 Total scores on the Williams scale of class A and class D participants (adapted from Cheung et al., 2010, p. 154).

These results are remarkable. All four teachers shared the same object of learning for all four learning studies, and basically for all lessons concerned with Chinese writing during the whole school year. Moreover, they worked according to the same theoretical framework. Obviously, however, as is also shown in Kullberg's (2010) study, referred to below, the enacted object of learning might differ importantly from the intended object of learning, and working with the same theory does not guarantee equally powerful lessons nor similar outcomes.

In order to avoid bias or preconceptions, those judging the variability of the compositions were ignorant of which classes belonged to the target group, but even if this had not been the case, both of these two classes belonged to the target group, so nobody could have had any expectation that there would be differences between them. This is also true, naturally, of the observers who rated the students' behavior on the Williams scale.

When we find such unexpected differences, we still maintain our assumption about the association between learning and the conditions of learning and try to describe both in such a way that the relation between them becomes apparent. This is the principle of contextual analysis, mentioned in Chapter 5. And when the classroom data was studied again, a major difference, and a possible explanation of the differences in outcome, could be identified. Cheung (2005) found that the teacher in class A structured the content of every learning study hierarchically, while the teacher in class D structured the same content sequentially, throughout the year.

In learning study 3, for instance, the students were asked to create an account of the cleaning day (a whole day) that they had just participated in the day before. In class 3A the cleaning day was dealt with in the context of life at school in a wider sense, the cleaning tasks were dealt with in the context of the cleaning day as a whole, the specific features of the individual cleaning tasks were dealt with in the context of the set of the different cleaning tasks, and this hierarchical structure was brought into correspondence with the time line.

In class 3D the different component parts were dealt with one at a time. The teacher and the students first talked about the major events during the day, then they talked about the preparation for the cleaning day, then the students were asked to act out some cleaning tasks, then they discussed the outline of the account that was to be written and the teacher reminded the students to pay attention to certain important aspects, such as time, location, characters, events. Finally the teacher pointed out the importance of using connectives in the account.

The differences between the two classes resemble the differences between the two classes in Chik's (2006) study, discussed earlier in this section. And, of course, the differences are differences between hierarchical and sequential structuring of the content, in both cases. No wonder that they are similar! And the differences in what happens in the classrooms are highly correlated with outcome measures in both cases, so the differences in outcome are similar too. But what about the most fundamental aspect of learning, according to this book: the object of learning? Well, they are different, it is true: seven Chinese words in Chik's case and creativity in Chinese writing in Cheung's study. How can differences in the mastery of such different objects of learning be related to differences in the same respect: the structural organization of the content?

According to the theory argued for in this book, it is of vital importance for the learners to separate things, to attend to one dimension at a time against a background of invariance in other dimensions. But the learner must be aware of what an aspect is being separated from, while simultaneously being aware of the aspect that is separated. And once the aspects are separated, they have to be brought together again. Words take on richer meanings in this way, as compared to when their different aspects are never taken apart (nor brought together).

But what about creativity? It is frequently thought about as a generic individual attribute: some people are creative, others are not. I do not subscribe to such a view. What people call "creative" has to do with the way we handle different tasks. You cannot be creative without doing some specific thing creatively. Boden (2004) says: "Creativity is the ability to come up with ideas or artefacts that are *new, surprising* and *valuable* [italics in original]." Ideas about *something,* artifacts used for *something,* I would add. But Boden continues, "'Ideas' here include concepts, poems, musical compositions, scientific theories, cookery recipes, choreography, jokes and so on. 'Artefacts' include paintings, sculptures, steam engines, vacuum cleaners, pottery, origami, penny whistles and many other things you can name" (p. 1).

In Cheung's (2005) case, the object of learning was "creativity in Chinese writing." I called it "variability in Chinese writing" because it is essentially variability that is rated in compositions and in the students' ways of acting (specifically: speaking) in the classroom: varied ideas, different ideas, novel ideas and so on.

As mentioned previously, learners will most likely gain more meaning from dealing with content that is structured hierarchically as compared to when the same content is structured sequentially. Gaining more meaning is likely to help you to fill in missing words in a text (which was the outcome measure used by Chik, 2006), and it is likely to help you to come up with a more varied account in a written composition and to talk about something in a more varied way in the classroom (basically the outcome measures used by Cheung, 2005). Moreover, "gaining meaning" is defined within the present framework as opening new dimensions of variation and focusing on them simultaneously. Although such a conceptualization might not be consistent with habitual ways in which the word *creativity* is used, it is consistent with "better learning" in Chik's, Cheung's and even Säljö's study. This explains the similarities between those studies, but at the same time it reflects the fact that the difference between hierarchical and sequential structuring is, unlike most things in this book, not content specific.

Keeping Things Apart and Keeping Things Together

It was mentioned earlier that while dimensions of variation have to be separated initially and brought together subsequently, the learners are supposed to be simultaneously aware of the values within the dimensions. The latter also applies to wholes and parts. The learners are supposed to be aware of both parts and wholes at the same time, just as they are supposed to be aware of a certain dimension and the values in that dimension.

Can the "Art of Learning" Be Learned?

According to the previous chapter, the "art of learning" amounts more or less to bringing about powerful patterns of variation and invariance. This is something that learners do spontaneously, and they do it to varying extents. But can the art of learning be taught? Most of the studies mentioned so far have been about learners becoming good at specific things, such as understanding what elegance in Cantonese opera is, how changes in demand and supply affect changes in price, how you can learn to discern Cantonese tones and so on (the previous section being a bit of an exception). But to what extent can we help learners to develop more general abilities? Can we help them in learning to learn, for instance?

Can Variation Theory Contribute to Developing Generic Abilities?

As was pointed out previously, in the discussion of creativity being an aspect of dealing with specific tasks, generic abilities exist, according to the theory, as general aspects of specific abilities. In that sense generic abilities are very appropriate objects of learning and the examples in this book are on widely differing levels of generalizability.[14] Reading and making sense of a text, for example, might have certain general aspects that we also recognize in the reading of other texts. But the general aspects exist only in relation to the reading of specific texts. Moreover, the most general ability is the ability to attend to the specific as fully as possible. And doing so can definitely be taught. Even better: it can be learned, too.

Preparing for the Unknown by Means of the Known, by Widening the Space of Learning

In this section, a comparison of ways of handling the same content is made from a specific perspective. As was mentioned in Chapter 1, the main dilemma of schooling is that the students do not see the need to learn things when they are expected to learn them, although their teachers try to persuade the students that they need to learn these things for use in the future. It is certainly a problem if the students do not see the relevance of learning, and another problem is how to prepare the students for a future that keeps becoming increasingly unpredictable. (We know less and less what the world will look like in 15 years—or even in 5.) At the same time, what the school has to offer is what is known today. How can we prepare our students for an unknown—and unknowable—tomorrow by means of what we know today?

The question of how to prepare for the unknown exists on all different levels of learning. The "unknown" may be something that differs from the known in what appears to be a very minor respect. However, it is still something that is unknown, and something that you may have to be prepared for. If you want to enhance children's skill in hitting a target from a particular angle, from a particular distance, with a particular kind of ball, under particular conditions, for instance, it might make sense for the children to keep practicing from the same angle, at the same distance, with the same kind of ball, under the same conditions. But if we want to enhance children's skill in hitting a target from any angle, from any distance, with any ball, under any conditions, repeating the features and the conditions of throwing is far from the best thing to do. If we want to prepare children to hit a target from any angle, we should let them try to hit the target from varying angles (as shown in Moxley, 1979, summarized in Chapter 3). And if we want to prepare them for throwing at any distance, with any ball, under any conditions, we should let them practice throwing at varying distances, with different balls, under different conditions. This follows from the theory and is also analogically implied by many empirical results (learning under varied circumstances seems to be conducive to the handling of novel tasks). This does not mean that the children have to try every angle and every distance (which cannot be done), but that they try *some* different angles, different distances and so on. By doing so, they get better at adjusting to variation and also at sensing the relationship between the variation in angle or distance on the one hand and their way of throwing on the other hand.

This might explain the interesting result in Kerr and Booth's (1978) experiment (see Chapter 3) in which the group practicing to hit a target with a shuttlecock from two different distances was better at hitting the target from a third—and for them—novel distance than another group, which had the same amount of practice from the same, third distance only. In other words, practice at distances x and y was more powerful in enabling the thrower to hit the target at distance z, than the same amount of practice at distance z. The only possible explanation I can think of is that forming a relationship between throwing and distance (by opening up the dimension of variation "distance" and "throwing from different distances") yields better learning than relating the throwing to one single value only. Mastering a dimension of variation, rather than dealing with a particular value, might be a more powerful approach to dealing with all values, including the one that has been the object of particular practice.

The main point here is that even if you cannot predict the different values the learner will encounter, by opening the relevant dimension of variation, the learner will be better prepared to handle any values than if that dimension has never been opened.

Generative Learning

Holmqvist, Gustavsson and Wernberg (2007) made an interesting observation in connection with several learning studies (see the next chapter) that were carried out. The outcomes of learning turned out to be better some time after the learning occasion than immediately after it in certain classes, usually in later cycles of the learning study. A possible explanation could have been that the teacher in those classes continued to deal with the same object of learning after the learning occasion observed had come to an end. But through a clever design, such class-specific effects were controlled for. The different classes were put together from randomly selected pupils from different classes in accordance with Figure 6.22. After the learning occasion, the pupils returned to their regular classes. In this way whatever happened in the real classes, after the learning occasion, affected the delayed measures in the different "synthetic classes" equally. Delayed measures of learning outcomes usually yield results that are less favorable than do immediate measures, because of students forgetting what they have learned. How can we possibly explain Holmqvist at al.'s results, which they saw as indicative of "generative learning"?

Such effects were found when the students interacted with more powerful patterns of variation and invariance than students in the other classes. They probably developed more powerful ways of seeing the object of learning (i.e., they got better at discerning its critical aspects). This means that after the end of the learning occasion, every time they encountered instances of the object of learning the likelihood of discerning those aspects was higher than for students from other classes. And every time they discerned critical aspects they became better at discerning critical aspects. Every encounter with instances of the object of learning was thus a new learning occasion. This was a "learning to learn" effect, though not general, but specific to the specific object of learning. They had learned the object of learning better, but also learned to learn it even better again. Such effects have been demonstrated in widely varying cases, such as, for instance, mathematics (Wernberg, 2009), Swedish (Gustavsson, 2008), English (Holmqvist & Mattison, 2009) for primary school children in Sweden; and reading comprehension (Marton & EDB Chinese Language Research Team, 2009), financial literacy (Pang, 2010), economics (Marton & Pang, 2007) for upper-secondary students in China, for instance.

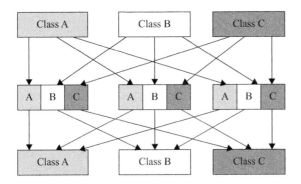

FIGURE 6.22 Design for studying generative learning (adapted from Holmqvist, Gustavsson & Wernberg, 2008, p. 116).

Learning to Make Sense of What You Read

In Chapter 5, differences between learners, in terms of making sense of the text being read, were described. One main point argued was that in each case examined, some learners turned out to do it better than others. Another main point was that "doing it better" meant noticing differences within the text as well as between things in the text and things in other texts, or more widely, in other contexts. This is because noticing something amounts to noticing a difference. Furthermore, noticing a difference amounts to being aware of two things (at least) at the same time. And this is what it takes to open a dimension of variation. Being good at learning something involves discerning the critical features and focusing on them simultaneously.

If a dimension of variation has been opened once, it is more likely that it will be available at a later point in time when attempting to master a novel task. Otherwise, we could never prepare ourselves for dealing with new tasks. A dimension of variation is an aspect of an entity (or actually of an unlimited number of entities differing from each other in the same respect). An "entity" is anything delimited—a part of the world.

"Reading an argumentative text" differs from "reading a narrative text" and from reading other genres. But one argumentative text can be different from another, for instance, in terms of how the text is structured. There are also differences in the meaning of the text as read by different students: there are differences in the perspective from which an account is given, and there are differences between arguments and the grounds for arguments and so forth.

The basic idea is that understanding an argumentative text amounts to being able to discern critical features of the text as text (what kind of text it is, what parts it consists of and how the parts are related to each other) in addition to being able to discern features critical for the specific content.

In accordance with this line of reasoning, Marton and EDB Chinese Language Research Team (2009) made an attempt to boost secondary students' (year 9) ability to make sense of argumentative texts. There were two classes taught by two different teachers in the target group, and two other teachers taught two other classes in the comparison group. Sequences of around 10 lessons, lasting about 1 hour each on average were spread out over a few weeks.

The idea that was put to test in the target group was based on the present theory, in accordance with what was said previously about the understanding of argumentative.

The principles underlying the program were the following:

1) In order to enable the learners to separate the act of learning (i.e. *how* they learn) from the content of learning (i.e. *what* they learn), the act of learning should vary while the content is the same. This can be achieved by inviting the learners to read a certain text in one way first (e.g. trying to memorize

it), and then to read the same text again, in a different way (e.g. trying to understand it). In this way the learners are likely to become aware of their own way of learning and of the potential variation in their way of learning. The learners certainly have experiences of going about learning from different texts in different ways, but exactly because in the past both the content of the text and the way of trying to learn from it have varied, it has not been easy to separate the way of learning (the act) from the content of learning.

2) In order to enable the learners to separate the meaning of the text from the words of the text, they should be invited to inspect different accounts (e.g. originating from other learners) of the meaning of the same text. By doing so they can see how the same text can be understood in different ways, i.e. the same words can have different meanings for different people. At the same time, they will find that different people can express the same meaning in different words.

3) In order to make learners aware of characteristics of different genres and enable them to separate those characteristics from the specific texts they read, they should read texts that differ as to genre (e.g. narrative, argumentative) but deal with the same theme and read texts belonging to the same genre but dealing with different themes.

4) In order to enable learners to discern the structure of different texts, they should read texts dealing with the same topic, but having different structures (e.g. sequential, hierarchical) and read texts which have the same structure but deal with different topics.

(Marton & EDB Chinese Language Research Team, 2009, pp. 138–139)

There is a specific curricular context to this study. In the first year of the new millennium, a new curriculum was introduced in Hong Kong with the trademark "learning to learn." Like other new curricula around the world during recent decades, it emphasizes generic abilities such problem-solving ability, creativity, critical thinking, learning by reading and so on (Education Commission, 2000). The research undertaking was an attempt to advance the last mentioned of these abilities:

> Argumentative texts are typically dealt with in secondary education in Hong Kong, but the comprehension of specific texts is emphasized rather than the enhancement of the capability of students to deal with new texts on their own.
> (Marton & EDB Chinese Language Research Team, 2009, p. 140)

This quote characterizes rather well the orientation of the teaching in the comparison group. This means that in different texts, the students try to find the main idea of each paragraph, the central idea of the text and they discuss its context. There is also a discussion of the features of the text, such as vocabulary, genre characteristics and so forth. The main difference between the teaching in the two conditions was the systematic use of comparisons and theory-grounded patterns of variation and invariance in the target group (for details, see Marton & EDB Chinese Language Research Team, 2009).

The students' ability to make sense of argumentative texts was observed three times, through a pre-test, a post-test and a delayed test (4 months after the series of lessons had finished). Each time the students read two argumentative texts and after reading each text, they wrote down what they thought the author was trying to say in the text. The proportion of students coming up with the most complex understanding, as determined by a phenomenographic analysis, was used as a descriptor of outcome on the group level. No difference was found between the students in the two conditions, either in the pre-test or in the post-test. Four months after the experiment, however, about 50% more of the students in the target group than in the comparison group expressed the most complex understanding of two novel argumentative texts.

This result appears to be an instance of the "generative learning" discussed in the previous section. If we assume that students did read some argumentative texts during the four months after the experiment, and if we assume that the likelihood of opening dimensions of variation in the future is increased by having opened them in the past, every encounter with an argumentative text was additional practice for most of the students in the target group.

There Are No Teaching Experiments

Earlier in this chapter, several studies were briefly summarized. In two of these (Pang & Marton, 2003 and Marton & Pang, 2006), efforts were made to create equal conditions for learning in a few classes, in all respects except for the teachers' insights into the particular theory advocated in this book. There was thus a difference in the conditions of learning, between "using the theory" in some of the classes and "not using the theory" in others. But as has been shown, all teachers use variation and invariance, and not infrequently in a way that is in agreement with the principles implied by the theory, in spite of the fact that they have never heard of it. Comparing "using the theory" with "not using the theory" is something very imprecise and hardly even meaningful. Actually, the theory does not tell us that it is better to use the theory than not. What it says is that in relation to particular aims and in relation to particular learners, certain patterns of variation and invariance are necessary conditions. Hence, using these patterns is a better idea than not doing so if we want to create powerful conditions for learning in that specific case. And in fact the emphasis in the two studies mentioned was more on the comparison between patterns of variation and invariance than between using and not using the theory. We found that the patterns that were in accordance with the theory were correlated with better learning to a greater extent than patterns less in accordance with the theory. It seems that such results give support to the theory.

The logic of experiments implies, however, that we can compare the effects of conditions defined *in advance*. The idea is that by randomization we make the conditions as near to equal as possible (in all respects that are likely to affect the outcome of the experiment, but one: that which is to be put to test) and by doing so we might gain support for our hypothesis (derived from—or at least commensurate with—the theory) or might be able to reject it, depending on whether or not the outcome is in agreement with the hypothesis. (The experiment may turn out to be inconclusive too, of course.) The problem is, however, that although we can plan the pattern of variation and invariance in advance, we can never define it prior to its coming into being. It can only be defined empirically, once it has taken place. The reason being that teaching is interactive: what happens in the classroom does not depend on the teacher only. And the more interactive teaching is, the more true the preceding sentences are. Teaching that is not interactive cannot be called teaching at all. In any case, it is not pedagogy, according to Premack's third criterion as presented in Chapter 1.

Beyond Patterns of Variation and Invariance: The Density of Rational Numbers

The limits of comparisons of conditions of learning, defined in advance, in terms of patterns of variation and invariance, was illustrated in Kullberg's (2010) study.

It builds on results originating from a so-called learning study (i.e., from a study in which a group of teachers choose an object of learning and plan a lesson together that aims to make it possible for the students to appropriate that object of learning). (Most of the next chapter deals with the idea and practice of the "learning study.") The original study—and, of course, also Kullberg's attempt to replicate some of the findings—was about the density of the rational numbers (i.e., about the fact that between any two rational numbers there are infinitely many rational numbers). Hence, the rational numbers are "dense." Gaining this insight was the object of learning for all the lessons, in the learning study as well as in Kullberg's study. To have "gained the insight" could mean that to the question, "Ann claims that there is a number between 0.97 and 0.98. John says that there is no such number. Who is right and why?" a student might answer, "Neither of them is right. There are actually infinitely many numbers between them, because any number and any interval between numbers is infinitely divisible." This question was used both in the pre-test and in the post-test in the learning study.

There was a striking difference in learning outcomes between the first cycle on the one hand and the second and third cycle on the other hand in the original study. The teachers seemed to have made a discovery, after the first cycle, and it was implemented in the second, as well as in the third cycle. In Table 6.8 we can see the rather dramatic difference between the lessons.

TABLE 6.8 Re-analysis of tasks on the understanding of the density of rational numbers, maximal score = 1.0 (adapted from Kullberg, 2010, p. 56).

	Lesson 1 (N = 19)			Lesson 2 (N = 17)			Lesson 3 (N = 17)		
	Mean	SD	Effect size	Mean	SD	Effect size	Mean	SD	Effect size
Pre-test	0.05	0.23		0.24	0.44		0.06	0.24	
Post-test	0.16	0.38	0.35	0.94	0.24	1.98	0.76	0.44	1.98

What made such a difference between the first lesson on the one hand and the second and third lessons on the other hand in the learning study? During the first lesson, the teacher introduced the topic by using the number line to represent decimal numbers. The point of departure was the question in the pre-test and the teacher demonstrated that there were indeed numbers between .97 and .98 (such as .971, .972, for instance). Then the students were asked to show their own answers to each other and to discuss the differences among their answers in groups. They were thus expected to gain the intended insight on their own. When the post-test was administered, it was obvious, however, that the teachers' expectations had not been met. The students did not come up with much better answers after the lesson than before. On the contrary: while none of the students said, "There are 9 numbers between .97 and .98, namely .971, .972 . . . 979" before the lesson, half of the class did so afterwards. The group of teachers agreed, after an in-depth discussion, that their way of using the number line might have created the impression that there were a finite number of decimals between .97 and .98. In accordance with the results of earlier research (e.g., Hart, 1981), they decided that an understanding of the decimal form of rational numbers should not be taken for granted but that the dimension of forms of representation should be opened up, including fractional numbers. Furthermore, the dimension of part–whole interpretations should also be opened up, by pointing to smaller and smaller parts of the same number, and by doing so demonstrating infinite divisibility. In concrete terms, this meant that the students could separate the quantity and its specific representation (for example, in the case of .97, by opening the dimension of variation of representations, this number could also be seen to be equivalent to e.g. 97/100, 97%). Furthermore, for each number represented fractionally they could separate the specific fractional representation by opening the dimension of variation of fractional representations of the very same rational number, such as 97/100 = 970/1,000 = 9,700/10,000 and so forth.

In this way the students became aware of the fact that each 100th is a part of a 10th, each 1,000th is a part of a 100th and so forth. We have parts and parts of parts and they are infinitely divisible: the students (most of them at least) discovered the mechanism for producing smaller and smaller parts ad infinitum (see Figure 6.23).

FIGURE 6.23 Two different dimensions of variation in which the density of rational numbers is experienced (adapted from Kullberg, 2010, p. 57).

However, by doing this, the focus was not so much on numbers as points on the number line (which contradicts any whole–part relations), but on the intervals between them representing the difference between the numbers. Judging from the results of the second and third cycles of the learning study (which were alike in these respects), by opening up all the previously mentioned dimensions of variation (corresponding to the critical aspects), the teachers managed to make it possible for the students to gain the insight aimed at, to a considerably greater extent than was the case in the first lesson.

Once we have arrived at a conjecture about the critical aspects and we want to put it to test, we can ask teachers to use them in some classes and not use them in other classes. We would then expect the students in the classes where the critical aspects are brought out to gain the insight in question to a greater extent than the students in the classes where the critical aspects are not brought out. Kullberg (2010) wanted to carry out such a study by asking four teachers to give the same lesson to two different classes, where the lesson in one class was taught in accordance with the design used in the first lesson in the previously mentioned learning study, and the other class was taught in accordance with the design used in the second and third lessons in the learning study.

Although this design is still far from foolproof, there was a group of teachers who declared themselves to be willing to teach the same topic in two different ways in two different classes each. Moreover, they seemed to be keen on finding out whether or not the conjecture held true. Of course, it might happen that although the teachers tried to teach with equal enthusiasm in both classes, they might not have succeeded in doing so. In any case, all the lessons were video-recorded and the researcher could again compare the patterns of variation and invariance in them.

There were thus four classes that were meant to be taught in accordance with the design in lesson 1 in the original study and four classes meant to be taught in accordance with the design in lessons 2 and 3 in the original study. When analyzing the lessons afterwards, it was found that in two classes in the latter group, one of the critical aspects (the divisibility aspect) was never brought out. While the difference in learning between the two designs resembled the difference observed in the original study, when the two classes in which the teachers did not follow the plan were excluded, the difference in learning between these two classes and those taught in accordance with the design in lesson 1 in the original study was negligible. This means that if we make the comparison in terms of what actually happened in the different classrooms the theoretical conjecture is strongly supported, but if we make the comparison in terms of predefined categories (of design) the conclusion is less clear cut.

In this case the difference between what was planned and what actually happened had to do with something that the teachers were supposed to do, but which they did not do (or at least that two of them did not do in one of the two cases they each taught). Interestingly, Kullberg (2010) carried out another similar study, trying to replicate some findings from a learning study about negative numbers. In this case, the teachers acted in accordance with the plans in all eight lessons (though changing the design a bit first), but as it happened, an alert student contributed to opening up the critical dimensions of variation that—for the purposes of the experiment—were not supposed to be opened in her class (pp. 137–139).

Kullberg's study shows that when we try to compare the effect of different conditions of learning, what we find by doing so in terms of pre-defined categories, might differ starkly from what we find by doing so in terms of what actually happens in the classrooms. And whether or not they differ, and how much they differ, we cannot tell without actually investigating what happens in the classrooms.

On the Dynamics of Content-Related Interaction

An interesting aspect of Kullberg's study is that it is more difficult to predict the flow and the outcome of a lesson with a lot of interaction than of one with less interaction. If you have developed a detailed design for the lesson, the closer attention you pay to the students' ideas and the more you adjust your teaching to them, the less can you follow the design of the lesson. At the same time, one of the most important effects of teachers' participation in learning studies is precisely that they pay more attention to their students' ideas and that they adjust their teaching more to the students (Al Murani, 2007; Al Murani & Watson, 2009). Paradoxically enough, the more the teachers act in accordance with this pedagogical implication of variation theory, the more difficult it is to put other pedagogical implications of the same theory to the test. The pedagogical implication that the teachers follow in this case is in accordance with Premack's third criterion of pedagogy: the teacher learns from the students in order to teach them better. The same idea has been foundational for "formative assessment" and for "assessment for learning," using information about the students' progress not so much for making a judgment about that progress but for enhancing it (see, for instance, Black, Harrison, Lee, Marshall & Wiliam, 2004). This is not an entirely new idea. It has been eloquently formulated already, in the 19th century, by the Danish philosopher, Sören Kirkegaard:

> If you want to bring a fellow human being to a certain goal, you must first find out where she is and start exactly there. If you cannot do this, you foul yourself, if you believe that you can help others. Although you must understand more than someone whom you want to help, but above all you must understand what she understands. If you cannot do that, knowing more is not enough. If you still want to show how much you know, it might be because you are vain and arrogant and want to be admired by the other person, instead of helping her. Genuine helpfulness begins with being humble to someone you want to help and to understand that helping someone is not wanting to rule, but wanting to serve. Without this, you cannot help anyone.
> (Quoted by Maunula, 2011, translation mine)

This means that communication in the classroom has to be bi- or multi-directional. It has to be interactive. And to a substantial extent it has to be related to the object of learning. Or as Maunula (2011) says: there has to be a dynamic content-related interaction.

Al Murani (2007) calls it "exchange systematicity" (see also Al Murani & Watson, 2009). He carried out a year-long study in the UK, in which a group of mathematics teachers from different schools worked together, trying to use variation theory as a point of departure for their teaching in algebra. The year-7 students taught by them did significantly better in mathematics (and not only in algebra) after that year than a comparable group of students taught with other kind of pedagogy. When analyzing the lessons carried out the most important difference between the target and the comparison groups was found to be that the teachers in the former made use to a much greater extent of the students' input as a resource in their teaching, a result very much in accordance with results of studies of the effects of participation in learning studies (see, for instance, Mårtensson, 2013).

Actually, the re-designing of the lesson before the second cycle of the learning study on the density of rational numbers that Kullberg (2010) tried to replicate was in part inspired by the following kind of content-related interaction during the first cycle:

Teacher: And zero point nine seven two [0.972] and what would come after that then?
Erika: (. . .)
Teacher: One, should we put one there [0.9721]?
Erika: It will never end.
Teacher: It will never end, see now something has happened in this discussion, from that we had, do you realize this now, from the beginning we had three groups that said that there were no numbers and we had one group that said there were nine numbers and one group that said that there was one number and now Erika says something very exciting she says it can never end, do I understand you correctly now?

Erika: Mm

Teacher: Okay Jennifer

Jennifer: But, it, I mean what is it called, we have [to] split them, zero point ninety-seven [0.97]

Teacher: Aha

Jennifer: To (0.975), so they are split in nine pieces and then you take every part and split it all the time so it will never end.

(Kullberg, 2010, pp. 52–53)

In this case the teacher's swift noticing and highlighting of a student's insight helps another student to develop it further, even if this insight was eventually thwarted by group pressure.

Putting Conjectures to the Test

Saying that an explanation is ad hoc means that it is not formulated in advance and put to the test but is an interpretation arrived at after having seen the results. According to Svensson's line of reasoning about contextual analysis (see Chapter 5), it may be that all explanation with regard to teaching is ad hoc. If teaching is genuinely interactive, it is impossible to predict its course or its effects. But it is possible to make sense of it, by using a theory as a tool, for instance.

There is, however, another option for testing theoretical principles about the relationship between learning and the conditions of learning. We can design a situation with an inherent, theoretically derived pattern of variation and invariance and "freeze" the parameters of the situation in advance. This means that we can carry out experiments about the relationship between learning and the conditions of learning, more specifically, the pattern of variation and invariance present in the situation. To the extent that we consider interactivity a defining feature of teaching, such experiments are, however, not about the relationship between learning and teaching. They are about the relationship between learning and the conditions of learning. Well then, how can this be done?

One of the most important conjectures of the theory, the challenge to induction, is that in order to discern critical aspects of the object of learning, the learner must experience variation in those aspects, one at a time, against a background of invariance in other aspects.

The conjecture has to do with the learners' experience, and thus it cannot be put to test. It is more like a definition or an axiomatic statement about what learning is. But in order to experience something, there must be something to be experienced. In experiments we can make it possible for the learners to experience a certain pattern of variation and invariance by making that pattern available to experience. However we can never make it certain that the experience will occur, hence the outcome will always be a stochastic variable (i.e., of a probabilistic nature). If a student has to experience a particular thing in order to learn, it is more likely that she will experience it if it is present in the learning situation than if it is not.

We can therefore formulate a secondary conjecture that indeed can be put to test:

It is more likely that the learner will discern critical aspects of an object of learning—if they vary, one at a time, while other aspects are invariant—than when this is not the case.

The interesting thing is that while "experience" is not observable, "discernment" (in terms of distinctions made) is. And so are "variation" and "invariance," of course.

Let us consider the secondary conjecture. It is made up of two component parts, that is, that the critical aspect varies, and also that other aspects are invariant. We have to compare the situation where this is the case with the situation where this is not the case. But there are different ways in which the pattern of variation and invariance is "not the case" (see Figure 6.24).

Consistent with the theory		Not consistent with the theory	
critical dimension	other dimensions	critical dimension	other dimensions
v	i	i	v
		i	i
		v	v

FIGURE 6.24 Patterns of variation and invariance, consistent and not consistent with the theory as far as necessary conditions for the discernment of novel aspects of the object of learning are concerned.

Comparing Contrast and Induction

This means that there are three ways in which the conjecture can be put to the test. First of all we can compare contrast with induction, which it is supposed to be an alternative to. The condition in which the critical dimension varies and other dimensions are invariant is compared to the condition when the critical dimension is invariant and other dimensions vary. Ki and Marton's (2003) study, described in Chapter 3, did just that. It was shown that varying tones (critical aspect) between Chinese words while the segments (other aspects) remain invariant is associated with better learning of tones than keeping the tone invariant and varying the segments. The results thus supported the conjecture.

Comparing Contrast With Invariance That Is Not Consistent With the Conjecture

The condition consistent with the conjecture can also be compared with the condition in which neither the critical aspect nor the other aspects vary. This means that the conditions are the same for every trial. This was done in Moxley's (1979) study, described in Chapter 3 and also discussed briefly in this chapter. The results showed that children who had practiced trying to hit a target from varying angles were better prepared to hit the target from a novel angle than were children who had practiced trying to hit the target from the same angle every time, under otherwise identical conditions. Again the conjecture was supported. The outcome was the same in Kerr and Booth's (1978) study, also discussed earlier in this chapter. In this case, it was demonstrated that children who practiced hitting a target from various distances did better in a test (involving hitting the target from a particular distance) than children who had practiced trying to hit the target from the same distance every time, even when the distance in the test was the distance that one of the groups used for practice throughout, while the group for which the distance varied did not practice from the test distance at all.

These studies reported results concerning the relationship between learning and the conditions of learning, and those results turned out to be consistent with the conjecture, even if the two last mentioned studies predate the conjecture by many years and thus were not designed to put it to the test. Furthermore, none of the three studies dealt with teaching: there was no interactivity, in the sense that the learners' ways of acting did not modify the conditions of learning. On the other hand, the expectations could be formulated in advance and the results were clearly related to the expectations.

Comparing Contrast With Variation That Is Not Consistent With the Conjecture

It has been tacitly assumed in the present line of reasoning that the different patterns of variation and invariance being compared were stated in terms of defining aspects of the object of learning (that have to be taken into consideration). As far as this third kind of comparison is concerned, Ki, Ahlberg & Marton (2006) have shown, for instance, that speakers of non-tonal languages learn Cantonese tones better when tone varies while segments are invariant, as compared to when both tone and segment vary. But what if a non-defining aspect varies? Does it have the same negative effect on learning? What if the words are read with varying voice qualities, even if the pitch level is the same? I do not know of any experimental studies of the third kind of comparisons, that between the critical aspect varying, and other (unfocused) aspects being invariant (consistent with the conjecture) on the one hand and the critical aspect varying, but other (unfocused) aspects varying too (not consistent with the conjecture) on the other hand.

This difference appeared, however, in several studies of teaching and was used in ad hoc explanations of the outcomes (which also supported the conjecture). Marton and Pang (2013) and Pang and Marton (2013) set out to try to replicate those findings in an experimental context.

In Chapter 4 as well as earlier in this chapter, Pang and Chik's (2005) study of an attempt to develop 10-year-old students' understanding of price and pricing, by means of a fictive auction, was referred to. The results were rather bleak, in spite of the fact that the pattern of variation and invariance was consistent with the theory, except in one single respect. The two focused aspects, demand and supply, varied one at a time, and it seemed likely that the two focused aspects had been discerned by most students and that the two were supposed to be related to each other. This would make it possible for the students to see the price of a commodity as a function of the relationship between demand and supply. Demand and supply were expected to vary simultaneously, while the commodity was invariant (so the students could separate demand and supply from the commodity). But the teachers introduced change in the commodity with the result that very few students reached the understanding aimed at. This was true in all classes but one. In this class the teacher happened to introduce simultaneous change in demand and supply, in combination with an invariant commodity, with the result that far more students managed to express the understanding of price aimed at.

It seems rather strange that such an apparently subtle detail can have such radical effects on the success of teaching. Marton and Pang (2013) decided to try to replicate this finding in an experimentally controlled situation. The same type of auction was carried out but involving individual students interacting with a computer. Each student had the same sum of money to begin with and they were supposed to buy as many items as possible during the auction. After the first round of the auction, the students were assigned "shopping money," but less in the second round than in the first. At the beginning of the third round they were given the same amount of money as in the second round, but the number of items available for them to buy was reduced. At last, in the fourth round, they got more money, but the number of items for purchase was further reduced. The students were supplied with statistics about the average price of the items per round, and the experimenter pointed out to the whole group that price went down when purchasing power (money) was reduced between rounds 1 and 2, price went up when supply was cut back between rounds 2 and 3, and price went up when purchasing power went up and supply of items went down between rounds 3 and 4. The students were randomly allocated to one of two conditions. In one condition (consistent with the conjecture) all the items offered for sale were the same within each round and throughout all rounds (the participants were simply supposed to buy as many chocolate boxes of the same type as possible). In the other condition (not consistent with the conjecture) all the commodities (within and between rounds) were different. The students participating in this condition were supposed to buy as many (different) sweets as possible during the auction. The difference between the two conditions was, of course, illusory. The number of the identical items was the same as the number of different items in each round, the base price was the same, and actually even the final prices were very close to each other. The students in the comparison group (the second one) could have neglected the visual differences between the items, as they were completely irrelevant from the point of view of pricing. But they turned out to have great difficulties in separating the unfocused aspects (the kind of the commodity) from the focused aspects (demand and supply), and the group dealing with the same commodity throughout (the first one) clearly outperformed the group dealing with different commodities.

In the case just dealt with, there were two focused aspects varying simultaneously, which had been discerned one at a time previously. The theory—and the results—indicated that in order to enable the learners to discern the relationship between them and its effect on price, the unfocused aspect (the commodity) should remain invariant, instead of varying simultaneously with the two focused aspects.

But what about the actual discernment of the two focused aspects? According to the theory, they should vary one at a time, while the other remains invariant (just as was the case in the study discussed here). As mentioned previously, Marton and Pang (2007) have indeed compared the effect of the pattern of variation and invariance just mentioned (consistent with the theory) with the effect of varying the two focused aspects simultaneously from the beginning ("fusion" throughout, not consistent with the theory). In this study the effect of change in the relative magnitude of change in demand and supply was the object of learning. A series of three lessons started with a concrete case aimed at developing an intuitive understanding in the students. It was followed up by a formal part, in which the relationships between the variables were illustrated and explained by means of graphs. As described earlier in this chapter, in connection with an account of Marton and Pang's (2006) related study, also dealt with in Chapter 4, the concrete case used had to do with changes in the price of face masks during the outbreak and disappearance of SARS in Hong Kong in February–August 2003. In the condition consistent with the theory, the students' attention was initially drawn to periods during which one of the two focused aspects (demand or supply) changed, while the other remained invariant, followed by pointing the learners to periods when the absolute magnitude of one of those aspects increased or decreased more and more, while the other remained invariant. At last the learners were invited to consider periods when all the aspects were in a flux. In the condition not consistent with the theory, the learners were asked to analyze and discuss cases of the last mentioned kind (changes in several respects simultaneously) from the beginning. This first part of the sequence of lessons was followed up with the formal treatment of the topic and was identical for both groups. Students learning under conditions consistent with the theory in the first part of the experiment again significantly outperformed the students learning informally under conditions not consistent with the theory.

Pang and Marton (2013) set out to replicate this study also, under controlled conditions. Both the informal part and the formal part were brought to the fore in a computer-implemented version. In this case, the students interacted individually with the computer for 3 hours, having been randomly allocated to one of the two versions of the sequence. Under both conditions, they were presented with information about the development of the price of face masks during the

SARS epidemic, supplemented with clips from local newspapers in Hong Kong, commenting on the situation (the epidemic, face masks, etc.) at different points in time. All the students were allowed the same time for analyzing and commenting (in writing) on different cases, referring to different points on the time against face-mask prices curve. The difference between the two groups was that the group working under conditions consistent with the theory started with cases where one aspect varied while the other was invariant (and then the other way around) and subsequently on cases where different aspects varied simultaneously while students in the group working under conditions not consistent with the theory were dealing with cases of the last mentioned kind (i.e., in which different aspects varied simultaneously) from the beginning and throughout the informal part of the learning sequence. Results were again clear cut: conditions consistent with the theory turned out to be significantly more powerful for learning than conditions not consistent with the theory.

The Power of Patterns of Variation and Invariance Is Relative to the Object of Learning and to the Learners

I have thus referred to a group of studies in which patterns of variation and invariance where predicted by the theory to be more powerful conditions for learning and were compared to patterns of variation and invariance predicted to be less powerful conditions for learning. In all of these studies the theoretical conjectures were supported in terms of statistically significant differences in outcome. But we know that conjectures can never be conclusively confirmed. We can only demonstrate that in a particular test they have not been rejected. And this is what we can say in these cases also.

The reason why we cannot confirm a conjecture, by showing that it works, is that the conjecture is a general statement, while any empirical test we put it to is necessarily specific, and however many specific tests we carry out they will never add up to a general statement. In Chapter 3 I pointed to the limitations of induction when it comes to *finding* a specific meaning; here the discussion is about the limitations of induction when it comes to *confirming* a specific meaning.

With regard to the possibilities for making generalizations about patterns of variation and invariance, the base line is that we can never say that a certain pattern is "better" (more powerful) than other patterns, full stop. However, one pattern may be better than another pattern in relation to a particular object of learning. In Ki and Marton's (2003) study about speakers of non-tonal languages learning Cantonese tones, discussed in Chapter 3, the pattern of variation and invariance that was consistent with the theory, and which turned out to be most powerful, was based on first comparing words that differ in terms of tones (they varied) but had the same segments (they were invariant). In the next phase, words that differed in terms of segments but had the same tone were compared. The different aspects were thus dealt with one at a time.

In Chik, Leung and Marton's (2010) study of the learning of seven Chinese words by 10-year-old Chinese children, the results were the other way around. Grouping three aspects (form, sound, meaning) together under each word (see Figure 6.11) was followed by more powerful learning than grouping the different words under one aspect at a time. Thus, in one case words grouped together in terms of aspects was better, while in the other case aspects grouped together in terms of words was better. How could two mutually exclusive alternatives be the best in two different cases? The answer to this question is that there were two entirely different objects of learning. In one case, the learners were expected to learn to distinguish between tones and relate them to meanings; in the other case, the children were supposed to bring together features of words, many of which they knew already (e.g., the pronunciation of the words and to a certain extent their meanings).

Then again, the objects of learning were also different because the learners were different in the two studies. Patterns of variation and invariance are relative to objects of learning, but also to learners. In the previous section, Marton and Pang's (2007) study, dealing with teaching and learning about the effect on prices of the relative magnitude of changes in demand and supply, was referred to. Varying one aspect at a time, while others remained invariant, and letting the different aspects vary simultaneously afterwards (consistent with the conjecture) was found to be superior to letting all aspects vary simultaneously from the beginning (not consistent with the conjecture). As previously mentioned, Pang and Marton (2013) wanted to replicate the Marton and Pang (2007) study in an experimental context, and they built the difference into two computer-implemented learning resources corresponding to the two different lesson designs in the 2007 study. Again, the condition consistent with the conjecture turned out to be associated with better learning, as compared to the condition not consistent with the conjecture (all aspects varied at the same time). But the two studies (the original and the computer assisted one) were carried out in schools very similar to each other. In Hong Kong, where the studies were done, students—and, in a way, also schools—are "banded"; that is, they are divided into three different levels according to ability (or rather achievement). This means that if a research study is carried out in a particular school, or in some similar schools, you get a sample which is not representative of the population, being taken from a rather narrow segment of it. This is why Marton and Pang (2013) wanted to go further and carry out a second computer-implemented replication of the original study, with students that better represented the whole population of Hong Kong students as far as their level of school achievement was concerned. In all other respects it was the same study as the one mentioned, yielding a significant difference between two patterns of variation and invariance as conditions of learning. No such difference was obtained in the new study, however. The two patterns seemed to provide the students with more or less equally powerful conditions for learning.

How could the results differ so much in two studies identical in all respects, except for the average and the spread of students' achievements? The explanation seems to be that, depending on what the students already knew before the session, they needed different experiences in order to learn more. If the students had already discerned demand and supply, they did not have to practice discerning them again, but they needed to bring them together. On the other hand, if they had not discerned demand and supply previously, they needed to do so before encountering simultaneous variation in both. If we break down the results for all participants into results for the students who had not discerned the two focused aspects previously and for those who had, we find highly pronounced differences between the effects of the two different sequences of patterns of variation and invariance, where one particular sequence produced better results in one group while the reverse order produced better results in the other. For the first group labelled "Low" in Figure 6.25 (who needed to learn to discern demand and/or supply and bring them together subsequently), the contrast-generalization-fusion sequence (labelled "A" in Figure 6.25) turned out to be best (because it enabled them to do this); for the second group, labelled "High"(who had discerned both demand and supply prior to the experiment but needed to bring them together), the fusion-only sequence (labelled "B") was found to be most efficient (because it enabled them to do this; see Figure 6.25). Actually, the contrast-generalization-fusion pattern could in principle have worked for the second group too, but they seemed to react against—or possibly were confused by—being forced to learn something that they knew already.

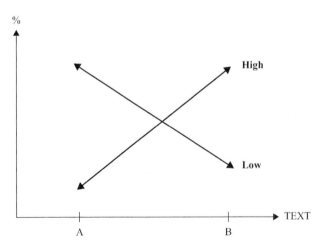

FIGURE 6.25 Interaction between how the content was handled in two learning resources and the participants' ways of handling the content before the experiment (Pang & Marton, 2013).

The Accidental Resurrection of the Idea of ATI

During the 1970s there was a strong movement in educational psychology called ATI (Aptitude-Treatment Interaction), whose core idea was that the suitability of teaching approaches (methods or arrangements) co-varies with individual differences (see, for instance, Cronbach & Snow, 1977; Gustafsson, 1976). Differences in teaching approaches were described mainly in terms of modality or representation (e.g., visual, auditory, logical, narrative), while differences between individuals were described in corresponding terms (such as, for instance, visual, auditory, logical, verbal ability). Pang and Marton's (2013) study also focused on the relationship between learning and the conditions of learning, and shares with the ATI movement the assumption that some conditions are better for some learners and other conditions are better for other learners. The important difference is that both the individual learners and the conditions of learning are described in general terms in the ATI tradition, while both are described in content-specific terms by Pang and Marton (2013), in accordance with the research tradition that their study—as well as this book—represents.

It can thus be concluded that variation theory does not generate statements about one pattern of variation and invariance being better or worse than any other. But in relation to specific objects of learning, characterized in terms of critical aspects, it predicts what pattern of variation and invariance is most powerful for learners for whom the critical aspects are critical. This has been shown in empirical studies, giving support to the theory, even if it can never be confirmed, which as Popper (1963) tells us, no theory can.

The Chinese Connection

Many of the examples in this book are from Chinese classrooms. One of the reasons for this is that I have spent a substantial part of the last 15 years in Hong Kong, and much of the work described in this book was carried out there. But there is another and more important reason. One can identify a Chinese pedagogy, mainly a theory in action, that the current theory resembles in important respects.[15] I will briefly summarize my understanding of some aspects of Chinese pedagogy, mainly in relation to the learning and teaching of mathematics (for a more elaborate presentation, see Chik & Marton, 2010).

Are Chinese Students Best in Math?

"Top scores from Shanghai stun educators," wrote the *New York Times* on December 7, 2010. More than five thousand 15-year-olds from Shanghai participated an international comparison of educational achievement in three subjects: mathematics, science and reading comprehension. The youngsters from Shanghai clearly outperformed the students from every other place, in all three subjects (and did so again, 3 years later; OECD, 2013). Even if it is not quite "fair play" to compare a sample from one big city with samples from entire countries, the results were a bit of a shock for many (and it included pretty reasonable comparisons, such as those between students from Shanghai, Hong Kong and Singapore, for instance). A number of different explanations were presented in the article, partly the journalists' own, partly from politicians (including President Obama) and educational experts. China's rapid modernization, the culture of education, emphasis on teacher training, more time spent on studying, among other things, were mentioned as potential factors contributing to the Chinese students' excellent performance. Interestingly, there was not a single word said about the things that this whole book is dealing with: how the different subjects are learned and taught. Could it not be the case that students are better at solving quadratic equations because they are taught to solve quadratic equations in more powerful ways? Could it not be the case that students understood Newton's laws better because they were taught Newton's laws in different ways from those who did not do so well? And could it not be the case that students were better at comprehending novel texts because they were taught to comprehend novel texts in a different way from those who had scored lower?

Why is it that what is actually taking place in the classroom, on the concrete level of what the students are expected to learn, is so rarely taken into consideration when we discuss differences in educational achievement? There is quite a bit of accumulated evidence of Chinese students' outstanding performance, especially in mathematics, during the last few decades at least. One of the most surprising studies was carried out by Stevenson and Stigler (1992).

They matched groups of students in big American, Japanese, Taiwanese and mainland Chinese cities from age 5 to 14 and compared them in mathematics tests (the content of which varied, of course, between age groups). American children were already lagging behind in the youngest group, but the differences widened for every age group. For the oldest students there was very little overlap in achievement between American and mainland Chinese students when the unit of analysis was schools: almost all the Chinese schools were doing better than all the American schools. Japanese and Taiwanese schools were in between, but much closer to the mainland Chinese schools, the three "Confucius heritage countries" forming a group.

During the 10 years from 1994 to 2003, mainland Chinese students had participated in the mathematics Olympiads nine times. They ended up as number one (of the 80 or so participating countries) six times, number two twice and number six once (Fan & Zhu, 2004, p. 26).

Students from other Confucius heritage countries or regions (Hong Kong, Taiwan, Singapore, Japan, South Korea) have occupied the top positions in all international comparisons in mathematics since the early 1970s (when such comparisons started). Mainland China had not participated until the PISA study, and the only country that recently managed to break into the top group was Finland (OECD, 2012).

Why Are Chinese Students Good at Math?

But let us focus on the Chinese students striking achievements in mathematics. There are many factors that might have contributed, but I would like to highlight only one. I would suggest that we consider the question of how the Chinese students have been so good at learning mathematics in relation to how they are taught mathematics. There is a particular feature of the teaching of mathematics in the Chinese culture, or to put it slightly differently, there is a distinctive way of teaching mathematics, called "teaching with variation" in China (Zhang, Li & Tang, 2004, p. 196). It is called *bianshi* (變式). My assumption is that a factor that contributes strongly to the Chinese students' excellent performance in mathematics is the way in which mathematics is taught. To define *bianshi* is, however, not easy. As Sun (2011) noticed, it is so widely practiced in the Chinese culture that it is nearly invisible to the participants. In consequence, although there are analyses of its different forms, functions or purposes, it seems difficult to find a statement about what is common to its different varieties. To the best of my knowledge, it was identified as a specific practice, or a specific feature of a practice by Gu (1991). He tried to find out what characterizes good practice in mathematics teaching and pointed to various patterns of sameness and difference that you can find in sets of tasks or examples used in powerful ways of teaching mathematics. Sun (2011) referred to it as "variation practice," and this is exactly what it is, in my understanding. It is not a theory, nor is it explicit for the most part. But it is 2,000 years or more old. The book, *Jiu Zhang San Shu* (九章算書) [*The Nine Chapters*], which has been a source of knowledge in mathematics for about 1,600 years and seems to have had a similar role in China to that which Euclid's *Elements* had in Europe, has several examples of highly systematic use of patterns of variation and invariance (Ma Li, 1999). Chapter 9, for instance, deals with what is now called "Pythagoras' theorem" but which was, in all likelihood, discovered independently in China. It is not presented as a theorem followed by many similar examples, but as a theorem presented through many different examples (any combination of two sides given, find the third side; the sum of any two sides and the third side given, find the two sides not given; difference between any two sides and the third side given, find the two sides not given, etc.). The idea of this practice is to draw the learner's attention to as many aspects of a certain kind of problem as possible. Instead of fearing complexity, things are not so much studied one at a time as together, in relation to each other.

What Is Bianshi?

One of the reasons that it is difficult to find a coherent, agreed-upon picture of *bianshi* (i.e., of the variation practice in the teaching of mathematics in China) is that in the attempts to characterize it, both patterns of variation and invariance and the purposes for which they are to be used are taken into consideration. Gu distinguishes, for instance, between conceptual and procedural variation, used to achieve different aims (Gu, Huang & Marton, 2005). Sun (2011), on the other hand, makes distinctions between different purposes that can be achieved by means of patterns of variation and invariance, such as introducing and solidifying concepts on the one hand and enhancing curriculum coherence and connectedness on the other hand.

I am looking at *bianshi* from the very specific perspective of variation theory, according to which distinctions as to content and function are captured in terms of differences between objects of learning. The only fixed categories refer to patterns of sameness and differences (contrast, generalization and fusion). These categories can be combined in an unlimited number of ways.

Bianshi can be characterized in terms of sets of tasks used in teaching, textbooks and so forth. Above all, the tasks are chosen to bring out certain relationships through the differences between those tasks. The differences may be ones that should be overlooked, where the learners are expected to become aware that certain cases, which they do not count as instances of a certain concept, are in fact instances. This means that features that learners take to be defining features should not be taken for defining features (such as different rotations of geometric figures, for instance). This amounts to generalization (e.g., a triangle is a triangle, even when it is "upside down").

On the other hand, cases might be juxtaposed in order to make the learners aware of certain distinguishing features that separate instances from non-instances. This amounts to contrast (e.g., an ellipse that does not have two foci is not an ellipse.)

In other cases, the teacher opens up for different ways of solving the same problem. This can also be done by inviting the students to suggest the different ways. By juxtaposing different solutions, the learners are supposed to realize that the same problem can be solved in different ways and also become aware of the specific nature of the different methods of solution. This is also contrast. Both these two patterns of variation and invariance are exemplified by Gu (1991).

In other cases, the path to mastering a certain problem is scaffolded by problems, the solution of which leads the learner to the solution of the target problem, by opening up one dimension of variation at a time. The basic (implicit) idea—as interpreted from the point of view of the theory of variation—is that a learner can discern one and only one new dimension of variation at a time. Hence all the dimensions of variation that the teacher suspects that the learner has not discerned previously are opened up in different steps.

In accordance with the theoretical framework adopted and argued for in this book, the best way of explaining what *bianshi* is, is to juxtapose it with what is not *bianshi*.

Sun (2011) made a comparison between how the same topics are dealt with in textbooks in the US and in China. The simplest example is how subtraction is introduced. In the American textbook there were three subtractions to begin with: $4 - 1 = 3$, $5 - 3 = 2$ and $3 - 2 = 1$. This was illustrated by

4 birds, of which 1 flew away. Question: How many left? Answer: 3
5 birds, of which 3 flew away. Question: How many left? Answer: 2
3 birds, of which 2 flew away. Question: How many left? Answer: 1

It seems that what the students had to do was to count the remaining birds and answer with the result of the subtraction (see Figure 6.26).

Separating
Write how many are left:

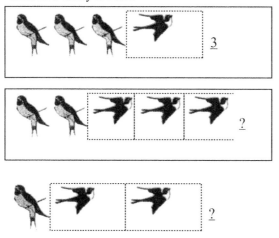

FIGURE 6.26 How subtraction is introduced in an American textbook (adapted from Sun, 2011, p. 71).

In the Chinese textbook, subtraction and introduction were introduced by means of three operations too (see Figure 6.27):

$1 + 2 = 3, 2 + 1 = 3$, and $3 - 1 = 2$

FIGURE 6.27 How addition and subtraction are introduced in a Chinese textbook (adapted from Sun, 2011, p. 70).

In this way addition and subtraction are linked together; the commutative nature of addition is illustrated, as is the part–whole relationship between the three numbers. The idea is that subtraction is easier to grasp if it goes with addition and that addition is easier to grasp if dealt with together with subtraction. Making something more complex does not necessarily mean making it harder, it might be—and frequently is—just the other way around. This is in accordance with the principle described in Chapter 3—you cannot grasp a specific quality without grasping the dimension of variation in which it is a value, nor can you grasp the dimension of variation without grasping the difference between values in that dimension (which requires at least two values).

Instead of introducing a method for solving problems of a certain kind, and then inviting students to solve problems of that kind, which mainly differ as far as the numbers are concerned (as it is mostly done in Western practices), the teacher has the students deal with problems chosen so that the differences between them enable the students to discern various aspects of the mathematical concepts embodied in the problems.

There are many other ways of using *bianshi,* or other purposes for doing so, but all the cases can be depicted in terms of patterns of sameness and variation. I would venture to argue that *bianshi* is characterized primarily by the systematic use of differences (between tasks, problems, solutions, examples, illustrations) in such a way that it draws the learner's attention to as many aspects of certain kinds of tasks as possible and thus prepares the learners for dealing with widely varying situations.

Now, the idea of *bianshi,* as it was characterized earlier, can hardly be expected to be unique to the Chinese or to Confucius heritage countries, and we cannot expect the way of bringing it about to be unique either. Watson and Mason (2006) speak about a set of tasks as *a single* mathematical object, which means that tasks are seen in relation to each other and that they are carefully constructed so as to bring out all the necessary features of the actual mathematical entity. Mason and Watson (2005) have gone through a great number of textbooks in mathematics used in England over the centuries and point to quite a few examples of the authors taking the relationships between tasks into consideration and thus constructing single mathematical objects of the tasks belonging to a particular topic.

With regard to the way of connecting tasks in order to scaffold learning, the most famous example of such a pedagogical method is to be found in Plato's *Meno* dialogue (Day, 1994). And of course, this approach of going step-by-step is recognized by all teachers around the world. The difference between Chinese pedagogy and other pedagogies is not qualitative but quantitative. There are no things done in Chinese classrooms that are not being done in any other classrooms, but there are things being done in Chinese classrooms that are done in other classrooms to a lesser extent and less systematically.

But there is another interesting issue. I would like to argue that the way of teaching mathematics, called *bianshi,* is actually not unique to mathematics but is the specific realization in mathematics of an aspect of Chinese pedagogy in general.[16]

Beyond Mathematics

As should be obvious from the many examples of teaching in China mentioned previously, variation and invariance are used highly systematically, not only in mathematics but also in other subjects. Some of the examples deal with the learning of Chinese as a mother tongue.[17] We have recently published a whole volume of studies of the learning and teaching of Chinese as a mother tongue (Marton, Tse & Cheung, 2010). In the different studies reported therein, the systematic use of variation and invariance is highlighted. While variation theory is inspired by Chinese pedagogy, these studies of learning and teaching Chinese are inspired by variation theory. What the theory does in this case is to analytically separate the principles from the practice and thus make the principles explicit and applicable to contexts in which they have not been used previously or have been used to a lesser extent.

Notes

1. For the distinction between first- and second-order perspective, see Chapter 4.
2. The same distinction was referred to by Mason (2011) in terms of implicit (primary) versus explicit (secondary) variation.
3. We have to remember, however, that what is a dimension of variation and what is a value is relative to the differentiation made.
4. This is a very good example (as is the lesson about the sloth, mentioned earlier in this chapter) of Laurillard's (2012) idea that the teachers should take advantage of the rapid development of information and communication technology by taking the lead in creating new tools of learning, specifically designed for specific needs.
5. Anderberg, Svensson and Alvegård (2008) have pointed out the problematic nature of this relationship as an important theoretical and methodological issue in research on learning.
6. Even if the present interpretation of the differences between Japanese and US classrooms may appear as a reasonable conjecture for explaining the differences in achievement between Japanese and American students, it might not be generalizable to differences between other countries, or even to differences between Japan and the United States at another point in time. For a comparison between mainland China, Hong Kong and Sweden, see Häggström's (2008) study, later in this chapter.
7. New values may open up a dimension of variation, of course. However repetition may close this dimension. If we were to use x, y, f, and g and only these all the time, the learners might get into difficulties with n and m. What a dimension of variation looks like is not finalized once and for all by means of an initial set of values. It can always change, by the repetition of values encountered and by encountering new values.
8. If a dimension of variation is present, it does not imply that it is opened up experientially (by the learners), but it does imply that it is opened up observationally (it is simply there to be seen).
9. Numbers within brackets refer to the different problems in Figure 6.9.
10. The original principal investigator was Professor Paul Morris at the University of Hong Kong (now at the Institute of Education, University of London), and the project

was financially supported by the Standing Committee on Language Education and Research in Hong Kong (SCOLAR).
11. One might object to such a move and refer to the risk of missing effects developing over much longer periods of time. Our ambition was, however, to start by establishing a particular way of looking at the connection between teaching and learning, mediated by a particular theory of learning. Subsequently, we have also studied the relationship between the students' learning and what happened in the classroom over much longer periods. Some of that work is described later in this chapter.
12. This is a test consisting of a text in which words are deleted and have to be filled in by the students.
13. We may wonder how two classes of equal standing in Chinese can do so differently after one lesson. If the quality of teaching Chinese is of decisive importance (which I assume it is), there should be a cumulative effect, should there not? Two things have to be said about this. One is that the classes were new for the teachers and the lessons took place at the beginning of the new school year. The other thing is more general and applies to all of the studies of the same kind discussed in this book. We might think of a cumulative effect during a whole school year, for instance. Take a certain student with certain skills and certain knowledge and put her in a particular class. After a year she could have reached a higher or lower level of achievement than if she had been placed in another class. How much difference does it make which class you happen to be in? Early in my own research career, I made an estimate of a lower bound of such an effect and reached the conclusion that depending on the subject, a lowest estimate of such an effect might be about 5% to 10% of the variation between students (Marton, 1967). Recent research actually supports this estimate: results seem to converge on 10% (L. Gustafsson, personal communication, January 29, 2013; Skolverket, 2009, p. 180; Nye, Konstantopoulus & Hedges, 2004). There are reasons to believe—thanks to several studies reported here, among other things—that the effect on the level of differences in learning during single lessons is higher than during a school year. The reason is that one teacher is more successful with one lesson, and another with another lesson, this being so because the design of the lessons rests more on intuitive than on theoretical grounds. Hence, in the long run the differences are to a certain extent equalled out. This also implies that if teachers manage to raise the quality of their teaching, as a result of relying on a theoretical ground consistently, the effect on the students' learning might be dramatically higher than has been suggested by estimates of upper bounds, based on current or past situations.
14. Consider, for instance, "integrated use of language skills" (Chik et al., 2010), "observing and describing" (Kwan et al., 2002) and "creativity in writing Chinese" (Cheung, 2005), all of which are discussed in this chapter.
15. There seem to be important similarities with the pedagogy practiced in other "Confucian heritage" countries and regions, such as Japan, South Korea, Singapore, Hong Kong and Taiwan (see, for instance, Emanuelsson & Häggström, 2008; Park, 2012).
16. If we can speak of a Chinese pedagogy, it is, however, to be expected that it would be characterized by repetition and memorization rather than by variation and understanding (see, for instance, Biggs, 1996). But as Marton, Dall'Alba and Tse (1992, 1996) pointed out, it does not seem very likely that students who show such good results as those of students from the Confucius heritage countries would do so mainly through repetition and memorization. This is the paradox of the Chinese learner. Marton et al. (1996) suggested, however, a solution to the paradox. Although Chinese pedagogy *is* characterized by repetition and memorization, it is also characterized by variation and understanding. Both approaches are seen to support each other and both are probably practiced more intensely than elsewhere. Here the focus has been on the latter approach.

17. Unlike the teaching of mathematics in today's China, the teaching of reading and writing Chinese characters has traditionally been dominated more by repetition than by variation. The students often have to copy the characters by drawing strokes (the component graphic elements of the characters) again and again in order to become able to retrieve them from memory. They start with graphically simple characters, which they might not have seen at all previously or for which the meaning is hard for them to grasp. Drawing on the current theory and on novel innovative practices in mainland China; Tse, Marton, Loh and Chik (2010) described an approach to the learning and teaching of characters that is based on their occurrence in the children's everyday world, on the relations of the characters to their spoken forms and to each other as far as meaning and structure is concerned. This means that the teaching starts with words that the children can recognize (even if they are graphically more complex), the words appear in context, and they are analyzed in terms of similarities and differences between component parts and their positions within the characters, corresponding to similarities and differences in meaning between characters. In Figure 6.28 a few such tasks are shown. They are meant as possible alternatives to traditional dictation tasks (where the teacher reads words, one at a time, and the students have to write them; performance is then judged in terms of accuracy of writing, for which the students prepare by learning the words by heart).

Example of new dictation task for learning Chinese characters

In order to help students perceive similarities and variations in characters, find out underlying astructure and relationships between characters, new exercises have been designed. Below are some examples:

1) Using specific component to form different characters
    氵: 泡, 河, 洗, 清, 海, 湯
    (water: blister, river, wash, clear, ocean, soup)

2) Use different components that form different characters (students may use any components in the table and form meaningful characters)

亻	口	忄	言
足	可	氵	虫
扌	木	食	青
火	白	包	日

   亻 + 白 = 伯 (human + white = old man)
   虫 + 青 = 蜻 (insect + green = dragonfly)
   氵 + 可 = 河 (water + permit = river)

3) Adding components to form different characters (students can put any components in the box that they think can form a meaning character)
   食 + 包 = 飽 (eat + bread = satisfy)
   氵 + 古 + 月 = 湖 (water + old + moon = lake)

4) Subtract component(s) from a character so that it becomes another character (students can put any components in the box that can be subtracted to form a meaningful character)
   頑 - 元 = 頁 (play - coin = page)
   火 - 包 = 炮 (fire - bread = cannon)
   胡 - 古 = 月 (northern - old = moon)

FIGURE 6.28 Alternative tasks for learning Chinese characters (adapted from Tse et al., 2010, p. 101).

This alternative approach has been found to be highly effective in boosting the students' reading/writing skills and their reading comprehension (see Tse et al., 2010, Table 5.1 and 5.2, pp. 91–92). It has been widely adopted in Hong Kong, where it was developed, and it has now also spread to other countries where Chinese is taught as a mother tongue. It has possibly contributed to the remarkable improvement of Hong Kong students in the internationally comparative Progress in International Reading Literacy Study (PIRLS) test of reading comprehension. Between the years 2001 and 2006 Hong Kong went from 14th to 2nd place (see Cheung, Tse, Lam & Loh, 2009).

7
LEARNING TO HELP OTHERS TO LEARN

What Teachers Have to Be Good At

What has been said about learning and teaching in this book so far rests on the assumption that the ideas promoted might be useful conceptual tools in teachers' work. This chapter looks at a way in which this could be brought about. As the chapter is about learning, primarily teachers' learning this time, and as I want to follow the principles argued for throughout the book, let us begin by looking at those things that teacher are expected to learn more about.

Like other professionals, teachers need to be good at a great many things in order to do a good job. One of those things, emphasized in this book, is handling the objects of learning in powerful ways. Although this is surely not all there is to being good at teaching, it is of decisive importance for the students' learning. Moreover, it is a defining quality of the teaching profession.

"The object of learning" was dealt with in detail in Chapter 2. It was pointed out that it has to do with what the learners are expected to become able to do, what they need to learn in order to achieve that, the learning that is made possible for them and what they actually learn. The difference between "what the learners are expected to become able to do" (the object of learning in terms of educational objectives) and "what they need to learn in order to achieve this" (the object of learning in terms of critical aspects to be discerned) was emphasized. The aspects of the object of learning that are discerned and focused on simultaneously define the way in which it is seen.

Without learning to see, you cannot learn to do. Knowing what the learner is supposed to become able to do does not suggest what we should do in order to help the learners to learn. For this, we must find out what the learner needs to learn to see. Finding out what the students have to learn to see in order to become able to do certain things, under certain circumstances, is the philosopher's stone of the "art of teaching all things to all men" (Comenius, 1657/2002).

In order to find the "philosopher's stone" we have to start with the question, "What does it take to see certain things in certain ways?" An answer has been suggested in the previous chapters. As the students can never see all there is to be seen, they have to discern what they see. They have to delimit entities and discern their necessary aspects and features. Accordingly, we (teachers) must have an idea of what ways of seeing something we are trying to help the students to develop, what entities and what aspects and features of those entities we hope that the students will be able to delimit, discern and then simultaneously attend to. We ought to have a reasonably clear idea about *the intended object of learning,* in other words. And we also ought to have a reasonably clear idea about the students' ways of seeing the entity that we are dealing with, at different points in time; that is, we ought to have a reasonably clear idea about *the lived object of learning.*

What the teacher does and what happens in the classroom should ideally reflect the intended object of learning. The teacher is trying to help the students to make it their own. According to the theory this can be done by bringing about certain patterns of sameness and difference among tasks, problems, instances and illustrations; by pointing out and explaining those patterns and relations and by bringing about *the enacted object of learning,* reflecting our aims and expectations.

There are thus two closely related core components of teachers' professional competence. First, teachers ought to have insights into the different ways that students see and handle (and should become able to see and handle) the various objects of learning. Second, teachers ought to have insights into the different ways in which *they* might handle those objects of learning in order to enable the students to handle them in ways that are as powerful as possible. Shulman (1986) identified the same two components and coined the term "pedagogical content knowledge," referring to both components together. And you cannot have pedagogical content knowledge without content knowledge: you can only have insights into the students' ways of handling the content of an object of learning in relation to your own way(s) of handling that content, and you can only contribute to enabling the students to handle that content in powerful ways in relation to your own insights into what it takes to handle it in powerful ways.

The two core components are described in this book in terms specific to the underlying theory. The first component refers to the identification of critical aspects, and the second component refers to the constitution of patterns of variation and invariance.

Nobody can teach "in general." Teaching always means teaching something in particular to someone in particular. To do this in a powerful way does *not* amount to ignoring differences between learners and between contents, and acting in accordance with principles that cut across different learners and different objects of learning. No, on the contrary, using powerful ways of teaching involves finding out what has to be done in particular cases, for particular learners and for particular objects of learning. Just as the learners have to learn how to handle variation between different objects of learning and between different instances of the same objects of learning, teachers have to learn how to handle variation between the learners they are teaching and between the objects of learning they teach.

What Is to Be Done

The theory put forward in this book suggests that for every object of learning and for every learner or every group of learners there are certain necessary conditions of learning, specific for that object of learning and for that learner or that group of learners. The rather straightforward implication of this pedagogical theory of learning for pedagogical practice is that in order to make learning possible we have to find and bring about the conditions of learning that are necessary for the particular object of learning and the particular learner(s), in every case of learning.

What does it take to make this happen? Well, there are a few critical steps, which are presented here in a sequence but in reality are very much overlapping. This sequence of steps is supposed to apply to any pedagogical unit of school work. Such a unit is defined by an object of learning, something that the students are expected to learn. It might be a lesson, a double lesson or a sequence of lessons, or even a school year. Pedagogical units form hierarchies; some are parts of others. The steps are ideally these:

1) Choose a learning target (specify what the students are expected to be able to do by the end of the unit).
2) Find out what the learners can do already and what they must learn in order to achieve the target (find the critical aspects).
3) Identify the pattern of variation and invariance that is necessary for the learners to discern the critical aspects of the object of learning and to focus on them simultaneously.
4) Find out what the learners have to do in order to appropriate the object of learning; that is, find out in what kind of activities the pattern of variation and invariance should be embedded.
5) Carry out the plan, adjusting it continuously.
6) Find out what the students have learned.
7) Draw conclusions by relating what the learners have learned to how the object of learning has been handled, and document your conclusions.

Learning to Handle Pedagogical Units in More Powerful Ways

Hopefully, while working with a unit the students learn from the teacher how to see and handle the object of learning, while the teacher learns from the students about their ways of seeing and handling the object of learning in order to be able to help them to learn.

This chapter is about how the ideas presented so far in this book might contribute to teachers becoming better at being teachers. Hence, we have to ask what the object of learning is for teachers engaged in learning about the theory described in this book and how they can use it in their teaching. Two components were singled out in the previous section: finding the critical aspects (actually finding out what is to be learned) on the one hand and finding the patterns of variation and invariance that make it possible for the learners to discern the critical features in different cases on the other hand. In accordance with the theory, you can only grasp the idea of critical features by simultaneously grasping *some* critical features, and you can only grasp the idea of patterns of variation and invariance by simultaneously grasping *some* patterns of variation and invariance.

How is this to be done? In the previous chapter we were dealing with how teachers can make it possible for the students to learn. In this chapter we are dealing with the question of how it can be made possible for the teachers to learn. The principle should be the same. We have to start with the whole (a concrete case of a pedagogical unit), from which the critical aspects and the patterns of sameness and difference will be discerned.

By doing so, teachers can find out and learn about that specific case but also increase the probability of dealing powerfully with novel cases in the future. This is what Bowden and Marton (2004) called "learning on the individual level." Those who participate in the activity learn. But in order to make schools better places for learning, the findings should be shared with teachers who have not participated in the specific activity. This is what Bowden and Marton call "learning on the collective level," or research, in this case leading to the enhancement of the conceptual resources shared by teachers as a professional collective.

It would thus be an advantage if teachers engaged in in-service training with a focus on objects of learning that are relevant to their own subject, as suggested, and it would be an advantage if they engaged in the production of their own professional knowledge (i.e., if they engaged in research with a focus on their students' objects of learning and exchanged the results of this research). There is, indeed, a particular form of in-service training of teachers to promote learning on the individual level.—it is called a "lesson study." And there is a form of research that could be used to help teachers to learn on the collective level, called "design research." In the next section I will briefly describe the lesson study, and in the section after that, design research. Then I will describe an arrangement that combines the two, as far as their functions are concerned, called the "learning study."

Lesson Study

The lesson study, used in Japan for in-service training of teachers, became internationally known through Stigler and Hiebert's (1999) book *The Teaching Gap*, mentioned in the previous chapter. The authors identified the lesson study as a factor that potentially contributed to the excellence of Japanese students in international comparisons—in particular, in TIMSS (Trends in International Mathematics and Science Study). In a lesson study, a group of three to six teachers, who teach on the same level and in the same subject, get together, possibly assisted by a researcher, frequently by a teacher educator. They choose a topic that their students are supposed to learn, something that is important and difficult and which can be taught in one lesson. The group creates a lesson plan and one of the teachers is nominated to teach her own class in accordance with the lesson plan. The others in the group sit in on the lesson and observe what is happening. Afterwards, there is a discussion in the group about what has taken place and, in light of that discussion, the lesson plan is revised. Another teacher is now nominated to teach her class according to the revised lesson plan; the others again sit in and observe. After a final discussion, the study is documented and the experiences can thus be shared with other teachers.

We (our research group in Hong Kong) found the idea of the lesson study very interesting, especially as teachers work together on trying to find powerful ways of helping the students to make difficult and important objects of learning their own. We understood that lesson studies are mostly content oriented and deal with specific objects of learning, such as sawing straight or adding and subtracting negative numbers, for example. But lesson studies could deal with any topic, including different arrangements for learning (e.g., problem solving in groups), not only focusing on the content of learning (National Association for the Study of Educational Methods, 2011).

Design Research

Through research we hope to gain new insights. What we find out might not only enlighten us but even contribute to making things work better through innovations. Research and innovations can be linked to varying degrees. When the findings of research "are fed back into further cycles of innovative design" (Bereiter, 2002, p. 325) and put to the test there, we talk about design research. Design research is thus characterized by the closeness of knowledge generation and product (design) development. Furthermore, the validity of the former is tested against the latter, cyclically. The research is thus driven by the design work, while the design work is facilitated by research.

Bereiter (2002, p. 321) quoted Alfred North Whitehead (1925, p. 92), who argued that it was during the 19th century that the advancement of knowledge first became intimately linked with the advancement of technology, resulting in "a process of disciplined attack upon one difficulty after the other." The heart of the matter is sustained innovation, where every improvement opens up possibilities for further improvements, and it was exactly such a cumulative development that Whitehead had in mind when he said that "the greatest invention of the nineteenth century was the invention of the method of invention." Bereiter gives as examples the evolution of combustion car engines during the whole of the

20th century and of the television receiver from the 1950s onwards. In both cases the basic idea has remained the same; nevertheless, the development has been spectacular. We should remember that the emphasis here is not on the actual production of car engines or television receivers but on the production of design (or prototypes). This is why we call it design research, and this is why it yields sustained innovation.

The point has been made that one of the main problems with the improvement of education is that educational research fails to support sustained innovation (Bryk, Gomez, & Grunow, 2010). Accordingly, the need for design research in education has been emphasized again and again over the last 2 decades (Holmqvist, Gustavsson & Wernberg, 2008; Morris & Hiebert, 2011).

Learning Study

In accordance with what was said previously, we combined the idea of the lesson study and with that of design research and developed an arrangement encompassing the aims of both: learning on the individual as well as on the collective level—in-service training of teachers and a research undertaking. We called it a learning study (Marton, 2001).

A small group of teachers (three to six) tries to handle a particular pedagogical unit in as powerful a way as possible. From the point of view of the students, this is just a lesson (or a sequence of lessons) among other lessons—a part of regular school work. From the point of view of the teacher, it is a pedagogical unit, handled together with other teachers and perhaps a consultant (from a university, school, etc.). There is more time and effort invested than is possible in everyday school work, and there is a greater emphasis on arriving at new and generalizable insights than is possible in the daily work in school.

The students' ways of making sense of the content of the unit, initially and afterwards, is more systematically explored, planning is more extensive, as is reflection and analysis. The plan for handling the unit is revised once or twice and the revised plan is carried out in another class. The case is documented subsequently. Let me comment briefly on the component parts, one at a time. These correspond roughly to the steps in handling pedagogical units listed earlier in this chapter. The reason is, of course, that a learning study is a study of handling a pedagogical unit.

Who Will Help Whom to Learn

First of all, a few teachers teaching the same subject, on the same level, in one or several schools, decide to do a learning study in several parallel classes. If they do not have sufficient experience of learning studies, they may ask one or two consultants to join them, one being an expert on learning studies, for example, and the other an expert on the subject. If the two kinds of expertise are combined in the same person, it is even better, of course. The consultant or consultants may come from a university or from a school—the participants' own or from another. When the teachers have gained enough experience, they can run learning studies on their own.

What Is to Be Learned

The teachers choose an object of learning—something important, something known to cause difficulties for the students. It should be possible to appropriate it during the pedagogical unit chosen (usually a lesson).

The group plans the lesson together, using three to four meetings of 2 to 3 hours each, and when they have done so they nominate one teacher from among themselves to teach it (usually in her own class). The other teachers sit in and observe the lesson, taking notes. But the lesson is recorded as well, for further inspection.

In Chapter 2 it was pointed out that the object of learning can be described on different levels: in terms of the content of learning, in terms of what the students are expected to become able to do (educational objectives) and what the students have to learn in order to achieve this (discerning critical aspects). When describing the object of learning, one goes from the first to the second level, and then on to the third level, which is the main focus within the current framework.

Finding Critical Aspects (Developing the Intended Object of Learning)

As argued earlier, finding the critical aspects of a particular object of learning for a particular group of learners is a key to helping those particular learners to appropriate that particular object of learning. What resources can we draw on to find the critical aspects? Teachers can build on their previous experiences of similar kinds of learners, dealing with the same objects of learning. Most teachers are familiar with difficulties that appear in connection with particular topics. Such difficulties are also frequently identified in relevant research and can be found in publications about the learning and teaching of the subject in question. But the best resource is the group of learners being taught. They reveal critical aspects by what they say and what they do. This process is, of course, facilitated by the teachers' questions and the tasks the teacher invites the students to engage in. In a learning study this is done in a systematic way, with the students taking a pre-test. Such a pre-test consists of one or, more frequently, several questions. The questions are phrased in everyday words, as they are asked before the object of learning and the terminology related to it have been dealt with. Furthermore, an important aim is to find out whether or not the students discern certain aspects (dimensions of variation) and thus the questions should not point out the aspects to be discerned.

Let us consider, as an example, one question asked in the pre-test in the study about students' understanding of price and pricing described in Chapter 4:

> Have you ever tried the hot dogs sold in our school tuck shop? Do you know how much they are sold for? Maybe you know or you don't know. Anyway, just for your information, hot dogs are now sold for HK$4.50. Suppose that you are the new owner of the shop. What price would you set for a hot dog? Would you set the current price, or a different price? What would you consider when you set the price?
>
> (Pang & Chik, 2005)

We want to find out what aspects of the problem the students spontaneously discern. Hence, the problem is phrased so they can discern any aspects they find relevant. And this is what they do: some of them point to the qualities of the object, others point to the demand for it, others again to the supply of it and so forth. Compare this question with another question that could have been asked:

> Have you ever tried the hot dogs sold in our school tuck shop? Do you know how much they are sold for? Maybe you know or you don't know. Anyway, just for your information, hot dogs are now sold for HK$ 4.50. Suppose that you are the new owner of the shop. When you start your new business, you find that there is a shortage of hot dogs in Hong Kong, and you cannot get as many to your shop as you can sell every day. What price would you set for a hot dog? Would you set the current price, or a different price? What would you consider when you set the price?

In this case, two different values of the same dimension of variation (supply) are compared (earlier and now), which means that it is the question that introduces that dimension of variation and not the students. They still have to discern it, but it is made possible—and even likely—for them to do so, by the question presented by the teacher. Actually, this second kind of question represents an instructional move. This is what the teacher does in order to help the students to learn to discern the supply aspect of pricing. In the actual study, variation in supply is introduced in the auction game, while demand remains invariant.

There are many other examples, in various places in this book, of questions used to reveal which aspects of a situation the learners spontaneously discern. The logic of the construction of this kind of question is dealt with in Chapter 4 in connection with the methodological aspects of phenomenography.

The pre-test might be the same for all students or may be taken in two parallel versions (covering the same content and of equal levels of difficulty) by two randomly chosen halves of the class. In the latter case, the two parallel versions should be swapped between the two groups after the lesson. By doing so the class will have taken the same test (or rather, the same two tests) before and after the lesson, while every student will have taken two different tests.

Bringing About Patterns of Variation and Invariance (The Enacted Object of Learning)

Once the teachers have managed to find out what the critical aspects of the object of learning are, they try to help the students to learn to discern them. This can be done through a sequence of patterns of variation and invariance, described in the previous chapter in the section, "Bringing About Learning: The Order of Things." The same sequence is repeated here, in relation to the learning study model:

1) The undivided object of learning (*instantiation*). Usually, a problem is presented for the students to tinker with, affording an experience of the kind of situation the learner is expected to learn to master and a perspective from which the learning situation might be seen (relevance structure). Actually, the pre-test might have this function too (in addition to establishing a base level and generating data for identifying critical features).
2) Variation in each focused critical aspect, one at a time, against a background of invariance in other respects (*contrast*).
3) Variation in the non-defining aspects (across which the learners are supposed to become capable of generalizing) against a background of invariance in the critical dimensions (*generalization*).
4) Variation in all critical dimensions (*fusion*). In addition to practice with varying instances, the post-test might also contribute to this component.

The meaning of the object of learning that we (the teachers) expect the learners to appropriate, is a function of the pattern of variation and invariance (i.e., the relationships between the instances juxtaposed—cases, examples, problems).

Embedding Patterns of Sameness and Difference in Learning Activities

The fact that the patterns of sameness and difference are available to the learners is not enough. They have to engage in some activity—they have to do something with those patterns. In the study about pricing, the activity was participation in an auction; in the study about Cantonese as a second language, the activity was to recall—or to guess—one of the aspects (e.g., meaning) when another (e.g., tone) was given.

Once the teacher knows what pattern of sameness and difference has to be brought out, she has also to find learning activities in which it can be embedded.

Finding Out What Has Been Learned (The Lived Object of Learning)

As the main question in a learning study is the relation between the enacted and the lived object of learning (i.e., between the learning that is made possible on the one hand and what is actually learned on the other; we also have to describe the latter). This is usually done by having the students repeat at the end of the lesson the test they did at the beginning of the lesson (in the same or in a parallel version).

The difference between results from the pre-test and the post-test is an indication of what the students have learned during the lesson. If the content of the lesson is entirely new for the students, the pre- and the post-test might differ, of course.

Drawing Conclusions and Revising the Lesson

The lessons are, as a rule, recorded. The group working on the learning study can thus make use of the recording, in addition to their direct experience of the lesson and the notes taken. Also, the results from the pre- and post-tests are resources for analyzing what has happened and for drawing conclusions. The idea is to determine what the students have learned and what it is that they were supposed to learn: What was the object of learning? Have we really captured it? How has the lesson supported the students' learning? Is there anything that could have been done better? Is there anything we should change if we were to run the lesson again? The group develops a revised lesson plan and nominates another teacher to teach another class (usually her own) according to the revised lesson plan.

Different Cycles and Documentation

The discussion after the first lesson and the development of the revised lesson plan resembles the initial planning of the first lesson. Then the second cycle is completed, usually ending with the development of a third lesson plan, which is used in a third cycle. The discussion and analysis after that should result in documentation, in order to share the findings with others. This is necessary in relation to the second aim of learning studies—the contribution to learning on the collective level. In any case, the findings should be presented to other teachers. A PowerPoint presentation is the minimum requirement for documentation. In principle, most learning studies should yield a publishable paper. Many such papers have been published, and there is a specific scientific journal for such studies, the *Journal of Lesson and Learning Studies*.

Lesson studies usually have two cycles, and learning studies mostly have three. But in addition to the prototypical learning study there can be learning studies made up of one cycle only, or two, or four. A cycle is usually a lesson, but it can be 2, 3 or 15. As a rule, comparisons are made between different cycles, but sometimes the handling and the appropriation of the object of learning in the learning study is compared with the handling and the appropriation of the same object of learning in one or several "control" classes.

One of the defining features of the learning study is that it is owned by the teachers: they have to decide what to do and how. Other features are that there is an object of learning identified and that the focus of the study is the relationship between learning and teaching—between the lived and the enacted object of learning. Furthermore, there has to be a theoretical grounding for how to describe the former and how to design the latter.[1]

Examples of Learning Studies

To Have and To Be

The first example illustrates generative learning, mentioned in the previous chapter as referring to a content-specific "learning to learn" effect. Holmqvist and Molnar (2006) reported on a learning study with year-4 students (10–11 years old) in which the object of learning was to distinguish between the use of *has* and *have* in English. In Swedish the corresponding word (auxiliary) has only one form: "har." As described in the section on "Generative Learning" in the previous chapter, students in three classes were divided into three groups at random. One such group from each of the three classes was put together into three "artificial classes" for the learning study lesson. The idea was that by distributing the students in the artificial classes over three "real" classes, possible differential effects of teaching after the lesson on long-term retention would be equaled out. On average, the students in the artificial classes would encounter the same teaching. During the first lesson in the learning study, the inflected forms of the auxiliary verbs "to have" and "to be" were contrasted. The reason for doing this was that the short forms of "to be" and "to have" in the third person singular are identical (*he's, she's, it's*). The two forms thus have to be told apart by means of contextual clues. The intention was to help the students to grasp that this is the case. The idea was thus that learning to deal with the ambiguity of *he's, she's* and *it's* would help the students to learn to distinguish between the use of *has* and *have*.

After the first lesson, the teachers were not entirely happy with the results, and they thought that the contrast between "to be" and "to have" made things too complicated. So in lesson 2 and lesson 3, this contrast was dropped. And as expected, the results after lesson 2 and lesson 3 were better than after lesson 1 (the students were better at distinguishing between *has* and *have*).

Four weeks later the test was repeated. To the great surprise of the team, the students who had participated in lesson 1 now outperformed the students who had participated in lesson 2 and 3. In order to check the reliability of the unexpected outcome, yet another delayed test was carried out. But the results were again the same: students from lesson 1 outperformed students from lessons 2 and 3 in the long run. This means that the students who had the opportunity to distinguish between "to be" and "to have" (i.e., to separate the two) in the third person) became better at distinguishing between *has* and *have*, probably thanks to the former having been made visible through separation from *is* by means of varying contextual clues.

Understanding Fractions

Karlsson and Malm (2010) interviewed eight year-1 students (7 years old) about their understanding of fractions. This was done by asking them to represent 1/4 of a pizza or of a rectangle, or divide it into three or four parts, for example. It seemed as if the students did not differentiate between parts and partitioning: the former was "shadowed" by the latter; they were focusing on the acts of partitioning without seeing the denominator as referring to equal parts, making up a whole together. "Dividing into three parts" could thus mean drawing three lines, yielding four parts; "dividing into four parts" could mean drawing four lines, yielding five parts (see Figure 7.1) This means that distinguishing between parts and partitioning—and focusing on the latter—was a critical aspect and a critical feature of handling fractions for some of the participating children.

Another critical aspect and critical feature was distinguishing between dividing a whole (such as a pizza, for instance) into a number of parts and taking that number of parts *within* the whole (i.e., where these parts do not add up to the whole; see Figure 7.2). A third critical aspect was the way in which something was divided into a certain number of parts: equal parts (critical feature) or different parts.[2]

This investigation was not a learning study but could have been the first part of one (finding the critical aspects). Actually, it was a 10-week project assignment, a part of the authors' pre-service teacher training. Nonetheless, the identification of

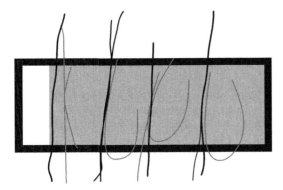

FIGURE 7.1 Dividing a rectangle four times instead of dividing it into four parts (Karlsson & Malm, 2010, p. 17, picture 7).

FIGURE 7.2 Taking four pieces of a pizza instead of dividing it into four parts (Karlsson & Malm, 2010, p. 15, picture 5).

the potential critical aspects and features of learning to handle rational numbers in powerful ways is of considerable general interest.

Learning Study on Negative Numbers

There is another study that Kullberg (2010) replicated under more controlled conditions (deciding on the design in advance). In the original learning study, new critical aspects were found throughout the cycles and the design changed accordingly. The first critical aspect was found through the students' answers to the pre-test but is available also in mathematics education literature. Many teachers are aware of this particular difficulty, which relates to the distinction between two senses of the minus sign meaning subtraction on the one hand and negative number on the other (also found in Olteanu's, 2007, study, referred to in the previous chapter).

It turned out to be easier to identify this critical aspect than to help the students to appropriate it, especially in the context of subtraction with negative numbers. There was another critical aspect that the students had to discern: the different metaphors used for making sense of subtraction. The thing is that you cannot use the most common metaphor of subtraction, —"take away"—with negative numbers. How do you take away -13 from -3, for instance? Instead of thinking in terms of taking away, you should compare the two numbers and focus on the difference between them instead of on the remainder. During the second lesson, yet another critical aspect was introduced in addition to subtraction as a difference: the perspective on subtraction. For example, if John is 12 years old and David is 9, we can say either that John is 3 years older $(12 - 9)$ or that David is 3 years younger (9 – 12). The difference has to be seen from the perspective of the first term, because subtraction is not commutative.

However, the results were still not great; even worse, during the third lesson a bolt of lightning struck the school, which caught fire. The fire was soon extinguished, but the lesson was ruined. Possibly thanks to this divine interference, during the fourth lesson, the teacher found that there is a fourth critical aspect. As we can see in Table 7.1 the students' learning improved considerably this time.

TABLE 7.1 Re-analysis of pre- and post-tests from the learning study on negative numbers (adapted from Kullberg, 2010, p. 69).

	Lesson 1 (N = 17)			*Lesson 2 (N = 17)*			*Lesson 4 (N = 21)*		
	Mean	*SD*	*Effect size*	*Mean*	*SD*	*Effect size*	*Mean*	*SD*	*Effect size*
Pre-test	0.82	0.88		1.35	1.22		0.81	0.98	
Post-test	1.35	1.00	0.56	2.06	0.90	0.66	2.24	0.83	1.57

What was the fourth critical aspect? During the lesson in the fourth cycle, the teacher tried to help the students discern the critical aspects of adding and subtracting negative numbers. But it became evident that something was missing when the teacher asked the students where to place the two numbers (–2) and (–1) in order to satisfy the expression (_ – _ = 1). It turned out that several students thought that –2 was the larger number of the two. The teacher realized that the nature of the number system was an additional critical aspect of the object of learning, and she said the following:

> I know what your problem is, and it was stupid of me not having considered this before. We have to find out which of the two numbers (–1) and (–2) is the biggest.
>
> (Kullberg, 2010, p. 68)

The students seemed to believe that 0 is the smallest number, and from that to the right the positive numbers get larger and larger, while to the left the negative numbers get larger and larger.

The Color of Light

Lo, Chik and Pang (2006) reported a learning study aimed at enabling year-3 students in Hong Kong (9 years old) to see sunlight as being decomposable into the seven colors of the rainbow, which may then be recombined into white light again. The arrangement used in two consecutive lessons is shown in Figure 7.3.

Two related critical features of the object of learning that were identified were the students' ability to see the colors of the rainbow as originating from—and

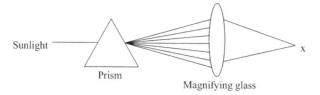

FIGURE 7.3 The demonstration set up for studying white light (adapted from Lo et al., 2006, p. 7).

being parts of—white light on the one hand and the ability to see the "tool nature" of the prism on the other hand. It was observed in connection with the pre-test that many students thought that the colors of the rainbow originated from the prism. Instead of seeing it as a tool diffracting the white light, they saw the colors of the rainbow as being produced by the prism. How can we then highlight the "tool nature" of the prism? When only the prism is used, its function and its tool nature are intertwined. Or to put it slightly differently, what is refracted (the effect) and what refracts (the agent) are not separated. In order to separate the two aspects, we have to introduce variation in the tool aspect (which is sub-ordinate to the functional aspect). We have to keep the function (diffraction) invariant and introduce other tools to perform it. This is the pattern that is called "generalization" in this book and it separates the tool nature of the prism from the prism. Its tool nature thus becomes visible.[3]

The alternative tools used in both classes were soap bubbles and water droplets, both diffracting white light into the seven colors of the rainbow. This intervention seemed successful in helping the students to see the tool nature of the prism, but they may still have not been aware of the white light as the origin of the seven colors. There could be a need for yet another action by the teacher. How can you contribute to making the learners aware of the presence of something? It is reasonable to think that this would happen through a contrast with the absence of that thing. In one of the classes, the teacher switched off the light for a second or two and thus made the learners aware of the importance of its presence. The gain scores relating to this insight were in this class very high indeed. (In the other class most students seemed to be aware of the role of light, even without the teacher introducing this contrast.)

What Is Straight?

Fröhagen and Ottander-Bjerkesjö (2009) carried out a learning study, together with three other teachers, in *sloyd* (handicraft). Year-5 and -6 students (12–13 years old) participated and they were expected to learn to saw straight by choosing the right kind of saw, fixing the wooden piece to be sawed, adopting a suitable position of the body and holding and moving the saw in an appropriate way. Two lessons

270 Learning to Help Others to Learn

were carried out. During the first one, the students were supposed to produce a wooden piece where all the angles were to be 90 degrees (see Figure 7.4). They were also asked to compare the suitability of different saws. The teacher told and showed the students how this should be done.

There was, however, not much improvement between pre- and post-tests in producing a straight sawed surface.

In the second lesson, the object of learning was adjusted towards developing a better understanding of what "sawing straight" actually means. Different ways of doing this were introduced, and it was emphasized that the angles might vary (do not all have to be 90 degrees) and that sawing straight can be done in many different ways (see Figure 7.5). The students had to choose and try out different saws for the different tasks. The teachers had realized that in order to discern the relationship between the angling of the saw and the surface produced (a critical aspect of the object of learning), the students had to experience variation both in the angling of the saw and in the surface produced. Those participating in the second lesson seemed to learn much better than those who had participated in the first lesson. By dealing with different tasks, they had to use different saws and use the same saw in different ways. In consequence, the relationship between their

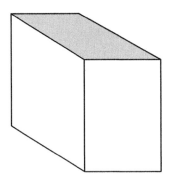

FIGURE 7.4 Wooden piece to be produced by the students during the first lesson (adapted from Fröhagen & Ottander-Bjerkesjö, 2009, p. 14).

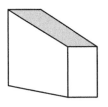 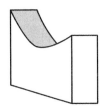 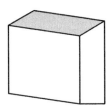

FIGURE 7.5 Wooden pieces to be produced by the students during the second lesson (adapted from Fröhagen & Ottander-Bjerkesjö, 2009, p. 14).

ways of handling the tasks and the results of their work became visible to them. Various ways of sawing were thus differentiated and linked to different outcomes.

Learning to Spell the tj Sound [C] in Swedish

Another study shows that the distinctions the learners can make—and have to make—in the learning activity are highly important for learning. A group of teachers, working with a researcher, designed a lesson that they thought would contribute to improving students' spelling of words with a *tj* sound [C] (Gustavsson, 2008). There are different ways to spell this sound, which conform to a rule-governed system (based on consonant–vowel combinations) with certain exceptions. One of the teachers carried out the lesson designed by the group. Afterwards, the group redesigned the lesson, and it was carried out by a second teacher with another group of students. The group revised the lesson again, and it was carried out by a third teacher with a third group of students. Just as in the first example of a learning study shown in this section, the students participating in three consecutive lessons came from different classes, and they were kept together for one lesson only, after which they returned to their own classes. All three groups took the same spelling test immediately after the lesson, again after 4 weeks, and once again after another 8 weeks. The first group lagged behind the other two groups initially but surpassed both groups sometime after the experiment. This group improved on each test, while the other two groups remained at the same level or became slightly weaker. The researchers investigated how the instructional treatments contributed to the differences across groups.

This study is similar to the first example ("to have" and "to be") in other respects in addition to having the same design. The first lesson was more complex than the other two: the immediate results were lower, the long-term results were higher. The central task of the students in this lesson was to underline all *tj* sounds [C] in a text given to them. This meant that the students had to differentiate between what signals a *tj* sound (should be underlined) and what signals an *sj* sound [S]—which is very close to the *tj* sound (should not be underlined). Thus, the students had to differentiate between different spellings of the same sound and different spellings of another sound.

In the second and third cycle this task was revised such that the students were given the same text but with all the *tj* sounds [C] removed, leaving gaps in their place. The students were asked to fill in the missing letters. In other words, the students did not have to differentiate between the *tj* sound and other sounds. Actually, they did not even need to read other words than those with missing letters. They had only to differentiate between the different spellings of the *tj* sound [C].

In order to explain why one group improved more than the two other groups after the learning occasion, the researchers conjectured that the students in the more successful group learned to pay attention to the differences between the *tj* sound [C] and the *sj* sound [S] (and other sounds), as well as to different spellings of the *tj* sound as compared to different spellings of the *sj* sound. The students became sensitized to a wider range of differences than the students in the other groups. Another way to put this is that the differences contributed to separating letter combinations and sounds, hence making them "visible." Accordingly, they had more opportunities for practicing what they had learned whenever they read or wrote something in Swedish, subsequent to their participation in the experiment. This condition was simply "better preparation for future learning," in the sense used by Bransford and Schwartz (1999).

An interesting aspect of this study is that the condition where students have to fill in letters ("fill-in condition") affords a more active role to the learners in a certain sense as they have to produce a particular spelling (among different possible spellings), while in the condition where students underline letters ("underlining condition") they only have to make choices between given alternatives. Still, the latter is correlated with better learning in the long run. This means that more contrast and less construction seems to be more conducive to learning than less contrast and more construction. In this case contrast means a comparison between words that are spelled differently and pronounced differently. Spelling and pronunciation are linked; hence, we cannot keep one aspect invariant while varying the other. In the fill-in condition the pronunciation is given, all the gaps are for some representation of [C] and the spellings vary. If the learners have previously noticed the difference between [C] and [S], this is generalization; otherwise it is induction (which should not work very well). The contrast between [C] and [S] is likely to emphasize the "[C]-ness" of certain combinations of letters and thus separate it from the specific words that are used.

From a more general perspective, this is yet another study in which a more complex pattern of variation and invariance yields weaker immediate results but stronger long-term results.

Reading the Clock

A group of Swedish teachers decided to run a learning study in three year-4 classes (students 11 years old). The object of learning was to be able to find out the amount of time that has elapsed between two given configurations of the clock (see Wernberg, 2009). The pre-test showed, however, that many students had difficulties with reading even one configuration. The teachers became curious and got some year-6 students involved in the study as well. Several of them also had difficulties with reading the clock (and they had problems with digital clocks as well). The teachers decided therefore to change the object of learning to simply "reading the clock." What did the students find difficult? It seemed that they could not see the relationship between the two arms, in terms of their functions. They did not realize that the fact that the long arm goes a full circle (12 sections) while the short arm moves one implies that the full circle travelled by the long arm is the one section travelled by the short arm magnified. If we had sharp enough eyes, we would not need the long arm at all. The students who had problems were not clear about configurations ("a quarter to," "a quarter past" "half. . . ," "half past"), not distinguishing between before and after whole hours. They could, for instance, read 6:25 as "five minutes to half six." Notice that unlike in colloquial English, *halv sex* (half six) in Swedish means 5:30, so when the student says that the time is five minutes before *halv sex* they are in fact wrong by an hour. In such a case, the learner seems to deal with the two arms separately. Focusing on the long arm first, she concludes that "it's five to half past." The question remains "half past what?" and the answer "6" springs from the fact that the short arm is closest to 6.

A substantial part of the first and second lesson of the learning study was spent on adjusting clocks to times given by the teacher in words, on reading out configurations produced by the teacher and getting feedback. The test after the lesson did not indicate that much learning had taken place, however. One of the teachers then made a somewhat radical change. Uncompromisingly, she removed the long arm of the practice clock. The theory advises us in such cases to let one aspect vary while the other is kept invariant. The two aspects of this particular situation (the two arms of the clock) are, however, correlated: if one moves, the other one moves as well. Removing the long arm is a substitute for keeping it invariant. Now the variation of the short arm is focused only and its function (meaning) is thus clarified. To the extent the function of the long arm is unclear to the students, it will very likely be made visible—paradoxically enough—through its absence, which makes the students unable to tell the time precisely. The results after the third lesson were slightly better than after the first and second one. But a delayed test after 6 weeks showed a much larger differences. Almost all of the students in the third group could answer all the questions, as compared to little more than half of the other two groups (see Table 7.2).

TABLE 7.2 Results in % for students participating in the three different cycles: pre-test (F), post-test (E1) and delayed post-test (E2), 9 weeks after the lesson (adapted from Wernberg, 2009, p. 111).

	Lesson 1A (n = 10)			*Lesson 1B (n = 8)*			*Lesson 1C (n = 8)*		
	F	E1	E2	F	E1	E2	F	E1	E2
1	50	60	40	63	63	63	63	63	88
2	100	100	60	100	100	88	75	100	100
3	30	50	60	50	50	50	50	63	75
4	30	50	40	25	25	50	38	63	63
5	40	55	60	63	50	63	50	63	100
M	48	62	53	60	56	63	54	69	88
SD	2.1	3.6	3.6	1.7	3.1	3.8	4.1	2.5	1.9

The Density of Rational Numbers

In this study, a group of mathematics teachers tried to help their students to understand that the rational numbers are dense (i.e., that there are infinitely many numbers between any two rational numbers). This is why, for example, we cannot say which is the smallest number higher than 3. This is the study that Kullberg (2010) tried to replicate under more controlled conditions, and it is described in the previous chapter. There we can see that the group of teachers failed to enlighten their students during the first cycle, when they focused on points on the number line and took the decimal representation of the rational numbers for granted. During the second cycle, however, the teachers found a more powerful way of teaching the density of rational numbers. They opened up the dimension of variation of representation and focused on fractions and on part–whole relations. In this way, the students realized that any fraction can be rewritten in terms of an infinite number of increasingly small units, and accordingly any interval on the number line can be divided into infinitely many parts. During the third cycle, they repeated the design with equal success, as was pointed out in the previous chapter.

"Learning Study in a Wider Sense"

The learning study has been characterized and exemplified in this chapter mainly as a particular arrangement for jointly choosing an object of learning and designing a lesson by a group of three to six teachers, teaching the same subject on the same level, with or without the support of an expert. The lesson is conducted by one of the teachers in her own class, and the students' understanding of the object of learning is explored before and after the lesson. The lesson is observed by the other teachers and discussed afterwards. The design for the lesson is revised by the group and then taught by another teacher in her class, again observed by the other teachers. This second cycle is mostly repeated once more, and after the third cycle and the final discussion the whole study is documented, often being presented to other teachers and possibly even published in some form.

In the previous chapter, several studies were reported that adhered to this model in several important respects, though they did not follow the model in every detail (for example, more than one lesson might have been used; there might have been one cycle only; in some cases one teacher might have planned the lesson or lessons on her own.). Pedagogical units of different kinds were introduced in the beginning of this chapter.

But even those studies have some important things in common with the learning study as it is described here: they have a theoretical ground, the teacher doing the teaching was involved in planning it, the students' understanding of the object of learning was explored somehow at the beginning and the end of the pedagogical encounter (which is ideally something that the teacher should focus on continuously). These are the characteristics of "learning study in a wider sense."

"Learning study" thus refers to a particular model for teachers' in-service training and research. "Learning study in a wider sense" refers to studies of the relationship between learning and the conditions of learning created by teachers, on their own or together with others. This is very much what Nuthall (2004) considered to be a very fundamental kind of pedagogical research, necessary for bridging the theory–practice gap.

Effects of Learning Studies

The model of the learning study was born as a response to an invitation for tender, sent out by the Ministry of Education in Hong Kong in 2000 to all universities within the territory. The idea was to solicit proposals for a project titled "Catering for Individual Differences." Hong Kong was at that point in the midst of an ambitious curriculum reform, part of which involved moving from a highly selective system towards one involving more heterogeneous classes. Handling differences between students in the same class, trying to learn the same thing, is a classical pedagogical problem. In the wake of the reform, this problem was expected to create much bigger problems than before. Could research address this dilemma?

I was a visiting professor at the University of Hong Kong, working with a wonderful group of people. We thought that our instruments (a focus on the object of learning; the search for critical aspects of the objects of learning and variation theory), would lend themselves very well to addressing the question. Our research was about why some students learn something while others fail to do so in the same classroom, but it was also about why students in a certain class manage to learn something that is taught there while students with the same relevant prerequisites fail to do so when the same thing is taught in another class. For us, catering for individual differences did not mean trying to match differences between students with differences in teaching arrangements across all kinds of content, such as using a concrete method for some and an abstract method for others, or to use a visual method for one group of students and an auditory method for another, or letting some students work on their own while others work in groups, regardless of what they were trying to learn. All these ways of categorizing students and categorizing teaching approaches cut across all kinds of contents and all kinds of objects of learning. But to the extent that students have problems with learning, they have problems with learning something (or many things) in particular. There are, undoubtedly, general problems with learning. But for every object of learning there are necessary aspects that the students have to discern in order to learn what they are expected to learn. This is true whether they are brilliant students or weak students, whether they are boys or girls and whether their parents are highly educated or not. We are thus less interested in differences between students across objects of learning than in differences between students *within* objects of learning.

The project "Catering for Individual Differences" was carried out in two classes in two different schools in Hong Kong, one in mathematics and the other in Chinese. Although the idea of a learning study was born in a research group at the University of Hong Kong, very soon afterwards, under the leadership of Professor Lo Mun Ling, a center for the development of the learning study model was set up at the Hong Kong Institute of Education, one of the world's biggest institutions for teacher education.

The learning study model spread in Hong Kong and also in some other parts of China, and subsequently in Sweden and quite a few other countries. I would guess that by the time this book is published, the number of completed learning studies will approach 1,000 altogether.

Marton and Pang (2013) summarized some of the main results of learning studies carried out so far:

- In nearly all of the studies, students' results were better after the lesson(s) developed than before (Lo, Pong & Chik, 2005). (Although this may appear self-evident, it is not. Unfortunately, there are many school lessons in which students learn nothing, or at least not what the teacher had hoped they would.)
- Students with fewer of the prerequisites for learning usually learn the most. Hence, not only does the average rise, but the difference between initially low- and high-achievers diminishes (Lo et al., 2005).[4]
- In cases in which what the students had learned was observed not only immediately after the lesson but also on a later occasion, the results were often found to be better at the later time (thus indicating a "learning to learn" effect, specific for the object of learning; Holmqvist, Gustavsson & Wernberg, 2008).
- Results on national achievement tests increased for classes that had participated in several learning studies, an effect that in all likelihood was mediated by changes in teachers' regular ways of teaching (Maunula, 2011).
- When the same object of learning is dealt with in a learning study and in a lesson study by groups of equally well-qualified teachers, the quality of learning turns out to be strikingly higher in the former (Marton & Pang, 2006, 2008; Pang, 2010; Pang & Marton, 2003).
- When the three cycles of a learning study are compared, the results from the third are usually better than those from the second, and those from the second are usually better than those from the first (Lo, Pong & Chik, 2005).

John Elliot, one of the founders of the action research movement in education, has evaluated two large-scale learning study projects carried out in Hong Kong. He concluded the following:

> The evaluation gathered convincing evidence of the positive impact of the process on teachers' and students' learning . . . . Learning Study is focused on realizing new kinds of pedagogical roles. From the evidence gathered in this evaluation it has enormous potential in this respect.
>
> (Elliott, 2004)

In Hong Kong the introduction of the learning study profited from the space and resources created by the curriculum reform. In a similar way, the introduction of the learning study model in Sweden profited from the space and resources created by a major governmental initiative to improve the teaching of mathematics. Schools could apply for projects aimed at improving the teaching and learning of mathematics. The most frequent projects included learning studies and/or applications of information and communication technology. In the report on the evaluation of these projects, the following was concluded:

> The evaluation shows that the learning study is an efficient method for improving teaching and thus enhancing the students' knowledge of mathematics. The teachers interviewed agree that working with the method is the best in-service training that they have ever experienced. The most rewarding aspect of the whole process was for them the opportunity to reflect, together with their colleagues, on how to present the mathematical content to the students in the classroom.
> (Skolverket, 2012, p. 32, translation mine)

Mårtensson's (2013) research pointed to what teachers get better at when they get better at teaching. She detected changes in the teachers' ways of referring to the object of learning. Initially they talk about mathematical entities such as linear equations, linear functions and graphic representations. These are objects of learning given in terms of content. From that they move to referring to capabilities, such as solving equations, representing functions graphically and matching mathematical expressions with their graphical representations. These are objects of learning given in terms of educational objectives. Eventually, they refer to differences in the students' ways of seeing the objects of learning. "Ways of seeing" or "meanings of mathematical entities" are separated by critical aspects. The teachers conclude that the students have difficulties with seeing the unknown x as a specific number or as a variable that can take different values. They may discover that students might have problems with matching linear functions represented algebraically and graphically for the simple reason that some students see "steepness" in relation to the x axis while others see it in relation to the y axis. This means that a new meaning, "reference axis," is a critical aspect with two values to be appropriated. These are examples of objects of learning given in terms of critical aspects and critical features. The major achievement of the teachers in this case is that they develop an understanding of critical aspects in terms of differences between different ways of seeing the object of learning. Or in other words, getting better at teaching might amount to getting better at finding out what the students have to learn.

Teachers' Research

In the beginning of this chapter a learning study was introduced as something in between a lesson study and design research, being at the same time both a kind of lesson study and a kind of design research. It differs from other kinds of lesson studies by focusing primarily on finding out something and secondarily on being an in-service training of teachers (instead of the other way around). It differs from other kinds of design research by focusing not only on finding out something and developing more powerful designs but also on being an in-service training.

Teachers' active involvement in the production of their own professional knowledge through research is certainly not a novel theme. According to Elliott (1991), "the teachers-as-researchers movement emerged in England during the 1960s" (p. 3). The context of this movement was a school-based curriculum reform in a school system that was highly differentiated (by means of exams, such as the "11+," with alternative paths thereafter and streaming within those alternative paths). "School-based curriculum reform" refers to attempts by teachers to change what was taught and how it was taught, and the attempts differed between schools in accordance with differences between students as well as between staff. This was the action research for educational change movement, most closely associated with Lawrence Stenhouse at the University of East Anglia: "The idea is that of an educational science in which each classroom is a laboratory, each teacher a member of a scientific community" (Stenhouse, 1975, p. 142). The point is that no behavioral objectives or learning targets on the national level can capture the diversity that exists in the educational system as far as the conditions and the enacted goals in different classrooms are concerned. If you want to find out what happens in each classroom and with what effect, the teachers have to explore the relationship between what happened in their classroom and the results obtained. "A particular kind of professionalism is implied: research-based teaching," Stenhouse said (p. 141). The idea of trying to capture the relationship between what is happening in the classroom and the students' learning is in agreement with what Nuthall (2004) considered to be the central question in educational research as well as with what we try to achieve with each learning study.

But can teachers' research be "real" (basic) research, and above all, can it be powerful research? Let us begin by considering the first of these two questions.

Can Teachers' Research Be Basic Research?

There is a deep-seated idea about research and knowledge production. According to this idea, we should find out what is generally true in all kind of contexts and in all kind of situations. Once we succeed, we have knowledge that is applicable in any contexts and any situations. This kind of research is called "basic research." Its driving force and the criterion of its success is its relevance to the advancement of knowledge. On the other hand, there is research aimed at solving specific problems. This kind of research is called "applied research"—its driving force and the criterion of its success being its usefulness for direct application. It builds on general knowledge produced by basic research and on specific knowledge of specific conditions. Such research can—in the view of many—hardly produce general knowledge of the sort that the first kind of research might. Basic research is then thought to be at one end of a scale and applied research at the other end. In between, there are various forms of research—more or less basic, more or less applied. As research is, in this case, ordered in one dimension, the two kinds of research appear as each other's opposites: the more basic, the less applied and the more applied, the less basic (see Figure 7.6)

In his book *Pasteur's Quadrant,* Stoke (1997) argued against such a one-dimensional view of the relationship between basic and applied research. The title of the book derives from the fact that Pasteur's discovery of micro-organisms that enter the body from the outside and cause diseases was made in the context of addressing some highly practical questions to do with the French wine industry. There are many other examples of so-called applied research leading to insights into fundamental scientific problems simply because the solution of highly practical and occasionally rather narrow problems requires such insights. Stoke's first point was that, instead of ordering basic and applied research in one dimension, as opposite ends of a scale, we should represent them in a two-dimensional space using two different driving forces and criteria (see Figure 7.7). If we do so, we will realize that there are not two but four different kinds of research: research that advances knowledge and is immediately useful, research that advances knowledge without being immediately useful, research that is immediately useful without advancing knowledge and research that is neither useful nor advances knowledge.

Stoke's second point was that we should go for more use-inspired basic research (research of the first kind). The learning study was actually introduced in Sweden

APPLIED--BASIC

FIGURE 7.6 The traditional view of the relation between basic and applied research (adapted from Stoke, 1997).

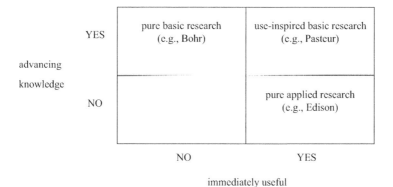

FIGURE 7.7 Rewriting the basic versus applied research dichotomy (adapted from Stoke, 1997).

in such terms (Marton, 2003, 2005). It was called "praxis-related basic research," a label seriously questioned by adherents of what was called "the traditional view" (see SOU:31, 2005). They argued that education is a societal sector, hence it cannot be the object of basic research.

Can Teachers' Research Be a Powerful Kind of Research?

The figure–ground reversal of research on learning does not have only epistemological but as organizational aspects as well, especially as far as the social distribution of knowledge production is concerned. Research with a focus on widely varying objects of learning has to be carried out in many sites, in widely varying contexts. One of the arguments for more diversified approaches to research that has probably made the greatest impact during the last two decades was Gibbons et al.'s (1994) *The New Production of Knowledge: The Dynamics of Science and Research in Contemporary Societies.*

The point made by Gibbons and his co-authors that is probably most relevant for the present discussion of teachers' research is about moving knowledge production towards the context of application. If it is the case that the very application of research findings is highly problematic and complex, which is indeed true as far as research on learning and teaching is concerned, it seems reasonable to include application in the research undertaking. Furthermore, as Nowotny, Scott and Gibbons (2003) remarked, when revisiting *The New Production of Knowledge,* "it is necessary to reach beyond the knowable context of application, towards the unknowable context of implication" (p. 192). But how can we reach towards what is unknowable, by means of what is knowable? Here we have the question, formulated earlier about learning on the individual level, raised as a question about learning on the collective level. The answer, however, must be similar: we can reach beyond the knowable by experiencing certain patterns of variation and invariance among instances of the known.

Following a similar point made by Cronbach (1980); Bryk, Gomez and Grunow (2010) argued for distributing knowledge production to many and varied sites that perform strategically different parts of the research work instead of trying to handle the whole in one place, at one site. This is probably not good advice as far as all research is concerned, but it is in all likelihood good advice as regards research on learning and teaching.

In School

In all the complexity of teachers' work, I would like to single out two things:

1) Focus on the object of learning and find the critical aspects that it is necessary to discern in order to appropriate it.
2) Find the patterns of variation and invariance that are necessary for learning to discern each critical feature, and bring these patterns about.

On what grounds can we single out these two things? On the grounds that they are necessary for learning and currently receive insufficient attention in school and in research.

What would it take for teachers to pay more attention to these two aspects of learning? First of all, they must see the point in doing so. I have written this book to convince them. Second, there are necessary conditions for this to happen. Again, I want to single out two of these conditions.

1) Teachers have to have time to explore the critical aspects of the objects of learning, to find and instantiate the necessary patterns of variation and invariance and to follow up what the students actually learn.
2) Teachers have to work with other teachers, striving for the same goals and teaching the same thing.

According to the McKinsey (2007) report on comparisons of educational achievement among nations, in the top-performing countries at least 10% of teachers' work consists of discussing what the students should learn next and how they can be helped to do this. In China, teachers work many hours per week but might teach only 6 to 14 lessons (see, for instance, Paine & Ma, 1993). The rest of their working time they spend analyzing curriculum documents, textbooks and other educational materials, having contact with students outside the teaching hours but above all planning and following up their teaching with their colleagues. It would probably be a very good idea to make the question of what is to be learned and how it should be dealt with a topic of conversation among teachers in schools everywhere.

For this to happen, teachers have to work with other teachers, teaching the same content on the same level. In China, teachers teaching the same content on the same level are organized into what is called a "teachers' research group." This way of organizing teachers' work is reflected on different levels (school, district, region). In Sweden, for instance, teachers are frequently engaged in working with other teachers teaching the same students (but mostly not teaching the same subject). Such a group is called *arbetslag* (work-team). What the teachers have in common are the students whom they all teach (though teaching them different subjects). The students themselves, and not the content of learning, become the shared topic of conversation. This is, of course, very good for discussing the students, their possible social, personal and motivational strengths or problems, but not for joint planning of teaching. Depending on how teachers are grouped together, they will have different things in common and hence might address different things in their discussions. If the focus is on what the students should learn and how the content should be dealt with, teachers teaching the same content on the same level have to work together. If the focus is on the students as individuals across different subject, teachers teaching the same students should work together. The best solution is probably to combine the two ways of forming teams.

We can thus identify two necessary conditions for following the suggested course of action with regard to the way in which teachers' work is organized: they need sufficient time for dealing with the objects of learning as well as with the learners, and they need colleagues with whom they share that time.

Notes

1. Does this theoretical grounding have to be variation theory? Of course not. Education suffers, more than anything, from the swift coming and passing of fads of all kinds. Variation theory is not supposed to be one of them. It is a pedagogical theory of learning, and it assumes a scientific attitude on the part of the user. The primary critical feature of such an attitude is the realization that you can be wrong. The theory has to be put to the test again and again, being modified, developed and complemented by other theories (for such an argument and an example, see Airey & Linder, 2009) or replaced if it does not serve its purpose.
2. Discerning critical aspects and features amounts to opening dimensions of variation. But going from dividing something into a certain number of parts in any way to dividing it into a certain number of equal parts may not sound like opening a dimension of variation. It rather seems that we go from more variation to less variation in this case. But what happens is that "the sizes of parts" are noticed when the dimension of variation is opened. This means that distinctions are being made that were not made before. It is in this sense that the space of learning grows.
3. It is assumed that the students are able to see things as tools for achieving certain purposes.
4. This particular finding has been replicated in practically every learning study (see, for instance, Lo, 2012) and looks a bit like a natural law. But how can that be so? The statistically sophisticated reader now probably thinks of these results as at least in part statistical artefacts. One thing that it is difficult to control is the ceiling effects (that those students who have high scores on the pre-test, cannot improve their results on the post-test as much as those who have low scores on the pre-test), another is that the scale on which gains are measured might not be (and in all likelihood is not) linear. This means, for instance, that a difference at the top of the scale may have a different meaning from the same numerical difference in the middle of the scale. On the other hand there is plenty of evidence for the conclusion that students with lower scores on the pre-test (i.e. with less complex understanding) gain more from the learning study as far as the specific object of learning is concerned than students with an initially more complex understanding.

    The explanation is that in a learning study, critical aspects of the object of learning are identified and focused on in order to enable the students to learn to discern those aspects which are vital in novel situations. Critical aspects are aspects that some students manage to discern, and others do not. Hence the teaching is geared towards things that some of the students have not mastered. This means that the other students are exposed to constituent parts of objects of learning that they have mastered already. One of our latest studies (Pang & Marton, 2013), discussed in the previous chapter, demonstrates, however, that when the teaching is differentially tailored for groups of students with different prerequisites, the gain is very similar for the different groups.

REFERENCES

Ahlberg, A. (1992). *Att möta matematiska problem. En belysning av barnens lärande* [Encountering mathematical problems]. Gothenburg, Sweden: Acta Universitatis Gothoburgensis.
Airey, J. & Linder, C. (2009). A disciplinary discourse perspective on university science learning: Achieving fluency in a critical constellation of modes. *Journal of Research in Science Teaching, 46*(1), 27–49.
Åkerlind, G. S. (2003). *Growing and developing as an academic: Implications for academic development, academia and academic work* (Unpublished doctoral thesis, University of Sydney, Australia).
Al Murani, T. (2007). *The deliberate use of teaching algebra: A realistic variation study* (Unpublished doctoral thesis, University of Oxford, England).
Al Murani, T. & Watson, A. (2009, August). *Exchange systematicity: Interactional dynamics of variation in mathematics lessons.* Paper presented at the bi-annual conference of the European Association for Research on Learning and Instruction, Amsterdam, The Netherlands.
Anderberg, E., Svensson, L. & Alvegård, C. (2008). The epistemological role of language use in learning: A phenomenographic intentional-expressive approach. *Educational Research Review, 3*(1), 14–29.
Anderson, L. W., Krathwohl, D. R., Airasian, P. W. & Cruikshank, K. A. (2000). *A taxonomy for learning, teaching, and assessing: A revision of Bloom's taxonomy of educational objectives* (Complete ed.). New York, NY: Pearson.
Ashton-Warner, S. (1963). *Teacher.* New York, NY: Simon & Schuster.
Athey, C. (1990). *Extending thought in young children: A parent-teacher partnership.* London, UK: Paul Chapman.
Barnett, S. A. (1973). Homo docens. *Journal of Biosocial Science, 5,* 393–403.
Bateson, G. (1980). *Mind and nature: A necessary unity.* Toronto, Ontario, Canada: Bantam Books.
Bauersfeld, H. (1988). Interaction, construction, and knowledge—Alternative perspectives for mathematics education. In D. A. Grouws & T. A. Cooney (Eds.), *Perspectives on research on effective mathematics teaching: Research agenda for mathematics education* (Vol. 1, pp. 27–46). Reston, VA: NCTM and Lawrence Erlbaum.

Behr, M., Harel, G., Post, T. & Lesh, R. (1993). Rational numbers: Toward a semantic analysis-emphasis on the operator construct. In T. Carpenter, E. Fennema & T. A. Romberg (Eds.), *Rational numbers: An integration of research* (pp. 13–48) Hillsdale, NJ : Lawrence Erlbaum.

Bereiter, C. (2002). Design research for sustained innovation. *Cognitive Studies, 9*(3), 321–327.

Bergqvist, K. (1990). *Doing schoolwork: Task premises and joint activity in the comprehensive classroom*. Linköping, Sweden: Linköping Studies in Arts and Science.

Biggs, J. B. (1996). Western misconceptions of the Confucian-heritage learning culture. In D. A. Watkins & J. B. Biggs (Eds.), *The Chinese learner: Cultural, psychological and contextual influences* (pp. 45–68). Hong Kong, China: CERC.

Biggs, J. B. & Collis, K. F. (1982). *Evaluating the quality of learning: The SOLO taxonomy*. New York, NY: Academic Press.

Biggs, J. & Tang, C. (2007). *Teaching for quality learning* (3rd ed.). Maidenhead, UK: Open University Press.

Björklund, C. (2007). *Hållpunkter för lärande: Småbarns möten med matematik* [Critical conditions of learning: Toddlers encountering mathematics]. Jakobsdal, Sweden: Åbo Akademi University.

Black, P., Harrison, C., Lee, C., Marshall, B. & Wiliam, D. (2004). Working inside the black box: Assessment for learning in the classroom. *Phi Delta Kappan, 81*, 9–21.

Bloom, B. S., Engelhart, M. D., Furst, E. J., Hill, W. H. & Krathwohl, D. R. (1956). *Taxonomy of educational objectives—Handbook I: The cognitive domain*. New York, NY: David McKay.

Boden, M. (2004). *The creative mind: Myths and mechanisms* (2nd ed.). London, UK: Routledge.

Bogdan, B. (1999). *Patterns of human growth* (2nd ed.). Cambridge, UK: Cambridge University Press.

Booth, S. (1992). *Learning to program: A phenomenographic perspective*. Gothenburg, Sweden: Acta Universitatis Gothoburgensis.

Boulton-Lewis, G. M., Marton, F., Lewis, D. C. & Wilss, L. A. (2004). A longitudinal study of learning for a group of indigenous Australian university students: Dissonant conceptions and strategies. *Higher Education, 47*, 91–112.

Bowden, J., Dall'Alba, G., Martin, E., Masters, G., Laurillard, D., Marton, F., Ramsden, P. & Stephanou, A. (1992). Displacement, velocity, and frames of reference: Phenomenographic studies of students' understanding and some implications for teaching and assessment. *American Journal of Physics, 60*, 262–268.

Bowden, J. & Marton, F. (2004). *The university of learning*. London, UK: Routledge Falmer.

Bowden, J. & Walsh, E. (Eds.). (2000). *Phenomenography*. Melbourne, Australia: RMIT University Press.

Bradley, F. H. (2008). *Appearance and reality*. New York, NY: Macmillan.

Bransford, J. D. & Schwartz, D. L. (1999). Rethinking transfer: A simple proposal with multiple implications. In A. Iran-Nejad & P. D. Pearson (Eds.), *Review of research in education, 24*, 61–100.

Brousseau, G. (1997). *Theory of didactical situations in mathematics*. Dordrecht, The Netherlands: Kluwer.

Brown, J. S., Collins, A. & Duguid, P. (1989). Situated cognition and the culture of learning. *Educational Researcher, 18*, 32–42.

Brumby, M. N. (1979). *Students' perceptions and learning styles associated with the concept of evolution by natural selection* (Unpublished doctoral thesis, University of Surrey, England).

Bryk, A. S., Gomez, L. M. & Grunow, A. (2010). *Getting ideas into action: Building networked improvement communities in education.* [Essay]. Carnegie Foundation for the Advancement of Teaching, Stanford, CA. Retrieved from http://www.carniegiefoundation.org/spotlight/webinar-bryk-gomez-building-networked-improvement-communities-in-education

Buck-Morss, S. (1975). Socio-economic bias in Piaget's theory and its implications for cross-culture studies. In K. F. Riegel (Ed.), *The development of dialectical operations* (pp. 35–49). Basel, Switzerland: Karger.

Burger, W. F. & Shaughnessy, J. M. (1986). Characterizing the van Hiele levels of development in geometry. *Journal for Research in Mathematics, 17*(1), 31–48.

Calvin, W. H. (1996). *How brains think.* New York, NY: Basic Books.

Calvin, W. H. (2004). *A brief history of mind.* Oxford UK: Oxford University Press.

Carlgren, I. & Marton, F. (2000). *Lärare av imorgon* [Teachers of tomorrow]. Stockholm, Sweden: Lärarförbundet.

Cassirer, E. (1923). *Substance and function: Einstein's theory of relativity.* Chicago, IL: Open Court.

Chase, W. G. & Simon, H. A. (1973). Perception in chess. *Cognitive Psychology, 4,* 55–81.

Cheung, W. M. (2005). *Describing and enhancing creativity in Chinese writing* (Unpublished doctoral thesis, University of Hong Kong).

Cheung, W. M., Marton, F. & Tse, S. K. (2010). Soaring across the sky like a heavenly horse: Enhancing creativity in Chinese writing. In F. Marton, S. K. Tse & W. M. Cheung (Eds.), *On the learning of Chinese* (pp. 147–162). Rotterdam, The Netherlands: Sense.

Cheung, W. M., Tse, S. K., Lam, J. W. I. & Loh, E. K. Y. (2009). Progress in international reading literacy study 2006 (PIRLS): Pedagogical correlates of fourth-grade students in Hong Kong. *Journal of Research in Reading, 32*(3), 293–308.

Chi, M., Feltovich, P. & Glaser, R. (1981). Categorization and representation of physics problems by experts and novices. *Cognitive Science, 5,* 121–152.

Chik, P. P. M. (2006). *Differences in learning as a function of differences between hierarchical and sequential organization of the content taught* (Unpublished doctoral thesis, University of Hong Kong).

Chik, P. P. M., Leung, A. & Marton, F. (2010). Learning words. In F. Marton, S. K. Tse & W. M. Cheung (Eds.), *On the learning of Chinese* (pp. 103–122). Rotterdam, The Netherlands: Sense.

Chik P. P. M. & Marton, F. (2010). Chinese pedagogy and a pedagogy for Chinese. In F. Marton, S. K. Tse & W. M. Cheung (Eds.), *On the learning of Chinese* (pp. 9–30). Rotterdam, The Netherlands: Sense.

Chomsky, N. (1959). Review of B. F. Skinner's "Verbal Behavior." *Language, 35,* 26–58.

Claparede, E. (1919). La conscience de la resemblance et de la différence chez l'enfant [The child's awareness of similarity and difference]. *Archives de Psychologie, 17,* 67–80.

Comenius, J. A. (2002). *Didactica Magna—Stora undervisningsläran* [The great science of teaching]. Lund, Sweden: Studentlitteratur. (Original work published 1657)

Crombie, A. C. (1953). *Robert Grosseteste and the origins of experimental science, 1100–1700.* Oxford, UK: Oxford University Press.

Cronbach, L. J. (1980). *Toward a reform of program evaluation.* San Francisco, CA: Jossey Bass.

Cronbach, L. J. & Snow, R. E. (1977). *Aptitudes and instructional methods: A handbook for research on interactions.* New York, NY: Irvington.

Csibra, G. & Gergely, G. (2006). Social learning and social cognition: The case for pedagogy. In Y. Munakata & M. H. Johnson (Eds.), *Processes of change in brain and cognitive development, attention and performance, XXI* (pp. 249–274). Oxford, UK: Oxford University Press.

Dahlgren, L. O. (1978). Effects of university education on the conceptions of reality. *Reports from the Institute of Education, University of Göteborg.*

Dahlgren, L. O. (1979). Children's conception of price as a function of the questions asked. *Reports from the Institute of Education, University of Göteborg.*

Dahlgren, L. O. (1985). *Quality and quantity in teaching and learning: Economics at university level as a case.* Unpublished manuscript, Department of Education and Psychology, University of Linköping, Sweden.

Davydov, V. V. (1990). *Types of generalization in instruction.* Reston, VA: National Council of Teachers of Mathematics.

Day, J. M. (1994). Introduction. In J. M. Day (Ed.), *Plato's "Meno" in focus* (pp. 1–34). London, UK: Routledge.

de Groot, A. D. (1965). *Thought and choice in chess.* The Hague, The Netherlands: Mouton.

Deleuze, G. (2004). *Difference and repetition.* London, UK: Continuum.

Derrida, J. (2001). *Writing and difference.* London, UK: Routledge.

de Saussure, F. (1916/1983). *Course in general linguistics.* Guildford, UK: Duckworth.

Education Commission. (2000). *Learning for life, learning through life.* Hong Kong, China: Government Printer.

Einhorn, S. (1998). *En dold Gud* [A hidden God]. Stockholm, Sweden: Månpocket.

Ekeblad, E. (1993). *Barn som pedagoger. Rapport nr 15 Institutionen för pedagogik* [Children as pedagogues]. Gothenburg, Sweden: Göteborgs Universitet.

Ekeblad, E. (1996). *Children, learning, numbers.* Gothenburg, Sweden: Acta Universitatis Gothoburgensis.

Elliott, J. (1991). *Action research for educational change.* Buckingham, UK: Open University Press.

Elliott, J. (2004). *The independent evaluation of the progressive and innovative primary schools (PIPS) project.* Hong Kong: Hong Kong Institute of Education.

Emanuelsson, J. (2001). *En fråga om frågor* [A question about questions]. Gothenburg, Sweden: Acta Universitatis Gothoburgensis.

Emanuelsson, J. & Häggström, J. (2008, March 24–28). *Algebra teaching and classroom evaluation in the west and the east: A comparative study of classroom interaction in relation to algebraic tasks.* Paper presented at the annual meetings of the American Educational Research Association, New York, NY.

Engeström, Y. (1991). Non scolae sed vitae discimus: Toward overcoming the encapsulation of school learning. *Learning and Instruction, 1,* 243–259.

Engeström, Y (2011) Personal communication.

Entwistle, N. & Marton, F. (1994). Knowledge objects: Understandings constituted through intensive academic study. *British Journal of Educational Psychology, 64,* 161–178.

Fan, L. & Zhu, Y. (2004). How have Chinese students performed in mathematics? A perspective from large-scale international comparisons. In L. Fan, N-Y. Wong, J. Cai & S. Li (Eds.), *How Chinese learn mathematics: Perspectives from insiders* (pp. 3–26). Singapore: World Scientific.

Feffer, M. (1988). *Radical constructionism: Rethinking the dynamics of development.* New York, NY: New York University Press.

Feldman, D. (1980). *Beyond universals in cognitive development.* Norwood, NJ: Ablex.

Ferreiro, E. & Teberosky, A. (1979). *Los systemas de escritura en el desarrollo del niño* [Writing systems in child development]. Siglo, México: Siglo XXI. (Quoted by Tolchinsky, 2003).

Fodor, J. (1980). On the impossibility of acquiring "more powerful" structures. In M. Piattelli-Palmarini (Ed.), *Language and learning: The debate between Jean Piaget and Noam Chomsky* (pp. 142–162). London, UK: Routledge.

Fröhagen, J. & Ottander-Bjerkesjö, H. (2009). *Att kunna såga rakt: Rapport från en learning study i slöjd [Sawing straight]* (Unpublished thesis, Stockholms Universitet, Sweden).

Fyrenius, A., Wirell, S. & Silén, C. (2007). Students approaches to achieving understanding—Approaches to learning revisited. *Studies in Higher Education, 32*(2), 149–165.

Galili, I., & Hazan, A. (2000). The influence of an historically oriented course on students' content knowledge in optics evaluated by means of facets-schemes analysis. *American Journal of Physics, 68*(7), 3–15.

Garner, W. R. (1974). *The processing of information and structure*. Potomac, MD: Erlbaum.

Gergely, G., Bekkering, H. & Kiraly, I. (2002). Rational imitation in preverbal infants. *Nature, 415,* 755.

Gergely, G. & Csibra, G. (2006a). Social learning and social cognition: The case for pedagogy. In Y. Munakata & M. H. Johnson (Eds.), *Processes of change in brain and cognitive development, attention and performance, XXI* (pp. 249–274). Oxford, UK: Oxford University Press.

Gergely, G. & Csibra, G. (2006b). Sylvia's recipe: The role of imitation and pedagogy in the transmission of cultural knowledge. In N. J. Enfield & S. C. Levenson (Eds.), *Roots of human sociality: Culture, cognition and human interaction* (pp. 229–255). Oxford, UK: Berg.

Gibbons, M., Limoges, C., Novotny, H., Schwartzman, S., Scott, P. & Trow, M. (1994). *The new production of knowledge: The dynamics of science and research in contemporary societies*. London, UK: Sage.

Gibson, E. J. (1969). *Principles of perceptual learning and development.* New York, NY: Appleton-Century-Crofts.

Gibson, J. J. & Gibson, E. J. (1955). Perceptual learning: Differentiation or enrichment. *Psychological Review, 62,* 32–41.

Glaser, B. G. & Strauss, A. L. (1967). *The discovery of grounded theory: Strategies for qualitative research*. New Brunswick, NJ: Aldine Transaction.

Goldenberg, P. & Mason, J. (2008). Shedding light on and with example spaces. *Educational Studies in Mathematics, 69,* 183–194.

Gould, S. J. (1997). *Life's grandeur.* London, UK: Vintage.

Gruber, H. E. (1974). *Darwin on Man*. London, UK: Wildwood House.

Gu, L. (1991). *Xuehui jiaoxue* [Learning to teach]. Beijing, China: People's Education Press.

Gu, L. Y., Huang, R. J. & Marton, F. (2004). Teaching with variation: A Chinese way of promoting effective mathematics learning. In L. H. Fan, Y. Wong, J. F. Cai & S. Q. Li (Eds.), *How Chinese learn mathematics: Perspectives from insiders* (pp. 309–347). Singapore: World Scientific.

Guo, J. P. & Pang, M. F. (2011). Learning a mathematical concept from comparing examples. *European Journal of Psychology of Education, 26,* 495–525.

Gurwitsch, A. (1964). *The field of consciousness*. Pittsburgh, PA: Duquesne University Press.

Gustafsson, B., Stigebrandt, E. & Ljungvall, R. (1981). *Den dolda läroplanen* [The hidden curriculum]. Stockholm, Sweden: Liber.

Gustafsson, J-E. (1976). *Verbal and figural aptitudes in relation to instructional methods: Studies in aptitude-treatment interactions*. Gothenburg, Sweden: Acta Universitatis Gothoburgensis.

Gustafsson, J-E. (2003). What do we know about effects of school resources on educational results? *Swedish Economic Policy Review, 10,* 77–110.

Gustavsson, L. (2008). *Att bli bättre lärare: Hur undervisningsinnehållets behandling blir till samtalsämne lärare emellan* [Becoming a better teacher: How the content of teaching is turned into topic of conversation between teachers]. Kristianstad, Sweden: Högskolan i Kristianstad.

Hacking, I. (1999). *The social construction of what?* Cambridge, MA: Harvard University Press.

Häggström, J. (2008). *Teaching systems of linear equations in Sweden and China: What is made possible to learn?* Gothenburg, Sweden: Acta Universitatis Gothoburgensis.

Hannula, M. M. & Lehtinen, E. (2005). Spontaneous focusing on numerosity and mathematical skills in young children. *Learning and Instruction, 15,* 237–256.

Hanson, N. R. (1958). *Patterns of discovery.* Cambridge, UK: Cambridge University Press.

Hansson, Å. (2010). Instructional responsibility in mathematics education: Modeling classroom teaching using Swedish data. *Educational Studies in Mathematics, 75*(2), 171–189.

Hansson, Å. (2011). *Ansvar för matematiklärande* [Responsibility for mathematics learning]. Gothenburg, Sweden: Acta Universitatis Gothoburgensis.

Harman, R. (2011). *Meno's paradox and Socrates' "theory of recollection."* Retrieved from www.eden.rutgers.edu/~journal/papers/harman.pdf

Harris, L. R. (2011). Phenomenographic perspectives on the structure of conceptions: The origins, purposes, strengths, and limitations of the what/how and referential/structural frameworks. *Educational Research Review, 6,* 109–124.

Hart, K. (1981). *Children's understanding of mathematics: 11–16.* London, UK: Murray.

Hatala, R. M., Brooks, L. R. & Norman, G. R. (2003). Practice makes perfect: The critical role of mixed practice in the acquisition of ECG interpretation skills. *Advances in Health Education, 8,* 17–26.

Hattie, J. (2009). *Visible learning.* London, UK: Routledge.

Hella, E. & Wright, A. (2009). Learning "about" and "from" religion: Phenomenography, the variation theory of learning and religious education in Finland and the UK. *British Journal of Religious Education, 31*(1), 53–64.

Helmstad, G. (1999). *Understandings of understanding. An inquiry concerning experiential conditions for developmental learning.* Gothenburg, Sweden: Acta Universitatis Gothoburgensis.

Holmqvist, M., Gustavsson, L. & Wernberg, A. (2007). Generative learning: Learning beyond the learning situation. *Educational Action Research, 15*(2), 181–208.

Holmqvist, M., Gustavsson, L. & Wernberg, A. (2008). Variation theory—An organizing principle to guide design research in education. In A. E. Kelly, R. A. Lesh & J. Y. Baek (Eds.), *Handbook of design research methods in education* (pp. 111–130). New York, NY: Routledge.

Holmqvist, M. & Mattison, J. (2009). Contrasting cases and their impact on learning: A replication of a learning study confirming the impact of contrasts. *Problems of Education in the 21st Century, 10,* 38–46.

Holmqvist, M. & Molnár, M. (2006). Att kunna tillämpa *have* och *has* i engelska språket. [Being able to use *have* and *has* in English.] In I. M Holmqvist (Ed.), *Lärande i skolan. Learning study som skolutvecklingsmodell* (pp. 151–176). Lund, Sweden: Studentlitteratur.

Hong Kong Examination Authority. (1992). *Annual report.* Hong Kong, China: Author. (In Marton & Pang, 2006)

Hong Kong Examination Authority. (1995). *Annual report.* Hong Kong, China: Author. (In Marton & Pang, 2006)

Horner, V. & Whiten, A. (2005). Causal knowledge and imitation/emulation switching in chimpanzees (Pan troglodytes) and children (Homo sapiens). *Animal Cognition, 8*(3), 164–181.

Illich, I. (1971). *Deschooling society.* London, UK: Marion Boyars.

Ilyenkov, E. V. (2008). *The dialectics of the abstract and the concrete in Marx's "Capital."* Delhi, India: Aakar Books.

Ingerman, Å., Linder, C. & Marshall, D. (2009). The learners' experience of variation: Following students' threads of learning physics in computer simulation sessions. *Instructional Science, 37,* 273–292.

Inoue-Nakamura, N. & Matsuzawa, T. (1997). Development of stone tool-use by wild chimpanzees (Pan troglodytes). *Journal of Comparative Psychology, 111*(2), 159–173.

Ireson, J., Mortimore, P. & Hallam, S. (1999). The common strands of pedagogy and their implications. In P. Mortimer (Ed.), *Understanding pedagogy and its impact on learning* (pp. 212–241). London, UK: Paul Chapman.

Itard, J. M. G. (1962). *The wild boy of Aveyron.* Newark, NJ: Prentice Hall. (Original work published 1801)

Jensen, M. (2007). *Lärande och låtsaslek* [Learning and pretending]. Gothenburg, Sweden: Göteborg Universitet, Kollegium SSKKII.

Johansson, B. (1975). *Aritmetikundervisning* [Data collection]. Gothenburg, Sweden: Göteborgs Universitet, Pedagogiska institutionen.

Johansson, B., Marton, F. & Svensson, L. (1985). An approach to describing learning as a change between qualitatively different conceptions. In A. L. Pines & T. H. West (Eds.), *Cognitive structure and conceptual change* (pp. 233–257). New York, NY: Academic Press.

Jusczyk, P. W. (1997). *The discovery of spoken language.* Cambridge, MA: MIT Press.

Kapur, M. (2008). Productive failure. *Cognition and Instruction, 26*(3), 379–424.

Kapur, M. (2010). Productive failure in mathematical problem solving. *Instructional Science, 38*(6), 523–550.

Kapur, M. (2012). Productive failure in learning the concept of variance. *Instructional Science, 40*(4), 651–672.

Karlsson, H. & Malm, E. (2010). Bråk i årskurs 1: Kritiska aspekter elever måste urskilja för att förstå det matematiska innehållet bråk [Fractions in year 1: Critical aspects that the pupils have to discern in order to grasp the mathematical content "fraction."]. Jönköping, Sweden: Högskolan i Jönköping, Högskolan för Lärande och Kommunikation.

Katona, G. (1940). *Organizing and memorizing.* New York, NY: Hafner.

Kerlinger, F. (1964). *Foundations of behavioral research.* Austin, TX: Holt, Rinehart & Winston.

Kerr, R. & Booth, B. (1978). Specific and varied practice. *Perceptual and motor skills, 46,* 343–347.

Ki, W. W. (2007). *The enigma of Cantonese tones: How intonation language speakers can be assisted to discern them* (Unpublished doctoral thesis, University of Hong Kong).

Ki, W. W., Ahlberg, K. & Marton, F. (2006, August). *Computer-assisted perceptual learning of Cantonese tones.* Paper presented at the 14th International Conference on Computers in Education, Beijing, China.

Ki, W. W. & Marton, F. (2003, August). *Learning Cantonese tones.* Paper presented at the 11th Biennial Conference of the European Association for Research on Learning and Instruction, Padova, Italy.

Kilborn, V. (1979). *PUMP-projektet—bakgrund och erfarenheter* [The PUMP project: Background and experiences]. Stockholm, Sweden: Liber.

Ko, P. Y. (2002). *The notion of teaching excellence in the People's Republic of China: The case of Chinese language teachers* (Unpublished doctoral thesis, University of Hong Kong).

Ko, P. Y. & Marton, F. (2004). Variation and the secret of the virtuoso. In F. Marton & A. B. M. Tsui (Eds.), *Classroom discourse and the space of learning* (pp. 43–62). Mahwah, NJ: Erlbaum.

Kroksmark, T. (1987). *Fenomenografisk didaktik* [Phenomenographic didactics]: Gothenburg, Sweden: Acta Universitatis Gothoburgensis.

Kroksmark, T. (Ed.). (2011). *Den tidlösa pedagogiken* [Timeless pedagogy] (2nd ed.). Lund, Sweden: Studentlitteratur.

Krutetskii, V. A. (1976). *The psychology of mathematical abilities in school children.* Chicago, IL: University of Chicago Press.

Kuhn, T. S. (1970). *The structure of scientific revolutions* (2nd ed.). Chicago, IL: University of Chicago Press.

Kullberg, A. (2010). *What is taught and what is learned: Professional insights gained and shared by teachers of mathematics.* Gothenburg, Sweden: Acta Universitatis Gothoburgensis.

Kwan, T., Ng, F. P. & Chik, P. (2002). Repetition and variation. In F. Marton & P. Morris (Eds.), *What matters? Discovering critical conditions of classroom learning* (pp. 39–58). Gothenburg, Sweden: Acta Universitatis Gothoburgensis.

Laurillard, D. (2012). *Teaching as a design science. Building pedagogical patterns for learning and technology.* New York, NY: Routledge.

Lave, J. (1988). *Cognition in practice.* Cambridge, UK: Cambridge University Press.

Lave, J. & Wenger, E. (1991). *Situated learning. Legitimate peripheral participation.* Cambridge, UK: Cambridge University Press.

Lénárt, I. (1993). Alternative models on the drawing ball. *Educational Studies in Mathematics, 24,* 277–312.

Libet, B. (2004). *Mind time: The temporal factor in consciousness.* Cambridge, MA: Harvard University Press.

Limberg, L. (1998). *Att söka information för att lära. En studie av samspel mellan informationssökning och lärande* [Searching information for learning]. Sweden: Högskolan i Borås.

Lindahl, M. (1996). *Inlärning och erfarande. Ettåringars möte med skolans värld* [Learning and experiencing. One-year-olds' encounter with the world of pre-school]. Gothenburg, Sweden: Acta Universitatis Gothoburgensis.

Lindahl, M. & Pramling Samuelsson, I. (2002). Imitation and variation: Reflections on toddlers' strategies for learning. *Scandinavian Journal of Educational Research, 46*(1), 25–45.

Lindström, B., Marton, F., Emanuelsson, J., Lindahl, M. & Packendorf, M. (2011). Pre-school children's learning of number concepts in a game-based environment. In J. Emanuelsson, L. Fainsilber, J. Häggström, A. Kullberg, B. Lindström & M. Löwing (Eds.), *Voices on learning and instruction in mathematics* (pp. 119–141). Gothenburg, Sweden: National Center for Mathematics Education, University of Gothenburg.

Lo, M. L. (2012). *Variation theory and the improvement of teaching and learning.* Gothenburg, Sweden: Acta Universitatis Gothoburgensis.

Lo, M. L., Chik, P. & Pang, M. F. (2006). Patterns of variation in teaching the color of light to primary 3 students. *Instructional Science, 34,* 1–19.

Lo, M. L., Hung, H. H. Y. & Chik, P. P. M. (2007). Improving teaching and learning through a learning study—Using variation to teach electro-chemical series in Hong Kong. *Curriculum Perspectives, 27*(3), 49–62.

Lo, M. L. & Marton, F. (2012). Towards a science of the art of teaching: Using variation theory as a guiding principle of pedagogical design. *International Journal of Lesson and Learning Studies, 1*(1), 7–22.

Lo, M. L., Pong, W. Y. & Chik, P. (Eds), (2005). *For each and everyone. Catering for individual differences through learning studies.* Hong Kong: University of Hong Kong Press.

Luhmann, N. (2002). *Theories of distinction. Redescribing the descriptions of modernity.* Stanford, CA: Stanford University Press.

Lundgren, U. (1977). *Model analysis of pedagogical processes.* Lund, Sweden: Gleerup.

Luria, A. R. (1978). The development of writing in the child. In M. Cole (Ed.), *The selected writings of A. R. Luria* (pp. 146–194). New York, NY: M. E. Sharpe. (Original work published 1929, quoted by Tolchinsky, 2003)

Ma Li. (1999). *A traditional Chinese way of teaching mathematics.* Periodical from American Mathematical Society (Mathematics subject classification 01A25, 97D50).

Ma, Liping. (1999). *Knowing and teaching elementary mathematics.* Mahwah, N.J.: Lawrence Erlbaum.

Magnér, B. & Magnér, H. (1976). *Medveten människa* [Being aware]. Stockholm, Sweden: Wahlström & Widstrand.
Markova, I. (1982). *Paradigms, thought, and language*. Chichester, UK: Wiley.
Mårtensson, P. (2013). *Lärares gemensamma kunskapsproduktion* [Teachers' collective production of knowledge]. Unpublished manuscript, Jönköpings Högskola, Sweden.
Marton, F. (1967). Reliabilitet och skolbetyg. [Reliability and school-marks]. Licentiatavhandlingar från Pedagogiska Institutionen, Göteborgs Universitet.
Marton, F. (1974). Inlärning och studiefärdighet [Study skills and learning]. Gothenburg, Sweden: Göteborgs Universitet, Rapporter från Pedagogiska Institutionen.
Marton, F. (1975). On non-verbatim learning. I. Level of processing and level of outcome. *Scandinavian Journal of Psychology, 16*, 273–279.
Marton, F. (1978). Describing conceptions of the world around us. *Reports from the Institute of Education, University of Gothenburg*.
Marton, F. (1981). Phenomenography—Describing conceptions of the world around us. *Instructional Science, 10*, 177–200.
Marton, F. (2001, November 26–27). *The learning study*. Keynote address delivered at the Hong Kong Subsidized Secondary School Council 30th Anniversary Education Conference, Hong Kong.
Marton, F. (2003). Learning study-pedagogisk utveckling direkt i klassrummet [Learning study—Pedagogical development right in the classroom]. In I. Carlgren, I. Josefsson & C. Liberg (Eds.), *Forskning av denna världen-praxisnära forskning inom utbildningsvetenskap* (pp. 43–50). Stockholm, Sweden: Swedish Research Council.
Marton, F. (2005). Om praxisnära grundforskning [On praxis-related basic research]. In I. Carlgren, I. Josefsson & C. Liberg (Eds.), *Forskning av denna världen II—om teorins roll i praxisnära forskning* (pp. 105–122). Stockholm, Sweden: Swedish Research Council.
Marton, F. (2006). Sameness and difference in transfer. *Journal of the Learning Sciences, 15*(4), 501–539.
Marton, F., Asplund-Carlsson, M. & Halász, L. (1992). Differences in understanding and the use of reflective variation in reading. *British Journal of Educational Psychology, 62*, 1–16.
Marton, F., Beaty, E. & Dall'Alba, G. (1993). Conceptions of learning. *International Journal of Educational Research, 19*, 277–300
Marton, F., Dall'Alba, G. & Tse, L. K. (1992). *The paradox of the Asian learner*. Paper presented at the Fourth Asian Regional Congress of Cross-Cultural Psychology, Kathmandu, Nepal.
Marton, F., Dall'Alba, G. & Tse, L. K. (1996). Memorizing and understanding: The keys to the paradox? In D. A. Watkins & J. B. Biggs (Eds.), *The Chinese learner: Cultural, psychological and contextual influences* (pp. 69–84). Hong Kong, China: CERC.
Marton, F. & EDB Chinese Language Research Team. (2009). The Chinese learner of tomorrow. In C. K. K. Chan & N. Rao (Eds.), *Revisiting the Chinese learner* (pp. 133–168). Hong Kong, China: University of Hong Kong, CERC.
Marton, F., Hounsell, D. & Entwistle, N. (Eds.). (1997). *The experience of learning* (2nd ed.). Edinburgh, Scotland: Scottish Academic Press.
Marton, F. & Månsson, M. (1984). Vad gör livet värt att leva? [What makes life worth living?]. In F. Marton & C-G. Wenestam (Eds.), *Att uppfatta sin omvärld. Varför vi förstår verkligheten på olika sätt* (pp. 143–160). Stockholm, Sweden: AWE/Gebers.
Marton, F. & Pang, M. F. (2006). On some necessary conditions of learning. *Journal of the Learning Sciences, 15,* 193–220.
Marton, F. & Pang, M. F. (2007). The paradox of pedagogy: The relative contribution of teachers and learners to learning. *Iskolakultura, 1*(1), 1–29.

Marton, F. & Pang, M. F. (2008). The idea of phenomenography and the pedagogy of conceptual change. In S. Vosniadou (Ed.), *International handbook of conceptual change* (pp. 533–539). New York, NY: Routledge.

Marton, F. & Pang, M. F. (2013). Meanings are acquired from experiencing differences against a background of sameness, rather than from experiencing sameness against a background of difference: Putting a conjecture to the test by embedding it in a pedagogical tool. *Frontline Learning Research, 1,* 24–41.

Marton, F. & Pong, W. Y. (2005). On the unit of description in phenomenography. *Higher Education: Research and Development, 24,* 335–348

Marton, F. & Säljö, R. (1976). On qualitative differences in learning I—Outcome and process. *British Journal of Educational Psychology, 46,* 115–127.

Marton, F. & Säljö, R. (1997). Approaches to learning. In F. Marton, D. Hounsell & N. Entwistle (Eds.), *The experience of learning* (2nd ed., pp. 39–58). Edinburgh, Scotland: Scottish Academic Press.

Marton, F. & Trigwell, K. (2000). Variatio est mater studiorum [Variation is the mother of learning]. *Higher Education Research & Development, 19*(3), 381–395.

Marton, F. & Tsui, A. B. M (2004). *Classroom discourse and the space of learning.* Mahwah, NJ: Erlbaum.

Marton, F. & Wenestam, C-G. (1988). Qualitative differences in retention when a text is read several times. In M. M. Gruneberg, P. E. Morris & R. N. Sykes (Eds), *Practical aspects of memory: Current research and issues* (Vol. 2, pp. 370–376) Chichester, UK: Wiley.

Marton, F., Tse, S. K. & Cheung, W. M. (Eds.). (2010). *On the learning of Chinese.* Rotterdam, The Netherlands: Sense.

Marton, F. & Booth, S. (1997, January 3–7). *Learning and awareness.* Mahwah, NJ: Erlbaum.

Marton, F. & Neuman, D. (1989). *The perceptibility of numbers and the origin of arithmetic skills.* Gothenburg, Sweden: University of Gothenburg, Department of Education.

Marton, F. & Säljö, R. (1976b). On qualitative differences in learning II—Outcome as a function of the learner's conception of the task. *British Journal of Educational Psychology, 46,* 115–127.

Marton, F., Watkins, D. & Tang, C. (1997). Discontinuities and continuities in the experience of learning: An interview study of high-school students in Hong Kong. *Learning and Instruction, 7,* 21–48.

Marton, F., Wen, Q. F. & Wong, K. C. (2005). "Read a hundred times and the meaning will appear . . .": Changes in Chinese university students' views of the temporal structure of learning. *Higher Education, 49,* 291–318.

Mason, J. (2011). Explicit and implicit pedagogy: Variation theory as a case study. In C. Smith (Ed.), *Proceedings of the British Society for Research into Learning Mathematics, 31*(3), 107–112.

Mason, J. & Watson, A. (2005, August, 23–27). *Mathematical exercises: What is exercised, what is attended to, and how does the structure of the exercises influence this?* Paper presented at the 11th Biennial Conference of the European Association for Research on Learning and Instruction, Nicosia, Cyprus.

Mathews, M. H. (1992). *Making sense of place: Children's understanding of large-scale environments.* Hemel Hempstead, UK: Harvester.

Maunula, T. (2011). *Dynamiska aspekter av innehållslig interaktion.* [Dynamical aspects of content-related interaction]. Unpublished manuscript, Faculty of Education, University of Gothenburg, Sweden.

Mayr, F. (1982). *The growth of biological thought.* Cambridge, MA: Harvard University Press.

McKenzie, J. (2003). *Variation and change in university teachers' ways of experiencing teaching* (Unpublished doctoral thesis, University of Technology, Sydney, Australia).

McKinsey and Co. (2007). *How the world's best-performing school systems come out on top.* New York, NY: Author.

Meltzoff, A. N. (1988). Infant imitation after a one week delay: Long term memory for novel acts and multiple stimuli. *Developmental Psychology, 24,* 470–476.

Montessori, M. (1987). *Barnasinnet* [The absorbent mind]. Stockholm, Sweden: MacBook. (Original work published 1949)

Morris, A. & Hiebert, J. (2011). Creating shared instructional products: An alternative approach to improving teaching. *Educational Researcher, 40*(1), 5–14.

Moxley, S. E. (1979). Schema: The variability of practice hypothesis. *Journal of Motor Behaviour, 2*(1), 65–70.

Mulhall, S. (1993). *On being in the world: Wittgenstein and Heidegger on seeing aspects.* London, UK: Routledge.

Murphy, G. L. (2004). *The big book of concepts.* Cambridge, MA: MIT Press.

National Association for the Study of Educational Methods. (2011). *Lesson study in Japan.* Hiroshima, Japan: Keisuisha.

Nemirovsky, R. (2011). Episodic feelings and transfer of learning. *Journal of the Learning Sciences, 20*(2), 308–337.

Nemirovsky, R., Tierny, C. & Wright, T. (1998). Body motion and graphing. *Cognition and Instruction, 16*(2), 119–172.

Neuman, D. (1987). *The origin of arithmetic skills: A phenomenographic approach.* Gothenburg, Sweden: Acta Universitatis Gothoburgensis.

Neuman, D. (2013). Att ändra arbetssätt och kultur inom den inledande aritmetikundervisningen [Changing ways of working and culture in the initial teaching of arithmetic]. *Nordic Studies in Mathematics Education, 18*(2), 3–46.

Newman, D., Griffin, P. & Cole, M. (1989). *The construction zone: Working for change in school.* Cambridge, UK: Cambridge University Press.

Ng, F. P., Kwan, T. & Chik, P. M. (2000). Analysis of a primary Chinese language lesson. *Curriculum Forum, 8,* 79–89.

Nishizaka, A. (2006). What to learn: The embodied structure of the environment. *Research on Language and Social Interaction, 39*(2), 119–154.

Nowotny, H., Scott, P. & Gibbons, M. (2003). Introduction. "Mode 2" revisited: The new production of knowledge. *Minerva, 41,* 179–194.

Nutbrown, C. (1994). *Threads of thinking: Young children learning and the role of early education.* London, UK: Paul Chapman.

Nuthall, G. (2004). Relating classroom teaching to student learning: A critical analysis of why research has failed to bridge the theory–practice gap. *Harvard Educational Review, 74*(3), 273–306.

Nye, B., Konstantopoulus, S. & Hedges, L. V. (2004). How large are teacher effects? *Educational Evaluation and Policy Analysis, 26*(3), 237–257.

OECD. (2012). *Education at a glance.* Retrieved from http://www.oecd.org/edu/eag 2012.htm

OECD. (2013) *PISA 2012 results: What students know and can do—Student performance in mathematics, reading and science* (Vol. 1). PISA, OECD Publishing.

Olteanu, C. (2007). *"Vad skulle x kunna vara?" Andragradsekvation och andragradsfunktion som objekt för lärande* ["What could x be?" Second-degree equation and second-degree function as objects of learning]. Kristianstad, Sweden: Högskolan i Kristianstad.

Örnkloo, H. (2007). *Fitting objects into holes: On the development of spatial cognition skills.* Uppsala, Sweden: Acta Universitatis Upsaliensis.

Paine, L. (1990). The teacher as a virtuoso: A Chinese model for teaching. *Teachers College Record, 92*(1), 49–81.

Paine, L. & Ma, L. P. (1993). Teachers working together: A dialogue on organizational and cultural perspectives on Chinese teachers. *International Journal of Educational Research, 19*, 675–697.

Pang, M. F. (2002). *Making learning possible: The use of variation in the teaching of school economics* (Unpublished doctoral thesis, University of Hong Kong).

Pang, M. F. (2010). Boosting financial literacy: Benefits from learning study. *Instructional Science, 38*, 659–677.

Pang, M. F. & Chik, P. P. M. (2005). Primary 4 general studies: Price. In M. L. Lo & W. Y. Pong (Eds.), *For each and everyone: Catering for individual differences through learning studies* (pp. 96–115). Hong Kong, China: Hong Kong University Press.

Pang, M.F., Linder, C. & Fraser, D. (2006). Beyond lesson study and design experiments: Using theoretical tools in practice and finding out how they work. *International Review of Economics Education, 5*, 28–46.

Pang, M. F. & Marton, F. (2003). Beyond "lesson study": Comparing two ways of facilitating the grasp of some economic concepts. *Instructional Science, 31*, 175–194.

Pang, M. F. & Marton, F. (2007). On the paradox of pedagogy: The relative contribution of teachers and learners to learning. *Iskolakultura Online, 1*, 1–29.

Pang, M. F. & Marton, F. (2013, January 23). Interaction between the learners' initial grasp of the object of learning and the learning resource afforded. *Instructional Science, 41*(6), 1065–1082.

Park, K. (2012). Two faces of mathematics lessons in Korea: Conventional lessons and innovative lessons. *ZDM Mathematics Education, 44*, 121–135.

Patrick, K. (1998). *Teaching and learning: The construction of an object of study* (Unpublished doctoral dissertation, University of Melbourne, Australia).

Patrick, K. (2002). Doing history. In F. Marton & P. Morris (Eds.), *What matters? Discovering critical conditions of classroom learning* (pp. 93–112). Gothenburg, Sweden: Acta Universitatis Gothoburgensis.

Pellegrini, A. D. & Gustafson, K. (2005). Boys' and girls' uses of objects for exploration, play, and tools in early childhood. In A. D. Pellegrini & P. K. Smith (Eds.), *The nature of play: Great apes and humans* (pp. 113–128). New York, NY: Guildford Press. (Quoted by Jensen, 2007)

Piaget, J. (1952). *The origins of intelligence in children.* New York, NY: Norton.

Piaget, J. & Inhelder, B. (1967). *The child's conception of the space.* New York, NY: Norton.

Piaget, J. & Inhelder, B. (1969). *The psychology of the child.* New York, NY: Basic Books.

Piaget, J. & Inhelder, B. (1974). *The child's construction of quantities.* London, UK: Routledge.

Polanyi, M. (1958). *Personal knowledge.* London, UK: Routledge.

Pong, W. Y. (2000). *Widening the space of variation-inter-contextual and intra-contextual shifts in pupils' understanding of two economic concepts* (Unpublished doctoral thesis, University of Hong Kong, China).

Popper, K. (1963). *Conjectures and refutations: The growth of scientific knowledge.* London, UK: Routledge.

Pramling, I. (1983). *The child's conception of learning.* Gothenburg, Sweden: Acta Universitatis Gothoburgensis.

Pramling, N. & Pramling Samuelsson, I. (2001). "It is floating 'cause there is a hole": A young child's experience of natural science. *Early Years, 21*(2), 139–149.

Pramling, N. & Pramling Samuelsson, I. (2011). Introduction and the frame of the book. In N. Pramling & I. Pramling Samuelsson (Eds.), *Educational encounters: Nordic studies in early childhood didactics* (pp. 1–14). Dordrecht, The Netherlands: Springer.

Premack, D. (1984). Pedagogy and aesthetics as sources of culture. In M. S. Gazzinga (Ed.), *Handbook of cognitive neuroscience* (pp. 13–35). New York, NY: Plenum.

Premack, D. & Premack, A. J. (2003). *Original intelligence.* New York, NY: McGraw-Hill.

Prosser, M. (1994). A phenomenographic study of students' intuitive and conceptual understanding of certain electrical phenomena. *Instructional Science, 22,* 189–205.

Quine, W. V. O. (1960). *Word and object.* Cambridge, MA: MIT Press.

Reis, M. (2011). *Att ordna, från ordning till ordning. Yngre förskolebarns matematiserande* [To order. From order to order. Toddlers' mathematizing]. Gothenburg, Sweden: Acta Universitatis Gothoburgensis.

Resnick, L. (1989). Treating mathematics as an ill-structured discipline. In R. Charles & E. Silver (Eds.), *The teaching and assessing of mathematical problem-solving* (pp. 32–60). Reston, VA: National Council of Teachers of Mathematics. Quoted by Schoenfeld (1992).

Roche, J. (1988). Newton's *Principia*. In J. Fauvel, R. Flood, M. Shortland & R. Wilson (Eds.), *Let Newton be! A new perspective on his life and works* (pp. 43–61). Oxford, UK: Oxford University Press.

Rovio-Johansson, A. & Lumsden, M. (2012). Collaborative production of pedagogical knowledge: Enhancing students' learning. *Journal of Applied Research in Higher Education, 4,* 72–83.

Runesson, U. (1999) *Variationens pedagogik* [The pedagogy of variation]. Gothenburg, Sweden: Acta Universitais Gothoburgensis.

Runesson, U. (2005). Beyond discourse and interaction. Variation: A critical aspect of learning mathematics. *Cambridge Journal of Education, 35*(1), 69–87.

Runesson, U. & Mok, I. A. C. (2004). Discernment and the question, "What can be learned?" In F. Marton & A. B. M. Tsui (Eds.), *Classroom discourse and the space of learning* (pp. 63–88). Mahwah, NJ: Erlbaum.

Ryle, G. (1949). *The concept of mind.* London, UK: Hutchinson.

Sachs, L. (1983). *Evil eye or bacteria.* Stockholm, Sweden: University of Stockholm, Stockholm Studies in Social Anthropology.

Säljö, R. (1979). Learning in the learner's perspective I. Some common-sense conceptions. *Reports from the Department of Education, Göteborg University,* no. 76.

Säljö, R. (1982). *Learning and understanding: A study of differences in constructing meaning from a text.* Gothenburg, Sweden: Acta Universitatis Gothoburgensis.

Säljö, R. (2000). *Lärande i praktiken* [Learning in practice]. Stockholm, Sweden: Prisma.

Säljö, R. (2001). The individual in social practices. Comments to Ference Marton's "The practice of learning." *Nordic Educational Research, 2,* 108–116.

Sandberg, J. (1994). *Human competence at work: An interpretative approach.* Gothenburg, Sweden: BAS.

Schmittau, J. (2004). Vygotskian theory and mathematics education: Resolving the conceptual-procedural dichotomy. *European Journal of Psychology of Education, 19*(1), 19–43.

Schmittau, J. & Vagliardo, J. (2006). Using concept mapping in the development of the concept of positional system. In A. Canas & J. Novak (Eds.), *Proceedings of the Second International Conference on Concept Mapping* (pp. xxx–xxx). San Jose, Costa Rica.

Schoenfeld, A. H. (1992). Learning to think mathematically: Problem solving, metacognition, and sense-making in mathematics. In D. Grouws (Ed.), *Handbook for research in mathematics teaching and learning* (pp. 334–370). New York, NY: Macmillan.

Schwartz, D. L. & Bransford, D. J. (1998). A time for telling. *Cognition and Instruction, 16,* 475–522.

Schwartz, D. L. & Martin, T. (2004). Inventing to prepare for future learning: The hidden efficiency of encouraging original student production in statistics instruction. *Cognition and Instruction, 22*(2), 129–184.

Séguin, E. (1977). *Idiocy and its treatment by the physiological method.* New York, NY: Columbia University Press. (Original work published 1866)

Shulman, L. S. (1986). Those who understand: Knowledge growth in teaching. *Educational Researcher, 5,* 4–14.

Signert, K. (2012). *Variation and invarians i Maria Montessoris sinnestränande material.* [Variation and invariance in Maria Montessori's materials for sense-development]. Gothenburg, Sweden: Acta Universitatis Gothoburgensis.

Signert, K. & Marton, F. (2008). Sinnenas skolning—variation och invarians i Maria Montessoris pedagogik [Nurturing the senses—variation and invariance in the pedagogy of Maria Montessori]. In H. Rystedt & R. Säljö (Eds.), *Kunskap och människans redskap: Teknik och lärande* (pp. 179–194). Lund, Sweden: Studentlitteratur.

Silén, C. (2000). *Mellan kaos och kosmos—Om eget ansvar och självständighet i lärande* [Between chaos and cosmos—On the learners' own responsibility and independence]. Linköping, Sweden: Linköpings Universitet, Filosofiska fakulteten.

Skemp, R. (1976). Relational understanding and instrumental understanding. *Mathematics Teaching, 77,* 20–26.

Skemp, R. (1987). *The psychology of learning mathematics.* Mahwah, NJ: Erlbaum. (In Schmittau & Vagliardo, 2006)

Skinner, B. F. (1957). *Verbal behavior.* Englewood Cliffs, NJ: Prentice Hall.

Skolverket. (2004). *Nationella utvärderingen av grundskolan 2003. Sammanfattande huvudrapport* [The national evaluation of the Swedish comprehensive school]. Stockholm, Sweden: Fritzes.

Skolverket. (2009). *Vad påverkar resultaten I svensk grundskola?* [What affects the results in the Swedish comprehensive school?]. Stockholm, Sweden: Fritzes.

Skolverket. (2012). *Tid för matematik: erfarenheter från matematiksatsningen 2009–2011* [Time for mathematics. Conclusions from the mathematics initiative]. Stockholm, Sweden: National Board of Education.

Smedslund, J. (1961). The acquisition of conservation of substance and weight in children. In I. E. Sigel & F. H. Hooper (Eds.), *Logical thinking in children* (pp. 281–286). New York, NY: Holt, Rinehart & Winston. (Quoted by M. Feffer, 1988)

Smedslund, J. (1970). Circular relation between understanding and logic. *Scandinavian Journal of Psychology, 11,* 217–219.

Snyder, B. (1973). *The hidden curriculum.* Cambridge, MA: MIT Press.

SOU:31. (2005). *Stödet till utbildningsvetenskaplig forskning* [Support for educational research]. Stockholm, Sweden: Fritzes.

Spencer Brown, G. (1972). *Laws of form.* New York, NY: Julian Press.

Spielberg, H. (1982). *The phenomenological movement: A historical introduction* (3rd ed.). The Hague, The Netherlands: Martinus Nijhoff.

Stenhouse, L. (1975). *An introduction to curriculum research and development.* London, UK: Heinemann.

Stevenson, H. W. & Stigler, J. W. (1992). *The learning gap.* New York, NY: Summit.

Stigler, J. W. & Hiebert, J. (1999). *The teaching gap: Best ideas from the world's teachers for improving education in the classroom.* New York, NY: Free Press.

Stilling, N. A., Weisler, S. E., Chase, C. H., Feinstein, M. H., Garfield, J. L. & Rissland, E. L. (1995). *Cognitive science: An introduction* (2nd ed.). Cambridge, MA: MIT Press.
Stoke, D. E. (1997). *Pasteur's quadrant: Basic science and technological innovation*. Washington, DC: Brookings Institution Press.
Sun, X. H. (2011). "Variation problems" and their roles in the topic of fraction division in Chinese mathematics textbook examples. *Educational Studies in Mathematics, 76*, 65–85.
Sutton-Smith, B. (1979). Epilogue: Play as performance. In B. Sutton-Smith (Ed.), *Play and learning*. New York, NY: Gardner Press.
Svensson, L. (1976). *Study skill and learning*. Gothenburg, Sweden: Acta Universitatis Gothoburgensis.
Svensson, L. (1977). On qualitative differences in learning, III: Study skill and learning. *British Journal of Educational Psychology, 47*, 233–243.
Svensson, L. (1997). Theoretical foundations of phenomenography. *Higher Education Research & Development, 16*(2), 159–171.
Svensson, L. (2009). *Introduktion till pedagogik* [Introduction to pedagogy]. Stockholm, Sweden: Norstedt.
Székely, L. (1950). Productive processes in learning and thinking. *Acta Psychologica, 7*, 388–407.
Szklarski, A. (1996). *Barn och konflikter* [Children and conflicts, in Swedish]. Linköping, Sweden: Linköping University, Department of Education and Psychology.
Theman, J. (1983). *Uppfattningar av politisk makt* [Conceptions of political power]. Gothenburg, Sweden: Acta Universitatis Gothoburgensis.
Thornton, R. K. & Sokoloff, D. R. (1998). Assessing student learning of Newton's laws: The force and motion conceptual evaluation and the evaluation of active learning laboratory and lecture curricula. *American Journal of Physics, 66*(4), 338–352.
Tolchinsky, L. (2003). *The cradle of culture and what children know about writing and numbers before being taught*. Mahwah, NJ: Erlbaum.
Top test scores from Shanghai stun educators. (2012, December 7). *New York Times*, p. 1.
Trankell, A. (1973). *Kvarteret Flisan: om en kris och dess övervinnande i ett svenskt förortssamhälle* [The neighbourhood Flisan: On a crisis and overcoming it in a Swedish suburb]. Stockholm, Sweden: Norstedts.
Tse, S. K., Marton, F., Loh, E. K. Y. & Chik, P. P. M. (2010). Learning characters. In F. Marton, S. K. Tse & W. M. Cheung (Eds.), *On the learning of Chinese* (pp. 75–102). Rotterdam, The Netherlands: Sense.
van Hiele, P. M. (1986). *Structure and insight, a theory of mathematics education*. Orlando, FL: Academic Press.
Van Rossum, E. J. & Schenk, S. M. (1984). The relationship between learning conception, study strategy and learning outcome. *British Journal of Educational Psychology, 54*, 73–83.
Vygotsky, L. S. (1986). *Thought and language*. Cambridge, MA: MIT Press.
Watson, A. & Mason, J. (2005). *Mathematics as constructive activity*. Mahwah, NJ: Erlbaum.
Watson, A. & Mason, J. (2006). Seeing an exercise as a single mathematical object: Using variation to structure sense-making. *Mathematical Thinking and Learning, 8*(2), 91–111.
Wenestam, C-G. (1978). Horisontalisering: Ett sätt att missuppfatta det man laser [Horizontalization: A way of misunderstanding what you read]. *Reports from the Department of Education, Göteborg University*.
Wenestam, C-G. (1980). *Qualitative differences in retention*. Gothenburg, Sweden: Acta Universitatis Gothoburgensis.
Wenestam, C-G. & Wass, H. (1987). Swedish and US children's thinking about death: A qualitative study and cross-cultural comparison. *Death Studies, 11*(2), 99–121.

Wernberg, A. (2009). *Lärandets objekt* [The object of learning]. Kristianstad, Sweden: Högskolan i Kristianstad.
Werner, H. (1948). *Comparative psychology of mental development*. New York, NY: International Universities Press.
Wertheimer, M. (1961). *Productive thinking*. London, UK: Tavistock.
Whalen, D. H., Lewitt, A. G. & Wang, Q. (1991). Intonational differences in the reduplicated babbling of French- and English-learning infants. *Journal of Child Language, 18*, 501–516.
White, S. H. (1989). Foreword. In D. Newman, P. Griffin & M. Cole (Eds.), *The construction zone: Working for change in school* (pp. ix-xiv). Cambridge, UK: Cambridge University Press.
Whitehead, A. N. (1925). *Science and the modern world*. New York, NY: New American Library. (Quoted by Bereiter, 2002)
Wilcken, P. (2010). *Claude Lévi-Strauss: The poet in the laboratory*. New York, NY: Penguin Press.
Williams, F. (1993). *Creativity assessment packet*. Austin, TX: Pro-Ed.
Wittgenstein, L. (1958). *Philosophical investigations* (2nd ed.). Oxford, UK: Blackwell.
Zhang, D., Li, S. & Tang, R. (2004). The "Two basics": Mathematics teaching and learning in mainland China. In L. Fan, N-Y. Wong, J. Cai & S. Li (Eds.), *How Chinese learn mathematics: Perspectives from insiders* (pp. 189–207). Singapore: World Scientific.

AUTHOR INDEX

Ahlberg, K. 64, 120n12, 220
Airasian, P. W. 116
Airey, J. 282n1
Åkerlind, G. S. 120n12
Alberti, L. B. 161
Al Murani, T. 235
Alvegård, C. 251n5
Anderberg, E. 251n5
Anderson, L. W. 116
Ashton-Warner, S. 31
Asplund-Carlsson, M. 148–9, 169
Athey, C. 130–1

Barnett, S. A. 2, 9, 11
Bateson, G. 80n9
Bauersfeld, H. 19n8
Beaty, E. 120n12
Bekkering, H. 7–8
Bereiter, C. 259–60
Bergqvist, K. 19n5
Biggs, J. B. 115, 116, 252n16
Björklund, C. 133
Black, P. 235
Bloom, B. S. 22–3, 116
Boden, M. 225
Bogdan, B. 161
Boklöv, J. 160
Booth, B. 70–1, 227, 239
Booth, S. 37, 60, 70, 89, 99, 107, 120n12, 148, 150, 216
Boulton-Lewis, G. M. 146–7
Bowden. J. 89, 120n12, 154, 156–7, 258

Bradley, F. H. 147
Brahe, T. 156–7
Bransford, J. D. 217, 219, 272
Brooks, L. R. 167
Brousseau, G. 13–15, 147
Brown, J. S. 11
Brumby, M. N. 157, 160
Bryk, A. S. 260, 280
Buck-Morss, S. 161
Burger, W. F. 115

Calvin, W. H. 131
Carlgren, I. 19n5
Cassirer, E. 45, 46, 74–5n3
Chase, W. G. 83
Cheung, W. M. 221, 224, 251
Chi, M. 83
Chik, P. M. 168, 171, 251n5, 268, 276
Chik, P.P.M. 101, 190, 193, 197–8, 213, 221–2, 224, 239, 243, 245, 253–4n
Chomsky, N. 210
Claparede, E. 54
Cole, M. 71
Collins, A. 11
Collis, K. F. 115
Comenius, J. A. 256
Confucius 246
Copernicus, N. 155–7
Crombie, A. C. 135
Cronbach, L. J. 245, 280
Cruikshank, K. A. 116
Csibra, G. 5–8

Author Index

Dahlgren, L. O. 100–1, 120n12, 196–7
Dall'Alba, G. 120n12, 252n16
Darwin, C. 1, 158–60
Davydov, V. V. 18, 80–1n10, 119n4, 134, 137–8, 166
Day, J. M. 250
de Groot, A. D. 83
Deleuze, G. 78–9n5
Derrida, J. 78–9n5
de Saussure, F. 45, 60
Duguid, P. 11

EDB Chinese Language Research Team 228–31
Einhorn, S. 43
Einstein, A. 74n3
Ekeblad, E. 4–5
Elliott, J. 276, 278
Emanuelsson, J. 82–3, 89, 252n15
Engelhart, M. D. 22–3
Engeström, Y. 36, 141
Entwistle, N. 99, 113
Euclid 247

Fan, L. 246
Feldman, D. 86
Feltovich, P. 83
Ferreiro, E. 29
Fodor, J. 42–4
Fosbury, R. 160
Fraser, D. 197
Fröhagen, J. 269
Furst, E. J. 22–3
Fyrenius, A. 143

Galili, I. 58
Garner, W. R. 45, 75–8n4
Gauss, G. F. 136, 162n3
Gergely, G. 5–8
Gibbons, M. 280
Gibson, E. J. 33–4, 36, 107–8, 119n9, 122n
Gibson, J. J. 33–4, 36, 107–8, 119n9
Glaser, B. G. 83, 121n
Glaser, R. 120–2n12
Goldenberg, P. 47
Gomez, L. M. 260, 280
Gould, J. 158
Gould, S. J. 1–2
Griffin, P. 71
Gruber, H. E. 158
Grunow, A. 260, 280
Gu, L. 188, 247–8
Guo, J. P. 70
Gurwitsch, A. 109

Gustafson, K. 131
Gustafsson, J-E. 19n7, 20, 245
Gustavsson, L. 131, 167, 227–8, 260, 271, 276

Hacking, I. 118
Häggström, J. 70, 185, 188, 195, 251n6, 252n15
Halász, L. 148–9, 169
Hallam, S. 11
Hannula, M. M. 31–2, 88
Hanson, N. R. 156
Hansson, Å. 12, 19n6
Harman, R. 42
Harris, L. R. 82
Harrison, C. 235
Hatala, R. M. 167
Hattie, J. 20, 214
Hazan, A. 58
Hedges, L. V. 252n13
Hegel, F. 36–7, 51, 139
Heidegger, M. 79n6
Hella, E. 120n12
Helmstad, G. 120n12
Hiebert, J. 181, 258–60
Hill, W .H. 22–3
Holmqvist, M. 227–8, 260, 265, 276
Hounsell, D. 99
Huang, R. J. 248
Hung, H.H.Y. 211

Illich, I. 12
Ilyenkov, E. V. 36
Ingerman, Å. 120n12
Inhelder, B. 122–3n13, 135
Inoue-Nakamura, N. 3
Ireson, J. 11
Itard, J.M.G. 79–80n7, 207

Jensen, M. 32, 131
Johansson, B. 91–2
Jusczyk, P. W. 28

Kafka, F. 99, 148–51
Kapur, M. 218–19
Karlsson, H. 266
Katona, G. 61
Kepler, J. 155–7
Kerlinger, F. 117–18
Kerr, R. 70–1, 227, 239
Ki, W. W. 62, 64, 66, 87, 220, 238
Kilborn, V. 15
Kiraly, I. 7–8
Kirkegaard, S. 235–6

Ko, P. Y. 177–8
Krathwohl, D. R. 22–3
Krathwohl, D. R. 116
Kroksmark, T. 80–1n10, 118
Krutetskii, V. A. 137–41, 162n4
Kuhn, T. S. 118
Kullberg, A. 223, 232, 234–5, 263, 267, 274
Kumar 221
Kwan, T. 168, 170

Lamarck, J-B. 2, 158
Laurillard, D. 251n4
Lave, J. 9–10
Lee, C. 235
Lehtinen, E. 31–2, 88
Lénart, I. 57
Leung, A. 190, 243
Levi-Strauss, C. 29, 78–9n5
Lewis, D. C. 146
Lewitt, A. G. 28
Li, S. 247
Libet, B. 112
Limberg, L. 19n5
Lindahl, M. 130
Linder, C. 120n12, 197
Lindström, B. 5
Ljungvall, R. 19n7
Lo, M. L. 72, 206, 208, 211–12, 268, 276
Loh, E.K.Y. 253–4n
Luhmann, N. 78–8n5
Lumsden, M. 120n12
Lundgren, U. 15
Luria, A. R. 29
Lyell, C. 158–9

Ma, Liping 16–17
Ma, L. P. 281
McKenzie, J. 120n12
Magnér, B. 44
Magnér, H. 44
Ma Li 247
Malm, E. 266
Malthus, T. R. 159
Månsson, M. 120n2
Markova, I. 37
Marshall, B. 235
Marshall, D. 120n12
Mårtensson, P. 236, 277
Martin, E. 217
Martin, T. 217, 221
Martineau, J. 59
Marton, F. 14, 19n5, 37, 60–2, 64, 66, 72, 79–80n7, 82, 87, 89, 91, 92–3, 99–100, 103, 105–7, 113, 117, 120n12, 121–2n, 142–4, 146, 148–51, 154, 156–7, 169, 171, 175, 177–8, 190, 200, 202, 216, 220, 222, 228–31, 238–40, 243, 245, 248, 251, 252n16, 253–4n, 258, 260, 276, 280, 282n4
Mason, J. 38, 47, 65, 80n8, 133, 139, 177
Matsuzawa, T. 3
Mattison, J. 228
Maunula, T. 236, 276
Mayr, F. 158–9
Meltzoff, A. N. 7–8
Meno's paradox 107
Mok, I.A.C. 178
Molnár, M. 265
Montessori, M. 79–80n7, 207
Morris, A. 260
Morris, P. 251n10
Mortimore, P. 11
Moxley, S. E. 68, 70, 227, 238–9
Mulhall, S. 79n6
Murphy, G. L. 40

Nemirovsky, R. 131
Neuman, D. 25, 28, 88, 92–6, 114, 120n12
Newman, D. 71
Newton, I. 10, 22–3, 84, 91–2
Ng, F. P. 168, 171
Nishizaka, A. 111
Norman, G. R. 167
Nowotny, H. 280
Nutbrown, C. 130–1, 168
Nuthall, G. 275, 278
Nye, B. 252n13

Obama, B. H. 239
Olteanu, C. 173–5, 193–4, 267
Örnkloo, H. 165
Ottander-Bjerkesjö, H. 269

Paine, L. 177, 281
Pang, M. F. 70, 91, 101, 103, 171, 175, 197–8, 200–2, 228, 239–40, 245, 268, 276, 282n4
Park, K. 252n5
Pasteur, L. 279
Patrick, K. 58, 120n12
Pavlov, I. 153
Pellegrini, A.D. 131
Piaget, J. 54, 88, 115, 118, 122–3n13, 129–31, 135
Plato 42, 250
Polanyi, M. 26
Pong, W.Y. 100–1, 106, 276

Popper, K. 245
Pramling, N. 27, 120n12, 220
Pramling Samuelsson, I. 27, 130, 220
Premack, A. J. 2–3
Premack, D. 2–3, 8, 11, 232, 235
Prosser, M. 120n12
Pythagoras 247

Quine, W. V. O. 39, 41

Reis, M. 5
Resnick, L. 19n4
Roche, J. 91
Rovio-Johansson, A. 120n12
Runesson, U. 131, 178, 182, 184
Ryle, G. 107

Sachs, L. 44
Säljö, R. 1, 14, 61, 99, 111, 120n12, 142, 152–4, 193, 221
Sandberg, J. 84–5
Schenk, S. M. 120–2n12
Schenk, S. M. 120n12
Schmittau, J. 80–1n10, 119n4
Schwartz, D. L. 217, 219, 221, 272
Scott, P. 280
Séguin, E. 79–80n7, 207
Shaughnessy, J. M. 115
Shulman, L. S. 256
Signert, K. 79–80n7
Silén, C. 142–3
Simon, H. A. 83
Skemp, R. 14, 147
Skinner, B. F. 153–4, 210
Smedslund, J. 12, 88–9
Snow, R. E. 245
Snyder, B. 19n7
Sokoloff, D. R. 92
Spencer Brown, G. 78–9n5
Spielberg, H. 36
Stenhouse, L. 278
Stevenson, H. W. 246
Stigebrandt, E. 19n7
Stigler, J. W. 181, 246, 258–9
Stilling, N. A. 112
Stoke, D. E. 279
Strauss, A. L. 121n
Sun, X. H. 119n4, 247–8
Sutton-Smith, B. 131

Svensson, L. 19n2, 60–1, 91, 120n12, 147, 251n5
Székely, L. 214–17, 219, 221
Szklarski, A. 121n

Tang, C. 105, 116, 122n, 144
Tang, R. 247
Teberosky, A. 29
Theman, J. 120n12
Thornton, R. K. 92
Tierny, C. 131
Trankell, A. 107
Trigwell, K. 89
Tse, L. K. 251, 252n16
Tse, S. K. 222. 253–4n
Tsui, A.B.M. 178

van Hiele, P. M. 115–16
Van Rossum, E. J. 120n12
Vygotsky, L. S. 1, 40, 43, 50, 54, 57–8, 73–4n1, 80–1n10, 118

Wallace, A. R. 159–60
Walsh, E. 89
Wang, Q. 28
Wass, H. 120n12
Watkins, D. A. 105, 122n, 144
Watson, A. 38, 38n2, 47, 80n8, 133, 139, 177, 235–6
Wen, Q. F. 143, 169
Wenestam, C-G. 120n12, 151, 154
Wenger, E. 9–10
Wernberg, A. 227–8, 260, 272, 276
Werner, H. 37, 214
Wertheimer, M. 123–7n14, 136–7
White, S. H. 11
Whitehead, A. N. 259
Wilcken, P. 29
Wiliam, D. 235
Williams, F. 222
Wilss, L. A. 146
Wirell, S. 143
Wittgenstein, L. 74n, 79n6
Wong, K. C. 143, 169
Wright, A. 120n12, 131
Wright, T. 131

Zhang, D. 247
Zhu, Y. 246

SUBJECT INDEX

abstract, to 36, 51
action research 276, 278
activity theory 108
adjustment 69
analysis 91, 116
application phase 55, 81n12
applied research 278–80
appropriate, to 14, 47–8, 52, 55, 64, 70, 117, 157, 177, 261, 263, 267
Aptitude-Treatment Interaction (ATI) 245
arbetslag (work-team) 281
ascending from the abstract to the concrete 36, 51, 139
aspects: critical 23–7, 33, 54–5, 85–8, 119n1, 147, 164, 234, 261–3; focused 52–3, 55, 81n11, 130, 168–9; necessary 14, 23–7, 158; non-necessary 33; novel 41, 43–7, 56–9; open up 33, 152; optional 51, 53; quantitative 31–2; unfocused 130, 239
assessment for learning 235
ATI (Aptitude-Treatment Interaction) 245
authentic learning 11–12
awareness 26–7, 33, 43, 54, 66, 108–9, 152

basic research 278–80
"Before the Law" (Kafka) 99, 148–51
beliefs 28
benefit of the doubt 88
bianshi 247–51, 252n16
Bloom's taxonomy 22–3, 116

categories 22–3, 46, 57, 71
category of description 99, 107, 114
"Catering for Individual Differences" project 275–6
central participants 8
centricity 155, 163n5
change of change 104
children, theories about 28
classical conditioning 152–4
cloze test 190, 252n12
collective learning 154–6, 160–1, 258, 260, 264, 280
communication 111, 236
comparisons 175–6, 214, 218
complexes 74
conceptions 28, 98, 101–3, 105, 117
concepts 41–2, 57–8, 177–8
conceptualize 17–18, 105, 225
conditions of learning 3, 21, 64, 153, 231–5, 243; necessary 49, 68, 165–6, 201–2, 206; primary and secondary 165–6
conjecture 237–8
consciousness 111
content 22–3, 37, 41, 116, 164, 175, 184–90, 210, 235–7, 256
contextual analysis 147, 224
contrast 46–7, 49–51, 130, 139, 165, 175, 177, 183, 187, 206–8, 238–42, 263
coordination 111
creating 116
creativity 131, 222–5

cultural difference 184–9
curriculum 230, 248, 275, 277–8

deep approaches to learning 14, 142–7, 151
delimitation 60–1, 152–3, 213–14
de-pedagogized learning 11–13
de-schooling 12
design research 258, 259–60, 278–9
diachronic simultaneity 68, 119n9, 146–7
didactic contract 13, 147
difference 66–7, 83, 109, 214
differences 28, 48–9, 56–9, 64–6, 80n9, 85, 92–3, 111; as changes 171–5; experienced 60–4; in learning 115–19, 173–4, 183, 185, 193–6, 208–10, 251n7, 251n8; origin of 166; in ways of reading 152–4
differentiate 18, 38n2
differentiation 33–7, 57, 59, 109–10, 214
direct object of learning 37
direct reference 39–40
discern, learning to 33, 43–7, 67–71, 74n2, 85–7, 214; *see also* open up
discerning 27, 32–3, 38n2, 40–7, 55, 57, 67, 119n10, 206–8, 251n8
discernment 58–9, 61, 66–7, 152, 154–60, 203, 238
distinctions 27–8, 33, 83, 92, 111–12, 238
distinguishing 53–4, 266, 282n2
documentation 264–5
dominance 111
dualism 34, 108
dynamic visualization 171–3, 175

ecological psychology 108
education, investment in 181
educational achievement comparisons 245–6
educational change movement 278
educational objectives 22–3, 110–11, 261
Educational Television Videos (ETVs) 170
Elements (Euclid) 247
emulation 6–8
enacted objects of learning 184, 188, 204–6, 256, 263
enrichment theories 33–6, 107–8
Essay on Population (Malthus) 159
Essays Philosophical and Theological (Martineau) 59
ETVs (Educational Television Videos) 170
evaluating 116
evolution 1–2, 6, 157–60

example space 139, 162
experienced variation 65, 151
explicit variation 65

features: critical 26–7, 38n1, 54–5, 188; discerning 37, 40–7, 73–4n1, 75–8n4, 78–9n5, 161; focused 40–1; necessary 26, 30–1, 48–9, 80n8; novel 41, 43–7, 56–9, 67; targeted 40; unfocused 62
figure-ground 157, 280
first methodological option 120–1n12
focal awareness 109
formative assessment 235
formula 173–5
Foundations of Behavioral Research (Kerlinger) 52, 64, 117
frames 15, 24, 53, 59, 108, 156, 223
funnelling 19n8
fuse 23, 85, 129
fusion 51–5, 91, 175, 193, 213–14, 220–1, 263
future learning 218–19

gaining meaning 225
generalization 33, 50–1, 53–5, 57, 129, 137–42, 210, 263; empirical 137, 140–1; theoretical 48, 80–1n10, 140–1, 166
generic abilities 168, 171, 222, 226
Gestalt school 108
goals 2, 7–8, 22–3
good teaching 177, 190, 252n11
grouping 46, 61–4, 73–4n3, 74–5n3, 166
guessing 94–6, 119n2–3

Hegel's principle 36–7, 51, 80n10
hidden curriculum 19n7, 69
Hidden God, The (Einhorn) 43
hierarchical structure 153–4, 191–3, 221–5
Hong Kong Institute of Education 276
horizontalization 154

imitation 7–8, 31, 40
implicit variation 65
inauthentic learning 11
indirect object of learning 37
individual consciousness 111
induction 40–3, 45–51, 62–4, 73–4n1, 74–5n3, 137, 183, 238–42
infinite regress 107
innate features 43–4
innovations 160–1
insights 237, 256
instantiation 220–1, 263

Subject Index   305

institutionalization of learning 11–12
instructional objectives 22–3
instrumental conditioning 153–4
instrumental understanding 14–15, 147
intended object of learning 256
interaction 235–7
internal relationship 147
internal representation 33–4, 108, 112
invarience 46, 48–54, 60–4, 135, 162n2, 201, 206, 220, 238–9
inverse teleology 6, 131
irrelevant aspects 33

Jiu Zhang San Shu (The Nine Chapters) 247
Journal of Lesson and Learning Studies 265

Karolinska Institute 43
knowledge, transmission of 2, 10
known, using the 67–71, 89

language 28, 45, 56, 60
learning: act of 12, 107, 147–52, 177–8, 229–30; aims of 9–11, 164–5, 202 –203; approaches to 12, 60–4, 142–7, 151–4; de-pedagogized 11–13; to discern 33, 43–4, 67–71, 74n2, 85–7, 197; generative 227–8, 231, 265–6; goals 2, 7–8, 22–3, 37, 278; to learn 3, 114–15, 210, 226–31, 276; organizing for 21; from others 5–8; outcomes 6–8, 21–3, 117, 147–51, 227–8, 232; pact 7–8, 13; path of 52–4, 220–1; pedagogized 3–5, 13, 19n7; phase 55, 81n12; practice-based 11; school-based 11–13, 278, 280–2; space of 14–15, 104–6, 119n8, 139, 169, 188, 226–7; study 197, 204–6, 208–9, 222, 224, 228, 232–6, 252n13, 260–77, 282n4; target 22–3, 116, 168; *see also* object of learning
learning by discovery 214
learning on the collective level 154, 256, 258–9
learning study group 202, 204
legitimate peripheral participants 9
lesson study 175–82, 202, 204–5, 252n11, 258–9, 277–8
location 107
logic 88–9

magnitudes of change 94, 103–5, 203, 205, 243
manyness 24–5, 94

mathematics Olympiads 246
mathematization 5
McKinsey report 281
meanings 33, 37, 44–5, 52, 64, 74–5n3, 106–7; novel 161–2; and structure 152; of words 39–42, 177
means-end structure 6–8
measurements 116
memorization 61, 105, 144–7
Meno dialogue (Plato) 250
Meno's paradox 42, 107
methodological options 120–1n12
misconceptions 28, 92
Montessori pedagogy 47, 79–80n7

New Production of Knowledge: The Dynamics of Science and Research in Contemporary Societies, The (Gibbons) 280
Newton's laws 92, 246
New York Times 245
Nine Chapters, The (*Jiu Zhang San Shu*) 247
non-authentic learning 11–12
non-dualism 34
novel aspects 41, 56–9
novel features 41, 56–9
novel situations 67, 90–1

object of learning 13–14, 22–3, 33, 52, 68, 89, 105, 115, 131–2, 164, 175–7, 236, 242–5, 277; direct 37; enacted 184, 188, 204–6, 256, 263; generic 171, 222, 226; indirect 37; intended 27, 104, 120n12, 176, 202–4, 256, 261–3; lived 27, 106, 116–17, 164, 180, 204, 256, 264–5
observable variation 65
open up 33, 50–1, 57, 89–90, 156, 160–1; *see also* discern, learning to
Organizing and Memorizing (Katona) 61
organizing learning 21
Origin of Species, The (Darwin) 157–60
orthogenetic law of development 214
outcome space 98, 100, 103–5, 117

participatory learning 7–11, 34–6, 184–9, 204–6
partitioning 61
parts and whole 80–1n10, 94, 119n4, 141, 145, 152, 175, 225, 229n4
Pasteur's Quadrant (Stoke) 279
patterns 94–6, 131, 251n5; experienced 165–6; random 83, 178
patterns of variation and invariance 48–54, 62, 128, 145, 166–8, 175, 187, 196–213,

231–2, 242–5, 263; experienced (primary) 49, 51–2, 65, 116–17, 161–2, 165–6; observed (secondary) 65, 165–6
pedagogical content knowledge 256
pedagogical contexts 46–7
pedagogical function 12, 19n5
pedagogy 3–5, 12, 19n2, 245; criterion of 2–3, 8–9, 235; practice of 11, 170, 211, 235–7, 250, 252n15–16, 257; science of 265, 275, 282n1
perception 34, 52–4, 56–7, 80n9, 107, 111–12, 171
perceptual learning 33
peripheral awareness 109
permissible range of change 47, 80n8
permissible range of variation 133
perspective 66, 87–8, 106, 118, 119n1, 151, 164–5, 217
phenomena 40, 73–4n1, 89, 118, 210, 215
phenomenography 82, 89, 98–9, 106–7, 113–16, 120–2n12
physical object 156
piloting 15, 19n8
PIRLS (Progress in International Reading Literacy Study) 254n
PISA study 246
play 131
pool of meanings 154
post-test 71, 167, 209, 231–3, 263–4
practice-based learning 9–11
praxis-related basic research 280
prerequisites for learning 96
pre-test 71, 167, 172, 202, 209, 231–3, 261–4
Principles of Geology (Lyell) 158
Productive Thinking (Wertheimer) 123–8n14, 136–7
Progress in International Reading Literacy Study (PIRLS) 254n
pseudo-concepts 57, 73–4n1
Pythagoras' theorem 247

qualitative differences 116–17, 122–7n13–14
quality *see* meaning
quantitative aspects 31–2
questioning 89–91, 100–1

randomization 232
Reading Gap, The (Hiebert, Stigler) 258–9
recursive teleology 6–8
reference, direct 39–40
relational understanding 14–15

relative magnitude 103–5, 171, 202–6
relevance structure 216, 219, 263
remembering 24, 29, 61, 64, 83, 116
repairs 111
repetition 143, 146–7, 168–9
research-based teaching 278

sameness 56–9, 109
scaffold learning 248, 250
schema 70–1
school-based curriculum reform 278
scientific concepts 57
second methodological option 120–1n12
seeing 15, 28, 58–9, 83–5, 89, 112, 119n10
sensitivity, pedagogical 5
sensory concrete, the 36
sensory information 33, 36, 107
separate, to 4, 10, 31, 33, 40, 51, 56–61
separation 53, 58–60, 75–8n4, 108, 123–7n14
sequential structure 153–4, 191–2
similarities 64–5
simple teleology 6
simultaneity 66–8, 109, 119n9
simultaneous change 202
skills 2, 10, 23, 28–32
Skinner box 153
Skolverket 12, 20, 277
SOLO taxonomy 115–16
speaking 28
Special Rank Teacher 177
specificity 70–1
spontaneous concepts 57
stochastic differences 66, 237
student achievement 12, 20, 181, 251n6
studying 111, 146
subject–object dualism 107
surface approaches to learning 14, 142–7, 151
syllabuses 22
synchronic simultaneity 68, 109
synthetic classes 228

tangibility 156, 172
targets, learning 22–3
teacher-led learning 12–13, 19n6
teachers' research group 190, 281
teaching, comparing ways of 180–90
teaching experiments 231–2
Teaching Gap, The (Stigler and Hiebert) 181, 258–9
teleological structure 6–8, 131
theory 117–118, 163n6

TIMSS (Trends in International Mathematics and Science Study) 181, 259
transfer of learning 72–3
Trends in International Mathematics and Science Study (TIMSS) 181, 259
turn taking 111

understanding 14–15, 88–9, 98–100, 105, 116, 144, 147, 152, 172, 236
University of East Anglia 278
University of Hong Kong Faculty of Education 190
unknown 67–71, 89

values 47–8, 79n6, 116–17, 160, 168, 187, 231n3
van Hiele levels 115–16
variation 46–54, 62, 65, 67, 79n6, 201, 220, 238; afforded 47, 151; and awareness 108–9, 113, 168–9; dimension of 71, 89, 109–10, 116–17, 120–2n12, 128–31, 133–4, 148, 151–2, 155–62, 168, 184–9, 229, 251n3, 251n8; experienced 65, 151, 206–8, 211–12; patterns of 116, 131–4, 144–5, 162n1, 169, 206; theory 89, 145, 171–2, 188, 211, 218, 226, 231, 245, 247–51, 265, 282n1
variation practice 247
visualization 171–3, 251n4

ways of experiencing 83, 106, 113
ways of seeing 15, 28, 58–9, 82–5, 89, 100–5, 107, 117, 119n5, 119n9, 120n11, 256; alternate 155–6; differences in 196; doing as 110–11
Williams rating scale 222–4
Word and Object (Quine) 39–40
words, meaning of 39–41, 73–4n1
work-team (*arbetslag*) 281
writing 28, 29–31

Printed in Great Britain
by Amazon